Psychological Factors in the Teaching of Reading

The Charles E. Merrill

COMPREHENSIVE READING PROGRAM

Arthur Heilman
Consulting Editor

Psychological Factors in the Teaching of Reading

Compiled by
Eldon E. Ekwall
University of Texas at El Paso

CHARLES E. MERRILL PUBLISHING COMPANY

A Bell & Howell Company   Columbus, Ohio

Published by
Charles E. Merrill Publishing Company
A Bell & Howell Company
Columbus, Ohio 43216

International Standard Book Number: 0-675-08965-4

Library of Congress Catalog Card Number: 72-96688

2 3 4 5 6 7 8 9 — 78 77 76 75 74 73

Printed in the United States of America

To four great teachers:

Roine Birky (Kempf)
Doris Fisher
Millard Seeley
Ruth Strang

Preface

Educators and researchers often decry the time lag between fruitful research and its implementation into actual classroom practice. Another complaint often voiced is that research and writing in the field of psychology are often not of a practical nature and thus have little or no application in the classroom. One purpose of this book is to bring together some of the best, most recent, and most usable research and writing in the psychology and pedagogy of reading. In an attempt to achieve this purpose, I have combined a book of readings with my own writing. The reader will note that chapters one, five, and seven contain other information in addition to that given in the articles chosen for these chapters. I believed that, although the information given in the articles was of considerable value, there was other information of which the reader should be aware. I have also written chapters six and eight since no article, or group of articles, could be found which were broadly representative of the information pertinent to these subjects.

All too many teachers, both prospective and practicing, complete a psychology course and learn about the importance of personality, self-concept, motivation, and other psychological factors, but when asked to describe how each of these relates to the teaching of reading, most are hard pressed to give a concrete answer. Therefore, a second purpose that I believe this book will fulfill is to help bridge the gap between theory and how one actually applies this theory in the teaching of reading.

Teachers, as well as doctors and lawyers, often receive poor or inadequate training. However, teachers, unlike doctors and lawyers, often fail to make up for these deficiencies through reading and study on their own after they enter the field. Consequently, a third purpose of this book is to provide reading material that is of a practical nature for self-improvement.

A fourth purpose of this book is to acquaint the reader with some of the problems we face in defining and using certain terms that seem to have caused a great deal of confusion. For example, certain words, such as "dyslexia," appear to possess one meaning for people in the medical profession and other meanings for people in education and psychology. Other terms, such as "psycholinguistics," are sometimes used where not appropriate. Although the information contained herein is not guaranteed to make the reader an expert on the use of these terms, the discussions presented should clarify some commonly held misconceptions and help the reader realize why the confusion exists.

It becomes a somewhat difficult task to categorize the various subjects for a book of this nature because there are no clear-cut boundaries for separation of certain subjects. For example, the subject of self-concept could be classified as a subcategory of personality; however, because of the extreme importance of this topic, it has been handled separately. I believe that the breakdown of the topics included here might best explain the various relationships involved. The reader will also note that each chapter contains a brief introduction written by the editor. Questions for discussion follow all but two articles. You may wish to read the discussion questions prior to reading each article.

The "right to read" philosophy demands an improvement in the quality of reading instruction. The future and practicing teacher and the practicing administrator should find within this volume many pertinent suggestions for program improvement. The researcher and college teacher also should find fertile ground for needed research in understanding the reading process as well as ways of implementing what we already know into the curriculum.

The articles for this anthology, when combined, represent hundreds of years of experience and research by some of the most competent people in the fields of psychology and/or reading; however, as one reads the series of articles contained herein, it also becomes apparent that there are many unsolved problems that need further research. It is my sincere hope that this book will be instrumental in making these problems widely known.

I would like to express my appreciation to the authors who have consented to have their articles appear in this volume. A note of thanks also is expressed to my former students whose questions and discussion have been so helpful in enabling me to learn more about the psychology of teaching reading.

My appreciation is extended to certain individuals who have helped in the preparation of the manuscript. Among these are Dixie Wicker and

Judy English (Solis). A special thanks is extended to Blanca Enriquez who helped in locating certain materials, collating information, and the typing of the final manuscript. Last, but not least, I would like to extend my sincere appreciation to Linda Gambaiani of the Merrill staff who spent many hours in editing the final manuscript.

E.E.E.

Contents

cai — computer assisted inst.

CHAPTER ONE

The

Reading

Teacher

Research during the past decade has led us to the conclusion that the teacher, and not the materials or program, is the most important ingredient in the classroom. For this reason is seems imperative that we concentrate our efforts on a study of the factors that are most important in developing and maintaining strong reading teachers. A large part of this chapter deals with these problems. The information presented by A. Sterl Artley, as well as that presented by the editor, indicates, however, that some of our commonly held beliefs are not really valid. One would think, for example, that one of the first steps in our effort to improve teaching in general would be to assess the competencies of practicing teachers. A second logical step would be to improve the training that teachers receive. As you will see, however, in reading the information contained in this chapter, we have not always been successful in doing either of the two.

The two articles in this chapter are somewhat different in nature. In the first article William R. Powell presents the criteria that *he* believes are essential for effective reading teachers. Although he does not state that these criteria are based on research, other information presented in this chapter should lead the reader to the general conclusion that he is at least partly correct as demonstrated by the results of the research. The information presented by A. Sterl Artley is based on his wide experience and on sound research. Artley also lists concrete steps which he feels should be taken to improve the effectiveness of the teacher of reading.

Following the articles you will also find further comments and research on the reading teacher which have been written by the editor.

1

This information deals with the effectiveness of teacher training, how the teacher should teach, and some further implications for the improvement of the reading teacher.

William R. Powell

The Effective Reading Teacher

Sometimes when I talk with my colleagues about "The Effective Reading Teacher," I feel as if I am bringing in the minority report. While some individuals spend their time and energies in the "lures" and "false images" of the endless controversies of

—grouping methods for teaching reading
   the ungraded school
      team teaching
         Joplin plan *— Multi age reading period.*
           family grouping *— small groups*
              middle schools, etc.

—this approach or that approach to teaching reading
   sight (look and say)
      phonics
         linguistics
           language-experience
              CAI, etc.

—this type of material versus that type of material
   phonovisual
      i.t.a. *Initial teaching Alph.*
         unifon
           Distar
              PKR
                 SRA
                    EDL
                      rebus, etc.

From William R. Powell, "The Effective Reading Teacher," *The Reading Teacher* 25, no. 7 (April 1969): 603-7. Reprinted with permission of William R. Powell and the International Reading Association.

I say we can begin to possess the skill of becoming an effective teacher of reading if we prepare ourselves with the basic and fundamental knowledge about the mission. That is where our source of strength and power emanates in the effective teaching of reading. Only after the "land has been possessed" should we as teachers concern ourselves with the related, but secondary, areas: grouping, approaches, materials, and the like. We must first, however, establish a baseline from which to launch our later priorities.

The Basic Issue

The most fundamental of basic questions: What are the first-order understandings that prepare us to be effective reading teachers? The same question stated with a little different perspective but with the same intent is: What makes a reading teacher unique—whether he is a classroom teacher of reading, a remedial reading teacher, a reading consultant, or an English teacher? What makes any teacher who teaches with and through written verbal material unique, that is, anyone who uses print at that teachable moment as the main avenue to learning? What distinguishes him from other teachers?

In these days of accountability, both fiscally and professionally, we had best be about the business of answering such a fundamental question. What follows is my own idiosyncratic reply to this crucial question.

Generally, there have been three approaches to the resolution of this issue. One approach is through studying, defining, and describing the characteristics of "effective" classroom teachers. Another approach for describing teacher behavior is through the technique of interaction analysis. The third alternative is to define and describe the basic competencies of such individuals. These three options are not necessarily mutually exclusive although past research efforts have tended to treat them as such. Neither are the approaches without their limitations. Perhaps the direction of research needed in this area is to design and conduct studies which include all three categories.

How do the people who pursue the characteristic approach describe the effective teacher? They say he or she is a person who is warm, friendly, understanding, responsive, businesslike, systematic, stimulating, and imaginative. But are these not descriptions of capable individuals regardless of their vocational field?

The "interactionists" attempt to describe the teacher through the manner in which communication is processed and facilitated in an instructional setting. They characterize their effective teacher as one who is focusing, accepting, controlling, extending, clarifying, ignoring, and the rest. While these characteristics are certainly qualities of a teacher, indeed, do they not equally describe an effective physician, minister, advertising man, lawyer, sociologist, or salesman?

Yet, aren't all teachers generalists and salesmen, too? So what makes us unique? Perhaps it is time we got around to the serious business of asking what it is we are selling and what leads us into the competence approach. What is it that we as reading teachers are supposed to be competent with or to master?

Competencies

First, we must have some conception of what makes up diagnostic teaching. For me, the effective reading teacher is one who teaches diagnostically. I view diagnostic teaching as a four-dimensional process. It involves the discriminating ability to collect data in the teaching-learning situation. (Oh, how the powers of observation become a most critical factor in effectively diagnosing.) Diagnostic teaching also includes clinical thinking. But to think clinically, one has to have something to think about and think with. In this second dimension, we need to have a clear-cut conception of the nature of and the components of the task we are to do. We have to develop conceptual maps of those items which are related to the task: the sound system, the cognitive system, the symbol system, the affective system, the error system, and the notion of syndromes. Unless one knows where he is going, a map is of no value; but once the destination has been identified, the accuracy of that map is of vital concern.

A third part of the diagnostic teaching is the ability to design and devise effective strategies for teaching. These strategies are based on the data from the other two previously mentioned dimensions. This involves our ability to match the performance level of the child, the difficulty level of the material, the valence of the interest value with the task, and the teacher's instructional ways and means of perfecting the match. Undergirding these three dimensions of diagnostic teaching is the development of a diagnostic attitude—the skill and technique which brings the other three major parts into congruence and consonance.

Second, the effective reading teacher knows how to determine the various reading levels inherent in each child in her charge—most important of which is the child's instructional reading level. This is indeed a unique characteristic of a reading teacher. Further, this technique encompasses a frame of reference for the reading teacher, a way to monitor oral reading behavior constantly, and a way to measure daily growth in reading.

Third, the effective reading teacher appreciates the value of, knows how to determine, and how to interpret accurately the potential of each student he has in his class. If we really believe in the development of each individual child to his fullest extent, then we must know something of his parameters. How do we know whom we should encourage greatly? With whom to act a bit more forcefully? Which youngster has a disability and to what degree? What is the range of individual differences we must attempt to meet? For whom is which mode of instruction most appropriate?

Fourth, we need as effective reading teachers to have a conceptual system of the organic nature of comprehension (cognitive system). We need to know the relationship between reading characteristics, the language basis for comprehending, the elements of the materials to be comprehended, and the specific comprehension skills we wish to develop. Instructional control of this vital skill area demands a conceptual map and even then any lack of knowledge about the process will lessen our effectiveness. Further, we need to see the direct effect of our ability to frame and present discriminating spiralling questions on the results of our instructional control.

Fifth, an understanding of the concept of readability (symbol system) is fundamental to an effective diagnostic teacher of reading. We need to know those message characteristics which influence the difficulty of the material and we need to be able to utilize this information on-the-spot. Diagnostic teaching demands instant replay and we do not have time to resort to specialized formulas from which our knowledge may have been derived.

Sixth, the basic ingredients of phonics, structural analysis and, more recently, linguistic patterns must clearly be perceived in our repertoire of knowledge and skills. We need to see the relationships between the auditory (phonic) and the visual (structure). Further, we should know the relationship between these two subreading tasks and linguistic patterns. Hopefully, we will have some idea of what constitutes the minimal requirements in this conceptual area.

These six competencies are basic, though I could mention one or two more. How, for instance, can we put it all together for teaching purposes, that is, the teaching of a reading lesson? Do we know the distinctive characteristics of that operation?

I cannot stress too much the importance of the completeness and the accuracy of these conceptual maps we hold concerning the primary systems of reading. A teacher who hasn't any conception or a very limited notion of these primary areas has untrained and uncontrolled perception. Faulty diagnostic teaching is probably related strongly to the incompleteness or the inaccuracies in conceptual maps.

As teachers we can operate at various levels of effectiveness. We can function at a verbal level, a performance level, or an automatic level.

At the verbal level of functioning, the correct words and jargon of the field are used. Unfortunately, people operating solely at this level often do not have the vaguest notion what those terms really mean nor how they are related. They just give the appearance of knowing.

A higher level of functioning is the performance level, of which there are two stages. At the preferred stage the teacher knows the primary systems, but they are applied only with conscious effort. The lower stage of this level occurs more frequently than we would like to admit. In the lower stage, the teacher has the knowledge and the maps but does not use them. This represents the most serious limitation to the competency approach. To know a task does not guarantee that the knowledge will be applied. Such reading teachers are not unlike the critic of whom James Russell Lowell wrote in 1848:

> It would be endless to tell you
>   the things that he knew,
> All separate facts undeniably true,
> But with him or each other they'd
>   nothing to do;
> No power of combining, arranging,
>   discerning
> Digested the masses he learned,
>   into learning
> A reading machine all wound up
>   and going,
> He mastered whatever was not
>   worth his knowing.

The highest level of functioning is truly the effective diagnostic teacher of reading. This is the automatic level. The knowledge, the maps, the strategies, and the attitude all become blended into one and become a part of the person. This teacher does correctly what comes naturally without conscious effort, but not without careful organization and preparation.

The Humanistic Touch

One can only hope the automatic teacher of reading will combine her more generalistic and humanistic qualities in arranging and conducting a teaching-learning environment. To do less may be to render their high levels of functioning ineffective. To paraphrase an old adage "It is not only what you do, but how you do it."

This humanistic touch probably is achieved, in a large part, through the quality of the covenant between the persons involved. In every teaching situation, there is a convenant, implicit though it may be, between the student and the teacher. The student comes expecting, however covertly, to give and receive. The teacher senses and accepts this responsibility and does likewise. The youngster has a right to expect to move progressively up a spiralling curricular ladder, commensurate with his potential, to new and more challenging levels of learning. When a teacher knowingly accepts a child he cannot and will not be able to help, implying that he will help, the covenant is made in bad faith. For maximum learning, a teacher must have the professional right and opportunity to enter into all covenants with his students in good faith.

Perhaps this Arabic proverb summarizes best:

He who knows not and knows not
he knows not,
   he is a fool—shun him;
He who knows not and knows he
knows not,
   he is simple—teach him;
He who knows and knows not he
knows,
   he is asleep—wake him;
He who knows and knows he
knows,
   he is wise—follow him!

The Reading Teacher

Powell — Questions for Discussion

Would you add any competencies to Powell's list of six that he feels are most important? Could the competencies mentioned by Powell be attained in most teacher education programs as they now exist? Would it be difficult to measure the teacher's attainment of the competencies mentioned by Powell? Does the research with which you are familiar tend to support or contradict Powell's thoughts about the effective reading teacher?

A. Sterl Artley

The Teacher Variable in the
Teaching of Reading

Certainly all educators are committed to increasing the level of achievement of their clients whether they be children, young people, or adults, and whether the area be mathematics, science, or foreign language. But with reading, a high level of performance is so important that no stone can be left unturned in our search for ways of facilitating growth and development. Society may raise only an eyebrow for one's inadequacies in spelling, mathematics, or ability to speak a foreign language; but, in one way or another, it castigates an individual who cannot read or read effectively.

It is no surprise, then, that to improve reading we have instituted research in all directions. Instructional materials have been examined and improved and new ones developed. Reading methods have been searched and researched, and the search continues for ways of improving instruction. Teacher education institutions have sought to strengthen their reading program by adding courses, modifying course content, or providing learning experiences that will strengthen the preparation their graduates are receiving. And above all, government funds have been poured into studies, programs, and projects, designed to discover ways of improving the level of reading attainment on all academic levels.

One of the best-known government sponsored studies is the Cooperative Research Program in First Grade Reading Instruction, reported in detail in the *Reading Research Quarterly* (Bond and Dykstra, 1967).

From A. Sterl Artley, "The Teacher Variable in the Teaching of Reading," *The Reading Teacher* 23, no. 3 (December 1969): 239-48. Reprinted with permission of A. Sterl Artley and the International Reading Association.

The master study, you recall, involved twenty-seven individual studies carried on in various places in the United States, and attempted to discover if there were an approach to initial reading instruction that would produce superior reading and spelling achievement at the end of grade one. Instructional approaches currently in use, including the linguistic, basal, language-experience, and i.t.a., were evaluated in terms of objectively measured reading achievement.

Though the study has some inherent limitations, its findings and conclusions are significant in relation to pupil achievement, and its implications for teacher education are cogent. It is to the issue of teacher education that I would like to direct attention starting from the recommendations of the First Year Study.

In the first place the study points out that children seem to learn to read by a variety of materials and methods. Accordingly, the authors state, ". . . no one approach is so distinctly better in all situations and respects than the others that it should be considered the one best method and the one to be used exclusively" (Bond and Dykstra, 1967). In other words, improved reading achievement does not appear to be a function solely of approach or method. And then the authors (1967) continue,

> Future research might well center on teacher and learning situation characteristics. . . . The tremendous range among classrooms within any method points out the importance of elements in the learning situation over and above the methods employed. *To improve reading instruction, it is necessary to train better teachers of reading rather than to expect a panacea in the form of materials.*

A similar statement has been made by others. Ramsey (1962), in an evaluation of three grouping procedures for teaching reading concluded, "The thing that the study probably illustrates most clearly is that the influence of the teacher is greater than that of a particular method, a certain variety of materials, or a specific plan of organization. Given a good teacher other factors in teaching reading tend to pale to insignificance."

A very recent study reported by Harris and Morrison (1969) reiterated the conclusions of the two other studies. These authors reported a three-year study and a replicated two-year study of two approaches to teaching reading, basal readers vs. language experience. They found as did Bond and Dykstra that differences in mean reading scores *within* each method were much larger than differences between methods and approaches. They write,

The results of the study have indicated that the teacher is far more important than the method. Costly procedures such as smaller classes and provision of auxiliary personnel may continue to give disappointing results *if teaching skills are not improved*. It is recommended, therefore, that in-service workshops and expert consultive help be provided for all teachers and especially for those with minimal experience. (P. 339)

In other words, these studies seem to be saying clearly—to improve pupil achievement in reading, one should look first at the teacher and his training. This, then, puts the responsibility squarely upon the shoulders of those who are engaged in teacher education, both pre- and in-service—teachers of methods courses, supervisors of practice teaching, and school- and system-wide reading supervisors, both elementary and secondary.

But to look at the teacher and his training poses a question in need of an answer. What teacher characteristics or teaching behaviors appear to differentiate the effective teacher of reading from the ineffective one? What seems to make a difference between "good" and "poor" reading teaching? Knowing the answers to such questions as these would make it possible for us to select as reading teachers those with certain characteristics or to prepare teachers with certain skills and understandings that appear to be associated with maximum pupil growth.

The writing and research in the areas of teacher education, teacher effectiveness, and teaching behaviors are voluminous, almost as voluminous as those in reading. And like the research in reading, their findings frequently leave much to be desired. I can certainly agree with Jackson (1966) who writes,

. . . Almost all of the noble crusades that have set out in search of the best teacher and the best method . . . have returned empty-handed. The few discoveries to date . . . are pitifully small in proportion to their cost in time and energy. For example, the few drops of knowledge that can be squeezed out of a half century of research on the personality characteristics of good teachers are so low in intellectual food value that it is almost embarrassing to discuss them. . . . (P. 9)

Part of the reason for the disappointing results, at least insofar as reading is concerned, is that the researcher was attempting to identify the good teacher and good teaching rather than the good teacher and good teaching of *reading*. And I have good reason to believe they are not the same. As a result they have described for us a kind of invisible, ghost-like person who, in fact, may not exist. She (he) has been found to be cooperative, sympathetic, and poised. She is well-groomed, healthy, imaginative, and cooperative. She gets along well with her co-workers and her principal, and she gets her reports in on time. As one of my friends said, "She has the same characteristics we would expect to find in a good bar-girl." We know nothing of what this person does in a reading class nor do we know anything about the achievement of her pupils. In short, the studies tell us little that we can put into the context of reading or that gives us helpful clues in planning programs of teacher education. Let me illustrate from several studies.

A widely quoted and certainly monumental study of teacher characteristics is the study reported by Ryans (1960). Ryans attempted to identify the general personal or social characteristics that would distinguish groups of teachers receiving high and low assessments as indicated by a self-report inventory and observations of classroom behavior by trained observers. Three dimensions of teacher classroom behavior were identified; namely, "X"—warm, understanding, friendly vs. aloof, egocentric, restrictive; "Y"—responsible, systematic, vs. unplanned, slipshod; "Z"—stimulating, imaginative vs. dull, routine. Further studies with the Teacher Characteristics Scale indicated that the "highly assessed" teachers received more favorable opinions of pupils and administrators than "low assessed" teachers, and that pupil behavior was rather closely related to teacher behavior, at least on the elementary school level.

A group of studies growing out of the work of Flanders and his co-workers (Flanders, 1960; Amidon and Flanders, 1963) deal with the development and use of a system of interaction analysis. Verbal behavior of teachers in the classroom was studied by trained observers and categorized as indirect (eliciting creative and voluntary pupil behavior) or direct (eliciting conformity and compliance). An indirect-direct (I/D) ratio was derived for each teacher studied. The rationale for the study of classroom interaction rests on the assumption that certain kinds of teacher statements, those that indicate acceptance, encouragement, and praise, encourage student participation, while other kinds indicating commands, criticism, statement making, and the like, inhibit student participation. The degree and quality of student participation, in turn, affects achievement. In verification of these assumptions Flanders was able to show that in seventh and eighth grade social studies and mathematics, students who were taught by teachers with a high I/D index achieve to a greater extent than those taught in a direct manner.

In another study conducted by Amidon and Giammatteo (1965) the authors were able to show that elementary teachers selected as "superior" by their supervisors and administrators showed a higher incidence of indirect teacher-talk when teaching language arts than that used by a randomly selected group of teachers. The authors conclude that, "The results . . . would seem to indicate that verbal behavior patterns of superior teachers can be identified and that these patterns do differ markedly from the verbal behavior patterns of other teachers" (P. 285).

Meux and Smith (1964) have developed still another approach to identifying significant teaching behaviors. They classify teaching behavior in terms of its logical qualities through observation of the teacher in the classroom. Classroom interaction is categorized into "logical dimensions of teaching" involving such functions as defining, describing, stating, explaining, etc., on the assumption that classroom discourse may be identified and analyzed in terms of rules of logic. On the basis of their analysis procedure they are able to show that increased pupil understanding and improved thinking ability are outcomes of instruction where teachers are taught to handle the logical operation involved in teaching.

The studies to which we have referred make important contributions to our understanding of what is involved in teaching, and could be justified solely on that basis. Teaching on any level is multi-dimensional and we need studies that will enlighten us as to the nature of the process. Yet looking at these studies for information relative to ways of improving reading instruction, and thereby pupil attainment, provides little that would be helpful.

In the first place, the teacher is being studied as a generalist, nonspecific to any teaching area or any grade level—elementary or secondary. Yet we know that there are differences among teachers in the way they handle given instructional areas and levels. A third grade teacher teaching in a self-contained classroom may be a very effective science teacher, but leave much to be desired in the way she handles reading. Or an eighth grade teacher may very skillfully teach reading through his literature, but would be completely lost as a teacher of second grade reading.

In the second place such studies as those mentioned have failed to give us any information about the teacher's teaching procedures, the content she teaches, the understandings she must have, or the commitment she has made to clinic teaching. It is conceivable that an observer might make use of one of the interaction analyses and derive for a fourth grade teacher a high score while observing an oral-reading-round class. The teacher-talk is at a minimum, she asks questions, she is accepting of the child's responses, she praises and encourages, yet who would accept this as an effective way of conducting a reading lesson? Or in another situation the teacher may be well groomed, poised, efficient, gracious, and get along well with her co-workers and principal, and yet never have had a course in the teaching of reading.

In the third place these studies are concerned only indirectly with the product of teaching, that is, changes in pupil behavior or with the cognitive aspects of learning in the way of skills, abilities, understandings, etc. It is not until we have seen the results of teacher characteristics or interaction, or behavior, or whatever, on pupil development that we will have something that we can use in teacher education.

Not for one minute are we deprecating the value and significance of the studies to which we have referred. They have made and are making a contribution to our understanding of the teaching process. I am certain that the researchers, themselves, would say that the studies are not designed to provide the kind of teacher education help to which we have referred. This being true we need, then, a different research approach. At least we need to ask different kinds of questions that will give us different kinds of answers, answers that we can use in developing our pre- and in-service teacher education programs.

Coming somewhat nearer to the type of studies we need in reading are those being carried on by Turner and Fattu (1960) at the University of Indiana. These investigators see teaching behavior as problem solving ability involving the use of learning sets and specific responses relevant to the teaching situation. In reading, a "Teaching Tasks in Reading" test was developed, assessing a teacher's understanding and application of skills in such areas as selecting appropriate instructional materials, grouping children, judging improvement, diagnosing word perception and the like. The authors found that the test differentiated between preparatory teachers, student teachers, and experienced teachers. It was interesting to find that their studies substantiated the observation that teaching skill in one area (reading) was not necessarily indicative of the level of performance in another (arithmetic). Moreover, they found that a given teacher may not perform evenly in a single curricular area when different problems were encountered.

A more recent side study was reported by Turner (1967) who found that an analysis of the data derived from a Teacher Characteristics Schedule (measuring nine selected personal-social characteristics such as friendly, organized, stimulating, child-centered, emotional adjustment, etc.) and a combined Mathematics teaching Task and Teaching Tasks in Reading scales made possible the identification of teacher characteristics associated with given types of problems of beginning teachers (discipline, management, forming instructional groups in reading, pupil expectancy, etc.). For example, teachers who had problems in reading appeared to be disorganized, to lack warmth or friendliness and a high level of imaginative behavior, and failed to have a favorable attitude toward democratic procedures. Turner suggested that a set of measures could be assembled by which problems of beginning teachers could be identified, and through counseling and in-service activities, steps could be taken to alleviate them.

The work of Bush and Gage (1968) at the Center for Research and Development in Teaching at Stanford University should be watched with interest, in view of the fact that one of the areas they are investigating is that of teacher behaviors and characteristics and their relationships to pupil achievement and changes. In fact, they indicate that one of their long-term goals of one project is to define a set of skills for effective teaching, to determine the effects of those behaviors, and to determine how to train teachers to use those skills. As a project effort this approaches the thing that I am concerned about. It will be interesting to note whether their "skills for effective teaching" will be general or whether they will be differentiated for various instructional areas and levels.

Lacking information about teacher competencies and related student behavior that could be translated into the context of reading, I would like to suggest a study or series of studies that might provide the needed information. I think we would have to admit that without research evidence all of us in teacher education have been operating pretty much on a series of hunches, on empirical evidence rather than objective. It may well be that if and when we do have the research evidence that clues us in on what "good" reading teachers do that "poor" ones do not, we may find only that our hunches have been confirmed. But at least we will know that.

Thinking about the two basic undergraduate courses, one for elementary teachers, the other for secondary, offered at our institution, here are the areas in which I would like information that would provide an objective base for what we try to do. First, I need consensus on the skills, abilities, understandings, and behaviors that we expect a mature reader to possess. Next I need to know the abilities, skills, knowledges, and competencies that a teacher will need to have if she is to promote sequential growth toward those desired learner competencies. Finally, I need to know the teaching procedures, the course content, the learning activities that I should use in my education classes in order to develop those teacher competencies.

To secure these kinds of information obviously requires a series of studies, each with the necessary research design that will yield appropriate findings from which conclusions may be drawn. It will be a prodigious task, but I am as certain as I am of anything in the reading area that Bond and Dykstra, Ramsey, and Harris and Morrison are right in saying that to improve reading achievement our efforts must be placed on the improvement of our teacher education program. This is our frontier for exploration. Believe me, I am not unaware of the problems to be encountered, but they should not deter us from action.

Let me try to indicate the broad steps the studies may take:

1. Formulating a broad and inclusive concept of reading maturity. By this I mean goals, or more appropriately, a series of goals, toward which reading instruction and guidance should be directed. I say, "broad and inclusive" because the goals must be more than ability to perceive words and comprehend meaning. I used the term, "maturity" not as a final point to be attained as an adult, but rather as a series of maturities, for a third grader may be a mature reader (i.e. meet the normal expectations for a child completing his third year in school), or he may be a mature reader going into high school, with yet a distance to go on a scale of maturity. Maturity is considered a process, a series of expanding concentric circles, rather than a final fixed point on a scale.

Coming to a decision with regard to what is involved in reading maturity will be no small problem, to begin with. However, spade work in this area has been done by Gray and Rogers (1956) and described in their *Maturity in Reading—Its Nature and Appraisal*. If you have read this monograph, you will remember that the authors defined reading maturity in terms of five dimensions: interest in reading, purposes for reading, recognition and construction of meaning, reaction to and use of ideas, and kinds of materials read. Each of these five dimensions was broken down into specific criteria which in turn, were assessed on a five-point scale. The authors of this study applied their scale to adults. Obviously if the idea is used with elementary and secondary aged children, intermediate maturity points would need to be established. Determining objectives for a reading program is little different from deciding where one is going on a vacation trip. One needs to know his destination before he backs the car out of the garage.

2. Making a series of decisions with respect to how the several correlates of reading growth referred to in number one will be measured. Apparently some of the areas may be measured by objective tests, others by observation, others by rather subjectively determined points on a scale. Suffice it to say that the ultimate criteria of the adequacy of a reading program and the effectiveness of teaching will need to be in terms of changes in the individual, with changes very broadly construed as indicated, but quantitatively assessed, none the less.

I am cognizant that learner change as a measure of teaching effectiveness has been avoided in the studies of teaching chiefly for the reason that it is difficult to measure. Substituted for it have been evaluations by principals, supervisors, peers, and even pupils. But in reading instruction we cannot compromise. The teacher is either good or poor in terms of what happens to the child. The principal as an evaluator is likely to be a questionable one, for he evaluates the generalist rather than the teacher of reading. Frequently he has never had work in reading and his assessment of the goodness of instruction may be in terms of his own biases and misinformation.

3. Ascertaining teacher characteristics and teaching practices assumed to promote in the most expeditious and effective manner the kinds of changes and types of growth decided on in number one and measured as in number two. Here the researcher's efforts will be in identifying the teacher variables that might differentiate the effective from the ineffective teacher. This could be done by making a series of kinescopes of reading instruction on a given label taught by a number of different teachers. Experienced observers would examine the tapes in terms of the concept of maturity established in number one to see if they would be able to identify and classify such factors as teacher talk, competencies developed, teaching style used, provision for individual needs, and the like.

4. Subjecting to measurement each assumed factor or teacher variable determined in step number three, and through experimentation determining its relation to pupil changes or growth in the various dimensions and levels of the mature reading act as established in number one and measured in number two. One might attempt in this step to identify groups of high and low achieving children, holding constant such factors as intelligence, socio-economic background, etc., and observe the teachers and their teaching to see if in truth the assumed variables determined in step number three differentiate the teachers of the high achieving pupils from those of the low achievers and to what degree. Or one could identify groups of teachers having and failing to have the variables derived in step number three, and determine if the pupils taught by those teachers were differentiated in terms of reading maturity. It is through step number four that we should be able to indicate that a teacher who possesses certain characteristics, who uses certain techniques and certain types of instructional media, and who provides in certain ways for the differentiated needs of children, will stand greater chances of having learners who are higher on a scale of reading

maturity than teachers who do not have these characteristics and understandings, and who do not perform these instructional acts.

5.   Using the information provided through step number four to improve the program of teacher education in reading. Since one now has objective evidence that certain teacher characteristics and understandings and certain teaching practices are productive of a higher level of pupil maturity than others, he can now begin to employ this evidence in his teacher education program in reading. One may discover that he needs to give more or even less emphasis to certain instructional areas than he did before. He may need to provide certain kinds of learning experiences to develop needed teaching competencies. In fact, a new dimension of research opens up for the teacher educator. Having evidence that teachers need to possess certain understandings and do certain things in certain ways to bring a desired level of achievement in their pupils, the teacher of the "methods" course finds it incumbent to discover the best ways to prepare his teachers in training. Answers will be needed to such questions as the following: How effective is lecturing in relation to other procedures? Will a four-minute single concept audio-visual tape be as much help as a thirty-minute film? How effective is microteaching in producing a particular understanding? Can one use effectively a group of students from his methods class to serve as a simulated group of third graders to demonstrate a given technique? Armed with the kinds of information described, one can begin to say with some degree of assurance that as teachers of reading teachers we have taken significant and objectively derived steps toward improving the quality of teaching, and thereby the quality of reading that children, young people, and adults are able to do. Teacher education is a rich and rewarding area within which to work. As for myself I would choose no other. We know now that the reading that children and young people do will not be improved by the administration of a capsule, by facilitating their creeping and crawling, by the use of a machine, or by method "x." We can give up these searches and concentrate on what we surmised was the case all along—that improved reading is the result of improved teaching, and in that pursuit many of us have a major stake.

References

Amidon, E., and Flanders, N. A. *The role of the teacher in the classroom.* Minneapolis: Paul Amidon and Associates, 1963.

Amidon, E. J., and Giammatteo, M. The verbal behavior of superior teachers. *The Elementary School Journal*, 1965, *65*, 283-285.

Bond, G. L., and Dykstra, R. The cooperative research program in first grade reading. *Reading Research Quarterly*, 1967, *2*.

Bush, R. N., and Gage, N. L. Center for research and development in teaching. *Journal of Research and Development in Education*, 1968, *1*, 86-105.

Flanders, N. A. *Teacher influence: pupil attitudes and achievement, final report, 1960*. (Project 397) Washington, D.C.: U. S. Office of Health, Education, and Welfare, 1960.

Gray, W. S., and Rogers, Bernice. *Maturity in reading: its nature and appraisal*. Chicago: The University of Chicago Press, 1956.

Harris, A. J., and Morrison, C. The CRAFT project: a final report. *The Reading Teacher*, 1969, *22*, 335-340.

Jackson, P. W. *The way teaching is*. Washington: Association for Supervision and Curriculum Development, 1966.

Meux, M., and Smith, B. O. Logical dimensions of teaching behavior. In B. J. Biddle, and W. J. Ellena (Eds.) *Contemporary reesarch on teacher effectiveness*. New York: Holt, Rinehart, and Winston, 1964.

Ramsey, W. S. An evaluation of three methods of teaching reading. In A. Figurel (Ed.) Challenge and experiment in reading. *International Reading Association Conference Proceedings*, 1962, *7*, 153.

Ryans, D. G. *Characteristics of teachers*. Washington, D. C.: American Council on Education, 1960.

Turner, R. L., and Fattu, N. A. Skill in teaching: a reappraisal of the concepts and strategies in teaching effectiveness research. *Bulletin of the School of Education*, Indiana University, 1960, *36*, 1-40.

Turner, R. L. Some predictors of problems of beginning teachers. *The Elementary School Journal*, 1967, *67*, 251-256.

The Reading Teacher

Artley — Questions for Discussion

P 14   What have been some of the shortcomings of past research when applied specifically to the field of reading? Have past studies in teacher behavior offered any clues that would be useful in assessing good teaching? P 16 If so, where might we start? Why is the good teacher and good teaching not necessarily the same as the good teacher and good teaching of reading? What are the problems involved in having principals evaluate teachers of reading?

Eldon E. Ekwall

The Reading Teacher —
Further Comments and Research

A further question that has been raised is whether or not the personality traits deemed necessary for a good teacher, or even a good teacher of developmental reading, are adequate or appropriate for a teacher of remedial reading. Dorothy Klausner (1967) points out the fact that because of the special problems of many disabled readers the teacher-pupil relationship is also changed somewhat from that of the teacher in a developmental reading program. For example, children in remedial reading usually have to work with methods and materials that may appear somewhat babyish to them. Helping these children then presents a situation where the teacher needs to be even more cognizant of each pupil's likes and dislikes and general attitudes. The remedial reading teacher also needs to administer more diagnostic tests and thus creates a situation where each child can easily experience a great deal of failure if special care is not exercised. The remedial reading teacher also deals with parents who are, because of the nature of their child's problem, somewhat anxious about his performance. Factors such as these would seem to require that remedial reading teachers possess personality traits and/or characteristics somewhat different from those of developmental reading teachers. Obviously a great deal of research will be required to help us answer the many unsolved problems in this area.

Can We Really Identify
Good Teaching?

Many of us who have served in a supervisory capacity in the public schools would probably have a tendency to feel that we have definitely been able to distinguish between good, mediocre, and poor teachers. Research results, however, do not tend to support this sort of conclusion; that is, if we define good teachers as those whose students achieve the highest and poor teachers as those whose students achieve the lowest. Albert Harris (1969) points out that the results of the cooperative first-grade reading studies indicated that the correlations between supervisor ratings of teacher effectiveness and class achievement averages ranged from .10 to .22. This was, as Harris states, "...hardly better than zero..." (p. 197). In referring to the Bond and Dykstra (1967) study Harris does, however, point out that there are some general characteristics of good teachers that can be identified. Harris states,

> When the five cooperative projects with the best results were compared to the five projects with the poorest results, the high-achieving projects had much higher percentages of teachers who were given good ratings in class organization and structure, class participation, awareness of and attention to individual needs, and overall competence. (Bond and Dykstra, 1967, p. 195.) But within each project the supervisors were not very successful in distinguishing the superior from the inferior teachers (p. 197).

It would appear at this point that we simply do not know very much about how to rate teachers. It also seems imperative that we should undertake large-scale research to attempt to locate those characteristics of good teachers and good teaching that produce superior student achievement. Furthermore, the techniques for observation and accurate rating of these characteristics must be incorporated into courses dealing with the training of supervisory personnel.

Does Teacher Training and Experience Help?

The instinctive answer to this question would be, of course, it does! However, a review of the research would seem to indicate that the answer may be either yes or no depending on a number of different factors. For example, a study by Rexel Brown (1969) indicated that no significant difference existed between the effectiveness of teachers with 0-3 years of experience, 4-10 years of experience, and 11-25 plus years of experience when pupil gain was used as the criterion. However, Brown reported that a significant difference did exist between the effectiveness of teachers with no graduate course in the teaching of reading, with one course in the teaching of reading, and with two or more courses in the teaching of reading. Brown reports that the mean pupil gain in vocabulary favored teachers with two or more courses in the teaching of reading and, while not reaching significance, the mean pupil gain in comprehension and total reading favored these teachers. A study by Carolyn Gracenin (1971), however, produced opposite results. Gracenin's study involved forty-two classrooms of first-year teachers who had all graduated from the same college. Pupils were divided into two groups which were supposedly taught in the same manner. One group was taught by teachers who had taken an additional course in reading, while the other group was taught by teachers who had not taken the additional reading course. There was no significant difference in the mean scores of either group.

One is always on dangerous ground when he attempts to second-guess the results of any study; however, the results of studies such as these may shed some light on the problem in spite of their contrasting results. For example, it is apparent that some kinds of teacher training are effective, although all kinds are not. The students in Gracenin's study had all graduated from the same college, and the study concerned itself with whether or not teachers taking an *additional* course made a significant difference in their pupils' mean gain. Perhaps all had received an excellent methods course to begin with, and the addition of one more course simply did not add appreciably to the teachers' knowledge of how to teach reading. One might also speculate on the nature and content of the additional course.

Further evidence of the effectiveness of certain training programs was presented by Empress Zedler (1970), who studied the progress of underachieving pupils taught by teachers with specific training in conventional as well as unconventional methods of teaching. Zedler's control groups were taught by teachers who were neither specifically trained nor supervised and used only "conventional methods." Zedler reports that the experimental group that was taught by specifically trained teachers made significantly greater gains in academic achievement and mental function than did the control group whose teachers lacked the special training.

Studies such as those of Arthur Heilman (1966) and Richard Burnett (1963) have also demonstrated the value of teacher-training programs and the ability of well-trained teachers to outperform those with less training. Although studies on the effectiveness of teacher-training programs do produce results that tend to be contradictory, the important point seems to be that certain types of teacher training are highly successful while other teacher-training programs appear to be of little or no value. Our research in improving the training of the reading teacher should no longer concern itself with whether or not training is effective, but rather with what type of training is most effective with teachers with various degrees of training and experience.

Teacher Training

Although no one approach to teacher training has proven completely satisfactory or superior to others, several approaches to both pre-service and in-service training appear to be somewhat successful. Performance-based teacher education is currently proving its value in a few teacher training institutions. Since we are striving to train teachers to perform certain tasks, the concept of a performance-based curriculum certainly seems logical. The typical course in a performance-based teacher education program no longer consists of a series of lectures, but rather of a set of behavioral objectives deemed necessary for the future teacher to accomplish. Courses usually contain a number of "modules," each of which is a complete teaching strategy for attempting to reach an objective. For example, a module might be constructed on teaching teachers to administer an informal reading inventory. The behavioral objective for this module might read as follows: "After completing the module on informal reading inventories, the student should be able to administer an informal reading inventory to a student via video-tape and obtain the same results as two other people who give the IRI simultaneously, *or* obtain the same results as those shown by the instructor as being correct." The general procedure for working through a module might be as follows:

1.   Take the pretest to determine if instruction is necessary. (Student could elect to omit this if he knew he did not know the material or could not meet the criteria as specified in the behavioral objective.)

2.   Take instruction via several routes such as:

a) Listen and watch a videotape lecture and demonstration of a student being given an IRI.

b) Read the International Reading Association monograph on how to administer IRIs.

c) Attend a lecture and audio-tape demonstration on administering IRIs.

3.   Take the posttest.

4.   If the posttest (behavioral objective) was passed, the student would move on to the next module; however, if it was failed, he might then elect to go back and be rerouted through another method of instruction.

As one can see, the principal difference between the traditional methods course and performance-based teacher education is that the student must demonstrate his ability to perform various tasks which the instructor feels are necessary to understand and "know" the material in his course. The use of modules is simply a convenient way of dividing what was typically a whole "course" up into measurable and/or workable units.

Although offering a great deal of promise, the concept of the performance-based curriculum is still only as good as the production of the teaching modules themselves. Many good instructors have essentially been using this concept for years in courses in reading diagnosis and also in courses labelled "practicum." The production of materials for modules is also very costly and many institutions simply lack the manpower and resources to develop adequate materials. However, as more institutions develop instructional modules, there should be an exchange of materials among various teacher-training institutions which should add to the overall capability of smaller, less endowed institutions to develop their own performance-based teacher education programs.

Another method of teacher training which has proven its worth at the secondary level is that of simply putting teachers through a course in which they actually learn the subject matter that they are to teach. Since many people maintain that we usually try to emulate our own former teachers, this method seems to make a great deal of common sense. Richard Smith and Wayne Otto (1969) report that such a program was carried out with nineteen junior and senior high school teachers in the Madison, Wisconsin, public schools. Students were given instruction in rate, interpretation, literal comprehension, and vocabulary on five consecutive Monday evenings. Two evenings were also spent on pre- and post-instruction testing. Although the authors reported that some of the teachers felt the need for more training, they did indicate that a course of this nature could be effective in getting content area teachers to teach reading skills in their subject matter areas.

Another method being used by some teacher-training institutions with a great deal of success is that of simply teaching methods courses at the site where the student teacher will be teaching. Florence Shankman (1971) describes such a program carried on between Temple University and the Philadelphia Public Schools. In this experiment, methods courses in reading were conducted within the elementary school. Half the period was devoted to discussion and lectures and the balance of the time was spent in actual elementary classrooms, where the student teachers taught individuals or small groups. This enabled the student teachers to immediately try out new ideas and provide for immediate feedback to the instructor. Students also made frequent visits to homes and businesses in the area to broaden their social perspective.

Many teacher-training institutions are also employing the use of micro-teaching. In micro-teaching a student teacher teaches a very short lesson (usually less than five minutes) to elementary or secondary students or to her peers. In some cases this lesson is videotaped. This lesson is then studied and criticized in detail. Albert Harris (1969) reports that a study by Davis and Smoot (1969) indicated that students using the micro-teaching technique improved more in eighteen out of twenty-two variables than students who took the same course where micro-teaching was not used.

Videotaping of entire lessons taught by student teachers has also proved its worth in a number of teacher-training institutions. In using this method the student teacher has the opportunity to view her own performance in private or with a cooperating or supervising teacher. This, of course, allows the student teacher the opportunity to point out her own errors, which is more likely to produce a lasting change in behavior.

How Should the
Teacher Teach?

Although the very excellent article by Artley has covered this subject to some extent, a research study by Roscoe Davidson (1969) contains some information which the editor believes is well worth knowing. Davidson used an interaction analysis system, patterned after that of Flanders, to study teacher-pupil interaction in grades two through six. He defines non-productive thinking as ". . . the absence of a response, or one that is incorrect, not pertinent, unclear, or in need of supporting evidence or reasoning" (p. 703). He lists the following characteristics of the classroom situation as those where relatively high proportions of critical thinking and low proportions of non-productive thinking took place:

1.   Questions were closely enough related to the material read or to a common background of experience to permit children to think critically about the questions and the answers given by other children.

2.   Questions inviting insightful and reflective answers were pursued until such responses were produced. In less productive discussions, characteristic teacher behavior was to turn to other questions, to provide the answers, or to accept unsupported answers.

3.   "Clarifying questions" were used frequently. These questions called for clarification or justification of a response. In less productive discussions these questions were asked infrequently.

4.   Teacher-pupil interaction was paced slowly enough to give children time to think. Where critical thinking was prominent, the teacher's control of class time seemed to be guided by a greater concern for the quality of verbal interaction.

5.   A comparatively small proportion of time was used in the teacher's repetition of questions, answers, and information contained in previous comments.

6.   Children who were incorrect or slow in responding were given clues and encouragement to develop their own answers. In similar

situations in less productive discussions the teacher usually called on another child or provided the answer; the focus seemed to be on the answer itself rather than on thinking processes that would lead to it.

7.   Children's responses that were germane and thought-provoking, but apparently not anticipated, were capitalized upon. In contrast, a frequent teacher reaction in less productive discussions was to pass over the unexpected response in pursuit of the answer the teacher was anticipating; the teacher's reaction was, in fact, "Yes, but that isn't what I was thinking of."

8.   Several kinds of inadequate and inappropriate pupil responses were identified by the teacher and were pursued with "clarifying questions." Interesting comments that were unrelated to the question, incorrect responses, repetition of previous answers, and expressions of feeling lacking in support did not go unnoticed.

Albert Harris (1969) also presents some research information on how the teacher should teach that should be useful to the teacher of reading. In discussing the effect of teacher criticism, Harris states,

> The effect of teacher criticism of pupils has been found to vary with the type of criticism. Mild criticism is not related to poor achievement. On the other hand, strong criticism has significant negative relationships with achievement. To put it differently, teachers should not hesitate to tell a pupil that he made a mistake, to correct him, or to give him direction. But use of shaming, sarcasm, and other forms of strong criticism is harmful to learning (p. 198).

Harris also says that "minimal reinforcement" using comments such as "uh huh" or "right" was related to positive achievement. He also points out, however, that frequent use of stronger praise did not seem to be related to positive achievement.

Harris also reports that studies have indicated that frequent verbal statements by the teacher that are intended to control behavior were associated with poor achievement. On the other hand, teachers whose pupils behaved themselves without frequent reminders tended to achieve higher than in those classrooms where the teacher constantly interrupted to control behavior.

Further Implications for the
Improvement of the Reading Teacher

In an article written about beginning reading in Norway, Malcolm Douglas (1969) states, "It is sometimes instructive to take a look at the ways of other people as they work with children; not because they warrant being copied, but rather for purposes of contrast so that one may be helped to entertain ideas that could lead to useful modifications in ways of helping children learn" (p. 17). This article certainly does contain a great deal of food for thought. Douglas states that in a survey conducted by Olaf Larsen (a member of the faculty of the Kristiansand Teachers College), teachers ranked inability of students to read as last among various instructional problems. He states that the percentage of disabled readers is only a fraction of that in the United States. Douglas also points out that dialect differences in Norway are often very pronounced and that many of the difficulties that we experience in teaching reading in the United States are also present in Norway. Why then are Norwegians so successful in an area in which we often experience a great many problems? Some factors that Douglas mentions are as follows:

1.   Norway has generally achieved a high standard of living for a majority of its population.

2.   Curriculum goals are spelled out in very great detail, but there is little or no interference in *how* teaching will be done or in how these goals will be accomplished.

3.   Although some effort is being made to individualize instruction, most reading instruction is still given *en masse* and systematic reading instruction is undertaken for all children only during their first year of school.

4.   The language is considered phonetically regular and instruction begins by instructing children in the sounds of a few letters. This then proceeds to a more analytic approach and eventually to what might be considered an eclectic approach.

5.   Although studies are being undertaken in which children are being taught by an approach which is perhaps more analytic, children appear to learn equally well either way. This evidently tells us what the First Grade Reading Studies did in the United States; that is, that materials and/or methods are not always the most important factors.

6.   Most children do not begin formal schooling until the age of seven. Although there are some kindergartens as in the United States, very little formal training is attempted at this level.

7.   In the first three grades the Norwegian child spends only about fifteen hours per week in school. Approximately five hours per week are spent in reading and writing instruction and the rest is divided among other subjects.

8.   The Norwegian child is likely to have the same teacher for at least four years; whereas in the United States, children usually

change teachers each year. Experiments are presently being conducted in which children will remain with the same teacher for. nine years.

9.   All grouping is done strictly on a heterogeneous basis so that there is no hint of difference in abilities.

10.   Coupled with the heterogeneous system of grouping is the expectation that all children will succeed. Since children will be with the same teacher for several years, there is less urgency that children learn a certain concept before they get to the next teacher.

11.   The teaching profession is held in high regard and it is more difficult to obtain admission to a teacher's college than to enter a university.

12.   Children who do need remedial help are given it at an early stage rather than waiting until the problem becomes more pronounced.

The information presented by Douglas contains some ideas that might be well worth incorporating into our future research in the United States. For example, might children do better if they were left with the same teacher throughout the school day and for several years providing we made an attempt to individualize instruction? Couldn't this system be used and still individualize instruction just as well as in some of our open concept schools? After all, aren't open concept schools really just an administrative device to allow teachers to move children into "groups" where they will receive individualized instruction? Don't we now have an ample supply of teachers so that our selection standards could be raised? Doesn't our research indicate that remedial or corrective reading programs are more effective if they are concentrated at an earlier stage, that is, on children who are just beginning to develop reading problems? Do we have any proof that early "formal" training in reading is effective? Might we be better off to extend children's background of experiences for another year before they begin formal training in reading? (Some studies have shown that early training in reading is effective, but do we have any real proof that a simple extension of a "good" readiness program for culturally deprived children and perhaps simply waiting another year for non-culturally deprived children might not produce equal or better results with less cost to our taxpayers?) Could children often profit more if they spent a greater amount of time in simply "free reading" books at their level and spent less time on actual drill activities? Since the Norwegians spend considerably less time in school in grades one through three, nothing seems sacred about the amount of time that children spend in school or on certain types of activities. How can we improve teachers' expectations for the success of their pupils?

References

Bond, G. L., and Dykstra, R. *Coordinating Center for First-Grade Reading Instruction Programs*. Final Report, Cooperative Project No. X-001. Minneapolis: University of Minnesota, 1967.

Brown, R. E. "Teacher skill and other variables associated with effectiveness in teaching reading." Doctoral dissertation, Indiana University, 1968.

Burnett, R. W. "The diagnostic proficiency of teachers of reading." *The Reading Teacher* 16 (1963): 229-33.

Davidson, R. L. "Teacher influence and children's levels of thinking." *The Reading Teacher* 22 (1969): 702-4.

Davis, O. L., and Smoot, B. R. "Effects on the verbal teaching behavior of beginning secondary teacher candidates' participation in a program of laboratory teaching."*AERA Paper Abstracts*, 1969, pp. 112-13.

Gracenin, C. T. "The effects of an additional undergraduate reading course with practicum on the beginning teacher's pupils' growth in reading." Doctoral dissertation, University of Pittsburgh, 1970.

Harris, A. J. "The effective teacher of reading." *The Reading Teacher* 23 (1968): 195-204.

Heilman, A. W. "Effects of an intensive inservice program on teacher classroom behavior and pupil reading achievement." *The Reading Teacher* 19 (1966): 622-26.

Klausner, D. C. "Screening and development of the remedial reading teacher." *Journal of Reading* 10 (1967): 552-59.

Shankman, F. "Innovations in teacher-training for inner-city schools." *The Reading Teacher*, 24 (1971): 744-47.

Smith, R. J., and Smith, Otto W. "Changing teacher attitudes toward teaching reading in the content areas." *Journal of Reading* 13 (1969): 299-304.

_____. "Elementary teachers' preferences for preservice and in-service training in the teaching of reading." *Journal of Educational Research* 63 (1970): 445-49.

Zedler, E. Y. "Better teacher-training — the solution for children's reading problems." *Journal of Learning Disabilities* 3 (1970): 106-12.

CHAPTER TWO

The Early Years and Reading

This chapter deals with some of the many important questions concerning readiness and early reading. One of these questions has been whether or not there is an "ideal" time to begin formal reading instruction and whether or not we can accurately determine when that time has arrived through the use of readiness tests. In the first article Dolores Durkin does an excellent job of providing some background information on these important questions and from her wide background of research and experience provides some answers to these questions. Durkin also discusses the kind of research that would be helpful in improving the assessment of early reading potential.

There are also many important questions concerning children's intellect. For example, if children are born with a fixed intellectual endowment or given proper intellectual stimulation, will their intellectual levels continue to rise? If children's intellects can be raised, we might then wonder just what is the limit of their potentials—or is there a limit? Also, is there an age level during which the intellect is most amenable to stimulation? Have we generally given children ample opportunity to achieve up to their potentials? In the second article in this chapter, Paul A. Witty provides some interesting answers to these questions. If Witty's information is indeed correct, then in many schools and preschool settings our educational structure should be changed.

The third article by John Downing was chosen because of the excellent insights it provides on children's thoughts about reading. The future and the practicing teacher can easily adapt this technique to gain further insights into their own children's thoughts about reading.

31

They should also be able to implement some of the information given by Downing.

The last article was included because of Jo M. Stanchfield's excellent review of the research and her concrete description of a successful pre-school program. In fact the kind of detailed, accurate description that she provides should make it most useful to others who wish to duplicate her methods.

Both Witty and Stanchfield have stressed the need for early stimulations of the intellect. One may wonder, however, if the child who learns to read at a very early age is really ahead of the child who learns to read in grade one. Perhaps the matter of economy of teacher time is an important factor; that is, if children who learn to read at a later date catch up with the younger readers anyway, does it really matter when the initial learning takes place? An important question is whether or not these children are ahead of the late starters several years later. Stanchfield does present some information illustrating that children read better later in their school career as a result of a good preschool program, but some studies have shown that there is little difference. Although some evidence is available to strengthen the argument for each side, more research is needed on this all-important aspect of early instruction.

Dolores Durkin

What Does Research Say About
the Time to Begin Reading Instruction?

Questions about the time to begin reading instruction are invariably bound up with the concept "reading readiness." Consequently, how they are answered directly reflects how this concept is interpreted.

When the term "reading readiness" was first used in the 1920's, the common interpretation was that readiness is the product of maturation; more specifically, of a certain stage in the child's development which equips him with the requirements for success in learning to read. Because this interpretation was generally accepted over four decades and, secondly, because it directly affected the readiness research that was done during the same 40 years, an understanding of why it was both proposed and accepted is important.

Although proposed in the 1920's, the initially assigned meaning stemmed from psychological ideas that were popular at the start of the century. One way to describe them is to describe some of the beliefs of G. Stanley Hall, for it was his teachings that dominated the psychological world at that time.

One teaching was that genetic factors determine the characteristics and abilities of each individual. With this as the accepted assumption, it was natural for the early years of the century to give attention to hereditary rather than environmental factors, and to the maturation process rather than to learning and practice.

From Dolores Durkin, "What Does Research Say About the Time to Begin Reading Instruction?" *Journal of Educational Research* 64 (October 1970): 52-56. Reprinted by permission of the author and the journal.

Another of Hall's influential beliefs was rooted in his acceptance of the doctrine of recapitulation, a doctrine defined briefly but clearly by Hall himself in a 1904 publication:

> The most general formulation of all the facts of development that we yet possess is contained in the law of recapitulation. This law declares that the individual, in his development, passes through stages similar through which the race has passed, and in the same order (14:8).

Hall's acceptance of the recapitulation theory led him to support this view of man: (a) Each individual, as he grows and develops, passes through certain stages, and (b) these stages follow each other in an inevitable, predetermined order. Because the learning process was being assigned only secondary importance, progress through these "inevitable stages" was explained with a reference to maturation.

Later, the special importance assigned to maturation was continued in the writings of Arnold Gesell, a student of Hall's who gave sustained support to his teacher's beliefs. As Gesell offered his explanation of development, he referred to processes like "intrinsic growth," "neural ripening," and "unfolding behavior" (9, 10, 11). Whatever the language, however, the contention was the same: Growth and development proceed in stages; progress from one to another is dependent upon spontaneous maturation or, put more simply, the passing of time. Such a contention met with little criticism during the 1920's, and, as a result, during this time "reading readiness" first entered the educator's professional vocabulary. This accounts not only for the original interpretation but also for the quickness with which it was accepted.

Why "reading readiness" became part of the educator's vocabulary in the 1920's can be explained with a reference to the Measurement and Testing Movement, which permeated both education and psychology by 1920 (22). Among other things, its concern for objective measurement led to an abundance of national surveys designed to uncover what and how much children were learning in school. Common among the findings was that the rate of non-promotion for first graders was considerably higher than for children at other levels and, secondly, that inadequate achievement in reading generally was the cause of retentions (5, 6, 20). What subsequently became as frequent as the reports of the two findings was the question: *Why* are first graders not succeeding with reading?

It would seem, at least in retrospect, that a multifactor explanation would be offered that might reasonably include problems related to— too large classes, too few materials, inadequate teacher preparation, wrong methodology, unmotivated children, and so on. This, however, was not the case. Because the 1920's were permeated by the ideas of Hall and Gesell, the *one* explanation that was both proposed and accepted placed the blame on the children's lack of readiness when reading instruction began. Or, in Hall-Gesell terminology, the children were having difficulty because at the time instruction was initiated, they had not yet reached that stage of development which would allow them to be successful. The solution? Within the Hall-Gesell framework, the obvious one was to have the schools postpone instruction until the children matured and became ready for it.

Mental Age Description

Once the "doctrine of postponement" was accepted, efforts were made to define that stage of development which equips children with the prerequisites for success in reading, and to define it in such a way that it could be measured and thus identified. Because of the new availability of group intelligence tests—another product of the Measurement and Testing Movement—the earliest of these efforts sought out a mental-age level that might define it. While other researchers were involved, the one whose findings were to be quoted for an unusually long amount of time was Carleton Washburne, a well-known leader in the then popular Progressive Education Movement. In a research report written by himself and Mabel Morphett in 1931, it was proposed that a child is ready to read when he has a mental age of 6.5 years, and it is only then that he should be introduced to reading (19).

Of interest is the fact that just a few years later Arthur Gates and his associates published a series of research articles in which the reported data went contrary to the Morphett-Washburne proposal. The findings of one study, for instance, led Gates to observe:

> Reading is begun by very different materials, methods, and general procedures, some of which a pupil can master at the mental age of five with reasonable ease, others of which would give him difficulty at the mental age of seven (7:508).

Because conflicting findings were being reported, it was only natural to wonder why the Morphett-Washburne data from a study of one teaching method in one school system (Winnetka, Illinois) were so readily accepted as being applicable to all children. I believe a combination of factors suggests an answer. For one thing, the Morphett-

Washburne proposal fit in perfectly with the temper of the times in which it was made. It gave support to the doctrine of postponement because most children entering first grade have not yet reached the mental age of 6.5 years. It also supported the notion that development proceeds in stages, and it honored the Measurement and Testing Movement by being precise and objective. Finally, any attempt to explain the unusual influence of the mental-age concept of readiness must take into account the prominence of Carleton Washburne. He was not only superintendent of the Winnetka schools—widely admired and copied in the 1930's—but also one of the most prestigious leaders of the Progressive Education Movement. As a result, what Washburne said was listened to—and not only in reading. Even earlier than 1931, for instance, he had made very specific proposals about what was to be taught in arithmetic and at which mental-age level (23).

With all these facts in mind, neither his mental-age description of reading readiness nor the influence it wielded should come as any great surprise. In fact, they simply demonstrate what still continues to be true of research: the quality and general applicability of a study are not always what determine the influence of its findings.

Reading Readiness Tests

While some researchers were pursuing a mental-age description of readiness, others were initiating studies designed to measure combinations of abilities which might also add up to readiness. These attempts to construct and evaluate reading readiness tests began in the late 1920's and have been continued right up to the present (2, 18).

Early forms of the tests, like many currently in use, typically included subtests said to evaluate vocabulary development and auditory and visual discrimination abilities. The most noticeable difference, when earlier editions are compared with the most current ones, lies in the visual discrimination subtest. Now the trend is to use letters and words; earlier, simple pictures and geometrical forms were the usual stimuli. It was, in fact, this use of stimuli other than letters and words that often resulted in low coefficients of correlation for readiness test scores and subsequent achievement in reading. Gates, this time in 1939, was one of the first to make this point when he reported on a very comprehensive study of readiness scores as predictors of success with reading (8). The general conclusion of that report was phrased this way:

> It should be noted that among the tests of little or no predictive value are many tests and ratings widely recommended in books and articles on reading readiness testing and teaching (8:54).

Once again, Gates and other researchers who also found a reason in their data to question the predictive value of readiness tests were generally ignored. In fact, during the 1930's, the 1940's, and even into the 1950's, the typical school practice was to use composite readiness scores, sometimes along with MA data, for making decisions about when to start teaching reading. Such a practice, it must be noted, in no way violated either the doctrine of postponement or the high esteem accorded the maturation process. Still assumed was that entering first graders are too immature to learn to read and would start the year by participating in a readiness program. It was only after such participation that administrators and teachers would begin to consider, with the help of readiness test scores, when reading instruction should begin.

The 1960's

Certainly there is no need now to explain with any detail why the 1960's are referred to as a revolutionary period for early childhood education. Suffice it to say that these years became an era in which unprecedented attention went to the young child; in particular, to the unique importance of the early years for his eventual intellectual development (3, 16). It was also an era in which the productivity of learning opportunities was stressed, with very little explicit attention going to the maturation process. Thus, at least for early childhood education, it was a time that contrasted sharply with the four prior decades.

With the sharp changes it was only natural to have questions raised about the traditional interpretation and use of the readiness concept. After all, an era which assigns critical importance to learning opportunities during the pre-first-grade period is not likely to be patient with school practices that postpone reading instruction beyond the start of the first-grade year and assume the passing of time will insure a readiness for it.

As the years have shown, the typical response to the impatience was neither complicated nor imaginative. For the most part, schools simply altered the timing of traditional practices. Readiness tests were administered earlier, often in kindergarten where readiness workbooks could be found too. In first grade, reading instruction usually was started sooner than was typical for the earlier decades—although readiness programs still could be found in some first grade classrooms, especially in school districts that had no kindergartens. In a few places the change in timing was more radical: they introduced reading in kindergarten. In other areas, however, opposition to this was as great and vocal as it had been in years gone by.

With such changes as these occurring in the 1960's, what was learned about readiness, and thus about the optimum time to begin reading instruction? Not much, and for a variety of reasons.

To begin with, the decade gave very little attention to the basic nature of readiness. In fact, some who were urging that reading be started even before the kindergarten year seemed either to ignore the factor of readiness or to take it for granted that all children are ready before the ages of 5 and 6. Those who did deal with the concept merely stressed that many aspects of readiness are learned and therefore can be taught.

Some of the learned and thus teachable aspects were like what was being evaluated in readiness tests; so, with some alterations, they continued to be used in great quantities throughout the 1960's. As was mentioned earlier, one common change in the visual discrimination subtests was the use of letters and words in place of pictures and geometrical forms. A change of more recent origin is the inclusion of a letter-naming subtest. Although this change has been explained with a reference to studies that show a significant correlation between letter-naming ability and later achievement in reading (4), it does not take into account the likelihood that the pre-reader's ability to name letters was the result of much more than something that might be labeled "readiness." More specifically, to assume that a young child's letter-naming ability in and of itself leads to success in reading is to overlook the strong likelihood that the research referred to measured as ability that was one product of an out-of-school environment that will always be contributing to the child's success in school.

This particular use of research is singled out here because it helps to underscore what has always been a serious flaw in readiness research. Here I refer to its unfortunate tendency over the years to present correlation data as if they indicated cause-effect relationships and, secondly, to omit attention to possible reasons for the reported correlations. In fact, the customary procedure has been one in which researchers collect readiness scores at one point in time and reading scores at another. Correlation coefficients for the two sets of data are then reported—and that is it.

Although, in more recent years, this type of research has decreased, it has been replaced only by equally nonproductive studies. For example, it is now common to find reports in which the researcher simply takes for granted the validity of some readiness test as he uses it to assess the value of the variable under study for preparing children to be successful with reading. Thus, in recent years readiness test scores have been used as the criterion measure for evaluating such things as the use of teacher aids, special science materials, a pre-first grade summer program, Frostig workbooks, and Delacato's crawling prescriptions (1, 13, 17, 21, 25). At other times they have been used to establish the relative value of attending kindergarten and not attending, of having mothers involved in a program and not having them, of one type of maternal behavior *vs* some other type, and so on (12, 15, 24). Underlying all the reports is the implicit assumption that readiness scores really do tell how well or poorly a child will perform when reading instruction gets underway.

While one can understand the desire of researchers to use instruments that will yield "objective" data than can be statistically analyzed—how else can one get "significant" findings?—one cannot help but be disappointed with their failure to point out the possible flaws in an instrument. In fact, if researchers continue to act as if the validity of readiness tests is unquestionable, then we can hardly expect school personnel to rise above traditional practices which should have been seriously questioned right from the start. Because the most important reason for questioning both the practices and the research on which they are based still exists, it will be dealt with now in some detail.

Wrong Question

For as long as the reading readiness concept has been with us—and this is true whether maturation or learning or some combination of the two is given credit for readiness—the assessment question posed by both educators and researchers has been, "Is the child ready?" Unfortunately, such a question is the wrong one to ask because it is incomplete. It focuses only on the child, thus omitting attention to an equally important variable; namely, the reading instruction that will be available.

Another way of making this same point is to say that the traditional way of asking the question neglects the *relational* aspect of readiness. It fails to recognize that whether or not a child is ready—that is, whether or not he will be successful in learning to read—depends not only on his own abilities but also on the kind and quality of instruction that is offered. Realistically, this means that a child might be very ready if one type of instruction can be made available, but unready if another is offered.

Since different kinds of instruction make different demands of the learner, this relational dimension also points out that readiness should not be equated with a single collection of abilities, as has been the traditional practice. Instead, we should be thinking in terms of readiness*es* in the sense that one collection of abilities makes a child ready for one kind of instruction, while a somewhat different collection might make him ready to cope with another.

A Second Major Flaw

Still another flaw exists in the kind of thinking and questioning that have been typical when readiness is the concern. This is the failure to realize that the process of learning to read does not require children to be ready to learn everything at once. All of the pieces that comprise "reading ability" are not taught at once; therefore, they need not be learned all at once. Yet, as questions about a child's readiness to read have been considered in the past, answers seem to assume that he must be able to do everything—and right away. Such an assumption needs to be replaced by one which recognizes that a child learns to read, a step at a time; and that the important readiness requirement is that he is able to learn the first step. Fortunately, success with that first step often prepares him to be ready for the second.

Implications for Future Research

If the two flaws which have been mentioned are valid criticisms of the way educators and researchers have traditionally thought about readiness, then certain implications follow.

For example, if readiness is dependent both on the child's abilities and, as Ausubel has phrased it, on *"the demands of the learning task,"* then future research efforts ought to go in the direction of (a) assessing more successfully than has been done up to now the relevant abilities of each child; (b) identifying the possible methodologies for reading as well as the learning demands of each; and (c) helping teachers match children in terms of their abilities, with methodology in terms of what it requires of the learner. It must also be emphasized that, once these basic tasks have been done, it is only *longitudinal* studies that will be able to pass judgment on their success.

If, in what seems like a staggering task, it is also kept in mind that a child does not learn to read "all at once," then what will also come to the forefront is the realization that those who make decisions related to readiness need only be concerned with the question, "Is this child ready to read, given the fact that such-and-such will be the first learning requirement?"

Admittedly, the suggestion of a more complicated picture of readiness than has been traditionally inferred in the question, "Is the child ready?" also suggests the need for more complex research than has been undertaken up to now. However, to let a wrong question guide research is to inevitably end up with wrong and meaningless answers. And, we have enough of them already.

References

1. Ayers, Jerry B.; Mason, George E., "Differential Effects of *Science: A Process Approach* upon Change in *Metropolitan Readiness Test Scores* Among Kindergarten Children," *Reading Teacher*, 22:435-439, February, 1969.

2. Berry, Francis M., "The Baltimore Reading Readiness Test," *Childhood Education*, 3:222-223, January, 1927.

3. Bloom, Benjamin S., *Stability and Change in Human Characteristics*, John Wiley and Sons, New York, 1964.

4. Chall, Jeanne, *Learning to Read: The Great Debate*, McGraw-Hill Book Company, New York, 1967.

5. Dickson, Virgil E., *Mental Tests and the Classroom Teacher*, World Book Company, New York, 1923.

6. Editorial, "Educational News and Editorial Comment," *Elementary School Journal*, 33:641-655, May, 1933.

7. Gates, Arthur I., "The Necessary Mental Age for Beginning Reading," *Elementary School Journal*, 37:497-508, March, 1937.

8. Gates, Arthur I.; Bond, G. L.; Russell, D. H., *Methods of Determining Reading Readiness*, Bureau of Publications, Teachers College, Columbia University, New York, 1939.

9. Gesell, Arnold L., *The Mental Growth of the Preschool Child*, The Macmillan Company, New York, 1925.

10. Gesell, Arnold L., *Infancy and Human Growth*, The Macmillan Company, New York, 1928.

11. Gesell, Arnold L., *The First Five Years of Life*, Harper and Brothers, New York, 1940.

12. Gil, Mohindra, "Relationship Between Junior Kindergarten Experience and Readiness," *Ontario Journal of Educational Research*, 10:57-66, Autumn, 1967.

13. Goralski, Patricia J.: Kerl, Joyce M., "Kindergarten Teacher Aides and Reading Readiness," *Journal of Experimental Education*, 37:34-38, Winter, 1968.

14. Hall, G. Stanley, *The Psychology of Adolescence*, D. Appleton and Company, New York, 1904.

15. Hess, Robert, "Maternal Behavior and the Development of Reading Readiness in Urban Negro Children," Self and Society, *Yearbook of the Claremont Reading Conference*, 32:83-99, 1968.

16. Hunt, J. McVicker, *Intelligence and Experience*, The Ronald Press Company, New York, 1961.

17. Jacobs, James N.; Wirthlin, Lenore D.; Miller, Charles B., "A Follow-Up Evaluation of the Frostig Visual-Perceptual Training Program," *Educational Leadership*, 26:169-175, November, 1968.

18. Johnson, Roger E., "The Validity of the Clymer-Barrett Prereading Battery," *Reading Teacher*, 22:609-614, April, 1969.

19. Morphett, M. V.; Washburne, C., "When Should Children Begin to Read? *Elementary School Journal*, 31:496-508, March, 1931.

20. Reed, Mary M., *An Investigation of Practices in First Grade Admission and Promotion*, Bureau of Publications, Teachers College, Columbia University, New York, 1927.

21. Stone, Mark; Pielstick, N. L., "Effectiveness of Delacato Treatment with Kindergarten Children," *Psychology in the Schools*, 6:63-68, January 1969.

22. Thorndike, Robert L.; Hagen, Elizabeth, *Measurement and Evaluation in Psychology and Education*, John Wiley and Sons, New York, 1969.

23. Washburne, Carleton, "The Work of the Committee of Seven on Grade-Placement in Arithmetic," *Child Development and The Curriculum*, Chapter 16, Thirty-Eighth Yearbook of the National Society for the Study of Education, Part I, Public School Publishing Company, Bloomington, Illinois, 1939.

24. Willmon, Betty, "Parent Participation as a Factor in the Effectiveness of Head Start Programs," *Journal of Educational Research*, 62:406-410, May-June, 1969.

25. Wingert, Roger C., "Evaluation of a Readiness Training Program," *Reading Teacher*, 22:325-328, January, 1969.

The Early Years and Reading

Durkin — Questions for Discussion

Why are correlational studies between reading readiness scores and reading achievement scores sometimes not only inadequate but also misleading? What is the major flaw in using readiness tests as the criterion measure of the effectiveness of preschool programs? Discuss the implications of the "right time" to begin reading instruction. Based on Durkin's discussion, are our presently-used readiness tests of any real value? If you could design an "ideal" readiness test, what might it include?

John Downing

How Children Think About Reading

Research on young children's thinking indicates five important conclusions about teaching reading:

1. Children's thoughts about reading, their notions or conceptions of its purpose and nature, present the most fundamental and significant problems for the teacher of reading.

2. The young beginner's *general* ways of thinking are extremely different from those of adults.

3. The very different logic of young children causes two serious difficulties in teaching them to read and write.

a. They have difficulty in understanding the *purpose* of the written form of their language.

b. They cannot readily handle the *abstract* technical terms used by teachers in talking about written or spoken language.

4. Teaching formal rules (e.g. of phonics or grammar) for their thinking is a] unnecessary and b] may cause long term reading difficulties.

5. It is vitally important to provide rich and individually relevant language experiences and activities which a] *orientate* children correctly to *the real purposes* of reading and writing, and b] enable children's natural thinking processes to *generate understanding of the technical concepts of language.*

From John Downing, "How Children Think About Reading," *The Reading Teacher* 23, no. 3 (December 1969): 217-30. Reprinted with permission of John Downing and the International Reading Association.

Why Children's Thinking Processes are of Central Importance for the Reading Teacher

Although this first point may seem commonsense to many classroom teachers, the curious fact is that most college textbooks about reading have no chapter on children's thinking. This topic is also notably under-researched, and comparatively few articles about it have been published in the journals. In contrast, there is a wealth of published material, for example, on visual perception in reading. Perhaps, this is due to the obvious need for a study of visual perception because printed symbols have to be looked at visually in reading. Perhaps thinking is neglected because it is an invisible process.

Yet, the most comprehensive and thorough review of research on children's failure in reading ever to be undertaken arrived at the conclusion that it was a breakdown in *the thinking processes in learning to read* which consistently appeared as the real problem in study after study. Vernon (1957), in her classic review, *Backwardness in Reading*, concluded: "Thus the fundamental and basic characteristic of reading disability appears to be cognitive confusion and lack of system." If *cognitive* confusion is the "fundamental and basic characteristic of reading disability", then clearly the *cognitive* processes of beginning readers must be the central concern of reading teachers seeking to prevent disability through any such confusion. Thus research says research resources and teachers' efforts should be directed more towards a concern for the child's own ways of thinking in learning to read.

The Child's Mode of Thought

It is impossible to understand the revolution which has occurred in British primary schools over the past two decades if one does not recognize the contribution to British educational theory made by the studies of Jean Piaget. His influence is most noticeable in math and science teaching, probably because part of his work was directly concerned with the development of mathematical and scientific concepts in children. However, Piaget's (1959) theory of the development of logic in children is a general one and must be applied to the child's learning of the written form of language too. His book, *The Language and Thought of the Child*, provides the starting point.

Piaget's concept and description of *ego-centric* language and thought in children below the age of about seven or eight years is fundamental to an understanding of the child's mode of thinking at the typical beginning reading age. It becomes clear that the logic of such young children is qualitatively different from that of adults. Marshall (1965) expresses simply and clearly what this means for the practical teacher. She is referring particularly to the revolution which started first in a change of teachers' attitudes towards art education. "The new conception of child art simply takes into account that children are not solely adults in the making, but creatures in their own right, as tadpoles differ from mature frogs, or caterpillars from butterflies." This statement is generally true of the thought of children before the age of eight years, and it is especially true of their thinking about reading.

Difficulties in Children's
Thinking about Reading

Vygotsky (1962) replicated and expanded the research started by Jean Piaget on the relationship between children's thought and language, and Vygotsky did turn his attention directly to the problem of teaching Russian children the written form of their spoken language. He describes his investigations designed to "account for the tremendous lag between the school-child's oral and written language." (Incidentally it is interesting to compare this great Russian educational psychologist's recognition of a "tremendous" reading problem in his country with the naive assertion that Ivan knows so much more than Johnny does!)

This fundamental Russian research led Vygotsky to draw just two main conclusions:

1. "Our studies show that it is the *abstract* quality of written language that is the main stumbling block."

2. The child "has little motivation to learn writing when we begin to teach it. He feels no need for it and has *only a vague idea of its usefulness.*" Both these conclusions could be predicated from Piaget's general theory of the development of thinking. At the conventional age for beginning reading, abstract ideas are least appropriate and the child's ego-centric view of his environment is not conducive to a natural understanding of the purpose of the written form of languages—an artificial two-dimensional product of civilization.

At the University of Edinburgh, Scotland, Reid (1966) has conducted an investigation which provides independent evidence to support Vygotsky's conclusions. Reid's original research will undoubtedly be recognized as one of the outstanding reading research contributions of this decade. Her method was to conduct intensive interviews with twelve five-year-old children in their first year in the infants' class at an Edinburgh city school. She interviewed them first when they had been two months in school, and then twice more, after five months and nine months of school.

Reid's protocols provide fascinating insight into children's thoughts about reading, and her article should be priority reading in every course for teachers of first grade reading. The first conclusion she reports is that, for these young beginners, reading "is a mysterious activity, to which they come with only the vaguest of expectancies." They displayed a "general lack of any specific expectancies of what reading was going to be like, of what the activity consisted in, of the purpose and the use of it."

The other finding of Reid's was that these children had great difficulty in understanding the abstract technical terms which adults use to talk about language, e.g. "word", "letter", "sound", etc.

New Research

Jessie Reid's original study stimulated the author of this present article to follow up her line of investigation. Her three focussed interviews are being replicated with thirteen five years olds in an infants' class at Hemel Hempstead, England. In addition, some experimental methods are being used to test predictions based on Reid's conclusions. Already, the first of the three interviews and experimental sessions has been completed with all the children. The results generally confirm Reid's findings and expand our knowledge of how the children think about reading. The following paragraphs provide an interim report of the new Hemel Hempstead research.

None of Reid's Edinburgh children could actually read, and all but one knew it. Some of the Hemel Hempstead children were beginning to read their basal (i.t.a.) readers, and this seems to account for the fact that seven children said they could read, two were uncertain, and four said "no". The children were fairly realistic about the extent of their reading. For example, Jane (5 years 0 months), answered the question, *"Can you read yet?"* by replying, "Not quite, I can read a little bit", and Felix (5 years 3 months) said "No. . . . I can read *something*. . . . I can read my Sam book" (A pre-primer).

What is in Books?

The question, *"What is in books?"*, produced responses at Hemel Hempstead which were quite similar to those of the Edinburgh children.

Only two children said "writing" and no child mentioned words. Four said "pictures". The usual response was to quote the names of characters in the basal reader (e.g. "Sam and Topsy") or in a story book at home (e.g. "Humpty Dumpty"). Three children quoted a specific phrase or sentence from the basal reader.

No child said anything to suggest that books conveyed information, and only one (William, 5 years 1 month), the most mature child in the class, said "stories" spontaneously. As Reid also had found that children did not think of books containing stories, the Hemel Hempstead children were asked specifically *"Do books have stories in them?"* Then, seven children agreed that they did, but it was usually books which had been read to them, more often at home, that they thought of as containing stories. Felix actually differentiated between the school books and the books he had at home, the former having no stories, while the latter did have them. One boy, Mark (5 years 0 months) denied that books have stories. He declared, that one gets stories "on the floor—near the piano." (This is reference to the teacher's arrangement for reading stories to the class.)

How Do Grown-ups Read?

Two of Reid's children did not know if their parents could read. Similarly, three of these Hemel Hempstead children were uncertain about their parents' ability to read.

Only one of the Edinburgh children mentioned symbols in trying to tell what their parents did when they were reading. At Hemel Hempstead the response was similar. Kay (4 years 11 months) said "They just look at the writing," and Sandra (4 years 11 months) said "They look at the numbers." The other children referred to the more obvious behaviour of adults when they read. For example, William simply said, "by looking," and both Tina (5 years 2 months) and Vanessa (5 years 2 months) said, "They sit down."

Questioning more closely, *"What part do they look at?"*, did not improve this vague picture of what their parents did when reading. Three then said "the pictures." But only William gave the most sophisticated reply "the words."

Because such young children have difficulty in verbalizing about a new experience, at this point in the Hemel Hempstead interviews a book without pictures was placed open before the child, with the comment. *"Show me what they look at."* Then six of the children used their fingers to indicate that it was the print, and more technical linguistic terms were used by the children. Four said it was "writing", one said "words", and two said "letters."

Reid asked the Edinburgh children, *"How does mummy know what bus to take?"* All but one said it was "by the number", and none mentioned the destination. The same question at Hemel Hempstead produced rather poorer results, only about half the children mentioning "the number."

A comment by Reid on this point is that, "In some cases it was unclear whether they really knew the number was visible, or whether they just thought of it as something the bus was called by ('the twenty-four')." To investigate this problem, after the Hemel Hempstead interviews, the children were shown three model buses each with different number and destination boards at front, back and on the side, and asked, *"How do you know which one to get on?"* When they were provided with this more concrete situation, all the children except one pointed correctly to the number and destination boards on the model buses. Felix cried, "There it is! That's the seven-oh-eight!" and "There's the one-oh-three!"

Another concrete aid added to the Hemel Hempstead interviews was a page with two pictures of cars. One car had an "L" ("learner") plate clearly visible. Eight of the thirteen correctly chose the "learner" car and pointed correctly to the "L" plate to show how they knew. William said the "L" was "the red number", but Jane and Kay called it "a letter."

The results with the model buses and the pictures of the cars are particularly interesting because, in comparison with Red's interview situation which depends solely on an exchange of spoken words, these young children could achieve so much more with actual concrete objects than they could in the more abstract verbal situation. This provides an example of the normal course of development in children's thinking. Actual understanding comes first, while ability to verbalize about it naturally comes later.

What Is Writing?

The Hemel Hempstead children gave identical responses to the request *"Can you write something for me?"* to those made by Edinburgh five-year-olds. All but one in both samples produced some kind of symbols. In both samples, just one child interpreted "write" as draw. At Hemel Hempstead, Michael (5 years 0 months) said, "I can write people with a round face," and drew a human figure which he said was "my Mum."

The larger majority of the Hemel Hempstead five-year-olds wrote recognizable numbers, letters, or words. Only two produced what appeared to be a row of unrecognizable hieroglyphs. Vanessa said they were "letters", but Gary (5 years one month) revealed that he was confused about the distinction between writing words and drawing pictures. He said, about his row of symbols, "that's about my Mum", and, when asked *"What are these* (the symbols) *for?"* added (pointing to one) "that's for the leg." Sandra, too, may have been demonstrating a similar confusion, because although she produced a quite well written "H", which she said was "for house", she pointed at a part of the letter and said it was "the door."

Asked, *"Tell me about what you have written?"* three children correctly named the numbers or letters which they had written, and one sounded the phoneme it represented. Tina mixed letter names and phonemes. She said "HOK" was "aitch, oh, kuh". Three children said correctly the word they had written. Two called the symbols correctly "letters" and one said they were "names."

Writing their own first name was spontaneously chosen as something they would write by three of the children. All the others were asked to do this as a second writing task. Of these, three were doubtful of their ability to do so, and one indicated that she could do it only with a fair copy, "I need some writing what it's like." All the children did try to write their names, but three of them produced only unrecognizable marks. Five children spelled their names correctly; but five others got only the initial letter correct, plus, in two cases, some other letters of their name. Such children usually said they had been taught to write their names by their mothers.

Mark made a spontaneous comment which provides supporting evidence for another of Reid's findings. Asked to write his name, he said, "You don't write muh." Asked, *"why not?"* he added, "Not the muh on the card." What he wrote was not recognizable, but he was probably referring to the lower case letter "m" as being on "the card", whereas he knew that his name began with a capital "M". He added an explanatory comment: "You write an older one". It is quite clear that young beginners perceive upper case and lower case letters as looking different, and they believe that this must have some special significance. Thus "m" is "muh" but "M" is not "muh."

This replication of Jessie Reid's first interview of five-year-olds clearly confirms her conclusion that such young children have only a vague notion of the purpose of the written language and of what activities are actually involved in reading. The Hemel Hempstead children, like the Edinburgh children, displayed a great deal of confusion over the use of abstract technical terms, such as word, number, letter, name, writing, and drawing. However, the concrete aids — the model buses, the pictures of cars, and the presentation of an actual book — stimulated motor and verbal responses which indicate that the Hemel Hempstead five year olds were groping towards an understanding of the technical concepts of language, although they were very much less able to use them accurately in verbal responses.

A Concept Attainment Experiment

Reid admits in a footnote that "the fact that a child does not, when given opportunities to do so, use a certain term is not proof that it is unknown to him. He may, for instance, understand it when someone else uses it."

The abstract technical terms "word" and "sound" often are used by teachers in talking to young beginners with the assumption that children understand just as well as adults do what "words" and "sounds" actually are. Reid's interviews suggest that this assumption may be quite unfounded, but her method leaves the problem unanswered. In an attempt to investigate this question further the following experiment was conducted with the thirteen Hemel Hempstead five-year-olds after their interviews.

The experiment began by training the children to give the type of response needed in the experimental test. This training was introduced as "the yes/no game". Each child was told that he would be shown some cards. On some of them he would see a picture of a bird. The others would not have a bird on them. The experimenter said, "Say 'yes' if you see a bird, and 'no' if you see something that is not a bird." All the children learned to make this discrimination response very quickly. To check that they could generalize the response to other discrimination tasks, they were tested on their ability to say "yes" when they saw a pencil and "no" when they were presented with other objects which were not pencils. All the children could do this at once after the training on the bird/not bird picture cards.

The hypotheses to be tested were:
1.   These five-year-old beginners are not able to discriminate between auditory stimuli on the basis of the concept of a "word."
2.   They are not able to discriminate between auditory stimuli on the basis of the concept of a "sound."

The test material for checking both these hypotheses consisted in a tape recording of twenty-five auditory stimuli of five types;

a. a non-human noise (e.g. bell ringing)
b. a phoneme (all vowel sounds)
c. a word (e.g. "milk")
d. a phrase (e.g. "fish and chips")
e. a sentence (e.g. "Dad's digging in the garden.")

The human utterances (b, c, d, e,) were spoken by a seven-year-old in the same school. Each stimulus was introduced by the experimenter's voice saying, seven seconds earlier, "get ready." Each type had five different examples, and the order of presentation of the types was randomized.

To test the first hypothesis, the child was asked to "listen for a word. Say 'yes' if you hear a word, and 'no' if you hear something which is not a word".

The tape began with a series of five stimuli for practice before the real test began. This made it possible to be certain that the child understood the instructions as far as he was able.

The second hypothesis was tested with the same tape, except that now the child was asked to respond "yes" for a "sound" and "no" for "not a sound".

Experimental Results

The results of these two tests were as follows:

The Word Concept

1. Five children made no *discrimination* between the auditory stimuli (one thought that none were "words", four that they were all "words").
2. Three children thought that all the stimuli were "words" *except the non-human noises*. i. e. What they thought was "a word", in actual fact, was anything from a single phoneme to a whole sentence.
3. Five children (one not certain—possibly belongs to category 2 above) thought that the *phonemes as well as the non-human noises were "not words."* These pupils were the most advanced in the attainment of the concept of "a word." The category "word" in their thinking included phrases and sentences as well as single words, but not phonemes.

The Sound Concept

1. Six children made *no discrimination* (four thought that all the stimuli were "sounds", two that none were "sounds").
2. Three children thought that all were "sounds" *except the non-human noises*.

3. Two children *excluded both phonemes and non-human noises.*
4. One child's category of "sound" *included only the non-human noises.*
5. One child *included both phonemes and non-human noises* in his category "sound."

Both hypotheses are strongly supported by these test results. "A word" for five of these thirteen children was a meaningless and useless category. Three had begun to connect it with human utterance, and five more had progressed a little further to connect it with a meaningful human utterance. *But none thought of it as the segment of human speech defined by adults as "a word."*

The term "sound" was even less well understood. About half the children could make no use of it as a category. Three more children associated it with any human utterance. Only two children had a narrow category for "sound". One seems to have used it to classify noises which were not human. The other added phonemes to this category.

No child thought of "a sound" as being exclusively the phoneme. But perhaps it is not surprising that "a sound" is not understood as meaning a phoneme. When we observe these children's confusion, it is clear that the term "sound" is in fact a confusing one, because, in everyday life outside the reading lesson, the word "sound" is used by people for a variety of noises. Perhaps reading teachers should learn from the experience of New Math and provide concrete experiences associated with accurate, clear, and rigorous terminology of a more sophisticated kind. There seems no reason why "phoneme" should not be used directly to the children *when* a technical term is needed for this unit of speech.

Experimental Conclusions

The replicated interviews together with this new experimental evidence provides emphatic endorsement of the earlier research of Vygotsky and Reid:

a. Young beginners have serious difficulty in understanding the *purpose* of written language.

b. They have only a vague idea of how people read, and they have a particular difficulty in understanding *abstract* linguistic terminology.

The Futility of Verbal Rules

These fundamental difficulties *in the essential nature of* children's thinking on the one hand and the written form of language on the other, pose the practical question for reading teachers—*How can we overcome these two problems?*

First they must beware of falling into the trap of believing naively that they need just *tell* their pupils how to think about reading. There is abundant evidence that teaching formal rules for thinking is both unnecessary and may even delay or prevent the development of the full understanding of the concepts essential in making children readers.

Unnecessary

Piaget's research led him to conclude, "A child is actually not conscious of concepts and definitions which he can nevertheless handle when thinking for himself." "Verbal forms evolve more slowly than actual understanding."

One has only to consider how very young children perform wonders in manipulating the grammar and phonemic structures of language, without anyone's telling them the rules or their being able to describe them, to see that it is quite unnecessary for rule following behaviour to be based on verbal formulation of the rules.

Dangerous

Teaching verbal rules is worse than unnecessary. It is likely to fool the teacher and delay or prevent the child from developing appropriate behaviour and atttiudes for reading.

Vygotsky's research led him to conclude:

Direct teaching of concepts is impossible and fruitless. A teacher who tries to do this usually accomplishes nothing but empty verbalism, a parrotlike repetition of words by the child, simulating a knowledge of the corresponding concepts but actually covering up a vacuum.

Such a vacuum is being covered up when a child can recite "When two vowels go walking the first one does the talking," but can't read "meat", "pie", "road", or "faint". Such ritualistic teaching methods go against all that research has revealed about the development of young children's thinking.

It is a serious error to assume that children always learn only what the teacher thinks she is teaching. This is why teaching methods are extremely important. They are important not for the usual reasons which people give, but *because of the concealed lessons which are unintentionally taught* by different methods.

Teaching verbal rules, before children have made generalizations from their own concrete experiences and arrived at an understanding of the nature of the tasks and problems they are required to undertake, reverses the natural order of development. The order in nature is from concrete experience, via understanding, to the ability to verbalize about such experience and understanding. Reversing this order confuses children about the purpose and nature of the skills of reading and writing.

When children are taught verbal rules about reading, they learn that reading is a kind of ritual which they have to perform to please adults. They also learn that reading and writing are dull and boring tasks which have little or nothing to do with the interesting things in their lives outside school. Thus, many children take a very long time to learn the essential truth about reading which is that it is to convey interesting information from the author to his reader. Quite a large proportion of pupils never learn this vital truth and so never become readers.

Foss (1967) has expressed this in more general psychological terms: "It is while learning to read that a child first meets symbolic representations, and one would expect the method of teaching and the age of learning to have important consequences for his later symbolic and non-symbolic behaviour."

Stranfi (1969) makes the point more specifically as regards the effects of such unintentional learning from beginning methods of teaching reading on later reading behaviour. In her lucid criticism of Chall's (1967), *Learning to Read: The Great Debate*, Strang comments: "To begin with the synthetic or code-emphasis method may 1] decrease the child's initial curiosity about printed words as he encounters and uses them, 2] deprive him of the experience of discovering sound-symbol relationships in words for himself, 3] give him the wrong initial concepts of reading, and 4] if pursued too extensively and too long, interfere later with speed of reading and maximum comprehension."

All these are unintentional learnings caused by beginning reading with synthetic phonics, but Strang's criticism number three, that this method may give the child "the wrong initial concepts of reading," seems the most serious ill effect of such methods. What makes this still more serious is that this ill effect may do long term damage to the child's development in reading.

Adapting Teaching to the Child's Thinking

Bruner's (1960) dynamic view of readiness is an application of the basic psychological research on children's cognitive development to the problems of teaching young children. His well known statement, "The foundations of any subject may be taught to anybody at any age in some form," has often been misunderstood because of insufficient consideration of its last three words, "in some form". This is filled out when Bruner adds in another place, "It is only when such basic ideas are put in formalized terms as equations or *elaborated verbal concepts* that they are out of reach of the young child, if he has not *first understood them intuitively* and had a chance *to try them out* on his own."

An object lesson in this is provided by two recent experiments on reading readiness. Tanyzer, *et al.* (1966) reported that "introducing a consistent medium such as i.t.a. to kindergarten children in a formal reading program does not result in significantly better reading and spelling achievement than that attained by children who begin formal reading instruction in first grade in i.t.a. when both groups are measured (in T.O.) at the end of first grade." But this is hardly surprising because the materials used were the i.t.a. Early to Read series *designed for six-year-olds!* In contrast, Shapiro and Willford (1969) used i.t.a. materials which were designed for *five-year-olds* (the i.t.a. Downing Readers and other special materials) and obtained significantly superior results from the children who began i.t.a. a year earlier. Similar errors with i.t.a. have been made in school systems. The i.t.a. Early-to-Read series designed for American six-year-olds was used with Canadian five-year-olds at Halifax, Nova Scotia with such poor results that i.t.a. was abandoned altogether. This was a pity because i.t.a. can be of great benefit *if taught in a way adapted to the thinking of younger children.*

The essential need of beginning readers, whether in i.t.a. or in T.O. at any age below seven or eight, is rich and personally relevant language experiences and activities which

a. *orientate* children correctly to the true purposes of reading and writing, and

b. enable children's natural thinking processes *to generate understanding* of the technical concepts of language.

Almy (1967) states: "An environment that provides the children with many opportunities for varied sensory and motor experiences is essential. So, too, is the presence of people who talk *with* (not merely to or at) the child, people who read and write and who share these activities with children."

When the non-reader shares a reading experience with a reader, he is having the most fundamental learning experience of his life, because he is learning the vital truth that reading is gaining information from the printed page. Similarly through creative writing experiences such as those proposed in Allen's (1961) *language experience approach*, children learn by induction what it means to be an author, and thus that writing and reading are essentially a purposeful and relevant means of communication. The British Plowden Commission report (1967) states: "Books made by teachers and children about the doings of the class or of individuals in it figure prominently among the books which children enjoy. They help children to see *meaning* in reading and to appreciate the *purpose* of written records."

In Britain, i.t.a.'s chief value has been in making this policy more effective, because children's independent authorship and the individualized approach to learning have come easier and earlier with i.t.a. Gayford (1969), headmistress of a Britsh Infants School, reports this in her new book on i.t.a., and the same theme is expressed by Warburton and Southgate (1969) in their report on i.t.a. for the British School's Council which has followed up the scientific experiments on i.t.a. conducted by the present author (Downing, 1967).

The new School's Council report says:

> The majority of teachers commented that the greater regularity and simplicity of i.t.a. enabled children to help themselves, far more than was possible with T.O. Children did not find it necessary to ask the teacher to tell them every new word they met. They soon discovered that they could 'puzzle it out for themselves'. The resultant change in procedure represented a swing away from instruction towards individual, independent learning.

It seems very sad that this aspect of i.t.a. has been missed by the majority of American schools adopting i.t.a. The American Early-to-Read i.t.a. series, for example, uses a formal synthetic phonics approach very different from the way in which i.t.a. has been introduced in British Schools. Featherstone's (1967) articles provide a fine description of the revolution in methods in British schools which has been achieved in recent years. In a private letter to the author of this present article, Featherstone comments:

> "Your justifiable concern that i.t.a. is being misused in America underlines the real danger: before we talk of i.t.a. or any innovation in teaching reading, however good, we must talk about making the whole approach to reading as flexible and individual as possible. When this is done, a useful innovation like i.t.a. will be very welcome, and there will be some chance that it will be used properly—that, for example, the children won't be set to memorizing the (forty-four) letters of i.t.a.'s improved alphabet, a spectacle that you and I would rightly agree in condemning."

Sadly, this is the common practice in many American i.t.a. classes, but fortunately not in all. The language experience i.t.a. program in Oakland County Schools, Michigan is the most notable exception, and a similar program has been developed in some of the i.t.a. classes in Stockton, California, for example. But in Britain, i.t.a. fortunately has been more generally recognized as an aid to individualized learning and the development of creative self-expression through teaching approaches which have been described so expressively by such intuitively great teachers as Marshall and Ashton-Warner (1963).

Such authors have the rare gift of being able to portray the special insight into and sympathy with children's special ways of thinking which good teachers use in adapting the demands of the adult world to the natural development of their pupils. Psychological researchers like Piaget, Vygotsky, and Bruner provide the scientific evidence which confirms the judgment and great artistry of these intuitive teachers.

References

Allen, R. V. More ways than one. *Childhood Education*, 1961, *38*, 108-111.

Almy, Millie C. Young children's thinking and the teaching of reading. In J. L. Frost (Ed.) *Issues and Innovations in the teaching of reading.* Chicago: Scott Foresman, 1967.

Ashton-Warner, Sylvia. *Teacher*. London: Secker and Warburg, 1963.

Bruner, J. S. *The process of education.* New York: Vintage Books, 1960.

Chall, Jeanne. *Learning to read: the great debate.* New York: McGraw-Hill, 1967.

Department of Education and Science. *Children and their primary schools.* London: Her Majesty's Stationery Office, 1967. 3 Vols.

Downing, J. *Evaluating the initial teaching alphabet.* London: Cassell, 1967.

Featherstone, J. *The primary school revolution in Britain.* Pamphlet reprinting of three articles in *The New Republic*, 1967.

Foss, B. A psychological analysis of some reading processes. In J. Downing, and Amy L. Brown (Eds.) *The second international reading symposium.* London: Cassell, 1967.

Gayford, Olive. *I.t.a. in primary education.* London: Initial Teaching Publishing, 1969.

Marshall, Sybil. *An experiment in education.* London: Cambridge University Press, 1963.

Piaget, J. *The language and thought of the child.* (Rev. Ed.) London: Routhledge & Kegan Paul, 1959.

Reid, J. F. Learning to think about reading. *Educational Research*, 1966, *9*, 56-62.

Shapiro, B. J., and Willford, R. E. I.t.a.—kindergarten or first grade? *The Reading Teacher*, 1969, *22*, 307-311.

Strang, Ruth. Is it debate or is it confusion? *The Reading Teacher*, 1968, *21*, 575-577.

Tanyzer, H., Alpert, H., and Sandert, L. *Beginning reading—the effectiveness of i.t.a. and T.O.* (Report to the Commission of Education) Washington, D.C.: U.S. Office of Education, 1966.

Vernon, M. D. *Backwardness in reading.* London: Cambridge University Press, 1957.

Vygotsky, L. S. *Thought and language.* Cambridge, Mass.: M.I.T. Press, 1962.

Warburton, F. W., and Southgate, Vera. *An independent evaluation of i.t.a.* (Schools' Council Report) Edinburgh: Chambers, 1969.

The Early Years and Reading

Downing — Questions for Discussion

If you assume that Downing's five important conclusions about teaching reading are correct, then what are some weaknesses of programs with which you are familiar? What are the implications for curriculum change based on Reid's initial research? What reading programs or materials with which you are familiar would less likely to be criticized from the standpoint of Piaget's and Vygotsky's research? In what ways do the essential points made by Witty agree with those made by Downing?

Paul A. Witty

Studies of Early Learning-
Their Nature and Significance

Research and writing by cognitive psychologists have, during the past ten years, brought a realization of the potentiality of young children for vast and extensive learning. Indeed, the results of efforts to teach young children have been so dramatic and far-reaching as to constitute a revolution in learning and to require far-reaching changes in our ideas and practices. Moreover, it is being recognized that the denial of early opportunities for learning may result in the child's failure to realize his intellectual potentialities and may impair his later learning. Thus, Maya Pine writes as follows:

> Millions of children are being irreparably damaged by our failure to stimulate them intellectually during their crucial years . . . from birth to six. Millions of others are being held back from their true potential (1, p. 1).

Pines stresses the child's potential for early learning and states that:

> The child's intelligence grows as much during his first four years of life as it will during the next thirteen . . . (1, p. 31).

Early Views of Intelligence

There has, unfortunately, been a great neglect of intellectual stimulation for young children at home (2). This condition has persisted in

---

Reprinted from the October, 1968, issue of *Education* magazine by permission of the author and the publisher. Copyright, 1968, by The Bobbs-Merrill Company, Inc., Indianapolis, Indiana.

many kindergartens and first grades. One reason is to be found in the long prevailing conviction among educators that intelligence, especially as shown by IQ, is largely unaffected by environmental factors.

For many years, the IQ was regarded as being chiefly an expression of an inborn capacity which developed according to a fixed rate. Hence, it was desirable to consider in teaching every subject the mental maturity of each child and to make adjustments accordingly. For example, it was held that in the area of reading, instruction should be postponed until a child had attained a mental age of six years or more when he could successfully be taught to read. Many teachers accepted this point of view and assumed that reading instruction should be delayed until the child had reached the necessary mental age. Accordingly, reading was considered an inappropriate activity for the kindergarten. And younger children were, of course, generally considered "unready" to read.

Some psychologists questioned these assumptions three or more decades ago and held that the IQ was much more changeable than was ordinarily assumed. At the present time, writers are emphasizing the possible changes in IQ associated with the provision of early childhood opportunities. Sometimes it seems that it is assumed that the discovery of IQ modifiability is of recent origin. We shall see that this is not the case. It is true, of course, that for many years textbook writers stressed a hereditarian point of view and cited with approval statements such as the following:

> The maximal contribution of the best home environment to intelligence is apparently about 20 IQ points . . . Conversely, the least cultured, least stimulating kind of American home environment may depress the IQ as much as 20 IQ points. But situations as extreme as either of these probably occur only once or twice in a thousand times in American communities (3, p. 309).

Moreover, writers held that the relative constancy of the IQ added support for the belief that by the side of heredity all other factors are "dwarfed in comparison." A leading investigator in the field of the gifted stated: "We can only say that the IQ is constant within narrow margins" (4). And L. M. Terman, perhaps the most outstanding authority, held that "from the ranks of gifted children (IQ 140 and higher) and from nowhere else our geniuses in every line are recruited" (5).

Importance of Early Learning

The writer objected again and again to these views and stressed the importance of factors such as drive, interest, and opportunity in determining the nature and extent of outstanding accomplishment. He indicated, too, the fact that a number of studies showed a great variability in IQ. For example, several investigations revealed large shifts in IQ with marked change in the character of children's homes and with the provision of nursery school experience (6).

One of the most conspicuous examples of IQ variability was revealed by the carefully controlled studies of Nancy Bayley in tests and retests of children during their first three years. These same children were given individual tests repeatedly until they were nine years of age.

> . . . a fourth of the group change 10 or more IQ points on retests made one year after the initial test; while an equal number change 17 or more IQ points over a three-year interval . . . (7, p. 20).

Case studies in the Psycho-Educational Clinic of Northwestern University also showed changes of large magnitude in the IQ's of many children. In evaluating factors contributing to changes, the writer stressed the importance of differences in maturation, interests and attitudes, opportunities for learning, extreme changes in environments and variations in the emotional state of the subjects. Although the importance of opportunity for early learning was considered, it was not treated as the only factor contributing to IQ change. Nor was it accorded the emphasis expressed by some writers today. For example, the case for the crucial importance of early learning is convincingly presented by Benjamin S. Bloom:

> We believe that the early environment is of crucial importance for three reasons. The first is based on the very rapid growth of selected characteristics in the early years and conceives of the variations in the early environment as so important because they shape these characteristics in their most rapid periods of formation. . . .
>
> However, another way of viewing the importance of the early environment has to do with the sequential nature of much of human development. Each characteristic is built on a base of that same characteristic at an earlier time or on the base of other characteristics which precede it in development. . . .
>
> A third reason for the crucial importance of the early environment and early experiences stems from learning theory . . . Although each learning theory may explain the phenomena in different ways, most would agree that the first learning takes place more easily than a later one that is interfered with by an earlier learning. Observation of the difficulties one experiences in learning a new language after the adolescent period and the characteristic mispronunciations which tend to remain throughout life are illustrations of the same phenomena (8, pp. 214-216).

Other writers also emphasize the importance of early learning in the mental development of the young child. For example, Bloom, Davis, and Hess state:

> Perceptual development is stimulated by environments which are rich in the range of experiences available; which make use of games, toys, and many objects for manipulation; and in which there is frequent interaction between the child and adults at meals, playtimes, and throughout the day. At the beginning of the first grade there are differences between culturally deprived and culturally advantaged children in the amount and variety of experiences they have had in their perceptual development (9, p. 13).

It is recommended that:

> Nursery schools and kindergartens should be organized to provide culturally deprived children with the conditions for their intellectual development and the learning-to-learn stimulation which is found in the most favorable home environments (9, p. 17).

The characteristics of superior home environments have been repeatedly shown. For example, the gifted children studied by the writer came from homes of superior socio-economic status. In these homes, abundant opportunities were given for varied experience and for exploration of the environment. Sensorimotor activities were usually rich and varied, as were language experiences. Many other opportunities for wholesome activity and intellectual stimulation were found in these homes. Moreover, the parents usually recognized the superior ability of their children and encouraged its expression and development.

It is plausible that the provision of similar experiences might improve the mental-test ratings of deprived and underprivileged pupils and of other groups for whom opportunities have been meager. It might also bring an increase in the numbers of superior and gifted pupils. These hypotheses will require careful testing. However, promising results have been reported already for slow-learning and for "disadvantaged" pupils who have been given early opportunities for learning (10, 11).

Not only have writers emphasized changes that are possible for the "disadvantaged" when they are offered opportunities for early learning, but they have also indicated that it might be possible to heighten the average intelligence rating. Thus, in a provocative book entitled *Intelligence and Experience*, J. Mc-V. Hunt states:

> . . . it is not unreasonable to entertain the hypothesis that, with a sound scientific educational psychology of early experience, it might become

feasible to raise the average level of intelligence by a substantial degree . . . this "substantial degree" might be of the order of 30 points of IQ (12).

It has been clearly shown that with early learning experiences, many young children are able to acquire remarkable proficiencies in reading ability, language, and other areas. Perhaps these acquisitions are associated with changes in capacity, as is suggested by Siegfried and Therese Engelmann:

A change in the activity of the environment results not only in a change in what the child learns but also in his *capacity* to learn. . . . Capacity to learn follows the activity of the environment (13).

These authors suggest procedures and materials for teaching the infant and the young child. The results reported in their book are indeed remarkable, but many persons will undoubtedly question not only the uniform procedures recommended, but also the value of some of the results. On the jacket of the book it is stated that if the parent follows the prescriptions in the book, the child will be able by the time he enters kindergarten to:

learn the basic rules of language . . .; learn the alphabet, learn the names of the geometric shapes, and begin counting . . .; learn to spell, tell time, add, subtract, multiply, divide, understand fractions and basic algebra . . .; learn to read . . .; learn to deal with such complex mathematical problems as the squares of numbers, equations, factors and exponents.

Early Reading Instruction

Attainment such as that just cited is so clearly in excess of earlier expectations that many persons will insist on more complete validation. Nevertheless, there is a large amount of evidence revealing outstanding accomplishments in young children. For example, several studies have shown the possibility of very young children learning to read. Conspicuous among these studies is Dolores Durkin's investigation described in *Children Who Read Early* (14). Many of the children had IQ's below 110. They were not a "special brand of children," but typically they came from homes in which their parents respected and encouraged early learning. Their superiority in reading persisted throughout the primary grades.

An example of successful reading instruction in the kindergarten is found in a large scale project in the Denver, Colorado, schools involving

4,000 pupils. Experimental groups totaling 2,500 pupils were given reading instruction for twenty minutes each day through the use of seven types of learning experiences. The experimental groups were compared with control groups that followed the regular kindergarten program. It was concluded that:

> Beginning reading can be effectively taught to large numbers of typical kindergarten pupils. . . .
> No evidence was found that early instruction in beginning reading affected visual acuity, created problems of school adjustment, or caused dislike for reading (15).

There is now sufficient evidence to justify modifying a commonly held concept of the role of reading in the kindergarten.[1] In some kindergartens, reading instruction and encouragement have been outlawed. Such a practice is unfortunate in terms of the potentiality of many children. Instead, it is perhaps desirable to introduce activities such as those Durkin has described for children who learned to read at home. These experiences might include, too, the making of simple charts from the children's dictation, the use of labels for pupils' names and for things in the classroom, and the provision of creative activities similar to those appropriately suggested by Torrance Fortson.

The fact that many children can succeed in reading at age four or earlier has been demonstrated recently. However, one of the most outstanding authorities in reading instruction stated in 1954:

> There are . . . factors which suggest that most children could learn to read in their fourth year. They learn to understand spoken language quite well by their second year, and psychologically there is little difference between learning, as it were "to read" spoken words and learning to read printed words. . . .
> If children are to learn to read at an earlier age, there seems little doubt that methods and materials different from those commonly used in the first grade should be employed. Modern facilities for printing, however, make it theoretically possible to provide an abundance of materials which would enable a child who can receive a bit of shrewd guidance, largely to learn to read by himself (16).

Materials are being developed and new approaches are being tried out in teaching young children to read. Successful results have been

---

[1]For opinions on early learning and reading, see Margaret Rasmussen (Editor) *Early Learning—Crucial Years for Learning* (Washington, D.C.: Association for Childhood Education International, 1966).

reported for the use of ITA in England with very young children. The ITA approach has also been introduced in many American schools. Adaptations of the Montessorri method and materials have been utilized successfully in other schools, particularly with "disadvantaged" pupils.

The *Talking Typewriter* has been employed by O.K. Moore in helping young children learn to read (17). And other relatively unstructured approaches such as the use of the *First Adventures in Learning Program* have proved of value in fostering reading ability in many homes (18). These materials designed for parents are found in a kit including books of high interest to young children which deal with topics such as sounds, colors, signs, and things around us. The effectiveness of these materials may be extended and reinforced by the use of the magazine *Highlights for Children*, and the related *Handbooks* (19).

Concluding Statement

We have recently become aware of children's outstanding capacities for early learning. Studies have shown the value of environmental opportunities in early childhood in fostering children's language and reading ability as well as in promoting attainment in other fields. It is believed that not only attainment but also *ability* is positively affected and enhanced by these early experiences. Moreover, failure to offer such opportunities may influence adversely children's later development. It is clear that millions of children probably lack adequate stimulation to develop their maximum potentialities. For the "disadvantaged," this neglect probably leads to later failures in school and results in frustrations that retard subsequent development.

It has been repeatedly pointed out that not only can we help the "disadvantaged" pupil by early stimulation, but that in this way we can also influence all children favorably. Thus, we may be able to increase the average level of intelligence to a substantial degree.

We are coming to believe that our expectations for children have not parallelled their true potentialities. For example, it is being repeatedly shown that many children can learn to read before they enter the first grade, an expectation that was formerly discounted. Accordingly, many kindergartens are now encouraging children to learn to read and are providing opportunities for them to use reading in various productive ways. Even at earlier ages, children are being given opportunities to learn to read. And, with appropriate provisions and motivation, many achieve remarkable success.

It is suggested that creativity is effectively cultivated in early childhood and that creative experience at this time may afford the basis for a rich creative life. But the neglect of this important area is evident. There have been relatively few programs developed to elicit creativity in early childhood as compared with a larger, although still inadequate, number designed to foster learning conventional subject matter such as reading, writing, and arithmetic. It is to be hoped that greater emphasis will soon be given to creativity in young children through the cultivation of productive efforts that involve imaginative, unique, and original behavior. Indeed, the field of divergent and productive behavior is a promising area which merits further careful exploration.

The results of experiments in early learning are indeed remarkable. The extent and nature of children's learning during the preschool years necessitate a revision in our thinking about the young child's potentialities. It is true, of course, that enthusiasts are voicing claims that are not fully substantiated. Nevertheless, the results already reported afford impressive evidence of the possibility of increasing intelligence and fostering more widespread productive learning during early childhood.

References

1. Pines, Maya, *Revolution in Learning—The Years from Birth to Six* (New York: Harper and Row, 1967).

2. Beck, Joan, *How to Raise a Brighter Child* (New York: Trident Press, 1967).

3. Burks, Barbara S., "The Relative Influence of Nature and Nurture upon Mental Development," *The Twenty-Seventh Yearbook of the N.S.S.E.*, Part I, 1928 (Distributed by the University of Chicago Press).

4. Hollingsworth, Leta S., *Gifted Children: Their Nature and Nurture* (New York: Macmillan Company, 1926).

5. Terman, Lewis M., in "Introduction" to *Education of Gifted Children* by L. M. Stedman (Yonkers-on-Hudson, New York: World Book Company, 1924).

6. Witty, Paul A., "Intelligence and Aptitude," Chapter Five in Charles E. Skinner (Editor), *Essentials of Educational Psychology* (Englewood Cliffs, N.J.: Prentice-Hall, 1959).

7. Bayley, Nancy, "Mental Growth in Young Children," *Thirty-Ninth Yearbook of the N.S.S.E.*, Part II, 1940 (Distributed by the University of Chicago Press).

8. Bloom, Benjamin S., *Stability and Change in Human Characteristics* (New York: John Wiley and Sons, Inc., 1964), Chapter Seven.

9. Bloom, Benjamin S., Davis, Allison, and Hess, Robert, *Compensatory Education for Cultural Deprivation* (New York: Holt, Rinehart, and Winston, 1965).

10. Bereiter, Carl, and Engelmann, Siegfried, *Teaching Disadvantaged Children in the Kindergarten* (Englewood Cliffs, N.J.: Prentice-Hall, 1966).

11. Kirk, Samuel A., *Early Education of the Mentally Retarded* (Urbana, Illinois: University of Illinois Press, 1958).

12. Hunt, J. McV., *Intelligence and Experience* (New York: Ronald Press, 1961).

13. Engelmann, Siegfried and Therese, *Give Your Child a Superior Mind* (New York: Simon and Schuster, 1966).

14. Durkin, Dolores, *Children Who Read Early* (New York: Teachers College Press, 1966).

15. Brzeinski, Joseph E., Harrison, M. Lucile, and McKee, Paul, "Should Johnny Read in Kindergarten?" *NEA Journal*, Vol. 56 (March, 1967).

The Early Years and Reading

Witty — Questions for Discussion

What beliefs have contributed to the neglect of intellectual stimulation in many cases? Do we have substantive evidence that many children could learn to read at an earlier age? Might one infer that the I.Q.'s of nearly all children could be raised to some extent, or could one expect this to happen only with culturally-deprived children? Do I.Q.'s really change or do we really not measure innate potential to begin with? Do some of us need to change our concept of what the I.Q.'s is if we admit that it can be raised?

Jo M. Stanchfield

The Development of Pre-Reading Skills in an Experimental Kindergarten Program

Current approaches to teaching reading are based on two assumptions. The first assumption is that success in beginning reading is crucial to subsequent achievement in school. The second assumption is that reading programs in the primary grades must be organized to assure this success. As evidence of the importance of initial reading instruction, one can cite the large number of research studies designed to find more effective ways of teaching beginning reading.

Recent research projects in reading readiness offer further evidence of the emphasis on early stages of reading. "Sesame Street," through the powerful teaching medium of television, has greatly increased interest in pre-reading skills. This innovative program accepts the premise that the pre-kindergarten years are a period of substantial and significant intellectual development (1). "Sesame Street" uses the techniques and the approaches of commercial television to help preschoolers develop skills necessary for a successful start in formal reading instruction.

An increasing number of authorities in early childhood education have recognized that children's formal education can, and should, begin long before the age of five or six. Many recent studies in readiness have been conducted with three- or four-year-old children in a structured learning situation. In research reported by Karnes in May, 1968, a traditional nursery-school program was compared with a highly structured program focused on specific learning tasks designed to promote

From Jo M. Stanchfield, "The Development of Pre-Reading Skills in an Experimental Kindergarten Program," *Elementary School Journal* 71, no. 8 (May 1971): 438-47. Copyright © 1971 by The University of Chicago Press. Reprinted by permission of the author and the publisher.

language and cognitive development. Four-year-olds were studied so that follow-up evaluation could be continued in kindergartens of public schools. At the end of the experimental period, results of the Metropolitan Readiness Tests showed superior performance by the experimental group in both reading readiness and numbers readiness. The University of Illinois researchers who conducted the study concluded that their findings offered evidence on the value of teaching cognitive skills as well as the value of social readiness for school activities (2).

In a four-year study in New York State, Di Lorenzo and Salter studied the effectiveness of an academic year preschool program for the disadvantaged. This longitudinal study extended from pre-kindergarten through second grade. The project was conducted in eight school districts whose basic curriculums emphasized language and cognitive development, but varied in comprehensiveness and methods of reading readiness instruction. At the end of the first two years of the study, the pre-kindergarten experience had proven beneficial for the subjects. The most effective pre-kindergarten programs were those that had the most specific structured cognitive activities (3).

Much of the work in reading readiness has been done with culturally and economically deprived children because they lack the background of information and skills that middle-class or upper-class children have when they begin their formal education. Traditional preschool classes are not adequate to prepare the disadvantaged child to compete with children of more privileged environments. Thus the gains that disadvantaged children make in structured programs to develop reading readiness contrast significantly with the gains of children in a California study by Prendergast. In his study, Prendergast compared the development of pre-reading skills in three groups of upper-middle-class children: a conventional day nursery class, a Montessori preschool class, and a non-nursery school group. The conventional school offered common enrichment experiences, while the Montessori class provided a structured program to develop skills through the use of special methods and materials. At the end of seven months, children were compared on perceptual motor skills and receptive language. In most areas evaluated, no significant differences were found among the three groups. The researcher attributed this finding primarily to the fact that the upper-middle-class home environment encouraged the development of reading readiness skills. The children from these upper-middle-class homes developed readiness skills without nursery-school experience (4).

At the kindergarten level, investigators at the University of Iowa studied the effectiveness of the Frostig perceptual motor method in developing reading readiness among 108 disadvantaged kindergarten children. Alley reported the findings after the children had had about eight months of training in sensorimotor and visual perceptual exercises (5). Results, as measured by the Marianne Frostig Developmental Test of Visual Perception and the Metropolitan Reading Readiness Tests, Form A, showed significant differences in favor of the experimental group.

The "nature versus nurture" controversy was considered by Bernabei in developing a reading readiness program in the schools of Bucks County, Pennsylvania. Do children grow into readiness, or is readiness a result of training and experience? Bernabei saw no immediate resolution of the controversy and undertook an interim, eclectic approach. His Extended Reading Readiness Program was organized to cover a longer period of time than the usual kindergarten curriculum of one year. During the program pupil learning experiences were devised, and materials were developed for a curriculum of readiness skills, including prereading and mathematics. An evaluation of the program after one year indicated significant differences between the skills of the interim class and the skills of the normal class (6).

Basic Pre-Reading Skills

Over the past seven years, the writer has been engaged in resarch with first-grade children in the Los Angeles city schools. Each year the studies involved about five hundred children of varying ethnic and socioeconomic backgrounds. The purpose of the research has been to experiment with a variety of materials and methods in teaching beginning reading to determine the effect on the reading achievement of first-grade children. During these years, it has become increasingly apparent to the writer, the teachers, and the administrators who took part in the studies that certain pre-reading skills were necessary if children were to succeed in reading. Through experimentation it was found that many children were not able to acquire proficiency in the reading readiness skills in the time that could be allotted in first grade.

Using this knowledge and findings from other reading readiness studies, the writer worked with teachers and administrators to develop a research design to teach pre-reading skills in a sequential, developmental order in six major areas. These areas included listening for comprehension of content, listening for auditory discrimination, visual discrimination skills, oral language skills, motor-perceptual skills, and sound-symbol correspondence skills.

To Develop Essential Skills

Through grouping and independent activities, the teacher taught lessons in the six areas to small groups of children. The skills of each lesson were developed in detail in the teacher's manual. These skills were taught and retaught, with sufficient practice periods, until the children attained an adequate level of proficiency. The objective of the study was to determine whether children who were taught pre-reading skills in a structured program would score significantly higher on a standardized test of reading readiness skills than children who had not been involved in such a program.

For the experimental program, seventeen schools were selected to provide a cross section of socioeconomic levels that represented blacks, Mexican-Americans, and other white children. Each experimental school was matched with a control school that had children of similar ethnic origins, academic achievement, and socioeconomic backgrounds. The teachers in the experimental and the control schools were randomly selected.

The teachers in the experimental program were given a teacher's guide for the reading readiness lessons and materials to implement their teaching. The pre-reading skills were taught in the language-arts block of time in the kindergarten program. During the fall semester of the school year, the teachers in the experimental program met each week after school at a designated school building to receive additional materials and to discuss the use of these materials. At these workshop-type meetings, the teachers also made instructional aids, such as puppets and flannelboard cutouts from patterns provided for them.

The teachers in the control schools followed the regular curriculum.

The Program

The teaching philosophy of the program was based on the premise that the skills in the reading process are the same on the pre-reading level as at the highest stage of reading development. The chief differences are those of degree and refinement. Therefore the materials and the techniques used in the research were developed to parallel the formal reading instruction that the children would receive as they progressed through the primary grades.

The materials for the program included the teacher's manual; picture cards; a large flannelboard; a large pocket chart; small, individual flannelboards, pocket charts, and chalkboards; flannelboard cut-outs; hand puppets; books; and phoneme boxes containing small objects.

Lesson plans were classified according to the six major areas of pre-reading skills. The purpose of each lesson was to improve one of these skills.

Each lesson plan included six sections: Purpose; Preparation; Presentation; Evaluation in Terms of the Purpose; Pupil Practice Materials; Additional Experiences. "Preparation" included materials needed in the presentation of the lesson. "Evaluation" established a quick check of what the children learned in terms of the purpose of the lesson. "Pupil Practice Materials" provided independent follow-up exercises for reinforcement of the skills taught in the lesson. At the close of the lesson, "Additional Experiences" suggested activities related to the skill to be developed by a specific plan.

The Materials

Picture cards were used in a variety of ways: to stimulate imagination, to help in noting details, for picture-reading, and for storytelling. The picture cards were also used to inspire paintings, to motivate dramatic play, and to stimulate creative language, including stories dictated to the teacher.

The large flannelboard and the pocket chart were big enough to be seen by a group of children. They were used by the teacher or by a child. The flannelboard held cutouts of story characters, objects, letters, and numbers. The pocket chart served as another illustrative aid.

There were small flannelboards, pocket charts, and chalkboards for each child in a group. Small groups were formed on the basis of specific needs. By having individual manipulative materials for each child in the group, the teacher could make sure that every child was involved in the activity and learning, and had instant feedback on individual progress.

Cutouts of the characters and objects from a story were used to illustrate the story on the large flannelboard. Children placed the cutouts on the board when a teacher was telling a story or when a child was retelling it. Other cutouts were used in teaching about shape, size, color, sight-sound-symbol correspondence, and numerals and simple number concepts.

In the experimental program, puppets were used to motivate oral language—for retelling stories and for creating stories or conversation. Children are likely to lose much of their self-consciousness when they use hand puppets. The children are intent on manipulating the puppet appropriately and actually become the puppet character.

The books for this program were chosen primarily because of their universal appeal for four-, five-, and six-year-olds. Other criteria the books met were those of high literary quality, worthwhile illustrations, and appropriate format. The collection included Mother Goose rhymes, poetry, fairy or folk tales, animal stories, an ABC book, and songbooks.

A phoneme box for each letter of the alphabet contained small objects with names that began with the sound of that letter. Later, objects from two or three boxes were combined for purposes of auditory discrimination of the beginning sounds of letters.

The Teaching Techniques

Descriptions of the teaching techniques used to develop the six major skills give an overview of the reading readiness program:

1. Listening for Comprehension of Content

The ability to listen is often taken for granted and is therefore seldom taught specifically. Efficient listening must be learned and practiced. In the research program, special attention was given to this area because it is important to speech, language, and reading.

The lessons in this part of the experimental curriculum centered on listening for pleasure and relaxation, comprehending what someone said or read, memorizing, remembering, and following directions. The children listened to poems, songs, and recordings, aware of the mood each work created. As the teacher read or told a story, the children listened to answer directed questions or to recall and tell parts of the story. The children listened to follow directions. At first the directions were simple. Later, they were more complex.

2. Listening for Auditory Discrimination and Development

As a prelude to the aural discrimination of words and word elements, the children had many directed listening experiences. After the children had learned to listen to the teacher, to each other, to music, and to sounds in their environment, the teacher began to develop the concepts of volume, pitch, direction, duration, sequence, accent, tempo, repetition, contrast, and distance. To develop these concepts, the teacher used a variety of recordings, tonal instruments, poems, jingles, and rhythms.

3. Visual Discrimination and Development

Observing and interpreting content. The interpretation of pictures and picture stories helped children develop such skills as arranging items in sequence, making inferences, predicting outcomes, getting the main idea, and noting relevant details. Before this part of the program, the teachers organized school excursions and walking trips to give children opportunities to observe and become acquainted with the world beyond their immediate neighborhood. These firsthand experiences helped the children understand concepts represented in the pictures and the picture stories, which otherwise might have had no meaning.

Visual imagery. Visual projection, or recognition of an object from its description, was developed by various techniques. The children guessed the answers to riddles about familiar objects. They painted pictures from vivid descriptions, or illustrated stories. The children practiced visual memory in a variety of simple exercises, such as describing objects or scenes from memory or locating, with eyes shut, familiar objects in the room.

Visual discrimination. The children were taught to note gross likenesses and differences before they made finer discriminations. Picture-matching games and the comparing and the contrasting of pictures, objects, and geometric forms were used to help the children make discriminations of size, shape, position, color, and small details. The development of these concepts laid a foundation for the further study of visual skills.

4. Oral Language Skills

The teachers provided experience in oral expression to develop the children's ability to express ideas to others, to develop the ability to speak with expression and with pleasing voice quality, to encourage the use of complete and well-structured sentences, to expand speaking, and to improve pronunciation and diction.

Varied and stimulating opportunities were provided for practice in oral expression. These ranged from spontaneous discussion of personal experience to participation in creative storytelling, recitation of poems, or choral speaking.

5. Motor-Perceptual Development

Through directed lessons, the children learned to co-ordinate vision and movement, to become aware of and to manipulate the parts of their bodies, and to perceive positions of objects in relation to themselves.

They learned body control through exercises, games, dances, and the interpretation of music. Later, opportunities for the development of finer motor co-ordination were provided through activities in construction, cutting, pasting, tracing, and coloring. Eventually the children were ready for paper and pencil exercises that further refined hand-eye coordination.

6. Sound-Symbol Correspondence

In the experimental classes, sound-symbol correspondence on increasing levels of difficulty was developed. Practice was given to reinforce the learning of the sounds of the letters of the alphabet. Auditory and visual recognition of letters of the alphabet was taught by the use of objects and pictures. Children associated letter sounds with the corresponding names and symbols. In the last step in the development of sound-symbol correspondence, the children learned to write the letters of the alphabet in manuscript form.

The ability to count from one to ten was developed by using the type of learning sequence that was used to develop letter recognition.

Results of the Research

At the end of the school year, the Murphy-Durrell Reading Readiness Analysis was given to the seventeen experimental classes and the seventeen control classes. With the data from this standardized test, a three-way analysis of variance was performed with sex, experimental-control, and ethnic group as the main effects. An analysis of the data permitted the writer to determine whether these variables or their interaction accounted for a significant part of the children's achievement, as indicated by the test scores.

The scores from the five tests of the Murphy-Durrell Reading Readiness Analysis were studied separately and in total. When the F-test was significant, it was followed by t-tests between the groups.

As Table 1 shows, the experimental group had a higher mean score than the control group in the total test and also in all the individual parts of the test.

As Table 2 indicates, the girls as a group had a higher mean score than the boys in the total test as well as in the individual parts of the test. However, this difference might have been due to chance in the first parts of the subtests on phonemes and on letter names.

As Table 3 indicates, the children in the "other white" group scored higher on the total test and on all individual parts of the test than the Mexican-American and the black children did. While the Mexican-Americans had a higher over-all average than the black children, the black children scored slightly higher in both parts of the Letter Names Test.

Table 4 reports the mean scores for the total test separated according to the three main effects: experimental-control, sex, and ethnic group. Table 5 presents the analysis of covariance for these three main effects and their possible combinations. In this analysis, mean scores reported in Tables 1, 2, 3, and 4 were tested for significant differences.

TABLE 1

Mean Scores for Experimental and Control Groups on Murphy-Durrell Reading Readiness Analysis

GROUP	PHONEMES TEST Part 1	Part 2	LETTER NAMES TEST Part 1	Part 2	LEARNING RATE TEST	TOTAL TEST
Experimental	15.92	18.57	20.51	21.71	10.80	87.50
Control	11.98	12.62	14.24	16.66	7.54	63.05

TABLE 2

Mean Scores for Boys and Girls on Murphy-Durrell Reading Readiness Analysis

GROUP	PHONEMES TEST Part 1	Part 2	LETTER NAMES TEST Part 1	Part 2	LEARNING RATE TEST	TOTAL TEST
Boys	13.72*	14.84	17.00*	18.35	8.64	72.56
Girls	14.19*	16.35	17.75*	20.01	9.70	77.99

*Differences on Phonemes Test, Part 1, and Letter Names Test, Part 1, not statistically significant. The differences could be due to chance.

TABLE 3

Mean Scores for Ethnic Groups on Murphy-Durrell Reading Readiness Analysis

GROUP	PHONEMES TEST Part 1	Part 2	LETTER NAMES TEST Part 1	Part 2	LEARNING RATE TEST	TOTAL TEST
Black	13.19	14.43	16.78	18.62	8.20	71.21
Mexican-American	13.45	14.91	16.57	18.45	8.87	72.24
Other White	15.21	17.45	18.78	20.49	10.43	82.38

TABLE 4

Means for Total Score on Murphy-Durrell Reading Readiness Analysis

Group	Black	Mexican-American	Other White
Boys	67.68	69.37	80.64
Girls	74.73	75.11	84.12
Total	71.21	72.24	82.38

	Black	Mexican-American	Other White
Experimental	82.68	84.57	95.27
Control	59.73	59.92	69.49
Total	71.21	72.24	82.38

TABLE 4 (continued)

	Boys	Girls	Total
Experimental	86.04	88.97	87.50
Control	59.09	67.00	63.05
Total	72.56	77.99	75.28

TABLE 5

Analysis of Co-Variance for Total Scores on Murphy-Durrell Reading Readiness Analysis

Source of Variation	Sum of Squares	Degrees of Freedom	Mean Square	F
Experimental-Control	205120.56	1	205120.56	315.28
Sex	10089.19	1	10089.19	15.51
Ethnic	34876.29	2	17438.14	26.80
Experimental-Control × Sex	2122.16	1	2122.16	3.26
Experimental-Control × Ethnic	464.45	2	232.22	0.36*
Sex × Ethnic	764.55	2	382.27	0.59*
Experimental-Control × Sex × Ethnic	714.53	2	357.27	0.55*

*Significant beyond the .01 level.

All three main effects showed significant differences:
1. The experimental groups had significantly higher scores than the control groups.
2. The girls, as a group, achieved significantly better than the boys in the study.
3. The "other white" group had significantly higher scores than the Mexican-American and the black groups. The experimental Mexican-American group and the experimental black group had considerably higher scores than the control group of "other white."

As Table 5 shows, combinations of the various possible groupings did not produce significant additional differences. That is, although the three main effects were significant, the interactions between the groups were not significant.

In summary, it may be said that the children in the kindergartens who were taught in a structured, sequential program with appropriate materials achieved significantly more than the children in the kindergarten who were taught the regular curriculum.

References

1. E. L. Palmer. "Can Television Really Teach? Preschoolers Watch Sesame Street Series," *American Education, 5* (August, 1969), 2-6.

2. M. B. Karnes and Others. "Evaluation of Two Preschool Programs for Disadvantaged Children: A Traditional and a Highly Structured Experimental Preschool," *Exceptional Children, 34* (May, 1968), 667-76.

3. L. J. Di Lorenzo and R. Salter. "An Evaluative Study of Prekindergarten Programs for Educationally Disadvantaged Children: Follow-Up and Replication," *Exceptional Children, 35* (October, 1968), 111-19.

4. R. Prendergast. "Pre-Reading Skills Developed in Montessori and Conventional Nursery Schools," *Elementary School Journal, 70* (December, 1969), 135-41.

5. G. Alley and Others. "Reading Readiness and the Frostig Training Program," *Exceptional Children, 35* (September, 1968), 68.

6. R. Bernabei. "An Evaluation of the Interim Class: An Extended Readiness Program." Unpublished research. Doylestown, Pennsylvania: Bucks County Public Schools, 1967.

The Early Years and Reading

Stanchfield — Questions for Discussion

What types of kindergarten programs does Stanchfield indicate have typically been most effective? Does the fact that children who have had kindergarten experience do well on readiness tests mean that they are also likely to attain higher achievement in reading? What are some basic differences between "traditional" kindergarten programs and the program described by Stanchfield? What are some of the reasons that children from lower socioeconomic levels need a prolonged and/or more intensive readiness program than do children from middle or upper socioeconomic levels? Could the kinds of activities carried on by Stanchfield in her research be easily implemented into other kindergarten programs?

CHAPTER THREE

Self-Concept
and Reading

A most important, although perhaps too often neglected, part of successful teaching is the building of positive self-concepts in students. Psychologists have been somewhat aware of this all-important problem for some time, but a great deal of credit should be given to Prescott Lecky, whose book *SELF-CONSISTENCY: A Theory of Personality* emphasized the phenomenon of fulfillment of the self-concept. From this book several works published on the subject of psychocybernetics have also given impetus to the subject.

If we as teachers are to deal effectively with children's self-concepts, then there are some very important questions that must be answered. For example, does the self-concept develop early in life, or is it an ever-continuing process? Once formed to some extent, can the self-concept be changed? If so, then how can it be done? As teachers of reading we are specifically concerned with the part that the self-concept plays in the teaching-learning of reading. For example, how does a child's self-concept affect his reading? Are there certain measures that the teacher can take to improve the child's concept that will in turn improve the child's concept of his ability to read?

The three articles chosen for this chapter do an excellent job of answering these questions. They also list several examples illustrating how one might implement procedures for the improvement of children's self-concepts.

Isabel Gillham

Self-Concept and Reading

"Don't bother about holding a chair for me," said fourteen-year-old Rick, as he climbed up to adjust the clock for the teacher. "My father always says that if I fall I'm OK as long as I hit on my head, because I'm too dumb for it to hurt me there!" Rick's remarks represent the types of self-image with which some parents inject their children before and after they start school.

"Everyone has an image or concept of himself as an unique person or self, different from every other self" (Hamachek, 1963, p. 2). In fact, each individual has many "selves," as pointed out by James (1890) many years ago. The concept the adolescent may have of himself as a fisherman could be quite different from the way he sees himself as a student, just as the concept he may have of himself as a brother or son could be quite different from the light in which he views himself as a member of a reading class. These ideas about himself did not come quickly.

Development of Self-Concept

Anderson (Hamachek, 1965, p. 2) maintains that "in the development of the self-image, the first year of life is the most important, each succeeding year becoming of lesser importance, until the image is essen-

From Isabel Gillham,"Self-Concept and Reading," *The Reading Teacher* 21, no. 3 (December 1967): 270-73. Reprinted with permission of Isabel Gillham and the International Reading Association.

tially completed before adolescence. This is not due to the fact that the earliest period of life is the most plastic or the most impressionable, but rather to the fact that the helplessness and dependency of the child are maximum in the earliest period, and therefore, his necessity is so much greater." The individual unconsciously builds his self-attitudes to reflect the love, acceptance and confidence—or lack of these qualities—shown toward him by his parents and significant others.

Building and rebuilding of these attitudes toward self (i.e. the self-image) is constantly occurring to some extent throughout life. The greater the sense of helplessness, the more the self-image descends, and vice versa. "Whereas people outside the family, such as contemporaries or teachers, may become significant ones, their influence and their impact tend to be less because of the advanced and, therefore, less helpless age at which they enter the picture" (Hamachek, 1965, p. 2).

"Once the psychological self-image has been formed, behavior . . . becomes compulsive" (Hamachek, 1965, p. 2). It is hypothesized that when he has decided what kind of person he is, the individual moves through life behaving subconsciously in a certain way so as to evoke the treatment or response to which he has adjusted. Moreover, he is comfortable with this anticipated response because it tends to reinforce his self-view.

According to Lecky (1945), the child not seen as bright by his parents, who has, therefore, come to see himself as stupid or incapable of learning, holds to this concept when he goes to school. In school, such a child may seem free to explore, to follow where his curiosity leads and to learn new things. But in reality, according to Lecky's theory, he is not free; he is restrained by the picture he has of himself as a non-learner. He must be faithful to this picture of himself or be threatened with loss of selfhood.

Jersild (1952) commented, "When a person resists learning that may be beneficial to him, he is, in effect, trying to protect or to shield an unhealthy condition. But, more broadly speaking, he is not actually protecting something unhealthy as such; he is trying to safeguard his picture of himself, his self-concept, the illusions concerning himself which he has built and which give him much trouble."

Sylvester and Kunet (1963), investigating why the child does not see himself as a potential learner, developed the theory of the inhibition of exploratory function. They reported the results of differential treatment of thirteen children, aged 8 to 13, who were under treatment for reading disabilities. In one case tutoring only was used; in another psychotherapy only; in the remaining eleven cases both tutoring and psychotherapy. They postulated that teaching alone was not enough—where tutoring alone succeeded it was because the tutor had intuitively met some of the emotional needs of the child. If the child's curiosity had been traumatically inhibited, anxiety became associated with curiosity. If this function had been over-indulged, the child became disorganized and again learning was adversely affected by anxiety. Thus, a reading disability becomes a defense against anxiety that may be aroused by curiosity. These writers believe that, in order to learn to read, a child must have preserved enough courage for active curiosity.

According to Lecky, theories of defense mechanisms help define the problem of self-concept and give a rather clear picture of the typical low-achiever.

> It is a picture of a child who sees himself as helpless and perhaps worthless. He sees himself, not as able to achieve or act constructively for his own enjoyment or benefit, but as having to be on the defensive in order to maintain integrity. He may simulate indifference or boldness; he may fight blindly and hopelessly, dig in his heels stubbornly, or withdraw into daydreams or unreachable passivity. While he may see himself as threatened and helpless, in the area of academic achievement, he can be the winner. No one can make him learn anything (1945).

It is important to note at this point, however, that this behavior has been learned, and that learned behavior can be modified and adjusted. The individual who has learned to see himself as stupid and insignificant is enslaved by this self-concept until some significant person or persons in his life help him see himself as capable and worthwhile. In early years this may be his mother and father. When he goes to school, it may be one or more of his teachers.

Changing Self-Concept

> If the teacher is to help free the pupil from his distorted picture of himself, she must *first* be significant to him. She must be able to see him as a more adequate person than others have seen him before. It is necessary to find the good in him and show it to him. (Lecky, 1945)

Often, the distortion previously mentioned is already so fixed by the time the student gets to junior high school that before he can learn, an area of non-academic success must be found and related to school in order to find a basis upon which to reorder his self-image. This is what one reading teacher was doing when she talked to Clare about what he liked to do. She found he liked to fly kites, and inquired if he thought he could build one. He thought he could, so arrangements were made with a kindergarten teacher in a nearby elementary school for Clare to spend an hour a day for a week with the kindergarteners. He showed them how to build a kite by actually constructing one in class with them, and then he accompanied them and their teacher on a field trip and helped them fly it. After that trip, his reading teacher saw him smile for the first time in seven months of school. Shortly after this, he requested special help with his reading. Even more significantly, at the end of the year when he evaluated his reading course, he wrote, "It helped me have more confidence in myself."

Earlier, a group of twenty eighth-grade students who were poor readers with inadequate self-concepts, were told that the kindergarten teacher in a neighborhood school had exceedingly large classes and no assistant. The eighth-grade class expressed wilingness to help her by preparing suitable stories and reading them to these beginners. Their reading teacher planned for them to visit the library and each student selected a book that he or she felt kindergarten children would enjoy. Careful preparation relating to reading the story meaningfully, handling children and their questions, and behavior expected of teacher-assistants paved the way for the successful experiences the junior high students gained. For an entire semester, the students read to a small group of youngsters once a week. (They changed books about once a month.) No one seeing the junior-highers returning could deny that they seemed to feel "ten feet tall." When other rooms in the elementary school began to request their services, the readers were infinitely proud to know they were doing such a good job. Every effort was made to give credit to these people . . . a newspaper article with their pictures and names appeared; at Christmastime they were remembered with cards the little folks had made; they were thanked publicly by the principal; other junior high students began to notice them. Wayne, who skipped as many of his other classes as possible, rarely missed reading class and never—until he was expelled—missed a morning when he was scheduled to read at the elementary school. This was one small area where he was achieving success and he was beginning to realize that it felt "good" to be respected and to respect himself. Unfortunately, for Wayne it was "too little, too late" to change academic and physical behavior in other classes.

Mike, who had always yearned to be in student council but who had never been elected, became the leader in the class. This new status, coupled with reading help, enabled him to gain four years in reading grade-level, bringing him to about middle seventh grade level.

Rick, referred to in the opening paragraph, was one of the students included in the kindergarten experience described above. His grades, after participating in the program, at the end of the semester were up in every subject. He said it was the best report card he had ever had. His parents were so impressed with his achievement that they told him *for the first time* that they felt he should complete high school—and they arranged for him to be enrolled in a work-study program the following year.

It is highly important for the student that parents express confidence in their children's abilities. Based on a previous study by Brookover (1962), a research project was conducted by Dr. Jean LePere with parents of low-achieving ninth-grade students. As a result of treatment for one semester, some parents changed their evolutions of their children's abilities to do better in school, and some students were so affected by the change that a gain in grade-point average was shown by 42 percent of them. This percent was raised significantly by the year's end. School systems and teachers need to be constantly searching for ways— new or old—that will help students realize their full potential.

References

Brookover, W., and LePere, J. *Self-concept of ability and school achievement in junior high school subjects.* Michigan State University, 1962.

Hamachek, D. C. *The self in growth, teaching, and learning.* Englewood Cliffs, N. J.: Prentice Hall, 1965.

James, W. *Principles of psychology*, vol. I. New York: Holt, Rinehart & Winston, 1890.

Jersild, A. T. *In search of self.* New York: Bureau of Publications, Columbia University, 1952.

Lecky, P. *Self-consistency: a theory of personality.* New York: Island Press, 1945.

Sylverter, E., and Kunet, M. Psycho-dynamic aspects of the reading problem. *Journal of Orthopsychiatry,* 1963, *13*, 69-76.

Self-Concept and Reading

Gillham—Questions for Discussion

Why are the early years of life of such great importance in molding the self-concept? According to Lecky and Jersild, why do some children resist learning? What are some possible symptoms of a child with a poor self-concept? What methods, other than those described here, might be used to build a better self-concept within a child?

Lucille Sebeson

Self-Concept and Reading Disabilities

The self-concept of an individual is viewed as a developmental phenomenon resulting from a dynamic interaction between the individual and his environment. It is generally accepted that the self-concept as a percept is not present at birth, but begins to develop gradually as perceptive powers develop. (Bodwin, 1959)

In their evaluation of self-concept, Bruck (1957) and Bodwin (1959) both stated that self-concept is composed of the following elements: liking for one's attainment, satisfaction with one's attainment, and feelings of personal appreciation for others.

Brookover (1964) says a relevant aspect of self-concept in school learning is the person's conception of his own ability to learn the accepted types of academic behavior performance in terms of school achievement in various areas.

Combs and Snygg (1959) state that:

The very perceptions we are able to make at a particular time are dependent upon the concepts we hold about ourselves and our abilities. Self is a basic variable affecting and controlling perception. Thus, if a man believes he is Napoleon, he will act like Napoleon or, at least, like his concept of Napoleon. How we act in any given situation will be dependent upon two things:
1. How we perceive ourselves.
2. How we perceive the situations in which we are involved.

From Lucille Sebeson, "Self-Concept and Reading Disabilities," *The Reading Teacher* 23, no. 5 (February 1970): 460-64. Reprinted with the permission of Lucille Sebeson and the International Reading Association.

They talk of the perceptual field and explain it as involving all an individual's perceptions including those about himself (phenomenal self) and those quite outside himself (phenomenal environment).

The phenomenal environment or "not-self" includes all the perceptions the individual has about himself *plus* perceptions about all things quite outside himself. The phenomenal self includes all the perceptions which an individual has about himself irrespective of their importance to him. This would be all the perceptions one has about himself in a given situation. This could also include others in his "me" such as "my mother," "my teacher," "my family," "my class," etc. Central to both kinds of perceptions are the very important ones involved in the person's individual behavior. This is the self-concept—the very essence of "me."

Once established in a given personality, the perceived self is thought to have a high degree of stability. The phenomenal self, with the self-concept as its core, represents one fundamental frame of reference, our anchor to reality. Even an unsatisfactory self-organization is likely to prove highly stable and resistant to change. Thus, even the person who regards himself as very inadequate or stupid, and with severe feelings of his level of worth, will likely be pleased by praise or even highly embarrassed, but will continue to act in the same old ways. So, the child who feels rejected may interpret his parents mildest rebuke as further evidence to prove what he already thinks—his parents do not love him. His resulting behavior may even cause his belief to come true.

Although the self-concept is ever changing and growing, it is the unifying force within the individual's personality, and change and growth derive direction from the existing self-concept.

How Self-Concept Develops and What Factors Influence It

Strang (1965, 1967) writes that distinguishing his own body is the first step in the child's development of selfhood. The approval or disapproval of the mother in regard to the way he responds to things his mother teaches as accepted values or attitudes in the culture give him a sense of a "good me" or a "bad me." Strang also states that parents, at this stage, have a great deal of control over the child's self-concept. By praise, punishment, love, rejection, or ignoring the child, they foster the feeling of good or bad in the way the child sees himself. Strang feels that reasonable freedom can give a child self-confidence, while unreasonable restrictions may produce anxiety or rebellion. A child who is constantly corrected will put a low estimate on his own worth and competence. He may give up trying.

Self-concepts are learned. They are built up in many subtle ways. They are derived, in part, by negative comments of parents, teachers and classmates and from repeated experiences of failure. The child becomes fearful of making mistakes, afraid and ashamed to be wrong again. Self-confidence, on the other hand, arises when others show a positive expectancy that the individual can close the gap between his present performance and his potential: it is reinforced by experiences of success.

Congreve (1966) agrees that one's self-concept is learned. The child develops his sense of identity, his feelings about himself, and his self-image from experience. These experiences include the attitudes, ideas, conduct, and self-concepts of significant others around him. Some children learn to accept defeat, frustration, and low position in life because they have taken over the self-concept of their defeated, frustrated, or impoverished families. The opposite, of course, could also occur.

According to Drews (1966), the child quite early takes on responsibility for his own learning. He may choose to "tune-in" on what is going on around him or not. In a conscious or unconscious way each child evaluates and chooses to focus on particular parts of the environment. He may learn the multiplication table during an arithmetic class or instead may simply count the number of times a teacher clears her throat. Something he chooses to learn or which he is excited about will be remembered longer than the correct spelling of a word if, for punishment, he had to write the word correctly a hundred times after misspelling it once.

Some of the behavioral symptoms that might indicate poor self-concepts are feelings of insecurity, inattention, antagonism, loneliness, and indecision. Poor readers may have a low motivation toward academic achievement. They often can not accept rules and will not try to adjust to them. They show other evidences of emotional instability, emotional immaturity, or lack of social confidence. Feelings of inadequacy and nervousness, or feelings of discouragement may indicate a low self-concept and result in under-achieving in academic subjects.

Smith and Dechant (1961) state that:

We wish to know how a child's personality traits may influence his reading and how reading failure or success may influence the development of the child's personality. The self has needs that demand satisfaction. Because reading, in our culture, is an essential developmental task, failure in reading can block the child's attempts to satisfy this need for self-esteem within the culture. Parents and teachers may compound the problem by nagging the child or by showing their worry, anger or discouragement.

How Can the Teacher Influence the Child's Self-Concept

Studies thus far have shown that self-concept develops through imitation, identification, and incorporation of the way the child perceives himself in relation to significant others. Plant (1966) indicates that "bossy and dominating parents" may lead a child to negativism, withdrawal, "defensive lies, blasé indifference, and braggadocio" as defenses against the "gaze and meddlesomeness of others."

Reading, because of its importance in society, assumes great importance as a developmental task and failure to master it may interfere with the development of a child's self-esteem. "Parents and teachers may compound the problem by nagging the child or by showing their worry, anger, or discouragement" (Smith and Dechant, 1961).

The fundamental aim of teachers, according to Drews, should be to help the child realize himself, help him develop his potentialities so he can move toward a more adequate self. Several specific suggestions to teachers follow:

1. "Basic to the acquisition of adequate and accurate self-concepts is the teacher who accepts each child as a unique person worthy as an end in himself, and who helps him in his growth toward self-realization" (Bledsoe, 1967).

2. Children are taught to speak of things outside themselves, but seldom anything having any relation to self. Teachers should get children to talk about what they think, what they believe, how they feel, what they are worried about or puzzled about. (Combs and Snygg, 1959)

3. Because many children come to school with very little self-confidence, the school must help the child acquire feelings of success and achievement. The teacher must seek some area where the child can find success so he will find acceptance among his peers. (Smith and Dechant, 1961)

4. Teachers must deal with the child's feelings of how he can relate what he has to learn in school to his own worth as a member of his immediate environment. From this he can react to the way he believes and the way his culture expects him to behave. (Fantini and Weinstein, 1968)

5. Both parents and teachers can aid the child in his struggle for self-realization. They can devise the techniques and develop materials that

will give all children a real opportunity for success in learning tasks, provide an example and a model of a good life, and be enthusiastic about their own lives. He feels that the excited, competent, alert, prepared teacher or parent can change the lives of children. When adults demonstrate to children that they care about them, the children begin to care about themselves. (Congreve, 1966)

References

Bledsoe, J. C. Self-concept of children and their intelligence, achievement, interests, and anxiety. *Childhood Education*, 1967, 436.

Bodwin, R. F. The relationship between immature self-concept and certain educational disabilities. *Dissertation Abstracts*, 1959, *19*, 1645-1646.

Brookover, W., and Shailer, T. Self-concept of ability and school achievement. *Sociology of Education*, 1964, 271-78.

Bruck, M. A study of age differences and sex differences in the relationship between self-concept and grade point average. Unpublished doctoral dissertation, Michigan State University, 1957.

Combs, A. W., and Snygg, D. *Individual behavior*. New York: Harper and Row, 1959.

Congreve, W. J. Not all the disadvantaged are poor. *P.T.A. Magazine*, 1966, 15-17.

Drews, Elizabeth. The child as evaluator. *The Instructor*, 1966, 22+.

Fantini, M. D., and Weinstein, G. Reducing the behavior gap. *NEA Journal*, 1968, 22-25.

Plant, J. S. *Personality and the cultural pattern*. New York: _____, 1966.

Smith, H. P., and Dechant, E. *Psychology in teaching reading*. Englewood Cliffs: Prentice-Hall, 1961. Pp. 297-304.

Strang, Ruth, McCullough, Constance, and Traxler, A. E. *The improvement of reading*. (4th Ed.) New York: McGraw-Hill, 1967. Pp. 22-24, 457.

Strang, Ruth. How the child's identity grows. *P.T.A. Magazine*, 1965, 28-30.

Self-Concept and Reading

Sebeson—Questions for Discussion

When does the self-concept begin to develop? Using the information given here, how might one best help a child to improve his self-concept? What factors contribute to the building of self-concept? Are the symptoms listed in this article as being typical of a child with a poor self-concept in agreement with those listed by Gillham? Are most classroom teachers equipped to do the things Sebeson suggests as beneficial in enhancing a child's self-concept?

Maxine Cohn
Donald Kornelly

For Better Reading — a More Positive Self-Image

The students had a defeatist attitude. Their records showed a history of reading failure extending over several years. They were far from enthusiastic about schoolwork, and their attitude spilled over into their relationships with their peers, their teachers and other adults. These students, now in junior high school, accepted failure as a certainty before they undertook any assignment.

Stanford Achievement tests the students had taken the year before confirmed their right to look at themselves as failures. Their test results in Grade 6 were studded with scores of 3.0, 4.3, 4.0, 3.6, and 4.4.

Could a program be structured that would offer help in the needed skill areas and, more important, provide a method to transform an ailing student? The defeatist syndrome of the poor readers would have to be shattered before they could benefit from any remedial help.

A heterogeneous seventh-grade class was selected for the pilot program. The students were reading at various levels: 30 percent were reading one to four years below national norms for seventh grade; 35 per cent were reading at grade level; 25 per cent were reading one to three years above grade level; 10 per cent were reading four or more years above grade level. The students intelligence quotients as determined by the Lorge-Thorndike Intelligence Tests ranged from 90 to 125.

Five students who were reading below grade level were individually tested by the reading teacher who used the Durrell Analysis of Reading Difficulty and classroom textbooks. Individualized programs, based on

From Maxine Cohn and Donald Kornelly, "For Better Reading — a More Positive Self-Image," *The Elementary School Journal* 70, no. 4 (January 1970): 199-201. Copyright © 1970 by The University of Chicago Press. Reprinted by permission of the authors and the publisher.

weaknesses indicated by the tests, were set up for each student. The programs were to be followed in the classroom.

While various materials were used, students preferred short selections on subjects that had special appeal for this age group. One series (1) that was used had individual books that ranged from Grades 2 to 8. Careful matching of student and reading level was possible to insure a successful experience. The answer sheets were simple enough to be used by the tutors. The students kept a record of their scores on each lesson. In this way they could easily see their progress. When a student did well for a period of time at one level, he was given the book for the next higher grade.

Each student was assigned a classmate tutor, and the children worked together on the readers for twenty minutes twice a week. The tutors were instructed to follow the general plan of the book, which had suggestions for vocabulary development, oral reading, strengthening of sight vocabulary, and comprehension. The areas emphasized were geared to fit the individual's diagnosed weaknesses.

A classroom library was set up using mainly paperbacks on subjects of interest to junior high school students. The books, which began at below third grade and progressed through adult level, accommodated the entire class. Paperbacks were emphasized because of their psychological acceptance by students at all reading levels. One set of paperbacks used had eighteen titles below third-grade level (2). The ease with which the stories were read contributed to the student's evolving successful self-image.

The teacher helped each student select a book that was not too difficult for him, and the student was given time in class to read. It was hoped that he would become involved in the book and become interested enough to take it home to finish. Reading skills were not taught at this time, but help with words was freely given when requested. No lengthy book reports were required, but time was given in class for sharing any enjoyable book. Mystery and sports books were especially well received (3).

The students showed immediate pride in their achievement. The realization that they could read was the first reinforcement which brought about a change of attitude. They felt they could read, answer questions, and give reports from real books, not just primer-type books. Some students volunteered oral book reports for the first time in many years. Other students asked for longer periods to work with their tutors.

More reinforcement occurred when the slow readers began tutoring each other. For the first time students were helping others with reading problems. They were no longer only on the receiving end, but could teach and were being depended on to help others. They felt capable and needed. They also enjoyed having the privilege and the responsibility of caring for the answer cards and of scoring their classmates' progress sheets.

These students were experiencing a pride in themselves—another step toward a positive self-image.

Scores on Stanford Achievement tests given ten weeks after the pilot program was begun were compared with scores of previous years. The test scores indicate a definite improvement in reading skills. The last test in the program, given in 1969, was administered ten weeks after the program was intiated and one year after the 1968 tests.

A short case study may give a sharper appreciation of the problems faced and goals attained.

Here was a thin, tall, sullen boy who never volunteered information and did not participate in class. He would not answer a direct question and would never look anyone in the eye. He was not able to follow in a reading group, but sought escape in daydreams.

His scores indicate one possible reason for his behavior: paragraph meaning—3.6, social studies—4.3, language—3.3.

Ten weeks later, we find a boy who has read four books, who has volunteered a four-page book report, and who has given an oral report on a book he obviously understood and enjoyed. He is now contributing in class and still appears somewhat surprised that his answers are accepted by the teacher and his "smarter" classmates.

His second set of scores on the Stanford Achievement tests registers the change in skills brought about by his new-found self-pride: paragraph meaning—6.4, social studies—5.3, language—5.1.

We cannot ignore the defeatist and negative attitudes of the junior high student when we deal with his reading needs. To ignore these attitudes is to court failure. To recognize them and try to change them is to pave the way toward a more successful learning experience.

References

1. "New Practice Readers." St. Louis, Missouri: McGraw-Hill Book Company, 1960.

2. "Pacemaker Story Books." Palo Alto, California: Fearon Publishers, 1967.

3. Among the books used were publications of the Benefic Press, of Westchester, Illinois.

Self-Concept and Reading

Cohn and Kornelly—Questions for Discussion

Was the group described by Cohn and Kornelly really a group of poor readers? Would any of the techniques discussed by Cohn and Kornelly require training beyond that usually possessed by the average classroom teacher? What type of commercially prepared materials would be especially useful in this type of program? What are the values and limitations of this article?

CHAPTER FOUR

Teacher Expectation- Self-Fulfilling Prophecies

The student's self-concept is so closely tied to the teacher's expectations that the material in the previous chapter could have been included very easily with this one. However, to focus attention on the extreme importance of teacher expectation and the implications of the research in self-fulfilling prophecies, the editor has chosen to separate the material into two chapters.

Anyone who has read the statistics concerning the percentage of boys vs. the percentage of girls who are retarded readers should immediately become aware of the fact that there are important factors working against the boys or extremely favorable factors working for the girls. One of these important factors is teacher expectation. Some foreign countries do not seem to encounter the sex difference in beginning readers that we do in the United States. However, teachers in these countries possess a different attitude toward boys than many teachers in the United States.

If we as teachers are to assure ourselves that we will succeed in developing positive self-concepts in our students, then we should be able to answer questions such as the following: What characteristics are normally associated with a positive self-concept? What characteristics are normally associated with a negative self-concept? What factors may lead to the deterioration of a student's self-concept? What can the teacher do to avoid developing negative attitudes or low expectations toward certain children?

In addition to the phenomenon of teacher expectation there are other self-fulfilling prophecies of which the serious researcher should become aware. Anyone attempting to do the kind of research that is often done in the field of education should familiarize himself with the work of Robert Rosenthal. The research done by Rosenthal over the past decade has helped us explain some of the reasons why results of similar research studies have varied.

Marvin Glock's article was placed first as an introduction to the topic of the self-fulfilling prophecy. Next, Robert Rosenthal's article gives a thorough account of the many factors involved in the self-fulfilling prophecy, and J. Michael Palardy's article describes in detail a study illustrating the phenomenon of teacher expectation.

Marvin D. Glock

Is There a Pygmalion in the Classroom?

Eliza Doolittle expressed it very well when she said, "You see, really and and truly, the difference between a lady and a flower girl is not how she behaves, but how she's treated."

It is time for teachers to redirect their thinking about the teaching of reading. It is time to stop arguing about whether a particular basal series, a linguistic approach, or a phonics approach is the best teaching method. It is not the method or approach that makes the difference; it is the individual teacher.

Flower Girls into Ladies

Can a child be made to "bloom"—in spite of what one might predict from test scores and other data—just because his teacher believes he will succeed? Some years ago a book entitled *Pygmalion in the Classroom* was published (Rosenthal, 1968). The book is an account of Professor Rosenthal's attempts to test this hypothesis in the classroom. Rosenthal gave children tests then picked boys and girls at random for various classes. He proceeded to tell the teacher that these randomly selected pupils had potential for "blooming." He assumed that the blooming would actually take place because of the assumption. Unfortunately, the design of the experiment and the interpretation of the data were both

From Marvin D. Glock,"Is There a Pygmalion in the Classroom?" *The Reading Teacher* 25, no. 5 (February 1972): 405-8. Reprinted with permission of Marvin D. Glock and the International Reading Association.

inadequate. Nevertheless, other research which led to the Rosenthal study suggests that such a phenomenon does exist.

During the 1970 Right to Read Conference Donald Davies, associate commissioner for Educational Personnel Development, struck on an important issue in stating that "Teachers are more important than the quality of the facilities, the quantity of materials and equipment or the level of financing." Indeed, there is a growing concern among educators to return to the concept of the basic importance of the pupil-teacher relationship.

What would be the result of such a "humanization" process? It would bring vitality, enjoyment and a satisfying self-image to the pupil in the classroom rather than the all too common punishment, boredom, shame or frustration. For it is the way a child thinks about himself that is most important in determining whether or not he can learn to be a good reader. His learning capacities often reflect whether he has a positive or negative self-concept.

Self-Concepts

How one views himself is most important. In a sense the individual's self-concept acts as a perimeter, as a boundary which defines the limits of his actions. Actions and thoughts which would lead to a new self-concept are limited by this perimeter and hence, changing one's self-concept is a most difficult process. An individual will steadfastly protect the image he has of himself even though it may interfere with achieving goals to which he and the society in which he lives aspire.

Why is the self-concept so difficult to change? First, the time factor has to be considered. One's self-concept has been developed extremely well and over a long period of time. Furthermore, a negative self-image has prevented the individual from learning responses which would have helped him overcome inferior feelings. The ability to take actions contradictory to that image is blocked by the image itself. A negative self-image is its own best defender.

What is a healthy, positive, self-concept, one that a teacher should help his pupils to develop? A person with a positive self-concept:
is able to accept himself as a person of worth
can realistically appraise his abilities and limitations
recognizes both his good and bad points
realizes he must be open to change both externally and internally
can accept his shortcomings without endlessly blaming himself
does not expect himself to be infallible

has a certain pride in his own thoughts and inclinations

feels he has a right to his individuality

In short, his self-concept has a degree of stability (Rosenberg, 1965).

In one study pertaining to self-concept, a national sample of eleven to thirteen year old boys was taken (SRC, 1960). As part of the study the boys were given a self-rating device. They were asked how they perceived themselves and how they believed significant people in their lives—mothers, fathers, teachers, friends and club leaders—perceived them.

Only 19 percent of the boys had highly positive self-concepts. Thirty-nine percent were rather ambivalent about themselves, while 41 percent lived with definite negative feelings concerning their own worth. Only 27 percent felt that their teachers perceived them in a positive light. Forty-seven percent of the group perceived their teachers' behavior and feelings toward them as negative. And it is the pupils' interpretation that makes the difference—not the teachers' judgment of his treatment of the pupils.

Removing Barriers

There is a happy note. Self-concepts can be changed no matter how difficult it is to do so. It is important for teachers to be aware of how they can help their pupils build positive, realistic self-perceptions. Just how can the teacher help move more pupils to achieve this important positive view of themselves?

Perhaps first one should look carefully at the educational system itself, which seems to have a built-in program of failure. According to the system a certain percentage of boys and girls are expected to fail. Unconsciously, through his own expectations, the teacher may be providing validity for this system.

As Lecky (1945) stated a quarter of a century ago, the mind is a unit, a system of ideas which must be consistent with each other. Resistance to ideas develops when the idea is incompatible with the organization of developed concepts. Boys and girls can develop such a resistance to any type of material, to any particular subject. Lecky found exceptional progress in all school subjects once pupils saw that certain learning tasks were in consonance with their feelings about their own abilities to learn.

Furthermore, a teacher can inspire confidence. Unless the teacher is confident that his pupil will be successful, the child will probably not change his self-image of being a failure in reading or in any other school subject.

The Teacher's Challenge

It is very difficult to hide one's true feelings from children. Their perceptions of adult expectations are derived from very subtle cues through an astute and complex process. A child can tell when an adult really has faith in him and when he is paying lip service to a belief.

A study reported in June 1970 (Rist, 1970) tells of a kindergarten teacher placing children in groups which reflected the social composition of the class. The different manner in which the teacher behaved toward the various groups became an important factor in determining each child's achievement.

Without the availability of any test scores or previous record of achievement, the children were placed at various tables on the basis of their supposed ability to learn. Children grouped at table one were designated as fast learners; those at table two were considered average; those at table three, slow learners.

Of course, once the teacher had seated the children on the basis of predicted learning ability, she was motivated to make these predictions come true. The children were informed of her expectations in the way in which they were treated. For example, the blackboard was long and opposite all of the tables. Nevertheless, all writing was done on the section opposite table one. One little girl at table three stood up to see as the teacher was demonstrating how to write an "o"; she was told to sit down. When she squirmed around to see the writing she was commanded to sit straight in her chair. This reprimand resulted in the child's looking away from the board and the demonstration. The little girl gave up completely and laid her head on the table.

By May of that year, during one full hour of teaching, one observer noted that all of the interaction was between the teacher and the pupils at table one except for two exchanges. These two exchanges were directed at table three—"Sit down!"

If there is a greater tragedy than being labeled a slow learner, it is being treated as a second class citizen. This teacher I am certain had no malice in her heart toward those designated as slow learners. Neither was she a poor teacher; the quality of her instruction was high. But her efforts were not directed toward all pupils alike. Undoubtedly she would have been crushed had the devastating effect of such behavior on these children been explained to her. But the effect on the pupils was just as serious as if her objective had been to destroy them. As the children passed on to other grades they tended to retain their original groupings. With time they perceived themselves as failures and their lack of performance in reading and in other areas reflected their self-concepts.

Certainly the task of replacing a child's negative self-concepts with a more positive image is most difficult, but obstacles to learning can be removed. And it is the teacher and the teacher's belief in the pupil's success that can inspire such a transformation.

References

Lecky, P. *Self-Consistency: A Theory of Personality.* New York: Island Press, 1945.

Rist, R. C. "Student Social Class and Teacher Expectations: The Self-fulfilling Prophecy in Ghetto Education," *Harvard Educational Review,* 40 (1970), 411-51.

Rosenberg, M. *Society and the Adolescent Self-Image.* Princeton: Princeton University Press, 1965, p. 31.

Rosenthal, R., and Jacobsen, L. *Pygmalion in the Classroom.* New York: Holt, Rinehart and Winston, 1968.

Survey Research Center, Institution for Research. "A Study of Boys Becoming Adolescents: A National Study of Boys Aged 11-13 in School Grades 4-8 Plus Other Boys in Grades 5-8." Ann Arbor: University of Michigan, 1960, p. 135.

Teacher Expectation—Self-Fulfilling Prophecies

Glock—Questions for Discussion

What does Glock mean by the "humanization" process? Can one's self-concept be easily changed? What characteristics are associated with a positive self-concept? Is it possible for the teacher to assess the self-concepts of the students in his class? What can the teacher do to avoid developing negative attitudes or low expectations toward certain children?

Robert Rosenthal

Self-Fulfilling Prophecies in Behavioral Research and Everyday Life[1]

Behavioral Scientists are said to be such a scientifically self-con-
scious group that there may one day be a psychology of those psychologists who study psychologists. That, for the most part, is in the future
but in the present there is a clearly developing science of the behavioral
scientist as he conducts his research with human and animal subjects.

The social situation which comes into being when a behavioral
scientist encounters his research subject is a situation of both general and
unique importance to the behavioral sciences. Its general importance
derives from the fact that the interaction of experimenter and subject,
like other two-person interactions, many be investigated empirically with
a view to teaching us more about dyadic interaction in general. Its
unique importance derives from the fact that the interaction of experimenter and subject, *un*like other dyadic interactions, is a major source
of our knowledge in the behavioral sciences.

To the extent that we hope for dependable knowledge in the behavioral sciences, we must have dependable knowledge about the experimenter-subject interaction specifically. We can no more hope to ac-

From Robert Rosenthal, "Self-Fulfilling Prophecies in Behavioral Research and
Everyday Life." Claremont Reading Conference. *Reading Conference Yearbook*
32 (1968): 15-33. Reprinted by permission of the author and the publisher.

[1]The research described in this paper has been supported by research grants
(G-17685, G-24826, GS-177, GS-714, GS-1741) from the Division of Social Sciences of the National Science Foundation. An earlier draft of this paper entitled
"The Psychology of the Psychologist" appeared in F. L. Ruch, *Psychology and
life,* 7th ed., Chicago: Scott, Foresman, 1967, pp. 645-652. In its present form,
the paper was also presented at the Fourth Annual Research Conference, North
Dakota State University, November, 1967.

quire accurate information for our disciplines without an understanding of the data collection situation than astronomers and zoologists could hope to acquire accurate information for their disciplines without their understanding the effects of their telescopes and microscopes. It is for these reasons that increasing interest has been shown in the investigation of the experimenter-subject interaction system. And the outlook is anything but bleak. It does seem that we can profitably learn of those effects which the behavioral scientists unwittingly may have on the results of his research.

Unprogrammed Effects of the Behavioral Scientist

It is useful to think of two major types of effects, which the behavioral scientists can have upon the results of his research. The first type operates, so to speak, in the mind, in the eye, or in the hand of the investigator. It operates without affecting the actual response of the human or animal subjects of the research; it is not interactional. The second type of experimenter effect is interactional; it operates by affecting the actual response of the subject of the experiment. It is a sub-type of this latter type of effect, the effects of the investigator's expectancy or hypothesis on the results of his research which will occupy most of the discussion. First, however, some examples of other effects of the investigator on his research will be mentioned.

Observer Effects. In any science, the experimenter must make provision for the careful observation and recording of the events under study. It is not always so easy to be sure that one has in fact, made an accurate observation. That lesson was learned by the psychologists, who needed to know it, but it was not the psychologists who focussed our attention on it originally. It was the astronomers.

Just near the end of the 18th century, the royal astronomer at the Greenwich Observatory, a man called Maskelyne, discovered that his assistant, Kinnebrook, was consistently "too slow" in his observations of the movement of stars across the sky. Maskelyne cautioned Kinnebrook about his "errors" but the errors continued for months. Kinnebrook was fired.

The man who might have saved that job was Bessel, the astronomer at Königsberg, but he was 20 years too late. It was not until then that he arrived at the conclusion that Kinnebrook's "error" was probably not willful. Bessel studied the observations of stellar transits made by a number of senior astronomers. Differences in observation, he discovered, were the rule, not the exception (Boring, 1950).

That early observation of the effects of the scientist on the observations of science made Bessel perhaps the first student of the psychology of scientists. More contemporary research on the psychology of scientists has shown that while observer errors are not necessarily serious they tend to occur in a biased manner. By that is meant that, more often than we would expect by chance, when errors of observation do occur they tend to give results more in the direction of the psychologist's hypothesis (Rosenthal, 1966).

Interpreter Effects. The interpretation of the data collected is part of the research process, and a glance at any of the technical journals of contemporary behavioral science will suggest strongly that while we only rarely debate the observations made by one another, we often debate the interpretation of those observations. It is as difficult to state the rules for accurate interpretation of data as it is to state the rules for accurate observation of data but the variety of interpretations offered in explanation of the same data imply that many of us must turn out to be wrong. The history of science generally, and the history of psychology more specifically, suggest that more of us are wrong longer than we need to be because we hold our theories not quite lightly enough. The common practice of theory monogamy has it advantages, however. It does keep us motivated to make more crucial observations. In any case, interpreter effects seem less serious than observer effects. The reason is that the former are public while the latter are private. Given a set of observations, their interpretations become generally available to the scientific community. We are free to agree or disagree with any specific interpretation. Not so with the case of the observations themselves. Often these are made by a single investigator so that we are not free to agree or disagree. We can only hope that no observer errors occurred and we can, and should, repeat the observations.

Intentional Effects. It happens sometimes in undergraduate laboratory science courses that students "collect" and report data too beautiful to be true. (That probably happens most often when students are taught to be scientists by being told what results they must get to do well in the course, rather than being taught the logic of scientific inquiry and the value of being quite open-eyed and open-minded). Unfortunately, the history of science tells us that not only undergraduates have been dishonest in science, but fortunately, such instances are rare. Nevertheless, intentional effects must be regarded as part of the inventory of the effects of the investigator himself.

Intentional effects, interpreter effects, and observer effects all operate without the investigator's affecting his subject's response to the experimental task. In those effects of the experimenter himself to be described
next, we shall see that the subject's response to the experimental task
is affected.

Biosocial Effects. The sex, age, and race of the investigator have all
been found to affect the results of his research. What we do not know and
what we need to learn is whether subjects respond differently simply to
the presence of experimenters varying in these biosocial attributes or
whether experimenters varying in those attributes behave differently toward their subjects and, therefore, obtain different responses from them
because they have, in effect, altered the experimental situation for their
subjects. So far, the evidence suggests that male and female experimenters
conduct the "same" experiment quite differently so that the different results they obtain may well be due to the fact that they unintentionally
conducted different experiments. Male experimenters, for example, were
found in two experiments to be more friendly to their subjects (Rosenthal,
1967).

Biosocial attributes of the subject can also affect the experimenter's
behavior which in turn affects the subject's responses. In one study, for
example, the interactions between experimenters and their subjects were
recorded on sound films. In that study it was found that only 12% of the
experimenters ever smiled at their male subjects while 70% of the experimenters smiled at their female subjects. Smiling by the experimenters,
it was found, affected the results of the experiment. From this evidence
and from some more detailed analyses which suggest that female subjects
may be more protectively treated by their experimenters (Rosenthal,
1966), it might be suggested that in the psychological experiment,
chivalry is not dead. This news may be heartening socially, and it is interesting psychologically, but it is very disconcerting methodologically. Sex
differences are well established for many kinds of behavior. But a question
must now be raised as to whether sex differences which emerge from
psychological experiments are due to the subject's genes, morphology,
enculturation, or simply to the fact that the experimenter treated his
male and female subjects differently so that, in a sense, they were not
really in the same experiment at all.

So far we have seen that both the sex of the experimenter and the
sex of the subject can serve as significant determinants of the way in which
the investigator conducts his research. In addition, however, we find that
when the sex of the experimenter and the sex of the subject are considered
simultaneously, certain interaction effects emerge. Thus male experi-

menters contacting female subjects and female experimenters contacting male subjects tend to require more time to collect portions of their data than do male or female experimenters contacting subjects of the same sex. This tendency for opposite-sex dyads to prolong their data-collection interactions has also been found by others (Rosenthal, 1967).

Psychosocial Effects. The personality of the experimenter has also been found to affect the results of his research. Experimenters who differ in anxiety, need for approval, hostility, authoritarianism, status, and warmth tend to obtain different responses from their experimental subjects. Experimenters higher in status, for example, tend to obtain more conforming responses from their subjects and experimenters who are warmer in their interaction with their subjects tend to obtain more pleasant responses from their subjects.

Situational Effects. Experimenters who are more experienced at conducting a given experiment obtain different responses from their subjects than do their less experienced colleagues. Experimenters who are acquainted with their subjects obtain different responses than do their colleagues who have never met their subjects before. The things that happen to the experimenter during the course of his experiment, including the responses he obtains from his first few subjects, can all influence his behavior, and changes in his behavior can lead to changes in subjects' responses. When the first few subjects of his experiment tend to respond as they are expected to respond, the behavior of the experimenter changes in such a way as to influence his subsequent subjects to respond too often in the direction of his hypothesis (Rosenthal, 1966).

Modeling Effects. It sometimes happens that before an experimenter conducts his study he tries out the task he will later have his research subjects perform. Though the evidence on this point is not all that clear, it would seem that at least sometimes, the investigator's own performance becomes a factor in his subjects' performance. When the experimental stimuli are ambiguous, for example, subjects' interpretations of their meaning may too often agree with the investigator's own interpretations of the stimuli.

Expectancy Effects. Some expectation of how the research will turn out is virtually a constant in science. In the behavioral sciences the hypothesis held by the investigator can lead him unintentionally to alter his behavior toward his subjects in such a way as to increase the likelihood that his subjects will respond so as to confirm his hypothesis or expectation. We are speaking then, of the investigator's hypothesis as a self-fulfilling prophecy. One prophesies an event and the expectation of the event then changes the behavior of the prophet in such a way as to make the prophesied event more likely. The history of science documents the occurrences of this phenomenon with the case of Clever Hans as prime example (Pfungst, 1911, 1965).

Hans was the horse of Mr. von Osten, a German mathematics instructor. By tapping his foot, Hans was able to perform difficult mathematical calculations and he could spell, read, and solve problems of musical harmony. A distinguished panel of scientists and experts on animals ruled that no fraud was involved. There were no cues given to Hans to tell him when to start and when to stop the tapping of his foot. But of course there were such cues, though it remained for Oskar Pfungst to demonstrate that fact. Pfungst, in a series of brilliant experiments, showed that Hans could answer questions only when the questioner or experimenter himself knew the answer and was within Hans' view. Finally, Pfungst learned that a tiny forward movement of the experimenter's head was the signal for Hans to start tapping. A tiny upward movement of the head of the questioner or a raising of the eyebrow was the signal to Hans to stop his tapping. Hans' questioners expected Hans to give correct answers, and this expectation was reflected in their unwitting signal to Hans that the time had come for him to stop his tapping. Thus the questioner's expectation became the reason for Hans' amazing abilities. We turn now to a consideration of more recent experiments which show that an investigator's expectation can come to serve as self-fulfilling prophecy.

Self-Fulfilling Prophecies
in Behavioral Research

To demonstrate the effects of the investigator's expectancy on the results of his research, at least two groups of experimenters are needed, each group with a different hypothesis or expectancy as to the outcome of its research. One approach might be to do a kind of census or poll of actual or potential experimenters in a given area of research in which opinions as to relationships between variables were divided. Some experimenters expecting one type of result and some experimenters expecting the opposite type of result might then be asked to conduct a standard experiment. If each group of experimenters obtained the results expected, results opposite to those expected by the other group of experimenters, we could conclude that the expectation of the experimenter does indeed affect the results of his research. Or could we? Perhaps not. The problem would be that experimenters who differ in their theories, hypotheses, or expectations might very well differ in a number of important related ways as well. The differences in the data they obtained from their subjects might be due, then, not to the differences in expectations about the results but to other variables correlated with expectancies.

A better strategy, therefore, than trying to find two groups of experimenters differing in their hypotheses would be to "create" two groups of experimenters differing only in the hypotheses or expectations they held about the results of a particular experiment. That was the plan employed in the following research.

Ten advanced undergraduates and graduate students of psychology served as the experimenters. All were enrolled in an advanced course in experimental psychology and were, therefore, already involved in conducting research. Each student-experimenter was assigned as his subjects a group of about 20 students of introductory psychology. The experimental procedure was for the experimenter to show a series of ten photographs of people's faces to each of his subjects individually. The subject was to rate the degree of success or failure shown in the face of each person pictured in the photos. Each face could be rated as any value from -10 to $+10$ with -10 meaning extreme failure and $+10$ meaning extreme success. The 10 photos had been selected so that, on the average, they would be seen as neither successful nor unsuccessful, but quite neutral, with an average numerical score of zero.

All 10 experimenters were given identical instructions on how to show the photographs to their subjects and were given identical instructions to read to their subjects. They were cautioned not to deviate from these instructions. The purpose of their participation, it was explained to all experimenters, was to see how well they could duplicate experimental results which were already well-established. Half the experimenters were told that the "well-established" finding was that people generally rated the photos as of successful people (ratings of $+5$) and half the experimenters were told that people generally rated the photos as being of unsuccessful people (ratings of -5). Then the experimenters conducted their research.

The results were clear. Every experimenter who had been led to expect ratings of people as successful, obtained a higher average rating of success than did any experimenter expecting ratings of people as less successful. Such clear-cut results are not common in behavioral research so that two replications were conducted. Both these subsequent experiments gave the same results; experimenters tended to obtain the data they expected to obtain. Other workers in other laboratories have also shown that the experimenter's expectation may affect the results of his research though the details cannot be given here (Rosenthal, 1966).

The combined probability that the results of all the relevant experiments might have occurred by chance is less than one in a million million.

Subsequent experiments in the program of research described here were designed not so much to demonstrate the effects of the investigator's expectancy as to learn something about the conditions which increase, decrease or otherwise modify these effects. It was learned, for example, that the subject's expectations about what would constitute behavior appropriate to the role of "experimental subject" could alter the extent to which they were influenced by the effects of the experimenter's hypothesis.

Through the employment of accomplices, serving as the first few subjects, it was learned that when the responses of the first few subjects confirmed the experimenter's hypothesis, his behavior toward his subsequent subjects was affected in such a way that these subjects tended to confirm further the experimenter's hypothesis. When accomplices, serving as the first few subjects, intentionally disconfirmed the expectation of the experimenter, the real subjects subsequently contacted were affected by a change in the experimenter's behavior to also disconfirm his experimental hypothesis. It seems possible, then, that the results of behavioral research can, by virtue of the early data returns, be determined by the performance of just the first few subjects.

In some of the experiments conducted, it was found that when experimenters were offered a too-large and a too-obvious incentive to affect the results of their research, the effects of expectancy tended to diminish. It speaks well for the integrity of our student-experimenters that when they felt bribed to get the data we led them to expect, they seemed actively to oppose us. There was a tendency for those experimenters to "bend over backward" to avoid the biasing effects of their expectation, but with the bending so far backward that the results of their experiments tended to be significantly opposite to the results they had been led to expect.

Individual differences among experimenters in the degree to which they obtain results consistent with their hypothesis have been discovered. The evidence comes both from additional experiments and from the analysis of sound motion pictures of experimenters interacting with their experimental subjects. Those experimenters who show greater expectancy effects tend to be of higher status in the eyes of their subjects and they seem to conduct their experiments in a more professional, more competent manner. They are judged more likeable and more relaxed, particularly in their movement patterns, while avoiding an overly personal tone of voice that might interfere with the business at hand. It is interesting to note that, although the influence of an experimenter's expectancy is quite unintentional, the characteristics of the more successful influencer are very much the same ones associated with more effective influencers when the influence is intentional. The more successful agent of social influence may be the same person whether the influence be as overt and intentional as in the case of outright persuasion attempts, or as covert and unintentional as in the case of the experimenter's subtly communicating his expectancy to his research subject.

We know that the process whereby the experimenter communicates his expectancy to his subject is a subtle one. We know that it is subtle because for six years we have tried to find in sound films the unintended cues the experimenter gives the subject—and for six years we have failed, at least partly. But there are some things about the unintentional communication of expectancies that have been learned.

We know that if a screen is placed between experimenter and subject that there will be a reduction of the expectancy effect so that visual cues from the experimenter are probably important. But the interposed screen does not eliminate expectancy effects completely so that auditory cues also seem to be important. Just how important auditory cues may be has been dramatically demonstrated by the work of Adair and Epstein (1967). They first conducted a study which was essentially a replication of the basic experiment on the self-fulfilling effects of experimenters' prophecies. Results showed that, just as in the original studies, experimenters who prophesied the perception of success by their subjects fulfilled their prophecies as did the experimenters who had prophesied the perception of failure by their subjects.

During the conduct of this replication experiment, Adair and Epstein tape-recorded the experimenters' instructions to their subjects. The second experiment was then conducted not by experimenters at all, but by tape-recordings of experimenters' voices reading standard instructions to their subjects. When the tape-recorded instructions had originally been read by experimenters expecting success perception by their subjects, the tape-recordings evoked greater success perceptions from their subjects. When the tape-recorded instructions had originally been read by experimenters expecting failure perception by their subjects, the tape-recordings evoked greater failure perceptions from their subjects. Self-fulfilling prophecies, it seems, can come about as a result of the prophet's voice alone. Since, in the experiment described, all prophets read standard instructions, self-fulfillment of prophecies may be brought about by the tone in which the prophet prophesies.

Early in the history of the research program on self-fulfilling prophecies in the behavioral sciences it had been thought that a process of operant conditioning might be responsible for their operation (Rosenthal, 1966). It was thought that perhaps every time the subject gave a response consistent with the experimenter's expectancy, the experimenter might look more pleasant, or smile, or glance at the subject approvingly, even without the experimenter's being aware of his own reinforcing responses. The experimenter, in other words, might unwittingly have taught the subject what responses were the desired ones. Several experiments were analyzed to see whether this hypothesis of operant conditioning might apply. If it did apply, we would expect that the subjects' responses gradually would become more like those prophesied by the experimenter—that there would be a learning curve for subjects, but no learning curve was found. On the contrary, it turned out that the subjects' very first responses were about as much affected by their experimenters' expectancies as were their very last responses. Since the very first response, by definition, cannot follow any unwitting reinforcement by the experimenter, the mechanism of operant conditioning can be ruled out as necessary to the communication of experimenters' expectancies.

True, there was no learning curve for subjects, but there seemed to be a learning curve for experimenters. Several studies showed that expected results became more likely as more subjects were contacted by each experimenter (Rosenthal, 1966). In fact, there was very little expectancy effect in evidence for just the very first-seen subjects. If the experimenter were indeed learning to increase the unintended influence of his prophecy, who would be the teacher? Probably the subject. It seems reasonable to think of a subject's responding in the direction of the experimenter's hypothesis as a reinforcing event. Therefore, whatever the covert communicative behavior of the experimenter that preceded the subject's reinforcement, it will be more likely to recur. Subjects, then, may quite unintentionally shape the experimenter's unintended communicative behavior. Not only does the experimenter influence his subjects to respond in the expected manner, but his subjects may well evoke just that unintended behavior that will lead them to respond increasingly as prophesied. Probably neither subject nor experimenter "knows" just exactly what the unintended communication behavior is—and neither do we.

Some Methodological Implications

The implications of the research on the effects of the experimenter's expectancy on the results of his research are of two general kinds; those that are primarily methodological and those that are more substantive. Our focus here will be more on some of the substantive implications but brief mention may be made of some implications for how we conduct research in the behavioral sciences.

To the extent that the results of behavioral research are affected by the expectation of the experimenter, we can only place a lessened confidence in these results. But to say that our confidence is weakened in the results of many experiments as they are actually conducted is not to say that our confidence is weakened in the basic logic of the experimental method. We must simply take those, only sometimes inconvenient, extra precautions required to prevent or reduce expectancy effects or those procedures designed to permit us to assess whether they have or have not affected the results of our research.

It is possible for research investigators to employ, as data collectors, research assistants who have not been told the purpose of the research. As long as the investigator's expectation can be kept from these data collectors, there should be no effects attributable to the investigator's expectation. There are some experiments in which the experimenter need have no direct contact with the subjects and, in such studies, automated data collection systems should be employed to reduce any possibility of the unintended influence of the experimenter's expectation. When a human data collector is required and that is often the case, at least the amount of contact between experimenter and subject can be reduced in order to minimize any opportunity for unintended communication.

Not only because of the danger of expectancy effects but also because of the general nature of other experimenter effects, it would be desirable to employ larger numbers of experimenters for each study than are now routinely employed. That would permit the assessment of the extent to which different experimenters obtained different results and, in any area of psychological research, that is a fact worth knowing.

Only one final technique for the control of expectancy effects can be mentioned here and that is the employment of special control groups known as "expectancy controls." In any experiment employing an experimental (treatment) and a control (no treatment) condition, two extra groups are added. In one of these added groups, the data collector is led to believe that no treatment has been administered when, in fact, it has. In the other added group, the data collector is led to believe that the treatment has been administered when, in fact, it has not. Such a research design permits the assessment of the effects in which the investigator is primarily interested as well as the assessment of the magnitude or complicating effect of the experimenter's expectancy (Rosenthal, 1966).

Self-Fulfilling Prophecies
Beyond the Laboratory

Perhaps the most compelling and the most general substantive implication of the research described here is that human beings can engage in highly effective and influential unintended communication with one another. More specifically, if we may generalize from experimenters to people more generally, it appears that one person's expectancy for the behavior of another may come to serve as a self-fulfilling prophecy. These implications invite further research. We will want to know how people communicate with one another nonverbally and unintentionally. We will want to know whether in everyday life, predictions become realities by the very act of prediction. When an experienced physician or psychotherapist tells the neophyte therapist that the neophyte's patient has a good or a poor prognosis, is the experienced clinician only assessing, or is he actually creating the poor or good prognosis? When the employer tells the employee that a task cannot be accomplished, does the accomplishment therefore become less likely? When a respected source suggests to a teacher that a child's intellectual ability will show marked gains will that prophecy be self-fulfilled? So far there are few answers to most of these research questions, except to the last, but before we describe that research from beyond the laboratory, let us return briefly to the lab for some background data.

In the course of the research program on expectancy effects it seemed important to learn whether these effects occurred only when the experimental subjects were humans. Accordingly, 12 experimenters were each given five rats who were to be taught to run a maze with the aid of visual cues. Half the experimenters were told their rats had been specially bred for maze-brightness; half the experimenters were told their rats had been bred for maze-dullness. Actually, of course, there were no differences between the rats assigned to each of the two groups. At the end of the experiment, the results were clear. Rats who had been run by experimenters expecting brighter behavior showed significantly superior learning compared to rats run by experimenters expecting dull behavior (Rosenthal & Fode, 1963). The experiment was repeated, this time employing a series of learning experiments each conducted in Skinner boxes. Half the experimenters were led to believe their rats were "Skinner box bright" and half were led to believe their animals were "Skinner box dull." Once again there were not really any differences in the two groups of rats, at least not until the end of the experiment. Then the allegedly brighter animals really were brighter; the alleged dullards really duller (Rosenthal & Lawson, 1964).

If rats became more bright when expected to by their experimenter, it seemed possible that children might become more bright when expected to by their teacher. Educational theorists had, after all, been saying for a long time that culturally disadvantaged children were unable to learn because their teachers expected them to be unable to learn. True, there was no experimental evidence for that theory but the two studies employing rats suggested that these theorists might be correct. The following experiment was therefore conducted (Rosenthal & Jacobson, 1966, 1968).

All of the children in an elementary school serving a lower socioeconomic status neighborhood were administered a non-verbal test of intelligence. The test was disguised as one that would predict intellectual "blooming." There were 18 classrooms in the school, three at each of the six grade levels. Within each grade level the three classrooms were composed of children with above average ability, average ability, and below average ability, respectively. Within each of the 18 classrooms approximately 20% of the children were chosen at random to form the experimental group. Each teacher was given the names of the children from her class who were in the experimental condition. The teacher was told that these children had scored on the "test for intellectual blooming" such that they would show remarkable gains in intellectual competence during the next eight months of school. The only difference between the experimental group and the control group children, then, was in the mind of the teacher.

At the end of the school year, eight months later, all the children were retested with the same IQ test. This intelligence test, while relatively nonverbal in the sense of requiring no speaking, reading or writing, was not entirely nonverbal. Actually there were two subtests, one requiring a greater comprehension of English—a kind of picture vocabulary test. The other subtest required less ability to understand any spoken language but more ability to reason abstractly. For shorthand purposes we refer to the former as a "verbal" subtest and to the latter as a "reasoning" subtest. The pretest correlation between these subtests was +.42.

For the school as a whole, the children of the experimental groups showed only a slightly greater gain in verbal IQ (2 points) than did the control group children. However, in total IQ (4 points) and especially in reasoning IQ (7 points), the experimental group children gained appreciably more than did the control group children.

When educational theorists have discussed the possible effects of teachers' expectations, they have usually referred to the children at lower levels of scholastic achievement. It was interesting, therefore, to find that in the present study, children of the highest level of achievement showed as great a benefit as did the children of the lowest level of achievement of having their teachers expect intellectual gains.

At the end of the school year of this study, all teachers were asked to describe the classroom behavior of their pupils. Those children from whom intellectual growth was expected were described as having a significantly better chance of becoming successful in the future, as significantly more interesting, curious, and happy. There was a tendency, too, for these children to be seen as more appealing, adjusted, and affectionate and as lower in the need for social approval. In short, the children from whom intellectual growth was expected became more intellectually alive and autonomous or at least were so perceived by their teachers.

We have already seen that the children of the experimental group gained more intellectually so that the possibility existed that it was the fact of such gaining that accounted for the more favorable ratings of these children's behavior and aptitude. But a great many of the control group children also gained in IQ during the course of the year. Perhaps those who gained more intellectually among these undesignated children would also be rated more favorably by their teachers. Such was not the case. The more the control group children gained in IQ the more they were regarded as *less* well-adjusted, as *less* interesting, and as *less* affectionate. From these results it would seem that when children who are expected to grow intellectually do so, they are considerably benefited in other ways as well. When children who are not especially expected to develop intellectually do so, they seem either to show accompanying undesirable behavior or at least are perceived by their teachers as showing such undesirable behavior. If a child is to show intellectual gain it seems to be better for his real or perceived intellectual vitality and for his real or perceived mental health if his teacher has been expecting him to grow intellectually. It appears that there may be hazards to unpredicted intellectual growth.

A closer analysis of these data, broken down by whether the children were in the high, medium, or low ability tracks or groups showed that these hazards of unpredicted intellectual growth were due primarily to the children of the low ability group. When these slow track children were in the control group so that no intellectual gains were expected of them, they were rated more unfavorably by their teachers if they did show gains in IQ. The greater their IQ gains, the more unfavorably were they rated, both as to mental health and as to intellectual vitality. Even when the slow track children were in the experimental group, so that IQ gains were expected of them, they were not rated as favorably relative to their control group peers as were the children of the high or medium track, despite the fact that they gained as much in IQ relative to the control group children as did the experimental group children of the high group. It may be difficult for a slow track child, even one whose IQ is rising, to be seen by his teacher as a well-adjusted child, and as a potentially successful child, intellectually.

The effects of teacher expectations had been most dramatic when measured in terms of pupils' gains in reasoning IQ. These effects on reasoning IQ, however, were not uniform for boys and girls. Although all the children of this lower socio-economic status school gained dramatically in IQ, it was only among the girls that greater gains were shown by those who were expected to bloom compared to the children of the control group. Among the boys, those who were expected to bloom gained less than did the children of the control group (interaction $F = 9.27$, $p = .003$). In part to check this finding, the experiment originally conducted on the West Coast was repeated in a small Midwestern town. In this study, conducted with Judy Evans, the children were from substantial middleclass backgrounds. This time the results were completely reversed. Now it was the boys who showed the benefits of favorable teacher expectations. Among the girls, those who were expected to bloom intellectually gained less in reasoning IQ than did the girls of the control group (interaction $F = 9.10$, $p = .003$). Just as in the West Coast experiment, however, all the children showed substantial gains in IQ. These results, while they suggest the nontrivial effects of teacher expectations also indicate the probable complexity of the effects of teacher expectations as a function of pupils' sex, social class, and very likely, other variables as well.

In both the experiments described, IQ gains were assessed after a full academic year had elapsed. However, the preliminary results of an experiment conducted with Don Anderson suggest that teacher expectations can significantly affect students' intellectual performance in a period as short as two months. In this small experiment, the 25 children were mentally retarded boys with an average pretest IQ of 46. Expectancy effects were significant only for reasoning IQ and only in interaction with membership in a group receiving special remedial reading instruction in addition to participating in the school's summer day camp program ($p < .03$. two-tail). Among these specially tutored boys those who were expected to bloom showed an expectancy disadvantage of nearly 12 IQ points; among the untutored boys who were participating only in the school's summer day camp program, those who were expected to bloom showed an expectancy advantage of just over three IQ points. (For verbal IQ, in contrast, the expectancy disadvantage of the tutored boys was less than one IQ point, while the expectancy advantage for the untutored boys was over two points.)

Another study, this time conducted in an East Coast school with upper middle class pupils, again showed the largest effect of teachers' expectancies to occur when the measure was of reasoning IQ (Conn, Edwards, Rosenthal, and Crowne, 1968). In this study, both the boys and girls who were expected to bloom intellectually showed greater gains in reasoning IQ than did the boys and girls of the control group and the magnitude of the expectancy effect favored the girls very slightly. Also in this study, we had available a measure of the children's accuracy in judging the vocal expressions of emotion of adult speakers. It was of considerable theoretical interest to find that greater benefits of favorable teacher expectations accrued to those children who were more accurate in judging the emotional tone expressed in an adult female's voice. These findings, taken together with the research of Adair and Epstein (1967), described earlier, give a strong suggestion that vocal cues may be quite important in the covert communication of interpersonal expectations.

We may conclude now with the brief description of just one more experiment, this one conducted by W. Victor Beez (1967) who kindly made his data available for the analyses to follow. This time the pupils were 60 pre-schoolers from a summer Headstart program. Each child was taught the meaning of a series of symbols by one teacher. Half the 60 teachers had been led to expect good symbol-learning and half had been led to expect poor symbol-learning. Most (77%) of the children alleged to have better intellectual prospects learned five or more symbols but only 13% of the children alleged to have poorer intellectual prospects learned five or more symbols ($p < 2$ in a million). In this study the children's actual performance was assessed by an experimenter who did not know what the child's teacher had been told about the child's intellectual prospects. Teachers who had been given favorable expectations about their pupil tried to teach more symbols to their pupil than did the teachers given unfavorable expectations about their pupil. The difference in teaching effort was dramatic. Eight or more symbols were taught by 87% of the teachers expecting better performance, but only 13% of the teachers expecting poorer performance tried to teach that many symbols to their pupils ($p < 1$ in 10 million).

These results suggest that a teacher's expectation about a pupil's performance may sometimes be translated not into subtle vocal nuances but rather into overt and even dramatic alterations in teaching style.

The magnitude of the effect of teacher expectations found by Beez is also worthy of comment. In all the earlier studies described, one group of children had been singled out for favorable expectations while nothing was said of the remaining children of the control group. In Beez' short-term experiment it seemed more justified to give negative as well as positive expectations about some of the children. Perhaps the very large effects of teacher expectancy obtained by Beez were due to the creation of strong equal but opposite expectations in the minds of the different teachers. Since strong negative expectations doubtless exist in the real world of classrooms, Beez' procedure may give the better estimate of the effects of teacher expectations as they occur in everyday life.

References

Adair, J. G. & Epstein, J. Verbal cues in the mediation of experimenter bias. Paper read at Midwestern Psychological Association, Chicago, May, 1967.

Beez, W. V. Influence of biased psychological reports on teacher behavior. Unpublished manuscript, Indiana University, 1967.

Boring, E. G. *A history of experimental psychology.* (2nd ed.) New York: Appleton-Century-Crofts, 1950.

Conn, L. K., Edwards, C. N., Rosenthal R., & Crowne, D. Perception of emotion and response to teachers' expectancy by elementary school children. *Psychological Reports*, 1968, *22*, 27-34.

Pfungst, O. *Clever Hans.* Translated by Rahn, C. L.; New York: Holt, 1911; Holt, Rinehart and Winston, 1965.

Rosenthal, R. *Experimenter effects in behavioral research.* New York: Appleton-Century-Crofts, 1966.

Rosenthal, R. Covert communication in the psychological experiment. *Psychological Bulletin*, 1967, *67*, 356-367.

Rosenthal, R. & Fode, K. L. The effect of experimenter bias on the performance of the albino rat. *Behavioral Science*, 1963, *8*, 183-189.

Rosenthal, R. & Jacobson, Lenore. Teachers' expectancies: determinants of pupils' IQ gains. *Psychological Reports*, 1966, *19*, 115-118.

Rosenthal, R. & Jacobson, Lenore. *Pygmalion in the classroom: Teacher expectation and pupils' intellectual development.* New York: Holt, Rinehart and Winston, 1968.

Rosenthal, R. & Lawson, R. A longitudinal study of the effects of experimenter bias on the operant learning of laboratory rats. *Journal of Psychiatric Research*, 1964, *2*, 61-72.

Teacher Expectation—Self-Fulfilling Prophecies

Rosenthal—Questions for Discussion

What does Rosenthal mean by interactional effects and non-interactional effects? How can we avoid non-interactional effects in educational studies? List some types of interactional effects and discuss methods of avoiding each of them. List some well-known research studies in the field of education and discuss the implications of the information presented by Rosenthal upon the results reported in each of these studies. Discuss ways in which the various effects listed by Rosenthal might affect your teaching as well as others' research.

J. Michael Palardy

What Teachers Believe — What Children Achieve

More than three decades ago, W. I. Thomas wrote, "If men de-fine . . . situations as real, they are real in their consequences" (1: 189). This theory has come to be known in the social sciences as the self-fulfilling prophecy. It is based on two assumptions. First, that the act of making a definition about a situation is also an act of making a prophecy about it. Second, that the act of making a prophecy about a situation is also an act of creating the conditions through which the prophecy is realized.

Recent research has presented some convincing evidence that the self-fulfilling prophecy may be at work in educational settings across the country. In a study by Rosenthal and Jacobson eighteen elementary-school teachers were told that certain of their pupils would show dramatic intellectual growth in the academic year ahead. Those pupils did make significantly greater gains in intelligence quotient than the other pupils in the same classrooms who had not been designated as "intellectual spurters." In reality, there was no difference between the two groups of pupils in their potential for "intellectual spurting." The only difference was in the minds of their teachers (2).

By using the rationale of the self-fulfilling prophecy, the study reported here investigated the effect of teachers' beliefs on pupils' achievement (3). The central purpose was to determine whether teachers' reported beliefs about first-grade boys' probable success in reading had

From J. Michael Palardy, "What Teachers Believe — What Children Achieve," *The Elementary School Journal* 69, no. 7 (April 1969): 370-74. Copyright © 1969 by The University of Chicago Press. Reprinted by permission of the author and the publisher.

any significant effect on the measured achievement in reading that the pupils in their classes attained. Of particular interest was the effect of these beliefs on the boys' achievement.

The major hypothesis tested was that there is no significant difference in mean scores in reading achievement between pupils classified according to sex and according to their teachers' beliefs concerning the probable success of first-grade boys in learning to read.

In December, 1967, a questionnaire was sent to the sixty-three first-grade teachers in an Ohio city. One item on this questionnaire was designed to elicit from the teachers a report of their beliefs regarding the probable success of first-grade boys in learning to read. The item read:

Assume that first-grade girls, on the average, achieve 80 per cent success in learning how to read. If this assumption were true, what per cent of success do you believe first-grade boys, on the average, achieve? (Please check only one.)

___100%	___50%
___ 90%	___40%
___ 80%	___30%
___ 70%	___20%
___ 60%	___10%

Forty-two usable questionnaires were returned. The teachers who responded were divided into three groups. Group A consisted of the ten teachers who had checked 80 per cent. These ten teachers reportedly believed that first-grade boys on the average are as successful as first-grade girls in learning how to read. Group B was made up of the twelve teachers who had checked 60 per cent and the two teachers who had checked 50 per cent. Reportedly, these fourteen teachers believed that boys are far less successful than girls in learning how to read. Group C consisted of the eighteen teachers who had checked 70 per cent. These eighteen teachers were eliminated from further consideration because it was thought that their reported beliefs were not sufficiently different from those of the teachers in Group A or in Group B.

Five teachers in Group A were then matched with five teachers in Group B. All the teachers were women, all were Caucasian, all had at least three years of first-grade teaching experience, all had bachelor's degrees, and all were employed in schools said to be located in middle-class neighborhoods. In addition, all the teachers reportedly had three reading groups in their classes, all were using the same basal reading series, and all were teaching in heterogeneously grouped, self-contained classrooms. And, finally, in individual interviews, all the teachers made statements supporting their reported beliefs concerning the probable reading success of boys.

In early May, reading achievement scores of fifty-three boys and fifty-four girls whose teachers constituted Group A and of fifty-eight boys and fifty-one girls whose teachers constituted Group B were obtained from the reading sections of the Stanford Achievement Test, Primary Battery, Form X. Each teacher administered the test to her own pupils, and all scoring was done by the investigator.

Several of the variables that might have contributed to a difference in the achievement among the four groups were accounted for. First, no pupils who were repeating first grade were included in the sample. Second, since all the Group A and Group B teachers were teaching in neighborhood schools said to be located in middle-class areas, it was decided that most of the pupils of the ten teachers came from middle-class families.

Third, only pupils whose age, as of January 1, 1968, ranged between six years and three months and seven years and three months were included in the sample. The mean chronological age by months of the fifty-three boys in Group A was 80.4; of the fifty-four girls in Group A, 79.7; of the fifty-eight boys in Group B, 80.7; and of the fifty-one girls in Group B, 80.5. On the basis of these mean ages, it was decided that there was no marked difference in age among the groups.

Fourth, only those pupils were used as subjects who scored in the average (60-68) and the superior (69-70) ranges on Ginn and Company's Pre-Reading Test, which was administered by their teachers in late September. The mean score in reading readiness for the boys in Group A was 66.6; for the girls in Group A, 66.6; for the boys in Group B, 66.0; and for the girls in Group B, 66.0. Based on these scores, it was decided that at the beginning of the school year there was no marked difference in readiness for reading among the four groups.

TABLE 1

Analysis of Variance of the Reading Achievement Scores of Pupils Classified by Sex and by the Beliefs of Their Teachers, with Pupils' Intelligence Quotient as a Covariable

Source of Variation	Degrees of Freedom	Sum of Squares	Mean Squares	F
Sex	1	519.460	519.460	1.787
Group	1	347.314	347.314	1.195
Interaction for sex $\times$ group	1	1184.152	1184.152	4.075*
Intelligence quotient	1	52860.063	52860.063	181.885†
Error	211	61321.656	290.624	
Adjusted Total	215	114853.983		

*Significant at the .05 level.
†Significant at the .001 level.

A two-way analysis of variance with pupils' intelligence quotient serving as a covariable was the method used to test the null hypothesis of no significant difference in mean reading achievement scores of pupils classified according to sex and according to their teachers' beliefs concerning the probable success of first-grade boys in learning to read. Levels of significance were set at .05, and all significant values were determined by an F test.

Since pupils' intelligence quotient was a covariable, the four groups of pupils were equated statistically on the basis of intelligence quotient before comparisons were made between and among them. Intelligence quotients were obtained in early March from Form J of the Otis-Lennon Mental Ability Test, Elementary 1 Level. Again, each teacher administered the test to her own pupils, and all scoring was done by the investigator.

Table 1 shows the analysis of variance of the reading achievement scores of the pupils classified by sex and by the beliefs of their teachers, with pupils' intelligence quotient statistically controlled.

As shown by the 181.885 value of F for the intelligence quotient variation, the effect of intelligence quotient on reading achievement scores was significant at the .001 level. This result was not unexpected. It means that pupils who scored high on the achievement test had high intelligence quotients and those who scored lower on the achievement test had lower intelligence quotients.

As shown by the 1.787 value of F for the sex variation, there was no significant difference between the mean reading achievement score of the 111 boys and the mean reading achievement score of the 105 girls. Similarly, the 1.195 value of F for the group variation indicates that there was no significant difference between the mean score of the 107 pupils whose teachers constituted Group A and the mean score of the 109 pupils whose teachers constituted Group B.

An inspection of the 4.075 value of F for the interaction effect, however, shows that there was a significant difference in the mean reading achievement scores of the pupils grouped both according to their sex (sex variation) and according to their teachers' reported beliefs concerning the probable success of first-grade boys in learning to read (group variation). A difference significant at the .05 level, in other words, was found among the mean scores of the 53 boys in Group A, the 54 girls in Group A, the 58 boys in Group B, and the 51 girls in Group B.

The interaction effect shown in Table 1, indicating that there was a significant difference in the mean reading achievement scores among the four groups of pupils, does not show specifically what this difference was. Consequently, an examination of the mean scores of the four groups was necessary. These scores are presented in Table 2.

As Table 2 shows, the boys in Group B scored much lower than the pupils in the other three groups did. The scores of these three groups were quite similar. Obviously, then, the combined effect of pupils' sex and teachers' beliefs resulted in a lower mean reading achievement score for the boys in Group B, those boys whose teachers reportedly believed that first-grade boys are far less successful than girls in learning to read.

TABLE 2

Mean Reading Achievement Scores for the Four Groups of Pupils

TEACHER GROUP	MEAN READING ACHIEVEMENT SCORE	
	Boys	Girls
A	96.523	96.241
B	89.207	96.686

Since it was of particular interest to investigate the effect of the teachers' beliefs on the achievement of the two groups of boys, their scores were compared by an F test. This comparison revealed a difference in mean scores that closely approximated significance favoring the boys in Group A ($F = 3.124$, $p < .08$).

Finally, when the pupils' scores on each of the four sections of the total reading test (word reading, paragraph meaning, vocabulary, and word study skills) were analyzed by the statistical procedure described earlier, the following results were found:

1. There were no significant differences between the 111 boys and the 105 girls in their scores on any of the four subtests.

2. In word reading and paragraph meaning scores, there were no significant differences between the 107 pupils in Group A and the 109 pupils in Group B. In word-study-skills scores, however, there was a significant difference favoring the pupils in Group A ($F = 13.115$, $p < .01$); and in vocabulary scores, there was a mean difference that closely approximated significance favoring the pupils in Group B ($F = 3.578$, $p > .05$).

3. There were no significant differences in scores for word reading and vocabulary among the 53 boys in Group A, the 54 girls in Group A, the 58 boys in Group B, and the 51 girls in Group B. But there were mean differences that closely approximated significance in scores for paragraph meaning ($F = 3.271$, $p > .05$) and in word study skills ($F = 3.386$, $p > .05$). Inspection of the mean scores of the four groups on these two tests, paragraph meaning and word-study skills, revealed that the boys in Group B did least well on both; and that, on both, there were no consistent differences among the other three groups.

The conclusions that can be drawn from these findings would seem to be quite clear and can be stated in two ways. The findings can be stated in terms of the major interest in the study: when first-grade teachers reported that they believed that boys are far less successful than girls in learning to read, the boy pupils of those teachers did achieve less well on a standardized reading test than a comparable group of boy pupils whose teachers reported that they believed that boys are as successful as girls in learning to read.

The findings can also be stated in terms of the self-fulfilling prophecy: when teachers in this study reported that they believed that boys are far less successful than girls in learning to read (when they defined a situation as real), the boys in their classes were far less successful than the girls (the situation was real in its consequences). Conversely, when teachers reported that they believed that boys are as successful as girls, the boys in their classes were as successful as girls.

Stated either way, the finding seems to have implications of some considerable consequence for educators.

References

1. W. I. Thomas. "The Relation of Research to the Social Process." In W. I. Thomas, *Essays on Research in the Social Sciences*, pp. 175-94. Washington: Brookings Institution, 1931.

2. Robert Rosenthal and Lenore Jacobson. *Pygmalion in the Classroom.* New York: Holt, Rinehart and Winston, 1968.

3. J. Michael Palardy. "The Effect of Teachers' Beliefs on the Achievement in Reading of First-Grade Boys." Doctor's thesis. Columbus, Ohio: Ohio State University, 1968.

Teacher Expectation—Self-Fulfilling Prophecies

Palardy—Questions for Discussion

Do you get a feeling as you read Palardy's article that the self-fulfilling prophecy phenomenon had some effect on his reporting of the results of the study? In what ways can the self-fulfilling prophecy phenomenon or the Hawthorne effect be used to advantage? What is the administrator's role in making sure that students are not harmed by this self-fulfilling prophecy phenomenon? Can teachers be trained to avoid unhealthy beliefs that consequently affect the achievement of their students?

CHAPTER FIVE

Personality
and
Reading

The article and other information in this chapter represent studies dealing with personality factors. The information also summarizes some past research and presents some difficulties involved in personality research. As mentioned in the preface, the area of personality may encompass some of the other factors included as units within this volume. The type of studies presented here should, however, help clarify the overall concept of personality.

Researchers and writers have long known of the relationship between personality factors and reading achievement. Many have stressed the extreme importance of these factors when dealing with children in the reading program. As one reads this material, it becomes obvious that the teacher of reading, especially remedial reading, needs to be cognizant of the research on personality and its implications for improving the reading program. Reading counselors and clinicians have learned that remedial treatment for retarded readers often cannot be successful without becoming involved in personality variables. Although some studies present slightly conflicting results, there is a trend in their results that should lead the reader to some rather definite conclusions.

Only one complete article is presented in this chapter due to the fact that researchers have so often duplicated many aspects of previous research. However, the editor has presented the results of a number of other research studies and has attempted to summarize and make some useful generalizations concerning their meanings. At the risk of boring the reader, several similar studies have been summarized. The editor believes, however, that each summary adds some relevant information not covered by Irla Lee Zimmerman and George N. Allebrand's article or the other research summaries that will help the reader to better understand the complex relationship between personality variables and reading achievement.

Irla Lee Zimmerman
George N. Allebrand

Personality Characteristics and Attitudes Toward Achievement of Good and Poor Readers

Children referred for remedial reading instruction are often characterized as poorly motivated toward school achievement. Current studies suggest that emotional problems are reflected in this negative approach to learning. The study of personal adjustment, attitudes toward achievement, and the relationship of these factors to reading success may throw light on the failure of certain children to develop adequate reading skills.

Review of the Literature

Results from studies to date have tended to point up aspects of the problem, and at least suggest the interrelationship between motivation and adjustment. For example, Karlsen (5) stressed the lack of social confidence and the low motivation toward school achievement in unsuccessful readers. Spache (8) noted the inability of retarded readers to acknowledge or accept blame, and an inability to search for solutions to conflicts. Granzow (3) reported that poor readers were not well adjusted to rules and often did not accept them.

Smith (7) in a review of contemporary studies, mentioned the high incidence of emotional disturbances in poor readers. Blackham (2), in a clinical study of underachieving readers, stressed the immaturity, emotional instability, and feelings of inadequacy in this group. Abrams (1) stressed the presence of insecurity, instability, and difficulty in both home and school adjustment.

From George N. Allebrand and Irla Lee Zimmerman, "Personality Characteristics and Attitudes Toward Achievement of Good and Poor Readers," *The Journal of Educational Research* 59, no. 1 (September 1965): 28-30. Reprinted by permission of the authors and the journal.

Purpose

The purpose of this study is to investigate the personality character-istics and attitudes toward achievement of two groups of school children differentiated in reading ability. As compared to the "good" readers (subjects reading at grade level or better), it is hypothesized that "poor" readers (subjects reading at least two years below grade level) will show less adequate personal adjustment and less productive attitudes toward achievement.

Procedure

Subjects in this study consisted of 71 "poor" readers, known as the "remedial" group, and 82 "good" readers, known as the "contrast" group, equated as nearly as possible for age, sex, ethnic composition, and in-telligence. The children were predominantly of middle to lower socio-economic status, and roughly half were of Mexican descent. Subjects were drawn equally from the fourth and fifth grade classes of an urban school district. Twice as many boys as girls were represented in the reme-dial group, and the same proportion was maintained in the contrast group. The subjects in the remedial group consisted of children enrolled in a remedial reading program. Children in this program were screened on the basis of having average or better intellectual ability (on a language and non-language test of intelligence, predominantly the California Test of Mental Maturity), and reading at least two years below grade level.

The contrast group consisted of children considered by achieve-ment test results and teacher judgment as reading at grade level or above, but otherwise matched to the remedial group. Both the California Achievement Test (primary and elementary form), and the Wide Range Achievement Test were used as screening devices.

The mean IQ of the remedial group was 102, while that of the contrast group was 105. The reading grade placement of the remedial group averaged 2.2, while that of the contrast group was 6.6. As an additional comparison group, a class of gifted children (IQs over 130) were given one portion of the test battery, TAT Card I (see below).

As a measure of personal and social adjustment, the California Test of Personality was administered to both the experimental and contrast group. As an approach to measuring attitudes toward achieve-ment, each child was asked to tell a story about Card I of the Thematic Apperception Test (TAT). This card is described by Murray (6) as "A young boy is contemplating a violin which rests on a table in front of him". Henry (4) describes the latent general theme of this card to be one of the relationship of personal demands to those of outside cultural agents, and secondarily, themes of self-direction and ambition.

Results and Discussion

A comparison of the results of good and poor readers on the California Test of Personality reveals significant differences in personality functioning. The good readers presented themselves as better adjusted in every area, and were rated average or above on all the subscales except Anti-social Tendencies (38th percentile). By contrast, the remedial group was below average (50th percentile) on all subscales. The average difference in percentile scores between the two groups was 20 points. Only on Anti-social Tendencies and Family Relations, where scores were relatively low for both groups, was there any tendency for scores to approach each other.

Analysing specific areas, the poor readers generally characterized themselves by marking items suggesting an awareness of nervous symptoms, limited personal freedom, feelings of isolation, as well as minimal social skills and standards. Good readers described themselves quite favorably, especially stressing personal worth, absence of withdrawal tendencies, and self reliance. Also strongly emphasized were their feelings of belongingness, good school relations, and absence of nervous symptoms.

TABLE 1

California Test of Personality Percentile Scores of Good and Poor Readers

CTP Scales	Good Readers N-82	Poor Readers N-71
Self-reliance	61	42*
Sense of personal worth	74	42*
Sense of personal freedom	52	30*
Feeling of belonging	58	30*
Withdrawing tendencies	70	46*
Nervous symptoms	54	33*
Total Personal Adjustment	55	30
Social standards	52	38
Social skills	54	38
Anti-social tendencies	38	27
Family relations	48	35
School relations	56	40
Community relations	48	28*
Total Social Adjustment	55	35
Total Personal and Social Adjustment	54	38

* Differences significant at the .05 level.

The major differences between the two groups appeared to be more in the area of personal rather than social adjustment, specifically, personal worth, feelings of belongingness, withdrawal tendencies, sense of personal freedom, nervous symptoms, self reliance, and community relations (differences significant at .05 level or better, Chi square test). Specific items relating to motivation and achievement revealed how typically the poor readers confessed to feelings of hopelessness and discouragement. Culturally realistic goals were seen as forced upon them by an unsympathetic environment, and neither accepted nor internalized.

Achievement attitudes were revealed by responses to the Thematic Apperception Test card I. Stories were classified in five areas as presented in Table 2.

Good readers most frequently composed a story stressing a positive acceptance of such middle-class goals as practice and study, with a pay-off of future success. Further analysis of these stories revealed specific themes of effort and the setting of long-term goals. For example, one good reader composed the following story:

> There once was a boy who wanted to play a violin but he didn't know how, and he felt awful about it. His friend knew how to play it, but he still didn't. He tried, tried, and tried again. Finally he did it, he can play it now. P. S. He's the best of them all. Title: Try, Try Again.

TABLE 2

Attitudes Toward Achievement Revealed on TAT Card I by Poor Readers, Good Readers, and Gifted Children

Story Classifications	Poor Readers N-71	Good Readers N-82	Gifted Children N-20
Ignore stimulus	11%	19%	0%
Neutral response or card description	4%	3%	5%
Escape from task	8%	13%	20%
Negative outcome	36%	1%	5%
Positive outcome	41%	65%	70%

The remedial readers were less inclined to accept the task, and when they did, the effort and long-term goal setting was frequently absent. For example, a poor reader reported the following:

> He's looking at a violin. He has his mind on playing it. Title: (none).

In general, the poor readers did not stress effort. When the outcome of their stories was positive, it was often a flat acceptance of the task (doing what one is told), with no, or only a very hazy, future implied.

An outstanding difference between good and poor readers was the negative tone of stories given by over a third of the poor readers. These tales emphasized the forcing aspects of authority, and ended most unfavorably. Several of these stories are given below:

> He's wishing he couldn't play a violin. (q) I don't know. Title: Violin Without a Noise.
>
> He's looking at the violin, he looks sad, he doesn't want to play the violin. He has to play the violin, but he doesn't want to. (q. outcome?) Bad. Title: Mad.
>
> He don't like to play his fiddle. He's sad. He would like to break it, tear it up, or something. His mother might make him play it. He wanted to play it but he found out he couldn't. He don't play it no more. Title: Sad Fiddle.

The contrast between the above stories and the story of a good reader which could also be classified as negative can be seen:

> A boy with a sad face looking at his violin. He was trying to sneak out when his mother told him to go practice his violin, and he didn't want to, so in his room he sat down and just looked at his violin. His mother will ask him why he isn't playing his violin, then he will start playing, but he will be thinking about playing baseball. I think a good title for it is: A Boy Can't Always Win.

As an additional comparison, the responses of a class of gifted children to the TAT card are classified in Table 2. Like the good readers, most of these children composed stories emphasizing a favorable outcome following effort.

Conclusions

In this report of the relationship between personal adjustment, attitudes toward achievement, and reading skills, a comparison is made of children reading at grade level or above and children showing a lag of two years or more in reading skills. As compared to the poor reader, the good reader is more apt to describe himself as well adjusted and motivated by internalized drives which result in effortful and persistent striving for success.

This study does not necessarily indicate that those good readers who proved to be such vocal proponents of "middle class morality" differ greatly from the poor readers. Rather, the good readers appear to have an excellent grasp of the concepts of adjustment and motivation prized by teachers and school psychologists, and they wish to present themselves in this light. The level of inculcation of these "adult" goals is in contrast to that of the poor readers, who willingly admit to feelings of discouragement, inadequacy, and nervousness, and whose proclaimed goals are often ephemeral or immediate—especially in avoiding achievement.

References

1. Abrams, J. C. "A Study of Certain Personality Characteristics of Non-Readers and Achieving Readers," *Dissertation Abstracts*, XVI (1956), p. 377.
2. Blackham, G. J. "A Clinical Study of Personality Structures and Adjustments of Pupils Underachieving and Overachieving in Reading," *Dissertation Abstracts,* XV (1955), p. 1199.
3. Granzow, K. R. "A Comparative Study of Underachiever, Normal Achiever, and Overachiever in Reading," *Dissertation Abstracts*, XIV (1954), pp. 631-632.
4. Henry, W. *The Analysis of Fantasy* (New York: Wiley and Sons, 1956).
5. Karlsen, B. "Comparison of Some Educational and Psychological Characteristics of Successful and Unsuccessful Readers at the Elementary School Level," *Dissertation Abstracts*, XV (1955), p. 456.
6. Murray, H. *The Thematic Apperception Test* (Cambridge: Harvard University Press, 1943).
7. Smith, N. B. "Research on Reading and Emotion," *School and Society*, LXXXI (1955), pp. 8-10.
8. Spache, G. D. "Personality Patterns of Retarded Readers," *Journal of Educational Research*, L (1957), pp. 461-469.

Personality and Reading

Zimmerman and Allebrand — Questions for Discussion

What might have been the results of this study if the authors would have divided each of their two groups into the boys and girls and then studied the same factors? What are the implications from this study for the teacher of remedial reading? Are the characteristics measured in this study the same as the characteristics studied in most of the following research studies summarized by the editor? Can the results of this study be compared with those of the studies which follow?

Eldon E. Ekwall

Personality and Reading —
Further Comments and Research

One of the earlier and perhaps more comprehensive studies dealing with the relationship between reading failure and emotional problems was done by Helen Robinson (1946) and a group of researchers. Robinson's research team consisted of a social worker, a psychiatrist, a pediatrician, a neurologist, three ophthalmologists, a reading specialist, and Dr. Robinson, who acted as a psychologist and reading clinician. Twenty-two disabled readers were tested and their progress was followed over a period of time. This enabled the researchers to do an intensive study and case analysis of each member of the group. Robinson concluded that 41 percent of the group had significant emotional problems and that emotional problems were the cause of reading disability in 32 percent of these cases. Robinson states, "The effects of emotional disturbances are so diverse and their manifestations so varied that they should never be overlooked during the examination of a poor reader" (p. 226).

One would certainly have to agree with Robinson's conclusion regarding her findings when we consider that one out of every three children we as remedial reading teachers are likely to encounter will have become a disabled reader because of emotional problems. Other researchers such as Arthur Gates (1941) have expressed the opinion that emotional problems are present in approximately 75 percent of the children who are disabled readers and are a *cause* of their reading disability in about one-fourth of these cases. This would, of course, mean that emotional problems are the actual cause of reading problems about 18.25 or approximately 20 percent of the time.

Glenn Chronister (1964) studied the relationship of reading comprehension to a number of personality variables. The personality variables identified in his study were ". . . self-reliance, personal worth, personal freedom, feeling of belonging, freedom from withdrawal tendencies, freedom from nervous symptoms, social standards, social skills, freedom from antisocial tendencies, family relations, school relations, community relations, cooperation, friendliness, integrity, leadership and responsibility . . ." (p. 254). Chronister measured the relationship of these variables to reading comprehension in a group of 167 fifth graders. Boys and girls were also divided and studied separately. He also attempted to determine which of the variables had the closest relationship (correlation) to reading comprehension for the entire group, for the boys, and for the girls. Chronister further attempted to determine which personality variables contributed to variance in measured reading comprehension for the entire group, for the boys, and for the girls.

Chronister's analysis of the results showed that for the entire group all personality variables had a correlation coefficient that was significant at the .01 level of confidence. All correlation coefficients were positive. When the results were analyzed for boys and girls as separate groups, Chronister found that all coefficients of correlation were also positive and significant for the boys. For the girls, however, only intelligence and freedom from nervous symptoms were statistically significant at the .01 level of confidence. Chronister found that the personality variables most closely related to reading comprehension for the boys were freedom from withdrawal tendencies, community relations, and cooperation. Those most closely related for girls were cooperation, friendliness, and integrity. In calculating the contributions to variance in reading comprehension of the variables for boys, Chronister found that intelligence, freedom from withdrawal tendencies, community relations, and cooperation accounted for 49.74 percent of the total. Intelligence, which was the control factor, contributed 31.20 percent of the total. This left 18.54 percent of the variance attributable to the three remaining factors. For the girls the contributions to variance of intelligence, cooperation, friendliness, and integrity accounted for 57.78 percent of the total. Intelligence, which was the control factor, contributed 50.51 percent of the total, which left 7.27 percent of the variance in reading comprehension attributable to the other three factors.

Chronister concluded that factors other than those studied in his investigation make a large contribution to the variance in reading comprehension. He believed that some of these factors might include instructional efficiency, cultural factors, health factors, and perceptive abilities. He also concluded that, of the personality factors studied in his investigation, the cluster of personality variables selected for study accounts for approximately 18 percent of the variance in reading comprehension for boys, but only about 7 percent for the girls. His recommendations were as follows:

   The teacher who is evaluating the work of underachievers in reading should give considerable attention to the appraisal of factors other than personality.

Success in interpersonal relationships has a greater influence on boys' progress in reading comprehension than on girls'. We may find here a partial explanation for the disproportionate number of boys who are handicapped in reading. We must look carefully at our approach to beginning reading instruction. Perhaps we should differentiate the experience of boys and girls in reading instruction (p. 259).

George Spache (1957) studied the personality characteristics of 125 children who were functioning on a reading level at least one year below their actual grade placement or were two years retarded in grades above the third. He used the Rosenzweig Picture-Frustration Test, which consists of a number of cartoon drawings depicting conflict among children or among children and adults. Each subject responds by saying what he thinks children in the cartoons would say. The test is designed to reveal information of such personality components as aggressiveness or hostility, feelings of martyrdom, self-blame, negativism or defensiveness, self-control, or tolerance.

Spache found that his disabled readers, when compared to Rosenzweig's normative group, showed significantly more hostility and overt aggressiveness toward others. They had less ability to acknowledge or accept blame and were relatively poor in knowing how to handle situations of conflict with adults. Disabled readers also tended to exhibit either a passive but defensive attitude or negativism toward authority figures. Spache states, "These generalizations about poor readers are, of course, applicable only to the great mass of cases. Within the group data, there are many individuals and small groups which present their own peculiar patterns of adjustment. It is highly desirable to identify and interpret these patterns in order to facilitate the matching of teacher personality with pupil personalities and the planning of the social climate of the tutoring situation" (p. 466).

Ralph Norman and Marvin Daley (1959) studied the comparative adjustment of superior and inferior sixth grade readers. The scores from the California Achievement Test were used to obtain two extreme groups in reading ability and the California Test of Personality was used as a measure of personality adjustment.

Norman and Daley found a significant difference ($p < .01$) between the personality adjustment of the superior and inferior readers. Superior readers scored higher on items dealing with behavioral maturity, interpersonal skills, social participation, satisfying work, and recreation. They also had more adequate methods and goals than did inferior readers. The researchers stated that their data did not permit them to state whether personality problems are a cause or a result of poor reading ability. The data only indicated that they are related.

R. Brunkan and F. Shen (1966) studied the personality characteristics of ineffective, effective, and efficient readers at the freshman level in college. The Reading Versatility Test was used to provide information regarding rate and level of comprehension in three reading areas. The Adjective Check List, which consists of 300 adjectives from which participants choose characteristics representative of themselves, was chosen as the measure of personality characteristics.

Brunkan and Shen found that both rate and quality must be taken into consideration, for as a whole there were more significant differences due to rate than to quality, and most of these differences existed in the efficient and effective quality groups. The "High-rate efficient readers" and the "High-rate effective readers" were described as well-adjusted, effective students. These participants were leaders. They were self-confident and had few self-doubts and guilt feelings, were independent, and needed little or no help in solving problems. They did not have an excessive need for heterosexual social relationships. The "Ineffective low-rate readers" displayed the poorest personality patterns for success in school work. These participants preferred to follow rather than lead, for they tended to be passive and dependent with a need for constant reassurance, especially from the opposite sex. Except for heterosexuality, this pattern was true also of the ineffective and middle rate readers. They needed fewer contacts with the opposite sex. The students in the "Effective middle and low-rate" reading groups were about average in both personality characteristics and ability; they were neither exceptional nor poor students.

A study of Alton Raygor and David Wark (1964), who used nearly the same type of students as those in the Brunkan and Shen study, produced somewhat similar results. They found that males who were poor readers differed from the normal students in that they have poor social skills with regard to girls and are somewhat less verbal. The poor male readers were somewhat more depressed, more irresponsible, and less comfortable in a social situation. They showed what the authors termed an ". . . almost medically significant shyness and withdrawal." The female students who were poor readers were more irresponsible and somewhat superficially more charming than good readers. In this study the authors felt that the results might have been biased since the participants in the poor reading sample were volunteers.

Summary and Implications

The study of Zimmerman and Allebrand and the summary of other studies by the editor clearly indicate that personality variables are related to reading achievement. There has been considerable disagreement on classifying personality variables as well as selecting which personality variables are the greatest contributors to either success or failure in reading. However, a review of the literature also indicates that a number of personality variables consistently correlate with success or failure in reading.

The implications for the teacher of reading, and especially for the teacher of remedial reading, can be summarized very well in the concluding statements of several authors who have either conducted studies dealing with the personality problems of disabled readers or who have done a thorough review of the literature. The first statement is that of Olive Sampson (1966). In reviewing the literature on reading and adjustment, Sampson states that there is disagreement among the studies over exactly which factors are involved in the reading failure. Sampson does, however, state that the important point made by evidence and studies is that regular instruction or remedial help will "fall flat" without the teacher's being fully aware of the "dynamics of emotions" in tutoring.

J. A. Thayer (1970) describes a study of twenty-one boys who were above or near grade level in grades four, five, and six. However, in grade seven their reading scores began to regress. Thayer states,

> It is doubtful that the usual remedial reading techniques would have proven significant in relieving the problem. What was necessary was to remove the cause of the reading problem.
>
> Teachers, counselors and principals should be aware of the effects of home conflict on school achievement and behavior. Teachers, especially, are in a position to compare annual reading achievement scores and should alert the counselors or principal when the regressive pattern appears.
>
> In the case of the 21 boys, reading was not the root problem. Reading regression was simply symptomatic of deep-seated home problems. When these problems were solved through group counseling, the boys were able to return to a relatively normal school life as evidenced by achievement scores and the testimony of the teachers, administrators and parents (p. 561).

James Hake (1969) studied the covert motivations of good and poor readers. He states,

> In general, the findings of this study support those of earlier studies that poor readers exhibit significantly more negative desires and wishes along with more maladjustive classroom behavior than do good readers. Also, as in previous studies, this research points up the fact that classroom teachers and reading clinicians must not only be concerned about

the poor reader's word recognition problems, but they must be equally sensitive to their emotional difficulties, which are indeed considerable. In this regard, the reading teacher should realize that much of the maladjustive behavior of poor readers is accompanied by negative self-concepts, anxieties, covert aggressive impulses, negative feelings about home and school, and an extreme distaste for reading and subject matter in general. When the reading teacher becomes aware of not only the overt behavior maladjustments of the poor reader but also his significant covert impulses, the way for helping the poor reader improve both his reading skills and attitude toward reading will greatly be enhanced (p. 738).

References

Brunkan, R. J., and Shen, F. "Personality characteristics of ineffective, effective and efficient readers." *Personnel and Guidance Journal* 44 (1966): 837-43.

Chronister, G. M. "Personality and reading achievement." *The Elementary School Journal* 29 (1964): 253-60.

Gates, A. I. "The role of personality maladjustment in reading disability." *Journal of Genetic Psychology* 59 (1941): 77-83.

Norman, R. D., and Marvin, F. D. "The comparative adjustment of superior and inferior readers." *Journal of Educational Psychology* 50 (1959): 31-36.

Raygor, A. L., and Wark, D. M. "Personality patterns of poor readers compared with college freshmen." *Journal of Reading* 8 (1964): 40-46.

Robinson, H. *Why pupils fail in reading.* Chicago: University of Chicago Press, 1946.

Sampson, O. C. "Reading and adjustment: a review of the literature." *Educational Research* 8 (1966): 184-90.

Spache, G. "Personality problems of retarded readers. " *Journal of Educational Research* 50 (1957): 461-69.

Thayer, J. A. "Johnny could read—what happened?" *Journal of Reading* 13 (1970): 501-6.

CHAPTER SIX

Intelligence
and
Reading

Questions often asked of professors who teach reading methods courses are: What is intelligence? What is the relationship between intelligence and reading ability? Does the lack of ability to read well influence various intelligence test scores? Are tests available that will give an accurate assessment of a poor reader's I.Q? Is there really a necessary mental age for success in beginning reading? Can I.Q. be used as a predictor of success in beginning reading? Does I.Q. change or can it be changed? Is the use of intelligence tests harmful or beneficial?

A great deal of the research that has been done over the years has concerned itself with the answers to only one, or a part of one, of the questions posed above. Furthermore, the research studies often contain a great deal of statistical information which is necessary for accuracy but which is often difficult to understand if one is not well grounded in statistics. For this reason, the editor has chosen to write this chapter himself. In doing so, an attempt has been made to summarize both early and recent studies which have made significant contributions to this field.

What is Intelligence?

Albert Harris (1963) states, ". . . psychologists have not been able to agree on a definition of intelligence, the three ideas that occur most frequently in definitions are that it involves ability to deal effectively with abstractions, to learn, and to respond appropriately in new situations" (p. 47). In terms of the evidence presented in the studies that follow, this definition would seem quite adequate. Harris indicates that there is still some disagreement whether intelligence is essentially unitary or whether it would better be conceived as a composite of inter-related but separate primary abilities. He points out that the interrelation of different abilities tends to be rather high at the primary level, but that various abilities become more distinct, or they have less relation-ship, as the child grows into adolescence.

In describing or defining intelligence the editor believes that the term "awareness of environment" is helpful in understanding an im-portant characteristic of intelligence. This would, of course, be some-what analogous to what Harris has referred to above as "ability to learn." Some people, however, seem to have an ability to learn in a structured situation but do not seem to profit from or be aware of the many opportunities to learn from their general environment, which is often quite unstructured. A typical example of this sort of unstructured learning is often evident in a child before a tester even begins the formal administration of an intelligence test. In gathering necessary data con-cerning the child, the tester will note that some children will know their age, birthdate, street address, and telephone number. On the other hand, other children of the same age will often simply say "I don't know" when asked for this information. The young child who can give the tester the sort of information listed above has often simply learned these things because he was *aware* of his environment, i.e., remembering things people say, things he has previously asked about, or things he has seen. This child has simply learned more about himself and the world about him than have others.

The factor of awareness or desire to learn has caused a great many psychologists to re-evaluate their thinking concerning intelligence. William Simmons (1968) points out that the more traditional view of intelligence was that it was the "capacity" to learn and was carried through the genes in the same way as the color of the eyes, the hair texture, and other physical characteristics. According to this theory, the way a person functions in different areas would depend on what he brought into the world in terms of intellectual potential. Environ-ment would still play an important role in acquiring experiences, but a person would be limited in gaining from these experiences in accor-dance with his innate intellectual potential. Simmons says that the modern view is that an individual is a product of his environment, and that intellectual functioning is not determined genetically but by the experiences acquired in many situations under many conditions.

An experiment performed in the laboratory of the famous psycholo-gist D. O. Hebb as reported by B. R. Bugelski (1964) is illustrative of the loss or lack of ability to reason when a stimulating environment is almost completely lacking. In describing one of Hebb's experiments Bugelski states,

> . . . in Hebb's laboratory, Scottish terriors were raised in boxes that allowed a view only of the laboratory ceiling. The puppies saw nothing but the sides of the boxes and the ceiling for a year and a half. During this time, they never saw a human or another living thing. When these puppies had grown to maturity, they were removed from this restricted environment and were compared with normally reared animals. In a sense, there was no comparison. The "restricted" dogs were more stupid, less aggressive, more "curious" and apparently unacquainted with pain. They would not retreat from flames held under their noses, would permit themselves to be pressed against hot radiators, would endure pin pricks, etc. Apparently these dogs had to *learn to sense pain*, have appropriate emotions, and eliminate a ubiquitious curiosity (p. 132).

In summary, it seems difficult to believe that intelligence could be conceived of as an "either-or" situation in regard to heredity or environment. A number of studies during the past decade have shown that by creating a stimulating environment a child's measured intelligence quotient can be raised from ten to twenty points or more in a period of from six months to several years. This can leave little doubt that at least measured I.Q. can be changed to some extent. Some might still, of course, contend that this simply happens due to the inability of present I.Q. tests to measure true innate potential. On the other hand, many experienced teachers would agree that it would seem fallacious to think that *any* given child in a classroom, given the proper stimulation and training, could become an atomic physicist, lawyer, or talented musician.

Relationship Between Reading and Intelligence

There are several ways of viewing the relationship between reading and intelligence. One of these is to look at the relationship of intelligence as a whole to reading as a whole. Albert Harris (1963) indicates that the correlation between reading and individual verbal intelligence tests, such as the Stanford-Binet, are approximately .60 to .70. He also says that the tests designed for primary age children in which the directions are given orally to the children and in which children respond by marking pictures have about the same correlation with reading as the Stanford-Binet. However, as children progress to the upper elementary grades and begin to take group intelligence tests that are more verbally-oriented, the correlation may range from .70 to .85. Nonverbal or nonlanguage group tests, however, have correlations ranging between .20 and .40. Since the relationship between group reading tests and group intelligence tests tends to be much greater at the upper grade levels, it is apparent that they are measuring a similar factor to a considerable degree. Researchers such as Donald Neville (1965) have concluded that for children in the intermediate grades, a 4.0 achievement level in reading is a critical minimum for obtaining reasonably valid I.Q. scores on a verbal intelligence test. Harris points out that there is now a tendency for test pubishers to call verbally-oriented group tests "scholastic aptitude tests" rather than intelligence tests. The reason for this is that they do correlate rather highly with scholastic aptitude or later academic progress. They do, however, fail to measure the true potential of disabled readers or culturally-deprived students.

Another way of viewing the relationship between reading and intelligence is to examine the correlation between various intellectual abilities and overall or specific areas of reading achievement. Berj Harootunian (1966) studied the relationship between fourteen intelligence variables and reading achievement. The intelligence variables were: First Letter, First and Last Letter, Reasons, Ideas, Groups of Things, Uses, Seeing Problems, Missing Facts, Incomplete Pictures, Incomplete Words, Concealed Figures, Best Answer, Critical Thinking, and Estimation. His subjects were 513 seventh and eighth grade students in two schools in suburban Philadelphia. Harootunian computed the product-moment coefficients of correlation between all pairs of tests (reading vs. intelligence factors) together with the beta coefficients. The use of the beta coefficient allows one to determine the relative weight or amount of the total contribution of each factor when taken in combination with all of the other factors. Harootunian found the combined coefficient of multiple correlation between reading and the combined variables to be .781. He states, "The highly significant product-moment coefficients of correlation between reading and each predictor test suggest that the various factors elicit abilities important for reading. But the contribution of each test to reading varies considerably" (p. 389). The subtest of Missing Facts was found to be the greatest contributor of the intelligence variables to reading (almost 41 percent), whereas the subtest of Uses contributed only 2 percent. Harootunian concluded,

> The results suggest two conclusions: first, that several of the tests measure variables that are relevant in reading; second, that these vari-

ables are not being elicited by intelligence tests. Among the most important variables were Missing Facts, Best Answer, Critical Thinking, and First Letter. The ideational fluency and closure factors made little independent contribution to reading. Taken in their entirety, the data strongly support the position that thinking abilites such as judgement, evaluation, and conceptual foresight have much in common with reading ability (pp. 391-92).

Harootunian also stressed the fact that he agreed with J. P. Guilford's studies in which he argued the point that we should not use a "single haphazardly-composed score" in interpreting intelligence.

Jean Braun (1963) studied the relation between concept formation ability and reading achievement among 139 boys in the third, fifth, and seventh grades. She also attempted to determine whether there was a greater degree of relationship between reading and concept formation or between reading and intelligence. Braun stated that her study supported the findings of E. A. Jay and L. L. Thurstone in that the concept formation factor is highly related to reading and that this factor is either a separate intellectual process or a component that is given little weight in existing intelligence tests. Braun also believed that a common misconception in cases of children with reading disabilities is that children with normal intelligence are suffering from emotional blocks or other psychogenic disorders. Braun believed that the children with emotional disorders did not have learning problems but performance deficiencies. She also questioned the use of intelligence tests as the basis for expectancy in reading clinics. She stated,

... the children referred by schools to reading clinics are those in whom intelligence is least closely related to reading achievement. What *is* apparently related to their achievement is their concept formation ability. We do not know, as yet, if these children are going to continue permanently low in this major cognitive process of concept formation or if they are simply unusually uneven in their development. In either case, it would seem futile to continue administering intelligence tests which do not tap concept formation and to prescribe remedial methods overly dependent upon perception factors until we have more systematic information about the nature of the handicapped (p. 681).

A number of researchers have studied the relationship between subtest patterns of various Wechsler (WISC, WAIS, W-B) tests and reading achievement. One of the earlier studies was done by E. Ellis Graham (1952). Graham's group consisted of ninety-six unsuccessful readers, ages 8-0 to 16-11, with a Verbal or Performance Scale I.Q.

of 90 or higher. On the Verbal Scale he found Comprehension and Similarities to be significantly high, with Comprehension the higher of the two. On the Performance Scale, the Object Assembly, Picture Completion, Picture Arrangement, and Block Design subtests were significantly above the mean. Subtests which were significantly below the mean were Digit Span, Information, Vocabulary, Coding, and Arithmetic, with Arithmetic much lower when the Performance Scale was higher than the Verbal Scale.

Graham formulated two hypotheses regarding the causes of reading failure: (1) the unsuccessful reader may have an inherent lack of verbal ability, and (2) there may be an interference with verbal ability due to repressions. These repressions, Graham thought, might be caused by the unsuccessful reader's resisting unconsciously the emotional climate of the school or home. He noted that Digit Symbol very closely resembles the beginning reading-learning situation and that Arithmetic, Digit Span, and Information involve rote memory and recall type questions, all common to much of our school work. Graham felt that if the repression hypothesis is valid, then we would expect unsuccessful readers to do poorly in these areas.

Woodrow Flanary (1953) studied the relation of the Wechsler-Bellevue subtests to the reading proficiency of ninety retarded readers and twenty normal readers between twelve and sixteen years of age. Flanary used a scatter diagram to show which subtests significantly differentiated the retarded reader from the normal readers. He also determined which subtests differed significantly from their combined mean. The scores of the retarded readers on Comprehension, Picture Arrangement, Picture Completion, Block Design, and Object Assembly were above the mean of the other subtests. The scores on Information, Digit Span, Arithmetic, Vocabulary, and Digit Symbol deviated significantly below the mean of the other subtests. The normal readers showed only a few significant deviations from the mean subtest scores. They were high on Comprehension and low on Digit Span.

Flanary believed, as did Graham, that retarded readers make the lowest scores in those subtests closely associated with school learning and the best scores on those least associated with school subjects. Flanary suggested that the low Digit Span score might indicate short attention span and inability to concentrate. He also believed that the low Arithmetic score confirmed their inability to concentrate. Flanary stated, "The Digit Symbol score is usually low, indicating that psychomotor speed is slow; that is, the individual thinks slowly and reacts slowly to any sort of stimulus involving visual-motor skills; consequently he is a slow learner" (p. 184). In his discussion of the normal readers Flanary stated,

Their memory function is good. They have a longer attention span than retarded readers and show definite signs of being able to concentrate better. They have a much better vocabulary than the retarded readers and demonstrate an ability to think on an abstract plane, rather than a low functional level characteristic of most of the poor readers. They indicate by their scores on Digit Symbol that they are relatively uninhibited in psychomotor speed and have a sort of "looseness" and "freeness" about them that makes learning relatively easy (p. 185).

A number of other researchers have since studied the WISC profiles of retarded readers. Among the more recent studies was one by Eldon Ekwall (1966). In this study Ekwall summarized the results of nine previous WISC profile studies. This summary is shown in table 1 (p. 34).

TABLE 1

*Summary of WISC Profiles of Retarded Readers
as Reported in Nine Studies*

Study	Control Group Used	I	C	A	S	V	DS	PC	PA	BD	OA	COD
Graham (1952)	No	L	H	L	H	L	L	H	H	H	H	L
Burks and Bruce (1955)	Yes	L	H	L					H	H		L
Altus (1956)	No	L		L		H		H	H		H	L
Robeck (1960)	No	L	H	L	H	H	L	H	H	H	H	L
Dockrell (1960)	No	L	H	L	H	L			H			L
Hirst (1960)	No			L			L	H	H	H?	H?	L
Kallos et al. (1961)	No	L		L						H		L
Neville (1961)	Yes	L		L				L	H	H		
Robeck (1964)	No	L	H	L	H	H	L	H	H	H	H	L
Total High		0	5	0	4	3	0	5	8	7	5	0
Total Low		8	0	9	0	2	5	0	0	0	0	8

Key:

      I = Information
      C = Comprehension
      A = Arithmetic
      S = Similarities
      V = Vocabulary
     DS = Digit Span
     PC = Picture Completion
     PA = Picture Arrangement
     BD = Block Design
     OA = Object Assembly
    COD = Coding

As one can see, the subtests of Information, Arithmetic, and Coding have been significantly low in most of the studies and the Digit Span subtest was significantly low in five of the nine. The Picture Arrangement and Block Design subtests have been somewhat consistent in being significantly high and the subtests of Comprehension, Similarities, Picture Completion and Object Assembly also have been significantly high in some studies. On the other hand, the Vocabulary subtests varied from significantly high to significantly low to neither significantly high nor significantly low.

Ekwall's study was done on forty-three retarded readers in grades four, five, and six. Twenty-one children were bilingual Mexican-Americans and twenty-two were unilingual whose ethnic background was not Mexican-American. The results of this study were somewhat similar to those of previous studies with the exception of the Comprehension and Coding subtests. For the entire group the Information, Comprehension, Arithmetic, and Digit Span subtests were significantly low, whereas the subtests of Picture Completion, Picture Arrangement, Object Assembly, and Coding were significantly high. Ekwall then compared the subtest means of the bilingual and unilingual groups. The Coding and Arithmetic means of the bilingual group were significantly higher than the corresponding means of the unilingual group. On the other hand, the Information and Vocabulary means of the unilingual group were significantly higher than the corresponding means of the bilingual group.

Analysis of various Wechsler subtest means has no doubt contributed to our understanding of the relationship between various aspects of intelligence and reading achievement. It appears that there are some very definite strengths which normal or good readers possess and retarded readers do not possess or at least have not developed. However, analysis of individual profiles within a group of retarded readers indicates that profiles often common to a group as a whole may vary considerably from individual to individual or from subgroup to subgroup, depending upon factors such as language or environmental background.

Another factor of which we should be aware is that studies in Wechsler profiles analysis have only shown general strengths and weaknesses in the overall intellectual makeup of retarded readers. And, although specific training designed to strengthen these weak areas may be successful in helping children to achieve higher scores on the various Wechsler subtests, there is now little evidence to indicate that strengthening these weak areas results in greater achievement in reading.

I.Q. and Beginning Reading

The question of whether or not there is a necessary minimum mental age for beginning reading instruction has been a subject of considerable controversy and much written discourse since the 1920s. Because of the voluminous amount of literature in various periodicals and textbooks, only a brief discussion dealing with this controversial subject is presented here.

A growing interest in the measurement of intelligence and achievement during the 1920s and the 1930s caused a number of educators to conclude that there was a necessary minimum mental age which children must reach before they can experience any substantial success in learning to read. Considerable impetus was given to this belief with the publication of a report by M. V. Morphett and C. Washburne (1931) in which the writers suggested that a mental age of 6.5 was necessary for success in beginning reading. In retrospect, it would seem logical that a number of researchers and writers would have seriously questioned Morphett and Washburne's proposal; however, this was not the case. A few writers and researchers, however, still remained unconvinced that there was a magical point in a child's mental age growth at which success in reading could be nearly guaranteed. Among these writers who held an opposing viewpoint was Arthur Gates. In an article published in the *Elementary School Journal*, Gates (1937) stated that it has not been proven that a mental age of 6.5 was a proper minimum for learning too read by "all" types of teaching skill and procedures. Gates, in fact, claimed to have gathered data which indicated that statements concerning the necessary mental age at which a pupil can be entrusted to learn to read were essentially meaningless. Gates stated,

It is quite conceivable — indeed the evidence in general tends now definitely to show — that the crucial mental age will vary with the materials; the type of teaching; the skill of the teacher; the size of the class; the amount of preceding preparatory work; the thoroughness of examination; the frequency and the treatment of special difficulties, such as visual defects of the pupil; and other factors (pp. 497-98).

The overall viewpoint represented by Gate's 1937 article is representative of modern day thinking on the subject of mental age and reading, although a few writers still cling to the former philosophy. It seems unlikely that mental age as it is now measured could be an accurate indicator of success. Research studies quoted earlier in this chapter, as well as a number of others, have shown that instruments presently used in assessing mental age (as derived from I.Q.) simply do not measure many of the factors that are evidently prerequisites for success in beginning reading.

Bruce Alcorn (1964) also cautions against attempting to derive mental age from most currently-used I.Q. tests. He points out that deviation I.Q.'s (such as those derived from the Wechsler Tests) should be interpreted only as normalized standard scores which indicate relative standing in a chronological age group. Alcorn stresses the fact that the relationship between mental ages and intelligence quotients for any given chronological age group differs markedly from one test to another; therefore, there does not seem to be a uniform or predictable relationship between mental age and deviation I.Q.'s.

The I.Q. as a Predictor
of Reading Ability

The question of whether or not the I.Q. is an accurate predictor of reading ability has traditionally been of special concern to the reading specialist. Since I.Q. scores are often readily available, the reading specialist may want to know, for example, if these can be interpreted as a measure of what children will be likely to achieve, or in the case of a specific child, whether there is a discrepancy between a certain child's potential as shown from an I.Q. test and his present ability as shown from a reading achievement test.

Louise Ames and Richard Walker (1964) did a study to determine whether or not reading achievement could be predicted from WISC I.Q.'s and Rorschach scores. Their sample consisted of fifty-four fifth grade students who remained from a larger group tested with the WISC and Rorschach at kindergarten level and retested with the reading section of the Stanford Achievement Tests at the end of the fifth grade. These researchers found a significant correlation between the Rorschach Prognostic score and later reading achievement, although it was only moderate: .53. The correlation between I.Q. and later reading score was again significant but only moderate: .57. The Rorschach and the WISC scores in a multiple correlation with later reading scores produced a correlation of .73, which was substantially higher than either alone. As a part of their conclusion Ames and Walker stated,

> The usefulness of the findings reported presumably does not lie in their employment for predicting fifth-grade reading scores. Rather, they offer support for the suggestion that individual subject characteristics other than either general intelligence or specific reading skills contribute to individual differences in reading at the above-average level as well as below average (p. 313).

The results of the Ames and Walker study are typical of those found in other studies, i.e., a relationship between I.Q. and later reading ability that is moderate to low in terms of their relationship as measured by studies of their correlation. The logical question that one might ask is, Does the fact that a moderate-to-low correlation exists between I.Q. and later reading achievement mean that I.Q.'s are useful in predicting later reading achievement? George Spache and Evelyn Spache (1969) express the opinion that I.Q.'s are of little value in predicting later reading achievement. They say,

> . . . research studies of school beginners show that intelligence test results are not highly predictive of early reading success. If pupils are arranged in the order of their reading test scores after a period of training, the order just does not neatly parallel a ranking based on mental age or intelligence quotient. Only the extreme cases, the very superior and the mentally retarded pupils, tend to agree in their ranks in reading and intelligence. The degree of reading success for most pupils is determined not by their exact level or rank in intelligence but by other more influential factors (p. 57).

Spache and Spache express the opinion that too much dependence is placed upon the results of mental tests as predictors of later reading success. They also point out that any broad intelligence test samples facets such as concrete reasoning, spatial relations, and quantitative thinking, which may have little relationship to reading. As Spache and Spache point out, children's ranks in reading and intelligence tend to agree or be predictable only for the extreme cases, i.e., the mentally retarded and the very superior pupils. It is, of course, these extreme cases that give us a statistically significant correlation between reading and intelligence.

Since it is evident that the relationship between I.Q. and reading is not great enough to make one a good predictor of the other, there is a question of whether or not expectancy formulas are really useful since many of them are based on I.Q. George Simmons and Bernard Shapiro (1968) compared the results of using the Bond-Tinker, Harris, and Los Angeles Reading Expectancy Formulas to determine reading expectancy for children of various intelligence levels. They stated,

> It is generally assumed that a student of "average" ability should be reading on a level roughly equivalent to his actual grade placement. Thus, it is not surprising to find that the three formulas are in close agreement for students in this middle ground. However, the major need for expectancy formulas is for students whose I.Q.'s are above or below average. Unfortunately, as this need grows greater (i.e., as the distance of the I.Q. from the mid-point increases), so do the differences in the

expectancies yielded by the three formulas. Thus, the expectancy formulas are least reliable for those students for whom there is the greatest need to determine expected reading level (p. 628).

Simmons and Shapiro stress the fact that if the difference between the actual and the expected reading grade level is based on commonly-used readability formulas, then the various formulas are quite likely to identify different students. For example, the Bond-Tinker formula would identify more students in the lower I.Q. ranges, whereas the Harris formula sets higher expectancies at the higher I.Q. ranges and would identify more students of superior ability. The authors, however, believe that if readability formulas are used with caution in conjunction with teacher judgment, reading test scores, student attitude, performance in relation to other members of the class, and perhaps the recommendations of a counselor or psychologist, then they can serve as valuable aids to teachers and administrators.

Does I.Q. Change?

As stated earlier in this chapter, there is a growing number of people, as well as an ever-enlarging body of research information, indicating that I.Q. is susceptible to development. For many years a number of people believed that I.Q. was a heritable trait and could not be changed. Henry Chauncey (1964) quotes Professor J. McV. Hunt of the University of Illinois, who indicates that I.Q. is suseptible to change. Hunt stated,

... the assumption that intelligence is fixed and that its development is predetermined by the genes are no longer tenable.

It is no longer unreasonable to consider that it might be feasible to govern the encounters that children have with their environments, especially during the early years of their development, to achieve a substantially faster rate of intellectual development and a substantially higher adult level of intellectual capacity (p. 23).

Chauncey also states that the same conclusion was reached by Professor Benjamin Bloom of the University of Chicago. In discussing Bloom's work Chauncey states,

He estimates that extreme environments (the difference between a very favorable environment and an underprivileged environment) each year in the first four may affect the development of intelligence by about 2.5 I.Q. points per year (or 10 I.Q. points over that four year period), while extreme environments during the period of ages eight to 17 may have an effect of only 0.4 points per year. Bloom believes that the cumulative effect of environmental influences during the whole first 17 years is on the order of 20 I.Q. points, when one contrasts deprived and abundant environments as they exist in America today (p. 23).

The tremendous change in some children's I.Q.'s is illustrated by the case of a child described by Shirley Aaronson (1965). The child was institutionalized in a state hospital at the request of his parents when he was seven years old. Aaronson states, "The diagnosis at that time was schizophrenia (childhood type). His behavior was marked by outbursts of violence directed towards his younger sister" (p. 91). At this time his WISC Verbal, Performance, and Full Scale I.Q. Scores were 74, 100, and 85 respectively. The child was released from the institution after about one year, at which time he showed improvement in his behavior problem. He then received remedial help for a period of time. Two years after his initial intelligence test (at age nine) his WISC Verbal, Performance, and Full Scale I.Q. Scores were 81, 114, and 96 respectively. The child was given more remedial help and, according to the author, gained a great deal of confidence in himself as well as competence in reading. At the age of eleven years he was again given the WISC. His Verbal, Performance, and Full Scale I.Q. Scores were then 96, 120, and 108 respectively. A comparison of the initial and the final I.Q. tests indicate that this child gained 20 or more I.Q. points on the Verbal, Performance, and Full Scale Scores.

It should be emphasized that unless children come from impoverished backgrounds or unless they appear to exhibit some type of emotional problems, their measured I.Q.'s (at least by the WISC) are not likely to change a great deal. Harold Tanyzer (1962) studied fifty retarded readers in grades four through eight who were average or above in intelligence but were reading one or more years below their mental age. Tanyzer reports that these children's mean per-month-gain in reading progress was statistically significant beyond the .001 level. Tanyzer reported a gain of 3.56 I.Q. points on the WISC Full Scale Score, which was significant at the .001 level but barely exceeded the standard error of measurement reported by Wechsler. Tanyzer also reported that the prediction of reading improvement from the WISC score was little better than a guess.

Richard Herrnstein (1971) quotes the writing of Arthur R. Jensen of the University of California at Berkeley, who believes that intelligence is affected more by inheritance than by environment. Jensen's now famous and controversial article appeared in the *Harvard Educa-*

tional Review. Some of Jensen's conclusions were based on studies of 122 sets of identical twins (224 individuals) who were reared apart from each other. Herrnstein states,

> Twins raised apart differ on the average by about seven points in I.Q. Two people chosen at random from the general population differ by seventeen points. Only four of the 122 pairs of twins differed by as much as seventeen points. Ordinary siblings raised in the same household differ by twelve points. Only nineteen of the 122 pairs differed by as much as that. And finally, fraternal twins raised in the same home differ by an average of eleven points, which was equalled or exceeded by only twenty-three of the 122 pairs (p. 55).

Herrnstein states that Jensen and most other experts conclude that heredity is responsible for approximately 80 to 85 percent of a person's intelligence, while environmental conditions are responsible for the remaining 15 to 20 percent.

It is evident that, for certain groups of children, measured I.Q. does change. On the other hand, the I.Q.'s of so-called normal children of school age who come from a socioeconomic level that is average or above do not seem to change greatly regardless of the type of instruction they receive. This may not, of course, be true at very young age levels. Thus, it would appear that, as many modern day psychologists believe, I.Q. can and does change to a limited extent. On the other hand, one can take the viewpoint that our presently used I.Q. tests simply do not accurately measure the innate potential of some children and therefore do not accurately reflect some children's true I.Q. in the beginning.

I.Q. — Harmful or Beneficial?

Typical of the feeling of many people at present concerning the overemphasis on I.Q. tests is that expressed in an editorial by Kenneth Winebrenner (1961). He states, "If this old world doesn't quite make it, and explorers from another planet eventually make some sense out of the ruins, it will be irony if they give credit for our stupidity to too much faith in the 'intelligence' quotient" (p. 48). Winebrenner believes that we are presently overemphasizing the importance of I.Q. in curriculum design, and he also believes that too much stress is being placed on inducing the "bright" student to attend "brainpower" colleges. He points out that we are not even sure that I.Q. really does measure the kind of action-oriented intelligence that he believes is called for. He states, "The kind of intelligence that we need so badly today is action-intelligence, not passive and esoteric intellectual capacity. This ability to invent new relationships and new forms, to conceive and create, is not measured by standard 'intelligence' tests and contributes little to the I.Q. score" (p. 48). Winebrenner also emphasizes that studies have shown that creative ability is just as important as intellectual capacity. For example, highly creative students do as well on achievement tests as high I.Q. students.

Perhaps one of the strongest indictments of intelligence tests is that they simply are not measuring enough of our total intellect. From an examination of some rather widely-used intelligence tests it is evident that only a few factors are being measured. Anne Anastasi (1968) points out that factorial research has produced a bewildering multiplication of factors. She states, "The number of cognitive factors reported to date by different investigators is well over 100" (p. 330). Typical of these is Guilford's Three-Dimensional Model of the structure of the intellect. Anastasi indicates that in this model there are 120 cells, and "in each cell one factor or ability is expected, and some cells may contain more than one factor" (p. 332).

Typical of the view that intelligence tests do serve a useful purpose is that of Louise Bates Ames (1968), who states,

> There is a very large percentage of the school population in this country (it might run as high as 15 percent) who will have difficulty in school simply because of their low intelligence. Many of these children will develop serious learning problems unless they are recognized early and taught and treated in a special way (p. 45).

Ames also states,

> Whenever a child is spectacularly failing in school, a routine intelligence test should be given as a first possible clue as to why he is having difficulty (p. 48).

It is evident that viewpoints on the usefulness of I.Q. scores range from those that believe they should not be used at all to those that believe that I.Q. scores are necessary for a thorough diagnosis. It is also evident that even among those persons who have spent a great deal of time studying intelligence and intellectual functioning many questions remain unanswered. Perhaps the most important thing for anyone working in this area to know, however, is that many questions concerning intelligence and intelligence tests *remain* unanswered. If any serious harm is being done by using intelligence tests and the information they provide, it is probably being done in most cases by those people who do not understand the limitations of our knowledge in this area.

References

Aaronson, S. "Changes in I.Q. and reading performance of a disturbed child." *The Reading Teacher* 19 (1965): 91-95.

Alcorn, B. K. "A study of the concepts of mental age and intelligence quotient." Doctoral dissertation, University of Iowa, 1964.

Altus, G. T. "WISC patterns of a selective sample of bilingual children." *Journal of Genetic Psychology* 83 (1953): 241-48.

Ames, L. B. "A low intelligence quotient often not recognized as the chief cause of many learning difficulties." *Journal of Learning Disabilities* 1 (1968): 45-49.

Ames, L. B., and Walker, R. N. "Prediction of later reading ability from kindergarten Rorschach and I.Q. scores." *Journal of Educational Psychology* 55 (1964): 309-13.

Anastasi, A. *Psychological testing.* 3rd ed. New York: Macmillan, 1968.

Braun, J. S. "Relation between concept formation ability and reading achievement at three developmental levels." *Child Development* 34 (1963): 675-82.

Bugelski, B. R. *The Psychology of Learning Applied to Teaching.* New York: Bobbs-Merrill, 1964.

Burks, H. F., and Burks, Bruce P. "The characteristics of poor and good readers as disclosed by the Wechsler intelligence scale for children." *Journal of Educational Psychology* 46 (1955): 488-93.

Chauncy, H. "Intelligence and the important early years." *The Education Digest* 29 (1964): 23-25.

Dockrell, W. B. "The use of Wechsler intelligence scale for children in the diagnosis of retarded readers." *Alberta Journal of Educational Research* 6 (1960): 86-91.

Ekwall, E. E. "The use of WISC subtests profile in the diagnosis of reading difficulties." Doctoral dissertation, University of Arizona, 1966.

Flanary, W. "A study of the possible use of the Wechsler-Bellevue scale in diagnosis of reading difficulties of adolescent youth." Doctoral dissertation, University of Virginia, 1953.

Gates, A. I. "The necessary mental age for beginning reading." *The Elementary School Journal* 37 (1937): 497-508.

Graham, E. E. "Wechsler-Bellevue and WISC scattergrams of unsuccessful readers." *Journal of Consulting Psychology* 16 (1952): 268-71.

Harootunian, B. "Intellectual abilities and reading achievement." *The Elementary School Journal* 66 (1966): 386-92.

Harris, A. J., ed. *Readings in reading.* New York: David McKay, 1963.

Harris, A. J. "Intellectual and perceptual development." In *Readings on reading instruction,* edited by A. J. Harris, pp. 47-52. New York: David McKay, 1963.

Herrnstein, R. "I.Q." *The Atlantic* 228 (1971): 43-64.

Hirst, L. S. "The usefulness of a two-way analysis of WISC subtests in the diagnosis of remedial reading problems." *Journal of Experimental Education* 29 (1960): 153-60.

Kallos, G. L.; Grabow, J. M.; and Guarina, E. A. "The WISC Profile of disabled readers." *Personnel and Guidance Journal* 39 (1961): 476-78.

Morphett, M. V., and Washburne, C. "When should children begin to read?" *Elementary School Journal* 31 (1931): 496-503.

Neville, D. "A comparison of the WISC patterns of male retarded and non-retarded readers." *Journal of Educational Research* 54 (1961): 195-97.

————. "The relationship between reading skills and intelligence test scores." *The Reading Teacher* 18 (1965): 257-62.

Robeck, M. C. "Subtest patterning of problem readers on WISC." *California Journal of Educational Research* 11 (1960): 110-15.

————. "Intellectual strengths and weaknesses shown by reading clinic subjects on the WISC." *Journal of Developmental Reading* 7 (1964): 120-29.

Simmons, G. A., and Shapiro, B. J. "Reading expectancy formulas: a warning note." *The Journal of Reading* 11 (1968): 625-29.

Simmons, W. L. "Human intelligence, the psychological view." *The Science Teacher* 35 (1968): 18-20.

Spache, G., and Spache, E. *Reading in the elementary school.* 2d ed. Boston: Allyn & Bacon, 1969.

Tanyzer, H. J. "The relationship of change in reading achievement to change in intelligence among retarded readers." Doctoral dissertation, University of Connecticut, 1962.

Winebrenner, D. K. "I.Q. road to mediocrity." *School Arts* 60 (1961): 48.

Intelligence and Reading

Ekwall — Questions for Discussion

Do we really know what intelligence is? What are some factors considered important in intelligence? Are the same factors that are important for scoring high on an intelligence test important for success in reading? Can measured I.Q. be increased in most students? Can measured I.Q. be increased more for some students than others? If I.Q. can be increased, then does this change our definition of I.Q.? What specific factors in reading have the greatest relationship to intelligence? Are the Wechsler Tests and/or subtests useful in predicting reading ability? What has been the greatest value of studies dealing with the analysis of the Wechsler subtests? Does the concept that a minimum mental age is necessary for success in beginning reading seem valid? Are reading expectancy formulas valid and worthwhile for most students? Has the use of I.Q. scores generally been harmful or beneficial?

CHAPTER SEVEN

Motivation
and
Reading

Educators have long realized the need for adequate motivation of students if they are to achieve near their maximum potential. One of the major problems, however, has been finding ways to adequately motivate all students. The articles in this chapter were chosen because they not only emphasize the complexity of the motivational factor but also explain why this complexity exists and give some concrete suggestions for improving motivation.

This series of articles also illustrates the importance of the teacher's becoming familiar with the various factors that motivate pupils to learn. For example, the key to the successful motivation of a certain student may lie within the student himself, and unless something is done to improve this factor, the events that happen within the classroom may have little or no reinforcing effect. The teacher may also need to become much more familiar than is often the case with student's backgrounds in order to realize what motivational factors may or may not be successful.

If the teacher is to be successful in motivating her students, then she must be able to answer questions such as the following: Is there a difference in the innate motivation of boys and girls? Is it possible to overly motivate students? What factors really do motivate students in school? Do students' requirements for motivation vary at different grade levels? Jack R. Frymier does an excellent job of answering questions such as these in the first two articles in this chapter.

Marion Martin, Keith Schwyhart, and Ralph Wetzel's article reports a study designed to bring motivation under the direct control of the teacher. The methods used to motivate students were, for the most part, only those which would be available to the average classroom teacher. This article again stresses the complexity of motivation and explains some of the conditions of which a teacher must be aware if he is to be successful in motivating students.

These articles do not cover all one needs to know about motivation. Furthermore, in some cases the reader may feel frustrated after reading them in realizing how many questions are still unanswered and how much more research really needs to be done. They do, however, contain a great deal of useful and practical information and should help us realize that this is an area which must not be neglected in the training of teachers or in actual classroom practice.

In addition to the three articles in this chapter, the editor also has added information concerning factors important in motivation, the kind of materials that seem to motivate students to read, and other practical ideas to motivate students.

Jack R. Frymier

Motivating Students To Learn

"What makes Johnny try hard in school? What can I do with Billy? He doesn't seem to want to learn." What is motivation? Can a teacher change a youngster's motivation level? Will this instructional technique or that set of curriculum materials affect a student's desire to learn?

During the last several years, staff members at the Center for the Study of Motivation and Human Abilities at Ohio State University have completed a number of research studies which deal directly with questions like these. Their findings suggest some clues that may help us understand what motivation is and what teachers can do to increase children's motivation to learn.

"What is motivation?" In general terms, it is that which gives both direction and intensity to human behavior. In an educational context, motivation to learn is that which gives direction and intensity to students' behavior in academic situations. If you say that the phrase *that which* is not very helpful, you are right. However, describing and understanding motivation to learn must begin at that point.

In many ways, the problem is similar to the one we face in dealing with intelligence in an educational setting. We always infer the nature and degree of intelligence from observations of a student's behavior. No one really knows what intelligence is, so we simply watch what a student does (or study his performance on standardized tests) and then make inferences about his intellectual ability. We never actually measure his intelligence, but only how he uses *that which* he has.

From Jack R. Frymier, "Motivating Students To Learn," *Today's Education: NEA Journal* 57, no. 2 (February 1968): 37-39. Reprinted by permission of the author and the journal.

We have to use the same process to understand *that which* gives direction and intensity to what young people do in school. Studies we have made of dropouts, underachievers, overachievers, medical students, delinquents, students in slum schools, students in plush suburban schools, and various other groups have led us to the following conclusions:

Generally speaking, girls tend to be more positively motivated to learn in school than boys. Also, students from more favorable socio-economic situations are, on the average, better motivated academically than those who come from less advantaged circumstances. Further, motivation to learn appears typically as a fairly constant and stable phenomenon. It will change, but only slowly and over extended periods of time, as the result of both intensive and extensive experiences. Finally, there can be such a thing as too much motivation, and for that reason we probably should try to think in terms of optimal rather than maximal motivation. Just as extremely high blood pressure is not conducive to health so the highest degree of motivation is not necessarily most conducive to maximum achievement in school.

Motivation is so complex that we must examine it from a number of angles in order to discover its nature. From the operational angle, our research reveals that students whose desire to learn in school is positive in nature and optimal in level differ in at least four ways from those whose motivation is less desirable: self-concept, values, orientation toward time, and openness to experience.

Highly motivated students tend to have a positive self-concept: "I count. I am competent. Other people like me. I can do it." On the other hand, students whose motivation is less positive tend to have a negative self-image: "I'm no good. Other people don't like me. I'm not sure that I can do it. I'm not as capable as others." Difference in self-concept is one of the most obvious factors research studies consistently show.

Another factor is a difference in values. Youngsters with a negative attitude toward school tend to value the concrete and specific, while optimally motivated students tend to value the abstract, aesthetic, or general. Considering the high positive correlation between social class and motivation, however, one cannot help but wonder which is cause and which, effect. That is, optimally motivated students generally come from middle- or upper-class homes, which provide them with more toys, books, and other material things than is the case with disadvantaged homes. If one were to remove these from the environment of the highly motivated, would their values change, and then their motivation? It may be that students from more prosperous homes are able to go beyond concrete concerns to the less tangible and more abstract because they already have the material things.

Positively and negatively motivated students also differ markedly in their perceptions of time. The low-motivated student is typically pre-occupied with the present, obsessed with the past, or fearful of the future.

Those students who really want to learn are generally conscious of the present, past, and future, but they do not freeze on one aspect of time as do their less adequately motivated counterparts. They are more open to experience than the relatively unmotivated. Less threatened, more curious and seeking in their behavior, they exhibit a kind of per-ceptual energy which enables them to pursue stimuli, so to speak.

Drawing upon these patterns which have become apparent in the course of our research, the staff at the Center for the Study of Motivation and Human Abilities has begun to reconceptualize a theory of academic motivation. Two generalizations have emerged to date.

First, whatever motivation is, it is neither intelligence nor creativity.

Second, any adequate concept of motivation to learn in school must encompass the fact that it involves at least three dimensions: internal-external, intake-output, and approach-avoidance.

Motivation to learn in school is in part a function of what resides within the individual and in part a function of the external world he encounters. Some positively motivated youngsters seem to draw most heavily upon forces located within themselves to enhance their learning. They believe in learning and knowledge, for example, and the new and novel excite them. Ambiguity and uncertainty intrigue them.

Other students, equally well motivated, seem to be most positively affected by the quality and quantity of stimuli which they experience in school. Exciting lectures, fascinating movies, vivid illustrations, and in-tense discussions are likely to spark these students' efforts.

In terms of the intake-output dimension, some students seem moved to consume the learning world around them, while others are producers. Students who are avid readers and thoughtful listeners—who seek information in every way—are "intake" types. They are consumers of information and experiences of every kind. Other students are "out-put" people. They write. They talk a lot. They generate ideas and con-cepts. Their motivations propel them to active rather than passive learning roles.

Finally, there are obvious differences in the way some students move toward teacher approval, marks, social acceptance, ambiguity, and the like, while others move away from such things.

Although the approach-avoidance dimension is a very real part of motivation to learn in school, not all positively motivated students move toward teacher approval or high marks, nor do all negatively motivated persons move away from such phenomena. The problem is more com-plex than that. For example, one student whose motivation to learn in school is positive might move toward (*approach*) reading (*intake*) an exciting novel (*external stimulus*). Another youngster whose motivations are equally positive might move away from (*avoidance*) teacher approval (*external*) in order to generate (*output*) a graphic description of social equality for his history course.

The point is, *that which* causes some young people to want to learn in school is complex rather than simple and requires a sophisticated rather than a naive professional response. Let's turn now to what teachers can do.

Traditionally, most teachers have approached the motivational problem from two directions: quality of the stimulus (subject matter) and variations in stress (instructional techniques).

The first approach is obvious. Those of us who teach have generally felt that if we could provide "good" content and "interesting" experiences, motivating students would be at least partially solved. And, according to the theoretical model described above, this will help some students. The approach will fail with other students because, for them, it simply does not get at the heart of the matter.

The technique of varying stress is equally elusive. Efforts to "raise standards," "bear down," or "require more hard homework" are all illustrations of our occasional attempts to place greater stress on the learner in the hope of affecting his achievement. Our common sense tells us that if we increase the stress, we may be able to raise his motivations and thus maximize achievement. Sometimes these techniques fail, however, because we do not recognize that the relationship between motivation and achievement is an extremely complex one, containing many separate but interacting elements.

Students who are more able tend to learn more than students who are less able. It is easy to move from that generalization to one which assumes that highly motivated students will learn more than poorly motivated students. Carrying the logic further, we then tend to assume that if we can somehow raise the motivational levels of the students in our classes higher and higher, they ought to learn more and more. The generalization is neat and logical, but only partially correct.

Students who are too highly motivated focus on a very narrow segment of their educational world and miss the relationships in learning which are so important. They are less able to see the pattern of events and to make meaningful interpretations of the complexities of learning stimuli.

Students whose motivation to learn is too low are unable to focus their perceptual energies long enough or clearly enough to engage in the kinds of experiences which are personally rewarding or which will be approved of by parents or teachers or both. And without some positive internal or external feedback, motivation to learn in school will eventually die.

Motivation to learn in school is so important and so complex that those of us who teach must seek out and use teaching techniques that produce positive results. In my opinion, our only hope is for a very subjective rather than objective approach. Capitalizing on research findings, we need to sort out the nuances of motivation and the variations among our students and then employ differentiated teaching strategies tailored to fit each individual student's learning needs.

Our short-range effort must be to start with each student where he is and to vary our instructional procedures to suit his immediate learning needs. Over the long run, however, we have to work in such a way that we help all our students to move to an optimal level of motivation.

Throwing away old clichés may be one place to begin. "We must treat all children alike" is one. Nonsense. Each student is unique. Our assessment of his motivations and other abilities demands that we use differentiated teaching techniques to help him learn.

And "Why doesn't Billy try to learn?" should probably be rephrased to "What can I do to help Billy learn to try?" Helping Billy learn to try means teaching him to become better motivated to learn in school. That, in turn, means to develop a positive self-concept, a set of values which includes the importance of learning, a tolerance for ambiguity, and a curiosity which just will not quit.

In the final analysis, this means that we must consciously and deliberately work at the business of personality development and personality change. This is an awesome and frightening task, but it will never go away. If we are seriously concerned about the possibilities of excellence in education, we must assume that responsibility.

Motivation and Reading

Frymier — Questions for Discussion

What factors do you believe account for the fact that girls are more positively motivated to learn in school than boys? Can motivation be taught? Specifically how could we motivate students using the information provided here? How can the teacher determine which factors in motivation are important to any one student? What are some of the reasons that teachers often fail in their attempts to motivate a student or some of a group of students? Are Frymier's suggestions practical and understandable?

Jack R. Frymier*

A Study of Students' Motivation
to do Good Work in School

Creating a learning situation in which students learn involves at least some understanding of what it is that motivates some young people to do good work in school. Some persons believe that motivation is essentially an inherent thing; that students come to school with their energies and enthusiasms for learning already a built-in part of their psychological framework. Others think that teachers must attempt to do something to learners "to motivate them" so they will want to learn.

Faced with the problem of trying to get a sharper picture of students' motivation, a group of interested principals, teachers, and parents posed the following question: "What motivates young people to try to do good work in school?"

The Procedure

To answer this question, a simple Sentence Completion Test-type instrument was administered to approximately 1050 students in six elementary, six junior high, and six senior high schools during the month of April, 1961. Approximately 400 fifth graders, 325 eighth graders,

From Jack R. Frymier, "A Study of Students' Motivation to do Good Work in School," *The Journal of Educational Research* 57, no. 5 (January 1964): 239-44. Reprinted by permission of the author and the journal.

*The author is grateful to the following persons for their assistance in conducting this study: Thomas Moffett, Jane Hobby, Dorothy Maxwell, Daisy Rash, Claire Westbrook, and Ruth McCall.

and 335 eleventh graders were asked to complete the following incomplete sentence two times: "I try to do good work in school when . . ."

This procedure, obviously, represents a relatively gross attempt to assess students' motivation. However, since the SCT is essentially a projective-type instrument, it was felt that this oblique way of probing youngsters' motivational structures might actually be more productive than a more direct approach.

Students were selected from the fifth- eighth- and eleventh-grade levels in an effort to determine whether there were important differences in student motivation according to grade in school. The schools selected represented various geographical and socioeconomic sections of Orange County, Florida. In each case the sentences were completed under the guidance of a parent specially instructed for the occasion. Students were directed not to sign their names.

Following the data-gathering sessions, responses from all students were put together and sorted into several broad categories. These categories were selected and defined after an initial inspection of several hundred responses. The complete sorting process involved four distinct stages.

First, six persons sat down together and went through all of the responses and sorted them into these major groupings: those which revolved around the teacher as a person or were related to something which the teacher did; those which clearly pertained to the individual student himself; and those which involved a miscellaneous group which included responses pertaining to the physical conditions of the room, an interest in the subject matter itself, recognition of some sort or other, and other things.

Following this initial sorting, the responses in each category were sorted a second time and then further divided into sub-categories. That is, if the initial sorting was incorrect, the response was placed in its proper category. Each of the original broad categories was then refined so that several sub-categories evolved.

Third, one person then sorted through all of the responses a final time, verifying placement in the broad categories and in the sub-categories. Fourth, following completion of this last sorting process, a final breakdown was made according to grade level.

The Results

There were 2128 usable responses from approximately 1050 students. Of these responses, approximately 26 percent related to the teacher, 38 percent related to the student, and 36 percent related to external factors of various types. Table 1 describes the proportion of these responses by grade level.

Several important observations are apparent from these data. First, no single category accounts for most of the responses. Second, there seems to be a definite indication of a shift in the focal point of responses from student to teacher between the fifth and eleventh grades. In other words, students in the secondary school apparently placed greater dependence upon the teacher to get them to try to do good work in school than students in the elementary school. This fact is probably exactly opposite from that which might have been expected. This point will be explored in more detail later.

Table 2 describes in more detail the responses in each of the sub-categories included in the general grouping under "teacher". For example, the following responses were included in these sub-groupings: "I try to do good work in school when. . .

"I am not angry at the teacher or when I feel good. Sometimes the teacher makes me angry by saying I did something when I did not do it."

"I am not tired and the teachers aren't mad and when we discuss the subject."

"the teacher starts the class off with a joke, a smile, or is just plain friendly."

"when the teacher is not in a bad mood. And when a teacher does not tear you down in class and make you feel you're stupid. And when they give you a little encouragement in class, also."

"when the teachers aren't crabby."

"the teacher gives me more freedom and doesn't gripe about every little thing."

"I enjoy the class, the teacher, and the atmosphere I am in, also the people I am around. Some teachers in this school and many others are very BORING."

"I can. That is most of the time. Sometimes when I am reading the teacher keeps on talking it bothers me, then she asks questions and I cannot answer her because when I was reading she was talking. Sometimes I cannot read the board so it is hard for me to do my work."

"I am not bothered by anyone and when I have the material to work by. I try to do good work in school when I know how to do the problems, etc. When I cannot get much help on something and get real discouraged I do worse work or sometimes when I do it by myself it comes out better."

"I have a good teacher. When I say good teacher I mean one who makes it clear what she's trying to explain. One who doesn't give you a lot of questions from the book then take it up."

"I have the cooperation of the teacher and can see that he wants to teach us as well as he can about that particular subject. If, however, the teacher is short on patience and easily gets mad, then I have very little desire to do my best for that teacher even though this action will hurt my grade."

"I know the teacher is helping you all he can, and it will help me in later life."

"I like the teachers that are teaching me, and when I am in a friendly class. When I get an urge to do good work."

"my teachers, principals, and schoolmates are interested in me. In other words, when my environment is fairly good."

"my teacher appreciates it and gives it due credit, and when I respect the teacher."

"I'm asked to or if the teacher tells me to do my school work. I will obey school rules. Whenever I am asked to do something I shall do it and not say anything."

"the teacher knows how to keep order. When there are discussions, and when the subject is interesting. But more than anything else I like a teacher who is not boring. (And when the class is not over-crowded)."

"conditions around me are pleasant. Some of the teachers bring about a kid not liking one subject—they really put a scare into them where they don't want to come to school. The teacher's personality and humor have a lot to do with a kid doing good work in school."

"the teacher likes me and when I like my teacher very, very much, and when I am happy and gay, and when my school friends like me I do my work as best I can in school."

"I am encouraged by the teacher and feel that they like me. It is much harder to do good work when I feel uneasy around the teacher."

Table 3 describes those responses which related directly to the student himself. For example, these responses were typical of statements included in this category: "I try to do good work in school when. . .

"I study, practice, and study some more. Also when I keep my mind on my work. I should go to bed early each night so I may do good work — but I don't. I'm a natural born oaf."

"I think it will help in my future plans. I also try to do good work so that I can make my parents proud of my work. I also try to get good grades so I can get ahead in the business world."

"I am good, when I am not scared or excited, when I am paying attention and not talking and not being fussed at."

"I feel confident that I may be able to do the work I am given."

"I set myself a goal and am encouraged to reach it."

"I want to, or when I am not too lazy. Sometimes I try to do good work, and I can do good work if I try, but I never try. I can get my class work and tests OK, but my homework I never do because I am too lazy."

"I am in a good mood. I really try to do good work any time in the year, because I want my grades to come up this year even if it is just a little bit. Thank you."

"I understand the work, feel like doing it, and have the ambition, which is seldom, because I'm usually worried about other things, and school work has no special appeal to me."

"I can. With the pull that is being put on students to participate in outside activities, this can prove to be very difficult at times. Church work, school work, club work — which is most important? I try to divide my time to include all three."

"I think of the importance of doing good school work. Making all 'A's' is not so important to me. The most important thing to me is doing my best in my school work."

"I think about it. I try to do good work but Dad and Mom say all I think about is boys. And I always sit in the back of the room and I hardly hear and I always have the urge to talk and I always do."

"I want to. When I want to do good work in school I can do good work. That is, if I have girls off my mind. Most of the time I have girls on my mind, and when I do I can't do good work."

"I am not nervous and my eyes do not hurt and when I feel good. I love school, but when I do not feel good, I hate it."

"I am not tired and I don't feel sick and I understand my work. And I try to do my best work when I don't have much work to do."

"I think of how our nation is advancing in knowledge. I believe that every student should do the best he can today in schools because most jobs in life today require more education than before. We must try to better ourselves more than our parents, who didn't have as much of an opportunity as we do today in our schools."

"I am not overloaded with extra school activities such as magazine drives, selling tickets to plays, etc."

"I see that my work is finished and checked before it is turned in."

"I feel good. Mostly I try to do good work all the time. When the teacher feels good and when I don't have a lot of pressure upon me."

"I get a good breakfast and get enough sleep, and when I am feeling well."

From these figures, it would appear that students' feelings are important in understanding their motivation to do good work in school. Further, it would also seem that older students are much more concerned about the relationship of school experiences to their future lives than younger students.

In Table 4 are described the proportion of students' responses which have been included in the category related to external factors. This category included statements which youngsters made about working for better grades, about what their parents might say, and the like. For instance, the following quotations were included in this category: "I try to do good work in school when . . .

"I need the money my dad pays me for good grades."

"there is an especially big test, when something I particularly like is being studied, when there is a chance to get ahead or make some money by doing well on a certain test, and when I just feel like working."

"ever my mother says she will give me one dollar for every 'C'."

"I think about my car being taken away, when I think about college, and when I think about the $5 I will collect for each 'A'."

"I don't have many things to do. I also do it for my parents, because I don't like to be called dumb."

"People don't come and boss me around and call me dumb, for that just doesn't go with me."

"I need to make up for previous low grades in order to have a high 'B' or 'A' for the six weeks grade. Also, I am pressured by my parents to maintain high grades."

"I am playing sports so that I won't be dropped from the team. I also try to do good work in school when I know I'm going to need my father's car."

"I know that if I don't I will be restricted. As an example, I was restricted this six weeks because I had made bad grades in three of my subjects. Therefore, to get off restriction I must work harder to get a better grade."

"I am required to do so to protect my pride and pass the year and watch my teachers smile at me for making a good grade."

"it is something I like to do and when the work is for my education."

"I can take the subject I want."

"I know that it is important to my grades. If there is an important test, I will study hard and do my best, but when I know it does not matter, I don't bother to do anything."

"ever I'm not bothered or distracted by other people, although some of my teachers just bore me stiff with stuff I already know."

"I especially want my parents to be proud of me and want them to know that I'm capable of their belief in me that I can do good work."

"Mother brags to others about my achievements, so that I will not disappoint her or myself and therefore I can maintain my record."

"I am trying to please my mother. She is so pleased when I make good grades, so I try to make good grades for her."

"I'm not pressured. Last year my grades were B+ and because of this my parents neither restricted me nor tried to force me to make good grades. This year my grades were not too good and right away I am restricted and am being pressured by my parents and teachers. I have lost the desire to work hard toward a college education."

General Conclusions

After a careful study of the data, two conclusions seem warranted. First, no single factor accounts for a significant proportion of the total number of responses, although five factors do account for approximately half of the responses. Second, there appears to be a definite shift in the sense of responsibility for doing good work in school from the student to the teacher over a period of time.

Throughout this study, it was apparent that students try to do good work in school for many reasons. Significantly, no single kind of response accounts for a large portion of the total responses. This would seem to imply that students' motivational patterns are both diverse and complex.

A careful examination of the data indicated that five types of responses did account for about half of the total number: interest in the subject matter, liking the teacher and the subject, grades and other forms of recognition, the students' physical and emotional status, and the physical factors in the classroom situation (light, temperature, distractions, etc.).

Perhaps the most remarkable generalization drawn from this study relates to the fact that there seemed to be an unmistakable shift in the sense of responsibility from student to teacher over a period of time. In other words, younger students seemed to evidence greater personal initiative and inherent motivation while older students apparently assumed that teachers ought to do something to make them want to learn. In effect, older students seemed to place greater dependence upon the teacher than younger students for their own learning, whereas, theoretically, at least, increased independence and personal initiative would be expected and hoped for among mature students.

Recommendations

Considering all of the data and the major conclusions described thus far, certain recommendations seem to be in order.

Since youngsters apparently are motivated by a whole host of factors, and since no single factor seems to be especially important to a sizable segment of any group, teachers should be urged to select and devise a variety of instructional techniques in their efforts both to tap and create students' motivations to do good work in school. Simultaneously, teachers should also strive to cultivate an intense awareness of each students' total way of behaving. That is, since some students seem to respond positively to approval, others to marks in school, others to direct instructions, others to optimum room conditions, and others to a variety of additional factors, teachers must continuously study their own students carefully for clues as to what it is that motivates them to do good work in school. In other words, in the opinion of the persons conducting this study, the most effective teacher will be that one who is most able to 'fit' his instructional techniques to each child's unique needs. In effect, the art of teaching may very well lie within this realm of "fitting" methods to each learner.

Finally, teachers should consciously strive to use their personality as a major tool to implement their educational purposes. The vigorous impact of a dynamic personality upon a learner may do more to promote motivation toward school than any amount of exhortation.

This study demonstrates the complex task facing teachers attempting to evoke or capture students' motivations. "Individualizing instruction" has to be more than a byword; it must be achieved.

If administrators are really concerned about devising circumstances in which a teacher can teach and a child can learn, they must provide innumerable opportunities for students and teachers to have close, intimate learning experiences. In effect, creative administrators will seek to contrive organizational patterns which maximize personal contacts between teachers and students. Large classes and large group instruction appear to facilitate those purposes of education which are directly related to the dissemination of information, but they also appear directly antithetical to increasing or tapping students' motivation. Providing information is not enough. Students must be helped to make this information an integral part of their lives. This task, which is difficult under the most favorable circumstances, is probably impossible when teachers have large classes every day.

Questions for Further Study

During the course of this research, several questions arose which seemed to warrant further study. They are listed below:
1. What do teachers think motivates students to do good work in school? How do their ideas compare with the results actually obtained from students in this study?
2. What do students really learn when their parents give them money for getting good grades in school? Are all of these learnings desirable?
3. What type of home situation is most conducive to fostering desirable attitudes toward school in general and learning in particular?
4. What type of organizational matter in a school will best enable teachers to utilize and promote students motivation?

If helping young people learn is important, these questions deserve careful study.

TABLE 1

Proportion of Responses in General Categories According to Grade Level

Category	5th Grade %	8th Grade %	11th Grade %
Teacher	20	30	31
Student	45	33	36
External factors	35	37	33
Total	100	100	100

TABLE 2

Proportion of Responses Related to Teacher

Sub-Category	5th Grade %	8th Grade %	11th Grade %
Material is presented clearly	2	3	2
Student likes teacher and subject	8	9	8
Teacher makes the subject interesting	1	2	8
Teacher is not grouchy	1	3	2
Teacher is in a good mood	0	2	1
Teacher is fair and understanding	1	2	2
Discipline is maintained	0	2	1
Teacher assigns work to be done	6	4	2
Teacher shows interest in student	1	3	5
Total	20	30	31

TABLE 3

Proportion of Various Responses Related to the Student

Sub-Category	5th Grade %	8th Grade %	11th Grade %
Use certain study habits	6	4	1
Enough time to study	2	1	1
Will be useful to me someday	1	4	13
When I feel good	16	12	11
When I am not afraid or worrying	1	1	0
When it is necessary	0	1	1
When I try	3	4	4
Whenever I can, all the time	16	6	5
Total	45	33	36

TABLE 4

Proportion of Responses Related to Various External Factors

Sub-Category	5th Grade %	8th Grade %	11th Grade %
When I get good grades or for a test	13	13	15
When I have the approval of others	1	3	3
When people don't push me around	0	1	1
Teacher is out of room	1	1	0
The room is quiet and cool	11	10	3
The subject is interesting	6	8	10
Miscellaneous	3	1	1
Total	35	37	33

Motivation and Reading

Frymier — Questions for Discussion

What are the merits and possible criticisms in the research design used by Frymier in this study? What are the implications for the teacher based on the research in this study? On the basis of this research, would our commonly held beliefs or methods used for motivation be successful? What are the implications for school administrators?

Marian Martin, Keith Schwyhart,
and Ralph Wetzel

Teaching Motivation in a High School
Reading Program

Two requirements stand out in successful teaching. The first involves an ordered set of learning tasks which presents material to the student in units which he can grasp, each step preparing him for the next. The second requirement calls for sufficient motivation to ensure that the student engages in the tasks that are presented. Teachers of reading have developed various methods of subdividing and ordering the process of reading into a series of simpler behaviors. They seek to lead the student from skills he possesses when he enters the learning environment into more and more complex skills. The development of efficient and effective materials has required a very careful analysis of the complex goal behavior of reading.

Motivation, on the other hand, has only recently been submitted to such a careful analysis. Teachers have usually relied upon materials to motivate the student, tried to develop techniques to "capture his interest," or just hoped that somehow or other his work behavior would be maintained. The analysis of pupil motivation is no less a challenge to the teacher of reading than the analysis of reading skills. This paper seeks to illustrate some ways in which motivation can be analyzed by presenting a technique which can bring pupil motivation under more direct control of the teacher.

Investigation of the teaching situation, both of skill sequences and motivation, has made productive use of the principles of operant learning.

From Marian Martin, Keith Schwyhart, and Ralph Wetzel, "Teaching Motivation in a High School Reading Program," *Journal of Reading* 11, no. 2 (November 1967): 111-21. Reprinted with permission of Marian Martin and the International Reading Association.

The segment of these principles most concerned with motivation is frequently called *reinforcement theory*. The central concept of reinforcement theory is that the occurrence of behavior is a function of the environment in which the behavior is imbedded. In particular, behavior is largely a function of the events which follow it. *Reinforcers* are defined as those events which increase the frequency of the behaviors which they follow. The analysis of motivation centers on the relationships, or contingencies, which exist between behaviors and certain environmental events.

A lack of motivation, then, is not viewed as simply a characteristic of the student, but as a characteristic of the whole teaching environment. When a pupil is not motivated to work, the events of the classroom often have little or no reinforcement value to him, or else they are not contingent on the appropriate behaviors. Adult attention, for example, has powerful reinforcing values, and all teachers are familiar with "attention getting" behaviors. In a series of research papers, Harris,[5,6] Hart, and Allen[7] have demonstrated that teacher attention may control a variety of behaviors, including withdrawal, regression, crying, and physical skills. The teacher may thus find himself in a position where his attention serves to maintain disruptive behaviors in the classroom rather than the appropriate work behaviors he seeks to develop, because of the contingencies that exist between his attention and pupil behavior. The attention or recognition given a child by his peers is another reinforcing event familiar to teachers. Others include special privileges, treats, and opportunities to play, to engage in a favorite activity, or to help in the classroom.

Token systems are one technique which has been used to explore the effect of reinforcers on pupil behavior. Items such as plastic chips, check marks, or stars are used as immediate reinforcers for specified behaviors. These tokens can then be exchanged for something of value, such as an object or event, much as money operates in our culture. A variety of motivational problems have been approached through the use of token systems. Whitlock[9] carried out a very successful program of remedial reading with a first-grade boy using a token system. Girardeau and Spradlin[4] were able to develop many desirable behaviors in institutionalized retarded children. Birnbrauer[3] has demonstrated that significant advances in the academic skill of retarded children can be obtained with appropriate contingency management.

The classroom environment is tremendously complex, and early analysis indicates that teachers are working under conditions more difficult than even they realize. Still, research relevant to the classroom can best be done in the classroom. In order to make effective use of token systems, teacher-experimenters must recognize the following principles of learning: 1) The behavior required for earning tokens must be in the repertoire of the student. Goals must not be set so high as to make reinforcement unavailable. Careful programming is needed to ensure that all pupils can engage in some behavior that will earn tokens. 2) The tokens must be given contingent on the appropriate behavior, and they must not be given unless the specified behavior has occurred. 3) The reinforcement must be delivered promptly. Tokens should be given as soon after the the occurrence of the specified behavior as is possible. This is especially important in making the relationship between the behavior and reinforcer very clear to the pupil. 4) The token must be exchanged for something that is of value to the individual; this will vary among individuals and even for a single individual over time.

The present paper describes the use of these principles in a token reinforcement system for high school remedial reading classes. An attempt was made to reorganize the contingencies between desired classroom behavior and reinforcing events usually available to the public school teacher. It is intended to demonstrate some of the techniques and advantages, as well as some of the difficulties of motivational analysis.

Procedure

All the remedial reading classes taught by one teacher, and one class taught by a second teacher, were included in the study, a total of six classes and 95 students. The token system was used in three classes (experimental E1, E2, and E3). These met during the last three periods of a day that ended at 6:40 p.m. The same teacher taught all the experimental classes, as well as control classes C2 and C3. Half way through the school year the teacher of control class C1 was reassigned to token rooms E2 and E3.

Description of the students appeared in Table 1. Most were of Mexican-American background and all were of lower socio-economic status. Curriculum was similar throughout, and the same lesson plan was used whenever possible. The program consisted mainly of assignments in reading and writing (including the SRA laboratories), class discussions, and individual work with the teacher.

The first step in the project was selecting the behaviors to be reinforced. This was done by asking the teachers what was most important to them. In addition to reading books and handing in completed assignments, such problem behaviors as excessive tardiness, failure to bring pencils and paper, and refusal to participate in class discussion were mentioned prominently. All the behaviors chosen appear in Table 2.

TABLE 1

Description of Experimental (Token) and Control Group Students

	CONTROL CLASSES			EXPERIMENTAL CLASSES			All Exp.	All Cont.
	C1	C2	C3	E1	E2	E3		
Grade Level	10	10	9	9	9	10		
Total Enrolled	13	13	18	18	17	16	51	44
Males	9	12	10	8	12	9	29	31
Females	4	1	8	10	5	7	22	13
Mean Age*	16.3	16.1	15.3	15.8	14.9	16.2	15.7	15.8
Mean Reading Grade Level*	3.9	2.4	3.0	3.8	4.1	3.1	3.6	3.1

* Reading Grade Level from Gray Oral Reading Tests and Ages for 59 students enrolled at the start of the school year

Consideration of others was chosen as a behavior incompatible with any of the multitude of disruptive behaviors in the repertoire of the students. Regular attendance, being on time, bringing pencils and paper, not creating a disturbance, and doing at least some of the work every day was sufficient to earn a grade of 3. Additional grading was done on a point curve.

About two weeks after the start of school, the students were told that something new was to be tried. A chart was posted on the bulletin board during each class period. On the chart was a list of work and behavior units for which points would be given and the point value of each (Table 2). Space was provided on the chart under each student's name where points, in the form of check marks, could be entered next to the appropriate work or behavior item, with one space ruled off for each day on which the class met.

At the beginning of each class period the teacher made check marks on the chart for each student present, on time, and prepared. During the class period, the teacher put additional check marks on the chart as they were earned by the students. In contrast to the familiar use of gold stars based on competition, where only the best performers can earn stars, any student in the token classes was able to earn points every day by coming to class and working to the best of *his ability*. Once earned, no points were taken away.

At the suggestion of the students, some minor changes were made in the system. "Books Completed," which included an oral or written book report, earned points with reference to the student's reading ability and the length and difficulty of the book. Make-up assignments were provided for some of the points missed during absences.

TABLE 2

*Sample Portion of Chart Showing Desired Behaviors
and Points Given for Each*

Student's Name	Points		Days	
Present	1			
On Time	1			
Prepared (paper and pencil)	1			
Considerate of Others	1			
Worked in Class	1			
Completed Assignment	1			
Participated in Discussion	1			
Completed a Color in SRA Laboratory	2		·	
Completed a Book	2+			
Overcame a Reading Difficulty	2+			

Back-up reinforcers were limited to those available to any classroom in the school. This ruled out spending any money to purchase items typically attractive to teenagers. The points were backed up by grades: the more points, the higher the grade. Letters of commendation were sent to parents and counselors for six-week's grades of 3 or above. Also, one excused absence to attend a school-sponsored activity (often missed by late session students) was given for every six-week's grade of 2, and two such absences for grade of 1.

Data Collection

A category system, based on the work of Bales,[2] was developed for time sampling classroom behavior. Beginning five minutes after the class bell and every fifth minute thereafter, an observer watched each student for 10 seconds, proceeding clockwise around the classroom. Behaviors observed were tallied into one or more of 11 categories on a record sheet. Tallies in each category were then totalled and expressed as percentages of all behaviors observed. Table 3 lists the categories used and their definitions. Agreement on three sets of ratings made by two observers was 98.2, 92.8, and 99.9 percent.

The same observer visited all the classes equally, usually for one class period per week. Her work was presented as part of a college research program on classroom behavior and the students were free to

TABLE 3

*Categories Used in Recording Classroom Behavior and
Definitions of Each*

Name of Category	Definition
WORK	Reading, writing, or doing an assigned task at desk.
RECITING OR LISTENING	Constructive participation in class discussion, or teacher-solicited recitation, or listening to the teacher or a reciting student, *including* looking directly at the speaker.
LISTENING OR TALKING PRIVATELY	Private conversation, topic irrelevant.
UNRULY	Shouting, banging desks, fighting or similar highly disruptive behavior.
SITTING AIMLESSLY	Sitting at desk but not falling into any other category; staring into space, doodling, fixing hair, etc.
UP AIMLESSLY	On feet but not falling into any other category.
UP WORKING	On feet, fetching or returning materials or doing an assigned task.
DOOR AND WINDOW	Standing or sitting by windows looking directly out or standing looking out the door.
PENCIL SHARPENER	Going to or from or using the pencil sharpener.
CHART	Standing or sitting at the bulletin board reading the chart.
OTHER	This included OUT OF ROOM and LIBRARY which were tallied separately.

observe the procedures and convince themselves that no record was being made of individual performances.

Records were kept by the teachers of absences, tardiness, assignments completed and handed in, and books read and reported on. The Gray Oral Reading Test was administered to all the students at the beginning and at the end of the school year. Metropolitan Achievement Test scores in Word Knowledge and Reading were available for 24 students from the beginning of the school year, and these were retested also.

Results

The token system was well accepted by the students. Teachers soon noted a variety of effects. Students in the token rooms tended to arrive on time and began to work independently, without waiting for the teacher to "settle them down" or to make an assignment. In fact, experimental room pupils often asked that no assignment be made so they could read their library books. Control classes waited for an assignment to be made and then expected the teacher to see to it that it was done. In a school that does not supply pencils and paper, a student without them is literally unable to do written work. Token room students made a point of bringing these supplies. Other teachers in the school began to show an interest when their students made remarks such as, "I don't have reading today, so I don't have a pencil."

Much more individual instruction was possible in the token rooms. Teachers also liked the quieter and more orderly atmosphere, the ease and accuracy of record-keeping on the charts, the advantages of making an evaluation of each student several times during each class period, and the more positive attitudes expressed toward reading.

Table 4 shows behavioral data for the year. It is evident that experimental class E2 was not nearly so much affected by the token system as the other two. This difference can also be seen in Figure 1, which summarizes *work related behavior*. This measure was obtained by combining *work, reciting* or *listening, up working,* and *library.*

During the last six weeks of the year, a new back-up reinforcer was added in room E2 only. A local drive-in theater manager agreed to donate some free passes. Two passes were made contingent on a grade of 1 for the marking period, and one pass for a grade of 2. The effect of this new contingency on E2 can be seen in Figure 1. Work-related behavior rose to a high of 71 percent of total recorded behaviors, higher than that for any other interval.

FIGURE 1

*Work-Related Behavior in Six High School
Reading Improvement Classes*

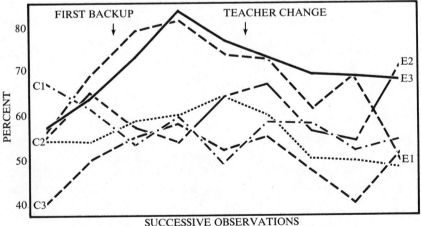

SUCCESSIVE OBSERVATIONS
Average percent per two observation periods shown.

TABLE 4

Mean Percents of Total Behaviors Recorded for One School Year

Behavior	Control Classes			Experimental Classes			All Cont.	All Exp.	T	P
	C1	C2	C3	E1	E2	E3				
Total Work-Related	58	56	49	69	60	70	54	66	4.59	<.01
Work	46	42	37	56	43	59	41	53	4.32	<.01
Reciting or Listening	9	10	10	7	8	8	9	8		
Up Working	3	2	3	3	5	3	3	4		
Library	0.1	1	0.2	3	3	0.6	0.4	2		
Talking Privately	12	11	22	11	15	10	15	12		
Sitting Aimlessly	20	25	23	16	16	17	23	16	2.44	<.01
Up Aimlessly	6	3	3	2	6	2	4	3		
Unruly	0.2	0.2	0.1	0.0	0.2	0.0	0.2	0.1		
Door and Window	2	2	0.2	0.3	0.2	0.2	1	0.2		
Pencil Sharpener	0.1	0.0	0.1	0.0	0.2	0.0	0.1	0.1		
Chart	0.0	0.0	0.0	0.0	0.2	0.0	0.0	0.1		
Out of Room	2	4	2	1	4	1	3	2		
Absent*	3.2	2.0	2.2	3.9	2.3	3.1	2.5	3.0	2.30	.05
Tardy*	0.7	2.6	0.5	0.3	0.3	1.3	1.3	0.6	3.30	<.01
Books Completed*	N.R.	0.0	0.3	1	0.8	0.9	0.2	0.9	3.43	<.01
Assignment Handed In*	N.R.	1.8	5.7	7.2	8.0	9.1	4.2	8.1	18.04	<.01

* Mean number per student for one school year

In spite of poorer overall results in token room E2, combined data show several significant differences between experimental and control classes. More work and total *work-related behavior* were recorded in the token classes, as well as less *aimless sitting,* less *tardiness,* more *completed assignments* handed in, and more *books read* and reported on. With the exception of absences, results on all other behaviors, though not statistically significantly different, were in the desired direction.

There was no significant difference in reading improvement between experimental and control classes on any of the measures used. Gains on the Gray Oral Reading Test, the Metropolitan Achievement Test, Word Knowledge and Reading scales for experimental and control classes, respectively, were 0.6 versus 0.7, 0.9 versus 0.4, and 0.9 versus 0.6 years.

Discussion

Riesman[8] urges that teachers of culturally deprived children strive for highly structured programs, clearly define what is to be done, and "perhaps the best overall principle is to be consistent." In addition, "every inch of progress on the part of the child calls for genuine praise." These stipulations are met by an effective token reinforcement system. The reinforcement may take various forms, including but not restricted to praise. Students vary as to what will function for them as reinforcers. Many work very hard for attention, praise, and grades. When the available reinforcement events are not maintaining a student's work behavior—when he is unmotivated—the teacher is challenged to rearrange the classroom environment so as to reinforce more consistently and immediately, and to begin a search for new reinforcers. The present study demonstrates that even very limited changes in contingency management can significantly affect motivation. There is substantial evidence that this will be true not only in exceptional classrooms, but in any classroom.

The student who lacks reading skills is not likely to enjoy his labored efforts; he is often very frank in stating that he doesn't *like* to read. Token systems offer a method for shaping and firmly establishing skill behaviors. The development of the skill will in itself enrich the possibility of reinforcement, as well as becoming potentially self-reinforcing. The student who reads well is rewarded in all aspects of his school work; often he develops a love of reading itself. Reinforcement theory suggests that by appropriate scheduling and development of reinforcers teachers can increase motivation as well as academic skill.

Reinforcement theory has developed largely in the psychology laboratory. Teachers interested in motivation can make lasting contributions to the applied science. A most important aspect is the careful keeping of records or data. Simple frequency counts of behaviors are often sufficient. The teacher begins by making systematic records of the behavior which he is interested in increasing—for example, arriving to class on time, or handing in completed assignments. This can often be done in the grade book. Perhaps a student teacher, aide, or even a pupil could be the data collector. Next, classroom contingencies are changed in some way, perhaps by introducing new reinforcers, or by rescheduling already existing ones. Subsequent records will then indicate whether the new system is working, how, and with which behaviors. What if the desired changes do not occur? The data are then telling the teacher that whatever system is being used, it is not an effective system and needs changing. Our results with token class E2 are an example. It may be that one or more of the principles listed in the introduction to this paper are not being satisfied. The next step is to change the contingencies in some way and again look at the subsequent data. As in playing music, a wrong note does not indicate that something is wrong with the piano. The data tell the teacher when it is time to alter his reinforcement system, thin out the schedule of reinforcement, or modify the character of the reinforcing events.

Another advantage in the systematic use of reinforcement is that it provides a better test of curriculum effectiveness. It is difficult to evaluate materials and their programming with poorly motivated students. A curriculum may be assessed negatively because motivation was lacking. On the other hand, the failure to learn may be blamed on poor motivation when it is actually a function of poor materials or methods. A reinforcement system such as the one described makes it more likely that the students are engaging in the requisite behaviors, thus allowing a more accurate appraisal of the curriculum.

The application of reinforcement theory in the natural environment has brought excitement and promise to intervention areas in which little progress has been made in the past. Such application requires both ingenuity and an attitude favoring experiment. Teachers are so placed that they are able to develop motivational research in the classroom environment.

References

[1]Allen, K. Eileen, Betty Hart, Joan S. Buell, Florence R. Harris, and M. M. Wolf. "Effect of Social Reinforcement on Isolate Behavior of a Nursery School Child," *Child Development*, 35 (1964), 511-519.

[2]Bales, R. F. *Interaction Process Analysis* (Cambridge, Mass.: Addison-Wesley, 1951).

[3]Birnbrauer, J. S., S. W. Bijou, M. M. Wolf, and J. D. Kidder. "Programmed Instruction in the Classroom," *Case Studies in Behavior Modification*, by L. P. Ullman and L. Krasner (N.Y.: Holt, Rinehart & Winston, Inc., 1965).

[4]Girardeau, F. L. and J. E. Spradlin. *A Cottage Program for the Retarded*, Parsons Research Project Working Paper #85 (1964).

[5]Harris, Florence R., Margaret K. Johnston, C. Susan Kelley, and M. M. Wolf. "Effects of Positive Social Reinforcement on Regressed Crawling of a Nursery School Child," *Journal of Educational Psychology*, 55 (1964), 35-41.

[6]_____, M. M. Wolf, and D. M. Baer. "Effects of Adult Social Reinforcement on Child Behavior," *Young Children*, 20 (1), 8-17.

[7]Hart, Betty M., K. Eileen Allen, Joan S. Buell, Florence R. Harris, and M. M. Wolf. "Effects of Social Reinforcement on Operant Crying," *Journal of Experimental Child Psychology*, 1 (1964), 145-153.

[8]Riesman, F. *The Culturally Deprived Child* (N.Y.: Harper & Row, 1960).

[9]Whitlock, Sister Carolyn. "Note on the Acquisition of Reading; an Extension of Laboratory Principles," *Journal of Experimental Child Psychology*, 3 (1966), 83-85.

Motivation and Reading

Martin et al. — Questions for Discussion

Do you believe that the methods described here are actually feasible for the average classroom teacher? What explanation might one possibly give for the fact that the experimental group did not achieve significantly more than the control group, even though they did appear to be more highly motivated? What are the implications contained within this article for further research? Would the results of this study possibly have been different if another, or more than one, teacher was used? Do you think that this type of motivational program could be successful if it were used by all classrooms within a school?

Eldon E. Ekwall

Motivation and Reading —
Further Comments and Research

In addition to the information presented in the three articles in this chapter, the editor believes that other currently available information can be of considerable help in planning for reading programs and in teaching reading. This information is presented in three sections. The first deals with some factors concerning motivation, with which the teacher should be familiar. The second deals with the kind of reading material that motivates readers, and the third deals with some practical ideas to motivate students.

Factors Important in Motivation

A factor that appears important in the motivation of students is that of identification with the material. Sara Williams (1968) studied the role of the identification process as a factor of motivational support for reading with young disadvantaged Negro children. She also attempted to measure the effects of intellectual capacity and sex on the operation of the identification process. In her experiment she used The City Schools Reading Program. It is a program designed specifically for culturally-disadvantaged minorities in a multicultural environment. Her control group used "conventional materials." Williams reported that, although for the entire group her analysis of covariance revealed no significant difference in reading achievement between the total experimental group and the total control group at the end of the study, there was a significant difference between the higher intellectual levels of the experimental and control groups. She found no significant difference between the total groups on the basis of sex. She did, however, find a significant difference, favoring the girls, between the boys and the girls of the control group, but there was no significant difference for the same measurement of the experimental group. This was interpreted to be indicative of the superiority of the experimental method for boys.

Williams believed that the operation of the identification process was directly and positively related to intellectual ability.

From Williams' study it would appear that children are more highly motivated to read material with which they can identify. It would also appear that the need becomes more pronounced when working with children of higher intellectual levels. This study also indicated that boys may do considerably better if materials were written about things, places, or events with which boys can identify. Since the ratio of boys to girls in remedial reading is often five-to-one or even higher, this is a factor that should not be overlooked or taken lightly.

The motivational factor involved in the use of certain types of materials was also illustrated by Lawrence Lowery and William Grafft (1968), who studied the effect of paperback books and reading attitudes of fourth grade children. Children in the Lowery and Grafft study were divided into several groups. One group was supplied with a number of paperback books which were placed in their classroom. All groups were encouraged to go to the library, where the same books were available in clothbound editions. Another group had the clothbound versions of the paperbacks available in their classrooms. The Projective Test of Attitudes was used to measure the children's attitudes toward reading at the beginning and end of an eight-week period. The authors reported that the attitudes of the children were significantly affected by the use of paperback books. The authors stated,

> . . . Boys and girls who used the paperbacks showed significant increases in their number of pleasant or positive attitudes and a decrease in their number of negative attitudes.
>
> Both experimental groups had the same titles and the same ready access to books in their classrooms, but the Experimental I group, with the clothbound books, showed no significant change in their post-test attitudes. It seems that there is 'something' about the paperback book which has an important and positive effect upon the attitudes of fourth grade students (p. 623).

The authors stated that no specific causes for changes in attitudes could be determined from their study. They did, however, suggest the following:

1. Perhaps clothbound texts become symbols of scholastic failure to many students. Perhaps such books impart negative feelings, because they represent assignments and homework rather than items of choice and pleasure. In the case of disadvantaged students, the clothbound

books certainly are not a real part of their world outside the school and the classroom and as such are not looked upon with favor.

2. Perhaps the attitudes toward reading and books are affected by the colorful covers, smaller size and/or ease of handling of the paperbacks. Clothbound library books do not lend themselves to being tucked into a pocket for easy carrying. Perhaps paperback books encourage a feeling of possession and are symbols of casual reading (p. 623).

Another important factor in motivating students to read is that of interest in the material. Margery Bernstein (1955) studied the relationship between interest and reading comprehension in 100 ninth grade pupils. She wished to determine whether or not there was a difference between the comprehension with which pupils can read a selection which is interesting to them and the comprehension with which the same group can read when the material is uninteresting to them. Bernstein's comprehension questions included identifying such things as the main idea, inferences, and the author's mood and purpose. She picked two passages, one of which was "The Get-Away Boy." It was picked for its clear style and teen-age hero. The other passage was from *The House of Seven Gables,* which was rewritten to make it of the same readability level as "The Get-Away Boy." In rewriting the passage from *The House of Seven Gables* the author included descriptive material, and hints of human action were removed which the author said tended to make it less interesting. Each story was six pages of about 200 words each. The author reported that the scores obtained showed that the group was significantly more interested in "The Get-Away Boy" and that the comprehension scores obtained were significantly higher. Bernstein stated that intelligence did not materially affect the intelligence-comprehension relationship, but the brighter pupils went to greater extremes in interest ratings. The students were then asked to state which story they preferred and why. They were also asked to write an additional chapter for each story. The indication that students were more highly motivated by the interesting story was illustrated by the fact that this story evoked fuller and more adequately written responses and also more creative responses. Students were evidently reading actively and thinking about the material as they went along.

Covert motivations are also extremely important in influencing children's reading ability. It is, of course, difficult to determine whether a child becomes a disabled reader because of negative covert motivations or whether negative covert motivations increase as a child fails to do well in reading. Apparently it works both ways, but the prevailing belief among those who have researched the problem is that children who are unsuccessful in reading develop negative covert motivations more often than the negative covert motivations cause reading failure.

The fact that significantly more negative covert motivations do exist among poor readers was illustrated by James Hake (1969), who studied the covert motivations of both good and poor readers. Hake used the Reading Apperception Test to study eighty sixth-grade pupils of average intelligence who were "below-average" and "above-average" readers as measured by the California Achievement Test. Hake concluded, ". . . below-average readers in the sixth grade exhibited significantly more negative covert motivations than did their above-average reading peers" (p. 736). In discussing the implications of his study Hake stated,

> In general, the findings of this study support those of earlier studies that poor readers exhibit significantly more negative desires and wishes along with more maladjustive classroom behavior than do good readers. Also, as in previous studies, this research points up the fact that classroom teachers and reading clinicians must not only be concerned about the poor readers' word recognition problems, but they must be equally sensitive to their emotional difficulties, which are indeed considerable. In this regard, the reading teacher should realize that much of the maladjustive behavior of poor readers is accompanied by negative self-concepts, anxieties, covert aggressive impulses, negative feelings about home and school, and an extreme distaste for reading and subject-matter in general. When the reading teacher becomes aware of not only the overt behavior maladjustments of the poor reader but also his significant covert impulses, the way for helping the poor reader improve both his reading skills and attitude toward reading will be greatly enhanced (p. 738).

Edward De Roche (1967), writing on the subject of motivation as an instructional technique, indicates that lack of readiness for a learning task leads to frustration which is "antimotivational." He stresses the fact that success is probably the most effective motivational device because it gives the pupil confidence in his ability and leads him toward self-motivation. Other motivational devices he mentions are comments of praise and encouragement written on childrens' papers, progress records kept by pupils so that they can compete with themselves rather than with other pupils, teacher enthusiasm, variety in teaching methods, familiar concepts used for illustrative purposes, summary statements by pupils, use of inventories to learn students' interests, and the use of professional, industrial, political and cultural community resources.

Materials That Motivate Students To Read

A number of studies have been done in the past concerning the reading interests of students at various age-grade levels. As a result of these studies, many teachers believed they could select books that would be highly interesting to children. However, there is some discrepancy in what teachers *think* children want to read about and what the children themselves often choose. Perhaps part of the problem has been that in giving children an opportunity to select reading materials on their own, we have in reality influenced their decisions. Furthermore, it is entirely possible that, because of the influence of television and the change in children's environment in general, their reading interests have changed and will continue to change.

Typical of the kind of information concerning teachers' inability to accurately judge the reading interests of their pupils is that which comes to us in an article by Eugene Baker (1968). Baker, who is the National Curriculum Director for Children's Press, tells of an experiment carried out with kindergarten, first, second, and third grade students. In this experiment children from two different socioeconomic groups were given a story preference test. Children were shown a number of pictures chosen from existing children's books. They were also read sentences that correlated with the pictures. They indicated which pictures they would most like to read about by marking a plus (+) beside that picture. A minus (−) was placed beside pictures that the children indicated they would least like to read about. After pictures were marked, the sentences that correlated with each of the pictures were read. Children marked the sentences in the same manner as they marked the pictures. The pictures represented six categories: (1) Children in general, (2) Children in ghetto areas, (3) Negro heritage, (4) History and science, (5) Animals, and (6) Fantasy. The author stated that children from the Watts-Compton School District near Los Angeles had approximately the same interests as children in the wealthy communities along Chicago's North Shore. Baker reported that, regardless of grade level, reading interests remained fairly constant and children did not usually simply guess but had specific likes and dislikes. Across the four grades "Negro Heritage" was by far the most popular category and "Animal" was the least popular. "Children in Ghetto" was high on the like side, whereas "Fantasy" was rated high on the dislike side. The author's most significant finding was that an alarming disagreement existed between the preferences of the children and the prediction of the teachers. Baker stated,

This simply means that *teachers generally don't know what their children prefer*. They don't know — whether advantaged or disadvantaged — that their children prefer stories which consist of situations showing action, antagonism, competition and adventure. So they continue to feed children a diet of sweet children and animal stories and fantasy.

The study further suggests that teachers must open their eyes, face reality and find out what their children are interested in. You can't hope to get through to ghetto children with white picket fences when they can only relate to overflowing garbage cans. It appears too, that children from the clean, white suburbs want to know about what goes on in the ghetto and will read stories on this subject (p. 106).

Baker suggests that teachers use tests of this nature to assess the reading interests of their own children. He cautions that in doing so they must be careful to emphasize free and open discussion and not to lead the discussion and suggest areas of interest. He feels that once this has been done, many children will simply "play back" the teachers' interests instead of pushing their own.

Practical Ideas That Motivate Students To Read

Recreational reading programs are not only relatively easy to set up and operate but also are one of the most effective means of motivating students to develop lifetime reading habits. The case for such programs is evident from information such as that given by Donald Fader. In a speech delivered to a convention of textbook publishers he stated that the Carnegie Foundation had done a survey of adult reading habits. They found that approximately one-half of the people with bachelor's degrees in the United States never read another book as long as they live!

Donald Pfau (1967) described a recreational reading program designed to motivate students to develop the reading habit. In discussing the need for programs such as these he stated,

Although there is obviously a syndrome of agents operative in causing many capable readers to appear disinterested in reading, much of the problem can be traced to the fact that young children encounter too many reading programs which are devoid of intrinsically rewarding reading experiences. Overly-narrow reading programs, often lacking enthusiastic endorsement of the teacher, deprive children of the enriching activities and materials which could foster personal enjoyment of reading. Such reading programs fail to differentiate between those experiences which build reading attitudes and habits (p. 35).

The fact that children can be motivated and *will* read when they *can* read is illustrated by a free reading program described by Eldon Ekwall (1969). In this program children in grades three through eight were given a free reading period of approximately forty-five minutes three days per week. During the other two days of the week children viewed full-length movies and other films and filmstrips. The purpose of using the various audiovisual aids was to broaden the children's backgrounds of experiences and to increase their reading comprehension.

Books were placed in each classroom on display racks built of plywood. This enabled students to view the covers of books rather than the spines. During the free reading period, teachers were asked not to "teach" but rather to read themselves and thus set an example for their students. Occasionally teachers read short selections from books to spark interest in certain subjects. Teachers also reminded pupils to maintain lists of the books they had read.

The time for the free reading period was taken from the time normally allotted to social studies and science. The researchers believed that this was justified since approximately one-half of the books used during the free reading period contained material relating to these subjects.

An evaluation of the program after one semester revealed that the children's ratio of learning during the program was 1.0 and 1.3 years in Vocabulary and Total Reading, respectively. Before entering the program their ratio of learning had been .80 and .88 years in Vocabulary and Total Reading, respectively. An analysis of the children's test scores in science and social studies vocabulary indicated that, although approximately one-half of their time from a "formal" class period was used for free reading, their vocabulary scores in these areas were slightly higher. The program was also evaluated in terms of the average number of books read by pupils in various classrooms. Typical of these results were the following:

A second grade class—137 books per pupil

A third grade class—369 books per pupil

A fourth grade class—62 books per pupil

These figures represent the average number of books read during one academic year after the program had been in progress for one and one-half years.

Teachers were also asked to respond by giving their opinions of the program. No teacher gave an unfavorable response. Typical of their comments is the following: "The free reading period and excellent films have been a real improvement in the school program this year. Interests have been expanded, curiosity aroused, and understanding increased" (p. 9).

An interesting motivational technique is described by Ralph Schrock and Milton Grossman (1961). In their hypothesis they stated,

> Children who continuously fail in reading acquire a negative outlook and defeatist attitude which prevents them from achieving in the reading area. They usually conform to the social and cultural pressures placed upon them, but cannot succeed in reading.
>
> It is believed that if these youngsters were given some special attention, and some possible reason for having failed previously, they would become motivated and improve in their reading ability (p. 119).

Since a relatively high percentage of the children who come to remedial reading classes have visual problems, the authors believed that visual training might help youngsters. They did not believe that the visual training per se would help the youngsters, but they believed that it would enable these children to receive some special attention and would provide them with a reason for failing in the past.

The researchers selected twenty seventh grade students with I.Q.'s ranging from 90 to 110 who were reading two or more grade levels below expectancy. All children were given the Keystone Visual Skills Test and the Lovelle Hand-Eye Coordination Test. The Gray Oral Reading Test was administered before and after the training period. Students were given two fifteen-minute periods of visual training each week. The authors did not describe the visual training, but they did emphasize that the visual training was designed to accomplish *nothing* from a visual standpoint and was done solely for the purpose of providing motivation through special attention and giving students a reason for past failure.

When the experimental and control groups were given the post-test, the experimental group was found to have gained seven months of achievement over a four-week period, as compared with an average loss of one month achievement for the control group. The difference of the means of the reading scores was significant beyond the .005 level of confidence. The authors stated, "The highly significant result of this project indicates that motivation or lack of it is a major factor in reading disabilities" (p. 120).

As this study indicates, children often need something to use as an excuse for past failures. It also illustrates that motivation and/or positive thinking can be extremely important factors in the success of a remedial reading program. The need of students to find an excuse for failure is also stressed in the article by Blau and Blau in chapter 11 of this volume.

Another important factor to be considered in motivating students is the kind of reward to be given. Some adults would perceive a gift of two tickets to an opera as a reward; however, there are others who would, no doubt, prefer to stay home. Thus, in reality they would perceive the opera tickets as punishment if they felt obligated to attend the opera to please the donor of the tickets. Teachers face the same sort of problem in attempting to determine which students will respond positively to a certain reinforcement. Numerous studies have shown that the kinds of things that normally motivate middle-class students are not always successful in motivating children from lower socioeconomic groups. For example, there is no guarantee that a student will perceive a smile or a pat on the head as a reward. On the other hand, it is difficult for a child who comes from a home where candy is always available to perceive a piece of candy as a reward.

Most researchers have been in agreement that there is a wide variation in the manner in which children are likely to respond to various types of reinforcement; however, some rather broad generalizations can be made. The results obtained by Tommie Hamner (1968) in studying the effectiveness of tangible and social reinforcements are typical of many studies. Hamner used three treatment groups in studying tangible and social reinforcements in culturally-deprived Negro children during instructional periods in individualized reading. His three treatment groups were: tangible reinforcement—a piece of candy, social reinforcement—"that's fine," and customary group instruction where several children were in a group and no planned or deliberate reinforcement was given.

The investigator measured the number of correct responses from each treatment group. He found that the tangible reward and the social reinforcement produced a significantly greater number of correct responses than did customary group instruction. He did, however, receive more correct responses by using the tangible reward treatment than by using the social reinforcement treatment.

Other researchers have found tangible rewards to be less effective than social reinforcement when used with children from middle or upper socioeconomic class groups. They have, however, obtained the same results as Hamner when studying the effectiveness of various reinforcement techniques with children from lower socioeconomic groups. One must remember that these are rather broad generalizations and that there are likely to be wide variations in the perceptions of children within any one group.

An interesting idea to stimulate motivation in disabled readers is described by Fred Schab (1967). Schab's article relates an interesting and rewarding attempt to rebuild the interests of students by a process of creative ego-involvement. The activity is described as a "core" unit and is an outgrowth from experiences the author had with a small group of retarded readers in a fifth grade class. Schab's objective was to re-kindle the interest of these boys and girls in reading.

After investigating the home background of the students in his class, the author felt that the most common element in the children's lives was the military experiences of their fathers or relatives. He noted that most of these students watched military shows on TV.

The group was polled to determine their desires in pursuing a study of their common interests. Schab related his experiences in the Pacific during World War II. This discussion led to the group organizing into a battalion of infantry preparing for battle. The instructor was chosen as the senior officer-in-command, and each student was to act as a company commander under him.

Under the guidance of the senior officer, the battalion was led through basic training and officer-candidate courses. The class learned about military protocol, dress, and weapons to be used in combat. To provide for the needs of soldiers entering battle, reading and discussion of information about history, geography, international affairs, climate, waters, and islands of the Pacific area was enthusiastically pursued by each student.

The group found that a study of mathematics, geography, and science was also necessary in order to complete their mission. Each company commander was entrusted to order the correct supplies for his group, thus using his knowledge of math. The group also studied the physics of light and sound, tides, and typhoons to conduct patrols of the Pacific area.

The group made a thorough study of the maps of the Pacific area. Since utmost secrecy was necessarily involved in military matters, the group devised a secret code. The messages, reports, orders, and letters written home in this code became the reading practice for the class.

The author states,

> ... the motivation was easily discernible as being unusually great. The constant variety of problems to be taken under consideration, with solutions appearing from the unified body of information the pupils had available from the various sources mentioned made remedial reading instruction a game instead of a boring task. These children saw the need to read in order to play the game. Even the frequent halts to discuss and analyze words were not objected to because of their eager pursuit of their goal. The usual gains were recorded on achievement tests at the end of the unit, but the most important result was that, once more, the retarded readers were interested in reading (p. 631).

References

Baker, E. H. "Motivation for the disadvantaged, special problems." *Grade Teacher* 85 (1968): 104-7.

Bernstein, M. R. "Relationship between interest and reading comprehension." *Journal of Educational Research* 49 (1955): 283-88.

De Roche, E. F. "Motivation: an instructional technique." *The Clearing House* 41 (1967): 403-6.

Ekwall, E. E. "Free reading-culture program." *Reading Quarterly* 2 (1969): 7-11.

Hake, J. "Covert motivations of good and poor readers." *The Reading Teacher* 8 (1969): 731-38.

Hamner, T. J. H. "The relative effectiveness of tangible and social reinforcement during individualized instruction of beginning reading." Doctoral dissertation, University of Alabama, 1968.

Lowery, L. F., and Grafft, W. "Paperback books and reading attitudes." *The Reading Teacher* 21 (1968): 616-23.

Pfau, D. W. "Effects of planned recreational reading programs." *The Reading Teacher* 21 (1967): 34-39.

Schab, F. "Motivation in remedial reading." *The Reading Teacher* 22 (1967): 626-27.

Schrock, R. E., and Grossman, M. "Pilot study: motivation in reading." *The Reading Teacher* 15 (1961): 119-21.

Williams, S. C. M. "Identification as a factor of motivational support for reading in young children." Doctoral dissertation, University of Denver, 1967.

CHAPTER EIGHT

Perception and Reading

A number of writers and researchers believe that inadequate perception may be the single most important factor contributing to disabilities in reading. This is especially interesting to note since other factors, such as intelligence, have often received considerably more attention. As one begins to study this field, the first question often asked is What is perception? Other logical questions are: What areas of perception are of special significance to reading? Are the commonly-used tests of perceptual difficulties really valid? Do children seem to benefit from perceptual training? Do children from low socioeconomic levels tend to be weak in certain perceptual skills? Do the commercial programs for the development of various perceptual abilities appear to be of value? What do we really know about perception after many years of research?

There is a fairly large volume of research and writing in the area of perception, but seldom does one find any one, two, or three articles which deal with the subject on a broad basis. For this reason the editor has chosen to write this chapter himself. In this chapter, the editor has attempted to define perception in simple terms and then answer some of the most commonly asked questions related to this field. Because there is still a great deal of disagreement over certain questions dealing with perception, truly definitive answers are impossible. Research, however, has given us some definitive answers and pointed to some rather definite implications in other cases.

What is Perception?

Perception might be defined as the process by which an organism receives and interprets certain information about the environment. The important point here is not only that perception is the process of receiving a stimulus, but also that it is the process of interpreting the stimulus. George and Evelyn Spache (1969) define perception as ". . . the preparation for a response, or as the processes which intervene between the presentation of a stimulus and the ultimate response to it" (p. 13). A student's perceptual field then consists of all of the various aspects of his external environment, which may include sounds, sights, words, and other events to which the student makes a discriminating response at any given time. It should be remembered, however, that in a student's perception we are dealing with the interpretations the student makes from these various stimuli rather than what is really there.

There are, of course, several kinds of perception. For example, the perceptual process may begin when an object is seen, when a sound is heard, when something is touched (both kinesthetic and tactile perception), and when something is smelled or tasted. The completed perceptual process occurs when the student interprets these various stimuli in light of his past experiences. Typical of the perceptual process in relation to vision is the following example: When our eyes are acted upon by some stimulus such as light, the stimulus acts on nerve endings called receptors. These receptors send a message (impulse) to the brain. If the brain can add nothing to the activity caused by the impulse, then we experience merely a sensation. If the brain, however, can add something to the impulse, then the experience becomes a perception. Thus memory, experience, and judgment all influence perception.

Perceptual Areas
Important to Reading

A casual study of the subject of perception will soon lead one to the conclusion that some areas of perception are more closely related than others. Obviously perception of taste and smell have some, but only minor, roles in the development of the ability to read. On the other hand, visual and auditory perception exert a major influence on reading proficiency. Tactile and kinesthetic perception also influence reading but evidently to a lesser extent.

In a discussion of the importance of the various learning modalities George Kaluger and Clifford Kolson say,

> In many ways, we consider the auditory modality to be most significant to the reading and learning process. This is a modality which is frequently underemphasized in diagnostic evaluation by too little testing.

We consider auditory perceptual abilities more important than visual above the third grade. Components of the auditory modality which are related to reading are (a) auditory acuity, (b) speech discrimination and (c) auditory memory and sequencing. We are concerned with auditory-verbal ability (ability to develop sound-symbol relationships) auditory comprehension or recognition of words, and degree of auditory awareness or alertness (pp. 149-50).

They further state, concerning the importance of the visual modality, that,

The visual modality is complicated by the fact that it has many aspects, some of which are perceptual and others mostly cognitive, also there may be a visual-motor involvement. Some of the visual elements to be tested are (a) acuity, (b) memory and sequencing, (c) with severe cases, figure-ground perception, and (d) with younger children, perceptual discrimination, form, and configuration. Generally visual-motor performance is also observed in connection with the other test of visual modality (p. 151).

Although a number of studies have concerned themselves with the relationship of tactile and/or kinesthetic perception and reading, the relationship is still not entirely clear. About this area Kaluger and Kolson state, "The significance of muscle patterns to reading and learning ability has not been fully determined, but there is considerable evidence to say that if motor patterns are not causative to reading development, then they certainly are correlated at least" (p. 153).

It further appears that most individuals develop more rapidly or learn more easily by using one modality than by using others. This is not to say that accurate development is unimportant in all perceptual areas, but only that some individuals have a predilection for one modality. This predilection is illustrated by a study reported by Barbara Bateman (1968). Bateman studied eighty-seven first graders who exhibited various preferences in modes of learning. She stated, "These data again confirm the earlier observation that children who prefer the visual modality are handicapped, relative to those who prefer the auditory modality in reading" (p. 109). The children who preferred the auditory mode became better readers than those children who preferred the visual mode. Some of the children who preferred the visual mode did, however, become good readers. Bateman wondered if the few visual subjects who became good readers by the end of first grade might have also become more auditorily-oriented.

Not only do certain perceptual areas have a tremendous affect on a child's ability to read, but certain abilities within any one perceptual area also may greatly impair a child's ability to learn to read. Typical of this situation are the children described by Joseph Wepman (1968), who stated,

> Some children have been known to be so deficient in auditory process-
> ing of signals that for most environmental situations they are function-
> ally deaf even though their hearing acuity is quite normal. One such
> child was incapable of recalling a telephone number or a single item from
> a list of ten items read to him. Another could not distinguish the letters
> of the alphabet at twelve years of age yet suffered no loss of visual acuity
> (pp. 2-3).

Some children not only have difficulty with specific perceptual areas but they also have trouble sorting out stimuli coming from various perceptual areas. For example, some children become confused by what they hear, see, taste, smell, and feel. In other words, one sense does not reinforce the message that another sense conveys. These children are not able to integrate their sensory experiences into a meaningful perception of the world about them.

The information presented here indicates that very little would be accomplished by arguing which perceptual areas are most important in learning to read. Evidently if a child is to be completely successful, he must develop normally in the visual and auditory areas. Although the exact relationships are not fully understood, the proper development of perception in the tactile and kinesthetic areas appears to correlate with normal reading development, if indeed these areas do not have a causal effect on proper reading development.

Perception and Maturation

Many authorities agree that a child who has not experienced normal perceptual development in the areas most important to reading by the ages of seven or eight years is likely to experience considerable difficulties in learning to read. Perceptual development would not, of course, have necessarily reached maturity by this age. Joseph Wepman (1968) states,

> For most children, the two major modalities seemed to reach a stage
> of equalization of function by the age of nine; that is, whatever lags in
> development were present seemed to be overcome by that time. Usually,
> however, the modality showing the most rapid development indicated the

child's predilection. Perhaps from this fact it might be said that a modality matures because of some neurological tendency—for the audile child, the auditory pathway matures earliest; for the visile child, the visual pathway. With maturation, there is an accompanying developmental sequence—again, earliest to mature nominates the earlier development of function. The audile child, then, not only matures earliest in an auditory sense, but also develops his more mature pathway with the greater ease. Here, use of the pathway assists with its development. It comes to complete function and use at an early age (p. 3).

Anne Morency (1968) reviewed the research on the auditory modality and its relationship to reading. She stated that there was a consistent increase in sound-discrimination ability with age, that children vary in the rate of development of both auditory discrimination and auditory memory, and that the development of auditory discrimination and auditory memory is not realized until most children reach the age of nine years. She states that auditory measures are not in themselves predictors of success or failure in reading. Morency, in discussing her study, also stresses the point that children vary in their development of various modalities. She states,

Thus, the notion of a developmental progression in perceptual ability is again confirmed in the performances of this population in the first three years of school. It should be noted, too, that the coefficients of correlation of improvement in the auditory modality with improvement in the visual modality are low, a finding which means that children who improve in one modality may or may not improve in the other. In other words, the study has shown that perceptual abilities develop significantly in the first three years of school in a normal population and that these abilities progress individually along lines of modality preference at differing rates in the same individual (p. 18).

In summary, the following conclusions seem justified:
a)   Modality preference seems to be related to the innate capacity of the child, with some children preferring the visual modality and some preferring the auditory modality.
b)   Visual and auditory perceptual abilities reach fruition around age nine.
c)   Growth or maturation in one modality does not necessarily assure growth or maturation in another modality.
d)   The modality preferred and used the most by a child is likely to mature or improve earlier than the less preferred modality.

Processes of Auditory and Visual Discrimination

Most authorities agree that, whether we are concerned with auditory or visual perception, we are dealing with acuity, discrimination, and memory. In a discussion of the processes of visual perception as described by M. D. Vernon, Jean Robertson (1968) says,

First, he is aware of the visual symbols standing out from the background of the page of the book, and then he sees essential similarities for the general classification of the word. Third, he classifies the visual symbols of the word within the general class. Last, he identifies the word, usually by naming it. Visual perception is a learned process which encompasses consideration of acuity, discrimination, and memory. Auditory perception may be viewed as a parallel process to visual perception taking similar account of acuity, discrimination, and memory (p. 93).

In discussing the processes of auditory perception, David Sabatino (1969) says,

The four major dimensions or processes of auditory perception are:
1.   The recognition of sound elements as meaningful information.
2.   The retention of these units of information.
3.   The integration of the symbolic relationships of these units as language concepts.
4.   The comprehension of language symbols through the three previous stages or steps of auditory perceptual functions (p. 730).

Perception is a Learned Function

As discussed earlier, perception deals with acuity, discrimination, and memory. If perception consisted of nothing more than acuity, then one could hardly consider it a learned function. However, as soon as we reach the stage of discrimination and memory, we are dealing with more than one factor, which automatically brings us to a situation which requires learning. Since perception is a learned function, it becomes susceptible to teaching. The fact that perception is a learned function then brings us to all sorts of problems. For example, if learning is required for accurate perception, then we are likely to encounter many instances in which children have come from environments which have not been conducive to the proper development of their perceptual areas. Because of various sociological conditions that are not conducive to normal development in certain perceptual areas, we find many children lacking the perceptual readiness required for success in reading.

The tremendous need for early experiences that contribute to the development of adequate or normal perceptual awareness has been observed in many classrooms and has also been demonstrated in the laboratories of psychologists who study the experiences necessary for the development of proper perceptual needs. It is, of course, not possible to purposely control the environments of humans to study their perceptual development; however, there have been a few cases where peculiar circumstances have given us a chance to observe the behavior of people who have been totally lacking in certain experiences. Cynthia Deutsch (1968) tells of a report by Von Senden. In this report he described the results of visual testing of subjects who were blind from the time of their birth or shortly thereafter but who had successful eye operations and subsequently gained vision. Deutsch states,

> While the studies were not so controlled as one would wish, the evidence shows that the people who had these experiences had serious visual perceptual deficits. In some cases, depending largely upon the age of the subject, fully normal visual perception was never achieved. Many of the subjects had difficulty with the function called "thing constancy," a term which refers to the ability to see an object as the same object no matter what its orientation in space or the angle from which it is viewed. One of the subjects reported by Von Senden, for example, could recognize an automobile easily when both he and it were on a level. That same subject when looking out a window was not able to recognize the objects he was seeing from the top and had to go all the way downstairs to satisfy his curiosity about what he was seeing: automobiles parked on the street. Similarly, some of the subjects did not acquire the ability to recognize geometric forms such as squares and triangles visually: they had to count the corners of the figures in order to designate them correctly (p. 83).

The development of the various dimensions of auditory and visual, and to some extent tactile and kinesthetic, experiences which ultimately lead to proper perceptual awareness for reading is one of the major tasks of teachers of kindergarten and beginning reading. Many children, of course, come to school with a background of perceptual experiences that permit the teacher to simply proceed with formal reading instruction. However, because perception depends on a child's innate ability, experiences, and interests, we are likely to find children entering school at all stages of perceptual development, including some children with serious perceptual deficiencies. Because this situation exists, a number of programs and various materials have been developed to promote perceptual awareness. The success of many of these programs, however, is questionable and will be discussed later in this chapter.

Perception and Environment

There is some disagreement among the studies as to the importance of the role of environment on perceptual development. For example, Wepman (1968), in discussing this question, states,

> The differential modality distinction appears to be related more closely to the innate capacity of a child than to any determinable environmental factor. No specific deprivation of stimulation could be found in the home or play environments of children with poor auditory learning or poor visual or poor tactile-kinesthetic learning. In fact, within the populations studied clinically, such children have been found to come from all types of homes, including the highly verbal university setting as well as the almost nonverbal disadvantaged environments. Some came from homes in which they were the only child and others from homes in which they were the eldest or youngest of multiple sibling groups (p. 3).

On the other hand, Warren Wheelock (1968) studied the visual discrimination abilities of kindergarten children. He stated, "While the pretest results very definitely favored those children who came from environments characterizing the upper extremes of the socioeconomic continuum within the district, the children from the lower extreme of the same continuum seemed to profit most from the training" (p. 104).

Deutsch (1968) also reports that some researchers have found that retarded readers from lower-class environments consistently have more difficulty with the auditory than with the visual channel on a variety of tasks. Deutsch reports that her own studies with the Illinois Test of Psycholinguistic Abilities indicate that lower-class children have greater difficulty with subtests tapping auditory input channels as compared with those presenting information visually. In interpreting this information, Deutsch states,

> It should be stressed that this emphasis on the relatively lower efficiency of the auditory channel for these children carries no intrinsic, anatomic, or structural implication. The hypothesis about the findings rests on the interaction of the process by which experience influences perception and the nature of audition as compared, for example, to vision (p. 85).

Deutsch also suggests the possibility that culturally-disadvantaged children may often be deficient not only in discriminative skills but also in their ability to do sequential patterning exercises and in their ability to shift modalities.

Other researchers such as Robert Dykstra have found that boys do not learn auditory discrimination skills as readily as girls do. Concerning these findings, Jean Robertson (1968) states,

> . . . the boys apparently learned auditory discrimination skills less readily than girls. It has been reasoned that boys spend more time outside of the home and do not have the same opportunities to hear their mother's speech patterns which are usually clearer than the less well-defined speech patterns of their young friends. In prereading activities in kindergarten, then, training periods in auditory discrimination could be held separately for the boys who need more help than the girls (p. 95).

Gaston Blom (1968) also believes that environmental and family conditions strongly influence the patterns of development of children's perceptions, language and cognition. This in turn affects their academic and psychological performances. Blom states that children from disadvantaged populations show inabilities for perceptual discrimination and sustained attention. Therefore, perceptual handicaps do not necessarily indicate central nervous system damage.

In spite of some rather convincing research, sometimes to the contrary, the visual channel is superior for poor readers and children from large families in low socioeconomic groups. On the other hand, for good readers and children from homes with stimulating environments just the opposite is true.

Causes and Diagnosis
of Perceptual Problems

The major causes of perceptual problems include intellectual, neurophysiological, physical, emotional, and environmental conditions. Whatever the causal factors, children with perceptual problems find it difficult to profit from normal reading instruction in the classroom. Furthermore, many perceptual problems are not detected until they have caused children to become seriously disabled in reading.

At the time when most children enter school, they are able to perceive simple forms without any difficulty. For example, most children can perceive various characteristics of letters that enable them to distinguish one from another. However, children with visual perceptual problems are unable to realize which of the parts of letters are significant in helping them to distinguish one letter from another. Such essential characteristics as height, shape, and direction often have little meaning to them. Some children also are unable to distinguish separate letters from whole words and are, therefore, unable to break them down into meaningful units necessary for the application of word attack skills.

Children with auditory perceptual difficulties, on the other hand, are often unable to perform the processes of auditory perception as described earlier in this chapter by Sabatino; that is, they are unable to recognize sound units as meaningful information and often fail in their ability to discriminate between different but somewhat similar sounds. Many also fail in their ability to retain these units until they can be integrated into symbolic relationships necessary for language concepts.

Many other symptoms of perceptual problems are listed in the literature, especially in the kinesthetic and/or tactile areas. However, the relationship between reading ability and these areas is still not fully understood, to say the least. For example, a number of researchers have found significant correlations between reading ability and various perceptual areas (in this case not auditory or visual), but information showing that specific training in these areas in turn improves reading ability is sadly lacking. Typical of the writing in these areas is that of Bruce Balow (1971), who states, "While motor and perceptual skills weaknesses are frequently found in learning disabled pupils, there is great likelihood that these are most often simply concomitants without causal relevance; thus the argument cannot depend upon assumed etiologies for learning disabilities" (p. 523).

A number of programs which provide appropriate remediation for difficulties in various areas where perceptual problems are encountered have been marketed in recent years. Most of these programs contain some type of diagnostic test or tests to determine areas of the program from which children are most likely to benefit. It should be noted, however, that the success of most of these programs has been somewhat less than satisfactory. Many of the tests that accompany these programs are either lacking in validity, or remediation in the weak areas simply does not produce a corresponding improvement in reading ability.

One of the best known tests of perceptual problems is the Frostig Developmental Test of Visual Perception (1966). In the administration and scoring manual for the test, Frostig states,

It is most important that a child's perceptual disabilities, if any exist, be discovered as early as possible. All research to date which has explored the child's general classroom behavior has confirmed the author's original finding that kindergarten and first-grade children with visual perceptual disabilities are likely to be rated by their teachers as maladjusted in the classroom; and not only do they frequently find academic learning difficult, but their ability to adjust to the social and emotional demands of classroom procedures is often impaired.

Identification and training of children with visual perceptual disabilities during the preschool years or at the time of school entrance would help prevent many instances of school failure and maladjustment caused by visual perceptual difficulties. Although some children may overcome these difficulties at a later age, there is as yet no method to predict whether a child will be able to do so without help. . .

The Developmental Test of Visual Perception can be used either as a screening device for nursery school, kindergarten, and first-grade children, or as a clinical evaluation instrument for older children who suffer from learning difficulties (p. 6).

A number of researchers have studied the relationship between the subtests of the Developmental Test of Visual Perception and various reading abilities. One of these was done by Arthur Olson (1966), who studied the relationship between school achievement, reading ability, and visual perceptual abilities as measured by the Developmental Test of Visual Perception. Olson reported that his analysis of the data indicated that there was only a small degree of relationship between the specific reading abilities tested and the individual Frostig tests. He believed that the Developmental Test of Visual Perception was of little value in predicting the specific reading abilities of the students tested in his study. He also stated that his results indicated that the test had little or no relationship to either mental age or chronological age. Frostig reports that her test seeks to measure five operationally-defined perceptual skills. These are eye-motor coordination, figure-ground, constancy of shape, position in space, and spatial relationships. Factor analysis studies such as those of Donald Hammill (1970) and Larry Boyd et al. (1970) have indicated, however, that the Frostig test does not, in fact, measure separate factors. In summarizing others' research Boyd et al. state, "In agreement with the Ohnmacht and Olson's study and Olson's review of the literature, the present findings suggested that the DTVP measures essentially one general visual perceptual factor" (p. 17). In summarizing their own research, Boyd et al. state,

In effect, the DTVP does not appear to reflect essentially different and independent perceptual abilities. Implications derived from the present investigation seriously question the content validity of DTVP and suggest that the Perceptual Quotient be used as a unitary measure of perceptual functioning rather than as a cumulative measure of five independent visual perceptual abilities (pp. 17-18).

Other researchers have attempted to use the DTVP as a predictor of reading achievement. Here again, the DTVP seems to fail. For example, James Jacobs et al. (1968) reported on a study in which the DTVP and the Metropolitan Readiness Test were both correlated with tests of later reading achievement. Jacobs et al. found that there was little relationship between Frostig scores and reading achievement. The Metropolitan Readiness Test was a better predictor of reading achievement.

The Illinois Test of Psycholinguistic Abilities (ITPA) has also been used as a test of perceptual difficulties; however, researchers have also found it somewhat unsatisfactory. Sabatino (1969) reviewed the research on its use. He found that the subtests of the ITPA have a relatively low correlation with academic achievement. In discussing the research of G. S. Hasterok, Sabatino stated,

> . . . visual and auditory difficulties as identified in ITPA profiles were unsuited to answering the important question of the relationship between learning problems and perceptual or sensory problems. He concluded that children cannot be matched for comparison purposes on the basis of sensory or perceptual problems. The problem is that the ITPA was designed as a measure of psycholinguistic skills and not perceptual functions (p. 730).

The Bender Visual-Motor Gestalt Test (1938, 1946) has also been used to a considerable degree for the purpose of measuring perceptual-motor difficulties. The success of the BV-MGT as a measure of perceptual difficulties is somewhat difficult to judge. For example, E. Koppitz (1964) reports that children with a disability in reading often do poorly on the test; however, children with other problems such as poor social or emotional environment exhibit somewhat the same symptoms. Frank Lachmann (1960) also reports that disabled readers' distortions of the designs of BV-MGT distinguish them from normal readers. On the other hand, Lachmann states, ". . . when emotionally disturbed, normal readers are compared with reading retarded children, the distortions do not distinguish so efficiently" (p. 431).

A further problem with the Bender Visual-Motor Gestalt Test is that it is somewhat difficult to interpret. Because of this, interscorer reliability is likely to be somewhat low.

The Block Designs subtest of the Wechsler Intelligence Scale for Children and the Wechsler Adult Intelligence Scale is also used as a measure of children's perceptual-motor abilities. A student who does poorly on the Block Design subtest may have perceptual difficulties, but as with the Bender Visual-Motor Gestalt Test, children with other problems may exhibit the same symptoms. For this reason, accurate interpretation of the results is very difficult.

The Purdue Perceptual-Motor Survey Tests (1966) are a battery of tests designed to measure perceptual-motor development. They consist of various movement tasks in walking, jumping, and identifying body objects. At this time little is known concerning the relationship between reading ability and perceptual-motor development. Some research has shown that there is at least a positive correlation; however, it is not known whether or not inadequate development in the perceptual-motor areas is a causative factor in cases of reading disability.

A number of attempts have been made to devise accurate tests of auditory perceptual difficulties. One of the most widely used tests is the Wepman Auditory Discrimination Test (Wepman, 1958). One of the strengths of this test, no doubt, lies in the fact that it is administered in a situation analogous to that of a child's beginning reading situation, i.e., he must discriminate between minimal word pairs. For example, Sabatino tried various types of subtests in an attempt to develop a test of auditory perception. He stated, "The subtests using digits (retention) and tapping (integration) were not good discriminators, indicating that meaningful language is necessary to discriminate between the auditory perceptual function of normal and neurologically impaired children" (p. 736).

Although the Wepman Test does a seemingly good job of measuring auditory discrimination, it is somewhat limited as an overall measure of auditory perceptual difficulties. For example, although some memory is required of the subject being tested, it does not necessarily measure auditory memory or auditory closure, both of which are highly important in the development of reading skills. This is not a criticism of the Wepman Test, however, since Wepman never claimed it measured these skills.

Sabatino developed an experimental test of auditory perception (TAP). He reports that his subtests of recognition, retention for sentences, and comprehension discriminated between neurologically-impaired and normal subjects at the .01 level when administered under normal testing conditions. In emphasizing the need for such tests, Sabatino states, "The data from the study indicated that visual and auditory perception are different behaviors requiring differential assessment, and that auditory perception is a complex function with specific behavioral components which must be assessed independently if classroom management of these behaviors is to be provided" (p. 736).

Programs For Perceptual Training

One of the most widely known programs for perceptual training is the Frostig Program for the Development of Visual Perception (Frostig and Horne, 1964). A great deal of research has been done on the effectiveness of the Frostig materials as a readiness program for both whole class groups and for children with specific problems as indicated by the Frostig Developmental Test of Visual Perception. John Sherk (1967) conducted a study in which the Frostig Program was used for thirty minutes daily with a group of disabled readers. A similar control group was given an equal amount of time with independent activity that was related to various aspects of reading. Sherk reported that no statistically significant results were attributable to the effect of the Frostig training program on any of the tests used. He concluded that the use of selected portions of the Frostig program for remediation of various visual perceptual problems was no more effective than an equal amount of practice time devoted to reading-related activities for a similar group of retarded readers.

James Jacobs (1968) used the Frostig program with a group of kindergarten children to determine whether or not these same children would perform better on the Developmental Test of Visual Perception after using the Frostig materials. He also wished to determine whether or not children using these materials achieve higher scores in future reading. Jacobs concluded that children who use the Frostig materials do show a higher level of visual-perceptual performance on the Frostig test in comparison to control pupils. He did, however, conclude that the children who used the Frostig program seemed to have no particular advantage as far as reading achievement is concerned.

Gordon Alley (1968) studied the effects of the Frostig Program on the reading readiness scores of 108 culturally-deprived kindergarten children. He reported significant differences in mean scores in favor of the group who used the Frostig materials vs. those children who did not receive the Frostig training. It should be emphasized, however, that the fact that these children achieved higher scores on readiness tests does not guarantee that they would therefore achieve higher in reading achievement at the end of the first or second grade.

Results somewhat similar to those in the three studies mentioned above were found by Richard Mould (1965), Robert Leibert and John Sherk (1970), Carl Rosen (1966), and Pearl Buckland (1969). The effectiveness of the Frostig Program seems highly doubtful as evidenced by the conclusions drawn by the following three researchers, who have all studied the literature and/or done research on the Frostig Program. Leibert and Sherk state, "Little evidence was found to support Frostig's contention that 1) specific relationships exist between performance on the Frostig Tests employed in this study and reading performance and 2) that 'normal' visual-perceptual development as measured by Frostig's tests must occur as a prerequisite to 'normal' ability to learn" (p. 137). Helen Robinson (1972), after discussing various research studies dealing with the Frostig Program, states, "The foregoing reports strongly suggest that the Frostig Program of visual-perceptual training is not effective in improving reading regardless of the school level at which it is introduced, the number of periods of instruction, the socio-economic level of the pupils, or the scores the pupils make on the initial visual-perceptual tests" (p. 139).

Another method of dealing with perceptual problems is that of Carl Delacato (1959). Delacato believes that specific "layers" of the brain mediate various motor functions. He believes that training in certain tasks, such as creeping and crawling, will influence various brain centers. These, he believes, will in turn influence the child's perceptual functioning in other areas. Delacato theorizes that the establishment of hemispheric dominance through training in unilateral functioning will improve the sensory functions. To insure that a dominant hemisphere is established, Delacato suggests, for example, that oral reading be done only in stage whispers. He states, "These children should not be asked to read orally other than to whisper the words. This activity tends to increase skill and to activate the dominant or skill hemisphere of the cortex while deactivating the subdominant or tonal hemisphere. By doing so, we increase the possibility of gaining laterality" (p. 25). Delacato also suggests that children in a remedial program should not listen to music, nor should they sing. He believes that this type of activity may activate the subdominant area which he believes would, in turn, interfere with developing the dominant hemisphere. In addition, he suggests that the use of certain sleep patterns or postural positions while sleeping will facilitate the development of unilaterality.

The Delacato Program has been well researched and severely criticized during the past decade, especially by the medical profession. Proof of the merits of the program is sadly lacking. For example, Patrick O'Donnell (1969) studied the effectiveness of the program on students in the second, third, and fourth grades. He found that the students engaged in the Delacato Program as a group did not make substantially greater gains in reading, nor did the proportion of students who developed consistent lateral expression during the study differ significantly from the students in his control group.

Bryant Cratty (1970, p. 256) points out that seven major medical and health organizations (the American Academy for Cerebral Palsy, the American Academy of Physical Medicine, the American Congress of Rehabilitation Medicine, the Canadian Association for Children with Learning Disabilities, the Canadian Association for Retarded Children, the Canadian Rehabilitation Council for the Disabled, and the National Association for Retarded Children) have stated that patterning was "without merit" and have chided its supporters for claiming cures without documentation. Cratty states, "The opinions of medical and research personnel thus seem almost unanimous in their condemnation of the methods and theories advanced by this method of reading remediation" (p. 256).

Another visual-perceptual program is that of G. N. Getman (1968), who places strong emphasis on the visual-perceptual processes. Getman, an optometrist, believes that children should be given tasks in eye patterning and tasks that are somewhat similar to those on intelligence tests. Research on Getman's theories and on the Getman-Kane Program is not nearly so abundant as in the case of the two previously mentioned programs. Carolie Emmons (1968) used the Getman-Kane Perceptual Training Program with one group and a Kephart experimental group exposed to selected gross-motor tasks of the Kephart Training Program. Her pupils were in the first grade. She concluded that neither program produced gains on the Metropolitan Readiness Test or the California Test of Mental Maturity that were significantly greater than a control group which did not receive the training, nor did one program produce significantly greater gains than the other. Emmons stated that within the limits of her investigation gross-motor training is effective only for slow learners. She believed that normal children especially by the age of six have reached a point in readiness that training such as that provided by the Getman-Kane or Kephart programs was ineffective in improving their academic skills.

In Cratty's summary of the research relating to the Getman Program and philosophy, he states,

> It is thus apparent that application of a program of visual training such as that suggested by Getman to large undefined populations of children suffering from mild to moderate educational difficulties is less than sound. Additional evidence is needed before a definitive statement can be made concerning the influence of visual training on ocular functioning, and the influence of ocular training on academic achievement has received only infrequent and cursory attention by investigators (p. 262).

Newell Kephart has written and co-authored several books on the subject of motor development and its relation to academic learning. He has also developed a series of films to explain his theories and has authored a test designed to diagnose difficulties in this area. Kephart's theories have gained a moderate amount of acceptance, although definitive research on his theories is still lacking. William Rutherford (1965) conducted a study to determine whether or not normal kindergarten children would show greater growth in reading, number, and total readiness as a result of a training program based on Kephart's suggestions. The Metropolitan Readiness Test was used as a measure of these criteria. Rutherford's experimental group's mean scores were significantly higher than the mean scores of his control group. He also found the program to be more effective with boys than with girls. Rutherford's study was, however, done with only a small group, and it is quite possible that any one variable —for example, teacher expectation—could have influenced the results more than the program itself. Furthermore, the fact that children achieved higher readiness scores using the program suggested by Kephart would not necessarily mean that these same children would achieve higher in reading at the end of one or more years of school.

Cratty (p. 252) reports a study by Margaret LaPray and Ramon Ross (1967), in which the latter used "Kephart's techniques" to study the effects of these techniques on reading. Cratty reports, as did LaPray and Ross, that the experimental group improved on perceptual-motor tasks, but not significantly more than the improvement of the control group in reading. In all fairness to Kephart, it should be pointed out, however, that LaPray and Ross only said that their study was " . . . ignited by studying the work of Kephart, Getman, Delacato, and others" (p. 530). To intimate that this was a "Kephart study" does not seem justified.

Cratty (p. 252) also reports that Eugene Roach (1967) studied the effects of another Kephart program and obtained results similar to those of LaPray and Ross. Again, in fairness to Kephart, it should be reported that the Roach group received their training for only an eight-week period of time. However, when certain individuals received continued training on an individual basis, they not only made significantly better scores on the Purdue Perceptual-Motor Survey, but they also scored significantly higher (.05 level) on the Gates-McKillop Reading Diagnostic Test than a control group who continued to receive group training.

It should also be pointed out that Kephart has been especially interested in the diagnosis and treatment of children on an individual basis and that in his clinic he has been quite successful in attacking perceptual problems from that standpoint. It seems unlikely that many of the so-called group "Kephart Programs" would have been called "Kephart Programs" by Kephart himself.

A review of the literature indicates that we have yet to prove that the various programs discussed here have generalizability and transferability to areas of academic learning. On the other hand, there is little doubt that in the majority of the cases there has been a rather clearly-demonstrated improvement in the perceptual skills directly related to those being taught. A well-designed study reported by Marion Faustman (1968) points out the possibility, however, that combining the ideas of several authors and the material from several programs may produce more positive results than any single program could have or has produced thus far. In the Faustman study, children in the fourteen experimental kindergarten classes were given perceptual training, while fourteen other kindergarten classes served as a control. Faustman describes the overall program as follows:

> The perception training consisted of use of materials and methods advocated by Frostig, Strauss, and Kephart, as well as materials and methods suggested by this writer. Teacher made materials following the five areas of visual perception identified by Frostig as Visual-Motor, Figure-Ground, Position-In-Space, Form Constancy, and Spatial Relations were also utilized. The Winterhaven Program for perception was added with template training and form recall. Template training was planned for no more than three times a week. Manipulating objects to ascertain relative size, shape, and texture, classifying into ordinate categories, and simple coding were also taught. Language experience and the learnings outlined in the kindergarten guide formed the basis for both the experimental and regular kindergarten programs. Perception training was added to the program for the experimental kindergartens (p. 99).

After their year of perceptual training in kindergarten, the pupils entered first grade mixed in with many other children who had not received perceptual training. The first grade teachers were not told which children had been through the perceptual training program. At the end of first grade, children who had been in the experimental groups scored significantly higher (.01 level) on the Gates Word Recognition Test than did the control group.

Bryant Cratty (pp. 264-65) believes that some programs have been somewhat successful because they provide certain children with much-needed individual attention. He also suggests that children who are kept at certain visual or visual-motor tasks for sustained periods of time may in turn simply learn to prolong their attention span. The results of studies on the effect of individual tutorial programs add credence to this belief.

At this point in the study of various perceptual training programs, a statement made by Bruce Balow (1971) in discussing perceptual-motor activities in the treatment of severe reading disability seems adroit in summarizing the state we are in. Balow says, "When some real answers are obtained, it is almost certain that they will be quite complex and will point to highly individualized programs of correction" (p. 513).

A Look To the Future

Any accurate prognosticating that is done concerning the future in the area of perceptual training for improving reading ability may be somewhat hazardous because of the often-conflicting research in this area. Certain trends, however, are appearing and each study, although often in conflict with others, may bring at least one important factor to the surface or may lend credence to the results of other studies. Some of these trends and factors as well as suggestions for future research are:

1.   There is considerable evidence that certain perceptual programs, although seldom helpful for groups of children, may be of considerable benefit to individual children. As more is learned about the functioning of the nervous system and about testing for various areas of perception and their relationships to each other, we are likely to see more theoretical models developed. Using these models we can then test and discard or test and retain until we have an accurate model upon which a diagnostic-prescriptive system can be based.

2.   A number of researchers such as Wepman and Morency agree that we must locate and capitalize on the strongest learning modality and build on the weaker modalities of each child. Wepman says, "To understand the effect of modality preference on such skills as reading, speech, and spelling, one must not only be able to isolate the preferred modality but also be able to assess the level of achievement and the potential for training of whatever modality is delayed in its development" (p. 3). Wepman also states, "Where a lag in the developmental process along any of the modalities can be determined, the remedial task seems most properly directed at that modality" (p. 6). In a discussion of her research on this subject, Morency states, "For the purposes of individual maximum potential education, ability grouping on the basis of modality preference as shown by the test results would seem in order" (p. 21). Morency notes that the notion of a developmental progression in perceptual ability was confirmed by the performance of the children in her study. She also states, "It should be noted, too, that the coefficients of correlation of improvement in the auditory modality with improvement in the visual modality are low, a finding which means that children who improve in one modality may or may not improve in the other" (p. 18).

3.   There is an indication that some children need to be desensitized to the reading or school situation before any learning can take place.

4.   Certain studies have indicated that individual children have improved as a result of perceptual training programs because of the development of their ability to attend and concentrate. Perhaps the development of programs solely for this purpose is in order.

5.   Although the use of drugs for perceptual problems may not be appropriate for most children, there is considerable evidence that for some children with perceptual problems drugs have been extremely effective. The problem is that the prescription of drugs in these cases has been largely a hit-or-miss situation. However, for the small percentage of children who do benefit from such treatment, the change is often nearly immediate as well as substantial. It seems quite possible that diagnostic instruments could be developed that would indicate which children are likely to benefit from treatment with drugs and that diagnostic instruments could also point to the prescription of the proper *type* of drug.

6.   Perceptual tests and perceptual programs have often neglected to test and/or teach auditory memory and visual memory. In reading, these skills seem to be of equal importance to auditory and visual discrimination. Tests and programs need to be developed which will test not just the ability to repeat digits forward and backward or that will test children's ability to remember the shape of a triangle or square. We need tests that will test these abilities in a situation analogous to what a child actually does when he reads. For example, auditory memory might be tested and taught by having a child attempt to remember phrases and sentences, and visual memory could be tested and taught by having children attempt to recall letter groups and words.

7.   There is ample evidence to support a statement that perceptual training closely related to actual reading is more likely to produce children who read better than perceptual training dealing with abstract symbols or eye-motor coordination. Typical of these findings and researchers' statements about them is that of S. Alan Cohen (1970), who studied various methods of teaching reading and/or training disadvantaged children in visual perceptual tasks. In summarizing his research he states, "To put it succinctly, on the basis of present data, I would play the visual perceptual game if I were in the visual perception or the I.Q. business. But in the reading field, the surest way to get urban ghetto kids to read is to teach them letters and words and to do it thoroughly" (p. 503).

References

Alley, G., and Snider, W. "Reading readiness and the Frostig program." *Exceptional Children* 35 (1968): 68-69.

Balow, B. "Perceptual-motor activities in the treatment of severe reading disability." *The Reading Teacher* 24 (1971): 513-25 ff.

Bateman, B. "The efficacy of an auditory and a visual method of first grade reading instructions with auditory and visual learners." In *Perception and Reading,* edited by Helen K. Smith. Proceedings of the twelfth annual convention of the International Reading Association. Newark, Del.: IRA, 1968.

Bender, L. *Bender visual-motor test and its clinical uses.* New York: Psychological Corporation, 1938, revised 1946.

Blom, G. E. "The concept, 'perceptually handicapped,' its assets and limitations." Denver: Colorado University, Denver Medical Center, April 1968, p. 2.

Boyd, L. et al. "Factor analysis of the Frostig developmental test of visual perception." *Journal of Learning Disabilities* 3(1970): 253-55.

Buckland, P. "The effect of visual perception training on reading achievement of low readiness first grade pupils." Doctoral dissertation, University of Minnesota, 1969.

Bugelski, B. R. *The psychology of learning applied to teaching.* Indianapolis: Bobbs-Merrill, 1964.

Cohen, S. A. "Studies in visual perception and reading in disadvantaged children." *Journal of Learning Disabilities* 2 (1969): 498-507.

Cratty, B. J. *Perceptual and motor development in infants and children.* London: Macmillan, 1970.

Delacato, C. H. *The treatment and prevention of reading problems.* Springfield, Ill.: Charles C. Thomas, 1959.

Deutsch, C. P. "Sociocultural influences and learning channels." In *Perception and Reading,* edited by Helen K. Smith. Proceedings of the twelfth annual convention of the International Reading Association. Newark, Del.: IRA, 1968.

Emmons, C. A. "A comparison of selected gross-motor activities of the Getman-Kane and the Kephart perceptual-motor training programs and their effects upon certain readiness skills of first-grade Negro children." Doctoral dissertation, Ohio State University, 1968.

Faustman, M. N. "Some effects of perception training in kindergarten on first grade in reading." In *Perception and Reading,* edited by Helen K. Smith. Proceedings of the twelfth annual convention of the International Reading Association. Newark, Del.: IRA, 1968.

Frostig, M. et al. *Developmental test of visual perception.* Rev. ed. Palo Alto: Consulting Psychologists Press, 1966.

Frostig, M., and Horne, D. *The Frostig program for the development of visual perception.* Chicago: Follett, 1964.

Getman, G. N. et al. *Developing learning readiness.* St. Louis: Webster Division McGraw-Hill Publishing Co., 1968.

Hammill, D. D. et al. "Diagnostic value of the Frostig test: A factor analytic approach." *The Journal of Special Education,* Summer-Fall 1970, pp 279-82.

Jacobs, James. "An evaluation of the Frostig visual-perceptual training program." *Educational Leadership* 25 (1968): 332-40.

Kaluger, G., and Kolson, C. J. *Reading and learning disabilities.* Columbus, Ohio: Charles E. Merrill, 1969.

Koppitz, E. M. *The Bender-gestalt test for young children.* New York: Grune and Stratton, 1964.

Lachman, F. "Perceptual-motor development in children retarded in reading ability." *Journal of Consulting Psychology* 26 (1960): 427-31.

LaPray, M., Ross, R. "Auditory and visual perceptual training." In *Vistas In Reading,* edited by J. Allen Figurel. Proceedings of the eleventh annual convention of the International Reading Association. Newark, Del.: IRA, 1967.

Leibert, R. E., and Sherk, J. K. Three Frostig perception Sub-tests and specific reading tasks for kindergarten, first, and second grade children." *The Reading Teacher* 24 (1970): 130-37.

Morency, A. "Auditory modality, research and practice." In *Perception and Reading,* edited by Helen K. Smith. Proceedings of the twelfth annual convention of the International Reading Association. Newark, Del.: IRA, 1968.

Mould, Richard, "An evaluation of the effectiveness of a special program for retarded readers manifesting disturbed visual perception." Doctoral dissertation, Washington State University, 1965.

O'Donnell, P. A. "The effects of Delacato training on reading achievement and visual-motor integration." Doctoral dissertation, Stanford University, 1969.

Olson, A. "The Frostig developmental test of visual perception as a predictor of specific reading abilities with second-grade children." *Elementary English* 43 (1966): 869-72.

Roach, E. G. "Evaluation of an experimental program of perceptual-motor training with slow readers." In *Vistas In Reading,* edited by J. Allen Figurel. Proceedings of the eleventh annual convention of the International Reading Association. Newark, Del.: IRA, 1967.

Roach, E. G., and Kephart, N. C. *The Purdue perceptual-motor survey.* Columbus, Ohio: Charles E. Merrill, 1966.

Robertson, J. E. "Kindergarten perception training: Its effects on first grade reading." In *Perception and Reading,* edited by Helen K. Smith. Proceedings of the twelfth annual convention of the International Reading Association. Newark, Del.: IRA, 1968.

Robinson, H. M. "Perceptual training — does it result in reading improvement?" In *Some Persistent Questions on Beginning Reading,* edited by Robert C. Aukerman. Newark, Del.: IRA, 1972.

Rosen, C. L. "A study of visual perception capabilities of first grade pupils and the relationship between visual perception training and reading achievement." Doctoral dissertation, University of Minnesota, 1965.

Rutherford, W. L. "The effects of a perceptual-motor training program on the performance of kindergarten pupils on metropolitan readiness tests." Doctoral dissertation, North Texas State University, 1964.

Sabatino, D. A. "The construction and assessment of an experimental test of auditory perception." *Exceptional Children* 35 (1969): 730.

Sherk, J. K. "A study of the effects of a program of visual perceptual training on the progress of retarded readers." Doctoral dissertation, Syracuse University, 1967.

Spache, George D. and Spache, Evelyn B. *Reading in the elementary school.* Boston: Allyn & Bacon, 1969.

Wepman, J. M. *Auditory discrimination test.* Privately published. Chicago, 1958.

_____. "The modality concept including a statement of the perceptual and conceptual levels of learning." In *Perception and Reading,* edited by Helen K. Smith. Proceedings of the twelfth annual convention of the International Reading Association. Newark, Del.: IRA, 1968.

Wheelock, W. H. "An investigation of visual discrimination training for beginning readers." In *Perception and Reading,* edited by Helen K. Smith. Proceedings of the twelfth annual convention of the International Reading Association. Newark, Del.: IRA, 1968.

Perception and Reading

Ekwall—Questioning for Discussion

What is the difference between perception and the simple reception of a stimulus? What perceptual areas are most important to reading?

Does there appear to be a developmental sequence to most perceptual abilities? Have the Frostig and/or Getman-Kane perceptual training programs been of any real value? Have they possibly harmed some pupils? How does a child's environment affect his perceptual abilities? What are some causes of perceptual difficulties? How can various perceptual difficulties be diagnosed? Based on past perceptual research, what recommendations would you make for further research?

CHAPTER NINE

Cultural
Influences
in Reading

The articles in this chapter present a summary of some of the many problems encountered by the disadvantaged child. They also contain some worthwhile suggestions for the improvement of presently existing programs as well as a description of the disadvantaged child who is successful in school. An important point stressed by Arthur B. Jensen in the first article is that we should not feel that since there is a great deal of writing on the culturally-disadvantaged child there should also be a lot of good research on good programs. Definitive research is lacking and sorely needed. As you read this series of articles, you will note that almost all of the authors are in agreement as to what needs to be done. Furthermore, almost all of these authorities agree that these suggestions can be and are being carried out in some schools without a great deal of difficulty. Yet, as one observes kindergarten and Head Start programs, it is often apparent that the training received by these teachers did not prepare them for the job that these authors say must be done. There is a gap between good research and writing and what is being practiced in many classrooms.

In the first article Arthur R. Jensen describes some interesting research concerning the I.Q.'s of various socioeconomic groups and discusses a number of other factors in relationship to the culturally disadvantaged. This article contains a good deal of food for thought, an excellent discussion of present compensatory education for the culturally disadvantaged, and some excellent recommendations for improving their education.

Dina Feitelson's article stresses that compensatory education for the culturally disadvantaged must contain provisions for developing cognitive skills, motor skills, and linguistic proficiency, as well as those abilities within the realm of the affective domain. She also offers some concrete suggestions for building self-confidence in children with poor self-concepts.

The articles by Alwin B. Coleman lists some of the factors that are common among disadvantaged children who are successful in school and summarizes those factors that he believes are responsible for this school success.

As you read this series of articles, you will be interested in the authors' comments concerning questions such as the following: Is there really a basic difference in the I.Q.'s of various ethnic groups? What kinds of programs have been successful with culturally-deprived children? Do we need to focus more attention on the cognitive, affective, or psychomotor domain, or are most culturally-deprived children deficient in all three areas? Does there seem to be a cluster of factors or symptoms that characterize the dropout? Do remedial procedures become more difficult as the culturally-deprived child grows older?

Arthur R. Jensen

The Culturally Disadvantaged:
Psychological and Educational Aspects

The literature on children called culturally disadvantaged that has recently proliferated is likely to give the impression to those who have not surveyed it in detail that much scientifically verified knowledge is now at hand as a sound basis for large-scale ameliorative action promising highly predictable and optimal results.

This is an incorrect impression. Although substantial knowledge about disadvantaged children, particularly of a demographic nature, is now available, the literature dealing with the psychological aspects of the problem is better viewed as a source of programmes for research and theoretical formulation. It is important to keep this in mind, not to discourage action programmes, which are obviously needed immediately, but to ensure that such action programmes are conceived of and conducted as research and not as the application of knowledge already established by research. This means that school programmes for the disadvantaged should be conducted, as far as possible, in the manner of scientific experimentation, which is to say with great attention to control and description of the "input" variables (what we do with the children, their parents, their environments, etc.) and the "output" variables (how the children respond). As in any investigation which attempts to evaluate the effects of an experimental variable, there should be appropriate control groups. Finally, there should be careful description of the population's social, economic, racial, family, and individual psychological characteristics.

From Arthur R. Jensen, "The Culturally Disadvantaged: Psychological and Educational Aspects," *Educational Research* 10, no. 1 (January 1968): 4-20. Reprinted by permission of the author and the journal.

The aim of this report is to indicate some of the main trends of thought and research on the psychology of disadvantaged children, to comment particularly on the research findings and hypotheses which seem to have the most direct implications for ameliorative action, and to point out a few of the most crucial gaps in our current knowledge and the controversies issuing from them.

Description and Assessment
of the Culturally Retarded

Descriptions of the disadvantaged have usually consisted of both environmental and personal characteristics. There is seldom any attempt to separate the causal, or background, factors from the supposedly resultant behavioural characteristics, of which the most important to the educator is the low educability of the disadvantaged child. In fact, low or mediocre intelligence (as assessed by standard intelligence tests) and particularly poor school achievement, are often included in the definition and identification of the "culturally deprived," along with such criteria as low socio-economic status and culturally impoverished home environment. The relatively rare slum child with a high IQ and superior school achievement is often not regarded as being culturally disadvantaged, while low-IQ, low-achieving pupils from what may appear to be very similar home backgrounds are characterized as disadvantaged and their poor school performance is attributed largely to this condition.

The question raised by this type of definition is not without important practical implications. If we assume that the low-IQ children actually have the potential both for higher intelligence and for normal progress in school, but have merely been "depressed" by an unfavourable environment, we must ask if average or above-average culturally disadvantaged children are similarly depressed. A slum child with an IQ of 115 might thus have the intellectual potential of the middle-class child with an IQ of 130 or 140, and he might be able to realize this potential more fully if he were provided with the right kind of cultural stimulation at some stage of his development. Thus, in looking for potential college material among low socio-economic status children, we might pin our greatest hopes on those already of at least average ability, despite a poor environment, and simply regard most low "socio-economic-status" children (whose IQ's are in the "dull" range of intelligence, that is, from 75 to 95), though capable of benefiting educationally from intervention programmes such as Head Start, as more or less destined for intellectual and occupational mediocrity. This widespread belief gives rise to various plans for watered-down, less intellectual, and less academic educational programmes tailored to the apparent limitations of a large proportion (at least one-half to two-thirds) of low socio-economic status children. This is a harmful and unjust set of beliefs, if acted upon, since some evidence now makes it reasonable (though surprising) to hypothesize that a greater absolute amount of educational potential may exist among the low socio-economic status children who, under present circumstances, obtain IQs in the range of 70 to 90 than among those whose measured IQs are in the above-average range from about 100 to 120. To state this proposition even more paradoxically, we can hypothesize that there is a greater chance of finding a potential IQ of 130, or 140, or 150 among the groups whose measured IQs are 70 to 90 than among the group whose IQs are 100 to 120, providing we are dealing with a population regarded by the usual criteria as predominantly culturally disadvantaged. All the evidence, which is massive, indicates conclusively that such a prediction with respect to children from middle-class families would be utterly ridiculous. With respect to low socio-economic status children (especially, in the U.S.A., Negroes; and possibly, in Britain, children of immigrant groups), however, it is a hypothesis worth investigating. No evidence as yet contradicts the hypothesis, and some evidence makes it seem reasonable, and, in fact, suggested this seemingly paradoxical idea in the first place (Jensen, 1963). But before we can elaborate on this line of thought, some supporting background information must be provided.

Differential Diagnosis of Cultural Retardation

In principle, intellectual and educational retardation can and must be clearly distinguished from what we will here refer to as primary retardation. Primary and cultural retardation are not at all mutually exclusive; one may exist without the other, or they may exist in independently varying degrees simultaneously. There is substantial evidence of some degree of correlation, albeit quite low, between primary and cultural retardation in the total population (Burt and Howard, 1956; Tyler, 1965).

Primary retardation can be subdivided into three main types, all having an essentially biological causation: (1) an inevitable consequence of what geneticists call the multifactorial or polygenic inheritance of intelligence; (2) a result of a single, major gene defect; and (3) a result of brain damage. Factors 1 and 3 and factors 2 and 3 are not mutually exclusive, but may occur singly or together. Factor 2, however, always overrides factor 1, so that when factor 2 is involved, factor 1 is of almost no importance.

Polygenic Inheritance

Intelligence is inherited in much the same fashion as height (Burt, 1955, 1958, 1966; Burt and Howard, 1956; Huntley, 1966; Pearson, 1903). It is the result of a large number of genes each having a small additive effect. Because of random assortment of these genes, the total additive effect will be normally distributed in the population. Thus, the hereditary mechanism (in effect a random lottery) that results in one person's being bright, results in another's being dull, and the person who is dull or mentally retarded for this reason is, biologically speaking, no more abnormal or pathological than the average or bright person or the short or tall person. He is simply a part of normal variation. Being at the very low end of the distribution may be a personal misfortune from an educational standpoint, but it is not an abnormality in a medical or psychological sense and is presumably not biologically or environmentally remediable. (In this respect dullness and brightness are genetically quite analogous to shortness and tallness of stature.) Persons at the low end of the distribution of intelligence need educational treatment somewhat different from that afforded average and bright persons. The majority of dull children in our schools who do not show neurological signs of organic impairment are of this type, regardless of their race or social class. For these children, education must be modified in accordance with their intellectual limitations, which is not to say that an appropriate education is not just as important for them as for the bright child. It must simply be a different kind of education, with different goals. The great misfortune of culturally disadvantaged children is that many are treated educationally (and they often perform accordingly) as if they were at the lower end of the genetic distribution of intelligence when, in fact, they may be in the middle or even at the upper end of the distribution. Failure to distinguish between hereditary retardation and cultural retardation, as well as being a social injustice, results in a waste of educational potential and talent. The consequences are especially damaging to the social progress of minority groups, and the costs are borne by our whole society. The discrimination between cultural and genetic retardation in the culturally disadvantaged is a difficult diagnostic problem which does not even arise in middle-class children, with exceedingly rare exceptions, since retardation in this group is almost always of the primary type. There are, of course, gradations of cultural retardation, just as there are gradations of primary retardation. But it is unlikely that the degree of cultural retardation is a simple linear function of the degree of environmental impoverishment. There is evidence that the environment may act as a threshold variable in such a way that a quite severe degree of environmental deprivation must exist in order to produce cultural retardation in a child of normal genetic potential. This idea is explicated more fully in a later section of this paper.

Major Gene Defect

Practically all severe forms of mental deficiency, where the IQ is below 50, are the results either of severe brain damage or of major gene defects (Ellis, 1963, p. 276). Examples of major gene defects are Mongolism, phenylketonuria, and amaurotic idiocy. Genetically these intellectual defects are analogous to dwarfism in the trait of stature. They are caused by Mendelian inheritance of a single gene or by a mutant gene, which for all practical purposes may be regarded as completely overriding the normal polygenic determinants of intelligence. The resulting severe degree of mental defect, which is generally easy to diagnose in the first days or weeks of life, is not of concern in the present discussion except to distinguish it from retardation which constitutes a part of normal variation.

Brain Damage

Brain damage, especially prenatal and perinatal, is a continuous variable; that is, its effects can range from the negligible to the disastrous, and the effects can be manifest at all levels of genetic potential. Thus, a child who would have grown up to have an adult IQ of, say, 150 may, as a result of the brain damage incurred by anoxia at birth, have an actual IQ of 140. The literature on the subject suggests that brain damage to a degree that makes a difference in measurable mental ability is sufficiently rare not to constitute an appreciable source of variance in intellectual ability in the total population. An upper-limit estimate would be about five per cent of the total variance of measured intelligence, which means that, on the average, brain damage lowers the IQ only slightly more than three IQ points (Corah, *et al.*, 1965; Eichenwald, 1966; Graham, *et al.*, 1962; Pasamanick and Knobloch, 1966). Of course, the effects of brain damage in individual cases may be intellectually devastating. There is also evidence that brain damage has a higher incidence in low socio-economic status groups in which the mother's nutrition, prenatal care, and obstetrical practices are substandard (Osler and Cooke, 1965). All possible efforts should, of course, be made to minimize these conditions in order to decrease the chances of brain damage, but these ameliorative efforts should prove considerably easier than combating the causal agents of *cultural* retardation *per se.*

All three types of primary retardation have three major effects in common: they result in below-average measured intelligence (IQ), in below-average educability in school subjects, and in a slow rate of what we shall refer to as basic learning ability. Cultural retardation, on the other hand, is distinguishable from primary retardation, at least in principle, on this third factor—basic learning ability. While cultural deprivation results in lowered IQ and lowered school achievement, it does not, except in extreme rare cases, result in lowered basic learning ability. This is a theoretically and practically important distinction, because it means that in trying to improve the educability of the culturally disadvantaged, we are trying not to make over genetically poor material but to allow sound innate learning potential to manifest itself. But now, to present further our thesis, we must clarify the special meaning we have given the terms *intelligence, basic learning ability,* and *educability.*

Intelligence, Learning Ability and Educability

Standard intelligence tests, such as the Stanford-Binet and the Wechsler, are measures of specific knowledge and problem solving skills which have been acquired by the testee at some time prior to the test situation. Mental age is determined directly from the amount of such knowledge and skill. By taking into account the amount of time the individual has had to acquire this knowledge, that is, his chronological age, we obtain a measure of learning rate expressed as the IQ. The validity of the IQ as a measure of learning ability, therefore, depends to a large extent upon equal opportunity for exposure to knowledge and skills that the test calls upon. Since intelligence tests were originally devised to predict school performance, they call upon knowledge and cognitive skills similar to the kinds of learning required in school—skills which are more or less prerequisite for school learning and which have considerable transfer value in the classroom.

Now, if IQ is a measure of learning rate, we should expect that learning tasks of the type used by experimental psychologists to study learning should show substantial positive correlations with IQ. This, in fact, is exactly what our research has found (e.g. Jensen, 1965). But here is the interesting thing: the correlation between IQ and learning ability, as measured directly in a controlled laboratory learning task, is much higher among middle-class children than among lower-class children (Jensen, 1961, 1963; Rapier 1966). Furthermore, in comparing level of performance (i.e. speed of learning) as a function of IQ level and of social-class (lower vs. middle), we have found in several studies that low-IQ (60-85) lower-class children are, on the average, markedly superior in learning ability to low-IQ middle-class children. In the IQ range above 100, on the other hand, there are not significant differences in learning ability between lower-and middle-class children matched for IQ. This suggests that once the IQ has exceeded a certain level (somewhere in the neighbourhood of 100 to 110), it gives a fairly accurate assessment of learning ability regardless of social-class level. In the lower IQ range (which, incidentally, contains the modal performance of lower-class children), the IQ test grossly underestimates learning ability among lower-class children. We are speaking here, of course, only of averages, for a certain proportion of lower-class low-IQ children are slow learners on the laboratory tasks just as are middle-class low-IQ children. The middle-class low-IQ group seems to be made up almost completely of slow learners. But the lower-class low-IQ group contains all levels of learning ability. The probability of finding a very fast learner (i.e. learning speed comparable to that of 'gifted' middle-class children) seems to be greater in the low-IQ low socio-economic-status than in the average IQ range of either social-class group. This suggests that the IQ is almost totally unpredictive of learning ability in the low-IQ range for low socio-economic-status children. It should be noted that the majority of low socio-economic-status children are in the below-average IQ range. This is especially true for Negroes in the U.S.A. On a national average only about 12 per cent of Negroes exceed the median IQ of the white population (McGurk, 1956; Tyler, 1965; Shuey, 1966).

In view of what has been said above, it might seem puzzling that the IQ is substantially correlated (correlations between .50 and .70) with school achievement regardless of social class. Ability for school learning may be referred to as *educability*. Educability is much more complexly determined than intelligence or learning ability. For one thing, it depends not only upon learning ability of the type measured in the laboratory, in which transfer from prior learning is relatively unimportant, but also upon a fund of prior knowledge, skills, and acquired cognitive habits, much of which is tapped by intelligence tests. But educability also involves much more than these intellectual abilities, as indicated by the fact that intelligence tests do not account for more than about 50 per cent of the variance in school achievement. A host of other factors must be taken into account to "explain" the remaining variance. These are usually described under labels, such as attitudes, motivation, work habits, regularity of school attendance, parental interest, and help in school work.

Another point of interest and educational implication lies in a comparison of the heritabilities of intelligence and of educability. Despite the popular denigration of the genetic study of intelligence in educational circles in recent years, it is entirely possible to estimate the relative contributions of heredity and environment to the total variation in intelligence in a given population. The numerous studies done in this field over the past fifty years show a great consistency (Erlenmeyer-Kimling and Jarvik, 1963). They indicate that in Caucasian populations above the poverty line (and this is an important qualification), some 80 to 90 per cent of the variability in measured intelligence can be attributable to genetic factors and about 5 to 10 per cent to social environmental factors (Burt, 1958). (The remaining variance is divided between biological environmental factors and error of measurement). The genetic component in school achievement or educability, on the other hand, is much less than for intelligence, accounting for only 40 to 50 per cent of the total variance (Burt, 1958; Jensen, 1967). Family influences largely account for the remaining variance. One of the obvious tasks of educational psychology and sociology is the analysis and isolation of these environmental influences on educability, so that they may be provided by one means or another when they are lacking in the child's natural environment. But before these environmental factors are discussed, a few other points need to be made concerning the inheritance of intelligence and the distribution of intelligence in the total population.

Environment as a
Threshold Variable

By virtue of a largely fortuitous set of conditions, the Stanford-Binet intelligence test, when used on a white American population, which for the most part excludes the lowest segment of the socio-economic-status continuum, yields a distribution of IQs which conforms almost exactly to the so-called normal or Gaussian distribution. This is the distribution one would expect on the basis of polygenic inheritance of intelligence (Burt, 1957, 1963). In this same population, estimates of the genetic component in the variance of intelligence range between 80 and 90 per cent (Burt, 1958). Even the seemingly rather large environmental variations within this bulk of the American population apparently contribute very little to the variance in intelligence, as measured by an excellently constructed test such as the Stanford-Binet.

However, if the Stanford-Binet is administered to a large and truly representative sample of the total population (or to the *entire* population of school children, as was done in Scotland in 1947), we find that the distribution of IQs departs in a very systematic way from the normal Gaussian distribution. There is a bulge (i.e. excess frequency) in the lower half of the distribution, especially in the IQ range from about 65 to 90 (Burt, 1957, 1963). This suggests the presence of some nongenetic influence which hinders intellectual development. (Another possible explanation is the differential fertility of dull and bright persons, there being a negative correlation of about -0.2 between intelligence and family size, which would result in there being a slight preponderance of low IQs. This theory is seriously undermined by the fact that by far the best explanation for the negative correlation between family size and IQ involves strictly environmental causation; there is no equally reasonable genetic interpretation of this correlation.) An American study shows that if low socio-economic-status subjects are removed from the distribution, and especially if Negroes are removed, the distribution again closely approximates the normal (Kennedy, Van de Riet, and White, 1963). There is always a slight bulge however, at the very lowest end of the distribution below an IQ of 50, due to major gene defects and brain damage (Zigler, 1967).

These facts taken together are consistent with the hypothesis that the environment influences the development of intelligence as a threshold variable. (Actually it is best thought of as a number of thresholds). That is to say, once certain kinds of environmental influences are present to a probably rather minimal degree, the individual's genetic potential for the development of intelligence will be more or less fully realized, and variations in the extent of these influences beyond this minimal threshold level will make only a slight contribution to the variance in measured intelligence. The situation is analogous to diet and physical stature. Once the diet is up to a certain minimal standard of adequacy with respect to vitamins, minerals, and proteins, the addition of more of these elements to the diet will not make any appreciable difference in physique; if they are present in the required minimal amounts, it will make no difference whether the person lives on beans and hamburger or on Oysters Rockefeller and pheasant-under-glass — the genes will entirely determine variations in stature. The case for intelligence seems much the same.

Another line of evidence is quite consistent with this threshold hypothesis, namely the studies concerned with upward changes in the IQ as a result of rather drastic environmental changes, either from "natural" causes or by means of experimental manipulation of the environment. Environmental changes or manipulations seem to affect to any marked degree only those children whose social environments are quite wretched and clearly below what is presumably the environmental threshold for the normal development of genetic intellectual potential. Thus, when children are removed as infants from very poor homes, in which the natural parents have subnormal IQs, and are placed in foster homes, in which the foster parents are of average or superior intelligence, the children will grow up to obtain IQs that may be from 10 to 30 points higher than would be predicted if they had been reared by their natural parents, and their educational attainments will be even higher (Skodak and Skeels, 1966). (Of course, due allowance is made here for statistical regression.) It is only when there is a great discrepancy between the early environmental background of the natural parents and the environment provided for their children by the superior foster parents that we find evidence of a substantial boost in the children's IQs. It is simply a case of innate intellectual potential receiving the nurturance needed for its full development. It is also instructive to note that even though the IQs of foster parents may span a fairly wide range, the IQs of foster children are not correlated in the least with those of their foster parents (Honzik, 1957). Again, once the threshold of adequate environment is attained (the adoption agencies see that this is nearly always the case in foster homes), practically all the variability in the children's IQs will be determined by genetic factors.

Social Class and Intelligence

It has been hypothesized that the bulge in the lower half of the distribution of IQs is due to the proportion of the population reared under conditions which are below the threshold of those environmental influences necessary for the full development of genetic intellectual potential. Thus, presumably, if these environmental lacks were eliminated, the bulge in the distribution of IQs would be smoothed out and the distribution would more nearly approximate to the Gaussian curve required by genetic theory. The portion of the population which contributed to the bulge would become redistributed at various higher points along the IQ scale; some would make only very slight gains, while others would make considerable gains in IQ. It would be difficult to estimate precisely the average expected gain, but it is likely to be somewhere between 10 and 20 IQ points.

Differences in mean IQ among various social classes and occupational levels are, of course, a well-established fact. But it is commonly believed that *all* of the socio-economic-status differences are due to environmental factors and none to differences in genetic potential. Though the evidence on this point is quite complex, and therefore cannot be presented in this brief paper, it suggests the conclusion that social classes probably differ in innate potential (Burt, 1961; Burt and Howard, 1956). Perhaps as much as half of the between-classes variance in IQ is genetically determined. Several lines of evidence lead to this conclusion. One of the most striking is the phenomenon of regression to the population mean, which can be most satisfactorily accounted for in terms of genetic mechanisms. Even though low socio-economic-status parents provide a poor environment for their children, their children, on the average, have higher intelligence than the parents; and though high socio-economic-status parents provide a good environment for their children — often better than the environment they themselves grew up in — their children, on the average, have *lower* IQs than the parents (Burt, 1961; Jensen, 1968). This would be almost paradoxical from an environmentalist point of view, while it is completely in accord with genetic expectations. Also, it should be pointed out that the greater the equality of opportunity in a society and the fewer the restraints on social mobility, the greater will become the genetic differences between social classes. The educational and occupational hierarchies act as an intellectual screening device. Genetic differences between social classes could be minimized only by means of imposing rigid and impermeable class and caste boundaries that would rule out social mobility for many generations. This obviously is the very antithesis of a democratic society which, strange as it may seem at first glance, actually tends to maximize genetic differences and minimize environmental differences as a basis of social and economic rewards.

Racial Differences in Intelligence

The above statements concerning socio-economic-status differences in innate potential cannot be applied to differences between racial groups when there are greater barriers to social and occupational mobility in one racial group than in another, as is clearly the case for Negroes and Mexicans as compared with Caucasians of European origin in the U.S.A. There are probably socio-economic-status differences in innate intellectual potential *within* any particular racial group, but these innate differences would be diminished to the extent that intellectually irrelevant genetic factors, such as lightness of skin color and other caucasoid features, are important as determinants of social and occupational mobility. Therefore, the fact that Negroes and Mexicans are disproportionately represented in the lower end of the socio-economic-status scale cannot be interpreted as evidence of poor genetic potential. For we know that there have been, and are still, powerful racial barriers to social mobility. Innate potential should be much more highly correlated with socio-economic-status among whites than among Negroes or other easily distinguishable minorities, who are discriminated against on the basis of intellectually irrelevant characteristics.

The Negro population in the U.S.A. as a whole has an average IQ about 15 to 20 points below the average for the white population, and the variance of Negro intelligence is less than 60 per cent that in the white population (Kennedy, Van de Riet, and White, 1963; Tyler, 1965). The Negro population (11 per cent of the total U.S. population) is thus largely bunched up in that lower part of the IQ distribution where we find the bulge or departure from the so-called normal distribution. Since we know that the Negro population for the most part has suffered socio-economic and cultural disadvantages for generations past, it seems a reasonable hypothesis that their low-average IQ is due to environmental rather than to genetic factors. A much larger proportion of Negroes (and Mexicans) than of whites probably grow up under conditions that may be *below* the environmental threshold required for the realization of genetic potential. It also appears that the economic condition of the Negro, which has markedly improved over the past two generations, does not bear a close relationship to the really crucial environmental threshold variables. It has been pointed out that the rise of the Negro IQ since World War I has not been nearly commensurate with the improvement of the Negroes' economic condition (McGurk, 1956). But the important environmental threshold variables, mainly interpersonal and psychological in nature, seem to be only incidentally correlated with economic status. Except in the most extreme cases, economic factors in themselves seem to have little causal potency as determinants of IQ and educability.

Environmental Influences on Intelligence and Educability

It remains now to identify those environmental factors presently thought to be the most potential influences in the development of intellectual and educational potential. In recent years there has been a shifting of emphasis by psychologists working in this area. The trend has been away from rather crude socio-economic variables towards more subtle intrafamily and interpersonal psychological variables. This shift in emphasis is given cogency by the fact that crude socio-economic variables, such as income, occupation, and neighbourhood, do not correlate as highly with intelligence and educability as do ratings of more psychological variables, such as whether the parents read to the children during the preschool years, whether the family eats together, whether children are brought into the conversation at the dinner table, and other features of parent-child interaction, especially involving verbal behaviour. The usual socio-economic variables found to correlate with IQ and educability have shown correlations in the range from .30 to .50. At most, only about 30 per cent of the variance in intelligence can be predicted from a composite of various indices of socio-economic status. Most variables that index socio-economic status, however, are better thought of as incidental correlates of IQ rather than as causal factors. The quality of the parent-child relationships, on the other hand, may be thought of as causal correlation, even though one cannot overlook the high probability that the quality of the parent-child interaction is influenced to a not inconsiderable degree by the genetic potential of both the parents and their children.

What are some of the environmental variables most highly associated with the development of intelligence? Wolf (cited in Bloom, 1964, pp. 78-9) found that ratings on 13 process variables, describing the interactions between parents and children, would yield a multiple correlation with intelligence of +.76. These variables may be classified as follows:

(a) Press for Achievement Motivation
   1. Nature of intellectual expectations of child
   2. Nature of intellectual aspirations for child
   3. Amount of information about child's intellectual development
   4. Nature of rewards for intellectual development

(b) Press for Language Development
   5. Emphasis on use of language in a variety of situations
   6. Opportunities provided for enlarging vocabulary
   7. Emphasis on correctness of usage
   8. Quality of language models available

(c) Provision for General Learning
   9. Opportunities provided for learning in the home
  10. Opportunities provided for learning outside the home (excluding school)

11. Availability of learning supplies
12. Availability of books (including reference works) periodicals and library facilities
13. Nature and amount of assistance provided to facilitate learning in a variety of situations

Specific Experiential Deficiencies of the Culturally Disadvantaged

More specifically, in terms of educational potential, what are presently thought to be the most crucial psychological deficiencies of the culturally disadvantaged can be grouped into three main categories: perceptual and attentional abilities, verbal and cognitive abilities, and orectic or motivational factors. A knowledge of the exact nature and etiology of deficiencies in these areas is, of course, highly germane to methods of prevention and remediation.

We have not mentioned motor abilities in connection with the disadvantaged, but because of current practices in some school programmes for the culturally disadvantaged, the topic deserves a few words. Retarded motor development, poor muscular co-ordination, balance, and the like, are known to be characteristic of mental retardation of the primary type, particularly of retardation associated with brain damage. There is no evidence [in fact, there is evidence to the contrary (Bayley, 1965)] that a greater proportion of culturally disadvantaged children are retarded in motor development or are in any way deficient in this sphere than the proportion in the total population. Yet in some kindergartens and primary grades we find culturally disadvantaged children being required to engage in various tasks intended to develop or improve motor co-ordination, such as "rail walking"—balancing on the narrow ledge of a two-by-four. Though such exercises may be found helpful for primary retardates, there is no reason to believe they are anything but a waste of school time for culturally disadvantaged children, unless these children also show definite signs of primary retardation or motor deficiency. This is one example of the mistaken notion, which unfortunately is rife in the field of education of the disadvantaged, that the educational methods suitable for primary retardates and slow learners are also the most effective methods for the culturally disadvantaged.

Perceptual Abilities

From the rather meagre research now available, it appears that low socio-economic-status children come to kindergarten or first grade with less well developed visual and auditory discrimination abilities (Jensen, 1966). The deficiency is not great in an absolute sense, but it is generally thought to hinder learning to read. Exercises in perceptual skills have been developed which apparently overcome these deficiencies fairly readily. Since ability to discriminate differences among shapes and sounds is an important prerequisite skill to school learning, these abilities should be assessed in kindergarten and compared with middle-class norms, and appropriate remedial training applied where deficiencies exist. Special tests, norms, and remedial techniques have still to be developed for this purpose, though some techniques already have been developed for experimental use. These remedial techniques can usually be played as games by small groups of children with the teacher, and the perceptual training can readily be combined with the much needed training in language skills.

Attentional Ability

Anyone who has observed culturally disadvantaged children in the classroom, particularly in the primary grades, notes as one of the most outstanding deficiencies these children's inability to sustain attention. This deficiency is not so conspicuous in kindergarten but becomes clearly manifest in the first grade, as soon as reading is introduced and other structured cognitive demands are made upon the child. I have noticed this attentional lack in culturally disadvantaged children in my own observations in classrooms, and it has also been described to me by numerous teachers of the disadvantaged. The recent literature makes little reference to attention, but some of the phenomena discussed here under this heading have come to be identified with the concept of motivation. An excellent discussion of attention, as the term is used here, and of its importance to educability is found in Sir Cyril Burt's *The Backward Child* (1937, pp. 479-85). Attentional ability presumably is innate but may be strengthened through reinforcement in infancy and early childhood. It develops differentially in various kinds of situations and is reinforced through the parent-child relationship. Typically, the disadvantaged child's attention is poorly developed with respect to the teacher's speech and whatever things the teacher tries to make the focus of the child's attention. These particular attentional abilities are developed in middle-class children from an early age, probably through certain features of the parent-child relationship (reading to the child, mutual play accompanied by relevant speech, etc.) which are presumably relatively lacking in lower-class parent-child relationships. These activities are mutually reinforcing to the parent and child: attentional behaviour on the child's part reinforces the parent's interaction with him, and the parent's interaction with the child further reinforces and shapes the child's attention. This shaping of attention in middle-class children is probably not only greater in sheer amount than in lower-class children but related to activities that more nearly resemble those of the school and of the pupil-teacher relationship.

Thus, attention is less well developed in the low socio-economic-status child at the time he enters school. In addition, I have observed a secondary phenomenon: there is an actual deterioration of the child's attentional ability, usually beginning in the first grade (Jensen, 1968). Some children begin actively to resist focusing attention on teacher-oriented tasks and activities. Normal attentional behaviour gives way to a kind of seemingly aimless and disruptive hyperactivity. This is an almost universal observation by teachers of the disadvantaged, especially disadvantaged Negro children. This behaviour can be likened to some extent to the phenomenon referred to by Pavlov as "experimental neurosis." In Pavlov's conditioning laboratory, dogs which were forced to learn discriminations beyond their capabilities became disturbed and resisted further attempts at training, even on much simpler tasks; they developed aversion to the entire laboratory setting and at times even lost previously conditioned habits. Though the analogy with culturally disadvantaged first-graders may seem far-fetched, it does suggest the possibility that the gap in difficulty between the tasks required of the disadvantaged child in the kindergarten and those encountered in the first grade might be too great in many schools. If the child cannot meet the tasks set by the teacher with *successful* performance (not merely receiving indiscriminate approval by the teacher for any quality of performance), the child gradually develops aversion to the school-learning situation. His attention is, as teachers are heard to say, "turned off," and distractability and aimless hyperactivity ensue. The gap between pre-school or kindergarten and first or second grade is not yet being bridged satisfactorily for the culturally disadvantaged child. The steps in the learning requirements are too big. For the middle-class child the transition from home to school is clearly a much less radical change from the activities and demands of the home.

Language Deficiencies

By far the greatest and most handicapping deficiencies of the culturally disadvantaged child are found in the realm of language. But the term language is here used in a much broader and psychologically more profound sense than is generally appreciated by teachers of English, speech therapists, and the like. The immediately obvious aspects of the language of the culturally disadvantaged—the lack of genteel English, incorrect grammar, poor pronunciation, use of slang, etc.—are psychologically the most superficial and the least important from the standpoint of intellectual development. This is not to minimize the social, economic, and occupational advantages of good oral and written English. It is simply important to realize that the language deficiencies of lower-class children have a much more detrimental psychological effect than the obvious social disadvantages of their language habits. Because the eschewal of certain lower-class language habits by the middle-class is perceived by some persons as undemocratic snobbery, there has grown up another utterly erroneous notion that lower-class language is just as good as any other kind of language, in the same sense the English, French and German, though obviously different from one another, are all equally good languages, as far as one can tell. Thus, social class differences in language habits are viewed as desirable or undesirable only according to one's acquired tastes, values and standards, and—to paraphrase the argument—who is to say that middle-class values are any better than lower-class values? This line of thinking can be quite discredited in terms of our growing understanding of the functions of language. Language not only serves a social function as a means of interpersonal communication but is also of crucial importance as a tool of thought. It is in this latter function that lower-class language deficiencies are most crippling psychologically.

General Language Characteristics

With respect to language functions, Metfessel (in Frost and Hawkes, 1966, p. 46) has listed the following general characteristics of culturally disadvantaged children:

1.   Culturally disadvantaged children understand more language than they use. Even so, by second grade the comprehension vocabulary of such children is only approximately one-third that of normal children, while by sixth grade it is about one half.

2.   Culturally disadvantaged children can use a great many words with fair precision, but not those words representative of the school culture. It has been estimated that something less than half the words known by middle-class pre-schoolers are known to slum children. Even such common name words as *sink, chimney, honey, beef* and *sandwich* are learned by culturally disadvantaged children one or two years later than by other children.

3.   Culturally disadvantaged children frequently are handicapped in language development because they do not have the concept that objects have names, and that the same objects may have different names.

4. Culturally disadvantaged kindergarten children use fewer words with less variety to express themselves than do kindergarten children of higher socio-economic status.

5. Culturally disadvantaged children use a smaller proportion of mature sentence structures, such as compound, complex, and more elaborate constructions. This is limited to the non-English-speaking child, but occurs among most children who come from a disadvantaged background.

6. Culturally disadvantaged children learn less from what they hear than do middle-class children. Part of this deficiency has been attributed to the fact that disadvantaged children come from a milieu in which radio, television, and the sounds of many people living together in crowded quarters create a high noise level, which the child eventually learns to shut out psychologically, so that verbal stimuli generally become less salient.

7. Culturally disadvantaged children are less likely to perceive the symbolic and conceptual aspects of their environment; the verbal means of abstraction and analysis are relatively undeveloped.

8. Culturally disadvantaged children frequently end the reading habit before it is begun; the cycle of mastery which demands that successful experiences generate more motivation to read, which in turn generates higher levels of skill sufficient to prevent discouragement, and so on, often never gets under way. These children, of course, have poor adult models for reading behaviour.

In general, it has been found that throughout the entire sequence of language development, from the earliest stages of speech in the first two years of life, there is retardation among culturally disadvantaged children (Bereiter and Engelmann, 1966; Jensen, in press; McCarthy, 1946, pp. 557-9). Furthermore, this retardation should not be thought of entirely as the disadvantaged child's merely lagging behind the middle-class child, with the same level of development merely being attained somewhat later. The characteristics of the language habits that are being acquired and the kinds of functions the language serves in the child's experience, actually shape his intellectual development, especially the development of the ability for abstraction and conceptual learning. Poor development of this ability places a low ceiling on educational attainment.

The most detailed analysis of social class differences in language characteristics, important to the development of cognitive abilities, has been made by Basil Bernstein (Bernstein, 1961). Except for minor details, his findings and conclusions seem to be applicable to social-class differences in the American culture as well as in the British, since social class differences in language behaviour of the type that concerns him are probably even more pronounced here than in England. It is especially important that Bernstein's type of socio-linguistic analysis be applied to some of the various American low socio-economic-status subcultural groups.

In characterizing social class differences in language behaviour, Bernstein distinguishes two main forms of language, which he refers to as *public* and *formal*. In formal language, the variations of form and syntax are much less predictable for any one individual, and the formal possibilities for sentence organizations are used to clarify meaning and make it explicit. In *public* language, on the other hand, the speaker operates in a mode which individual selection and permutation are grossly restricted. In formal language the speaker can make highly individual selection and permutation. Formal language, therefore, can fit the speaker's purposes with much greater subtlety and precision and does not depend to any marked degree upon inflection, gestures, facial expressions, and a presupposed prior mutual understanding of the main gist of the communication, as expressed in the highly frequent use of the phrase "you know what I mean" in lower-class speech. While middle-class persons can understand and use public as well as formal language, lower-class persons are more or less restricted to public language. Public language is almost completely limited to the single function of social intercourse within a community of tacit common understandings and values. It is not designed for expository functions, for detailed representation of past events or future plans, or for manipulating aspects of one's experience abstractly and symbolically. In public language, the quantity of speech is not reduced, but the variety of functions which speech can serve is limited. This becomes especially important in the realm of private or internal speech, where the person must use language to recall, review, structure, or otherwise mentally manipulate his past or his anticipated experiences, aims, plans, problems, and so on. Bernstein lists the following characteristics of public language:

1. Short, grammatically simple, often unfinished sentences with a poor syntactical form stressing the active voice.

2. Simple and repetitive use of conjunctives (so, then, because).

3. Little use of subordinate clauses to break down the initial categories of the dominant subject.

4. Inability to hold a formal subject through a speech sequence; thus, a dislocated informational content is facilitated.

5. Rigid and limited use of objectives and adverbs.

6. Infrequent use of impersonal pronouns as subjects of conditional clauses.

7. Frequent use of statements where the reason and conclusion are confounded to produce a categoric statement.

8. A large number of statements/phrases which signal a requirement for the previous speech sequence to be reinforced: "Wouldn't it?" "You see?" "You know?", etc. This process is termed "sympathetic circularity."
9. Individual selection from a group of idiomatic phrases or sequences will frequently occur.
10. *The individual qualification is implicit in the sentence organization: it is a language of implicit meaning.*
In contrast, the following are characteristics of formal language:
1. Accurate grammatical order and syntax regulate what is said.
2. Logical modifications and stress are mediated through a grammatically complex sentence construction, especially through the use of a range of conjunctions and subordinate clauses.
3. Frequent use of prepositions which indicate logical relationships as well as prepositions which indicate temporal and spatial contiguity.
4. Frequent use of the personal pronoun "I."
5. A discriminative selection from a range of adjectives and adverbs.
6. Individual qualification is verbally mediated through the structure and relationships within and between sentences.
7. Expressive symbolism discriminates between meanings within speech sequences, rather than reinforcing dominant words or phrases, or accompanying the sequence in a diffuse, generalized manner.
8. It is a language use which points to the possibilities inherent in a complex conceptual hierarchy for the organizing of experience.

Robert Hess, of the University of Chicago, has found considerable evidence of these two modes of language behaviour in the parent-child interactions of lower-class and middle-class Americans observed in situations in which the mother is required to instruct her child in learning a simple task (Hess and Shipman, 1965). The language of the lower-class mother does not provide the child with cues and aids to learning to the same extent as the language of the middle-class mother. Since children tend largely to internalize the language of their home environment, mainly that of the parents, the low socio-economic-status child acquires an inferior set of verbal techniques to apply on his own in learning and problem-solving situations.

Verbal Mediation of Cognitive Functions

From the standpoint of the development of intelligence, the most important aspect of language is its relationship to a variety of processes listed under the general heading of *verbal mediation* (Jensen, 1966).

We have hypothesized, and some supporting evidence is already available (Jensen, in press), that one of the crucial psychological differences between low and middle socio-economic-status children is in the spontaneity of verbal mediation, especially in ostensibly non-verbal learning or problem-solving situations. In short, low socio-economic-status children are much less likely than middle socio-economic-status children to talk to themselves as an aid to "thinking." On ostensibly non-verbal tests and learning tasks, which nevertheless require private verbal mediation, culturally disadvantaged children perform especially poorly. This is the main reason that so-called non-verbal intelligence tests are not by any means "culture free" or "culture fair."

Several main processes of verbal mediation, that is, covert language, can be identified.

1. Labelling

In middle-class children the habit of labelling, or naming objects and events in the environment, becomes automatic and unconscious. It is practically impossible to look at, say, a chair or a book, or any object, without these stimuli eliciting a verbal (usually covert) response of naming. Perception and verbalization are more or less unified, so that one cannot see a chair without thinking "chair," at least when the chair is the focus of one's attention. At first, in very young children, this naming tendency is overt; it gradually becomes covert. Most middle-class children enter school with this particular form of verbal equipment already fairly well developed. Lower socio-economic-status children do not. Apparently the conditions under which the lower-class child spends his pre-school years are insufficient to instil the habit of naming or labelling. Experimental evidence has shown conclusively that verbal labelling greatly facilitates learning, retention, and problem solving. Furthermore, this type of verbal mediation is learned in a particular environment; it is not an innate aspect of learning ability. It is a form of behaviour which must become habitual and automatic in children, if they are to develop their educational potential.

2. The Associative Network

Words in context acquire associations. These verbal associations have other associations, and so on, to form an elaborate, ramifying verbal associative network. This network is thought to act, more or less automatically and unconsciously, as a broad source of transfer for conceptual learning and retention. It is the psychological background or "net" which enmeshes the child's experiences in the classroom. Word association experiments on children indicate that low socio-economic-status children have a less rich associative network. Even the words they know and use have, in this sense, less associative meaning to them, and the associations are not as structured in terms of hierarchial characteristics that facilitate categorization, conceptual analysis, and the like. The quality of the child's verbal environment is the chief determinant of the richness and structure of his associative network. All children who can speak have an associative network, but the network of associations of culturally disadvantaged children is more like that of middle-class children who are two or three years younger (Entwisle, 1966).

3. Abstraction and Categorization

Conceptual learning, which includes much of school learning, involves the ability to abstract and to categorize things in terms of various abstracted qualities. For example, plates, wheels, doughnuts, and pennies, have in common the abstract property of being *round*. Young middle-class children and old culturally disadvantaged children are not likely to perceive anything in common among these disparate objects; in short, the objects as stimuli do not arouse abstract associations, and consequently the number of ways the objects can be grouped will be limited or entirely idiosyncratic, depending upon the child's particular experiences with the objects, such as the fact that his mother may have served him *doughnuts* on a *plate*. The ability to disassemble what is registered by the senses into various conceptual attributes is an important ingredient of educability, and it is greatly facilitated by, if not wholly dependent upon, verbal behaviour, either overt or covert.

4. Syntactical Mnemonic Elaboration

The ability to respond to one's experiences on the verbal level in a way that makes use of the structuring and ordering properties inherent in the syntactical aspects of language, greatly facilitates learning, comprehension, retention and retrieval of, and reasoning involving various kinds of experience, both verbal and non-verbal. Language imposes its structure upon raw experience and structures and organizes it in ways that the subject is able to recall for use at a later time. This ability is limited for the person who either has not acquired or does not habitually use the logical and structural properties contained in formal language.

Compensatory Education for the Disadvantaged

The most radical, yet probably most successful, of the pre-school programmes for the culturally disadvantaged is being conducted at the

University of Illinois by Carl Bereiter and Siegfried Engelmann (Bereiter, 1965; Bereiter and Engelmann, 1966). It focuses intensively on training disadvantaged children to use the language in ways that facilitate learning and thinking.

The Bereiter programme is based on the premise that it would be practically impossible to make up every environmental disadvantage that slum children have experienced, and that we must therefore concentrate all our efforts only on those which are most crucial to the development of educability in a normal school setting. These crucial skills, Bereiter maintains, are concerned with the use of language as a tool of thought. His programme consists of drilling the kinds of language habits we have described into children by methods that produce high motivation, unanimous participation, and maximal concentration and effort on the child's part, with a minimal waste of time. The specific techniques have been described in greater detail elsewhere, and Bereiter and Engelmann have a book on their methods for use by pre-school teachers of the disadvantaged (Bereiter and Engelmann, 1966).

Bereiter correctly maintains that disadvantaged children must learn at not a normal but a superior rate in order to compete successfully with middle-class children. Otherwise they will never catch up to grade-level.

The Bereiter programme attempts through direct and intensive training to remedy lacks in the following types of language skills, which Bereiter and his colleagues believe to be most crucial to early academic learning. This list is far from exhaustive, consisting only of the most basic language tools.

1.   Ability to use both affirmative and "not" statements in reply to the question, "What is this?": "This is a ball. This is not a book."

2.   Ability to handle polar opposites ("If it is not_____, it must be_____.") for at least four concept pairs; e.g.. big-little, up-down, long-short, fat-skinny.

3.   Ability to use the following prepositions correctly in statements describing arrangements of objects: *on, in, under, over, between.* Example: "Where is the pencil?" "The pencil is under the book."

4.   Ability to name positive and negative instances for at least four classes, such as tools, weapons, pieces of furniture, wild animals, farm animals, and vehicles. Example: "Tell me something that is a weapon." "A gun is a weapon." "Tell me something that is not a weapon." "A cow is not a weapon."

5.   Ability to perform simple "if-then" deductions. Example: The child is presented a diagram containing big squares and little squares. All the big squares are red, but the little squares are of various other colours. "If the square is big, what do you know about it?" "It's red." (This use

of *if* should not be confused with the antecedent-consequent use that appears in such expressions as, "If you do that again, I'm going to hit you," which the child may already be able to understand.)

6.   Ability to use "not" in deductions: "If the square is little, what else can you say about it?" "It is not red."

7.   Ability to use *or* in simple deductions: "If the square is little, then it is not red. What else can you say about it?" "It's blue or yellow."

Other Intervention Programmes

Other systematically developed intervention programmes for culturally disadvantaged preschoolers are more or less typified by those of Martin Deutsch in New York City, and Susan Gray in Nashville, Tennessee (George Peabody College). These programmes cover a broader spectrum of activities and experiences than the Bereiter programme, though the emphasis is still on stimulating cognitive development. It is generally agreed that the traditional middle-class nursery curriculum, with its emphasis on personal-social adjustment, is inappropriate and inadequate as a means of pulling lower-class children up to the developmental level of his middle-class age-mates. The Deutsch and Gray programmes are described in articles by these investigators (Deutsch, 1962; Gray and Klaus, 1965).

Unfortunately, as of this date, the evidence regarding the efficacy of any of these programmes is still meagre. It is insufficient merely to report gains in IQ, especially when this is based on retest with the same instrument or an equivalent form of the test, and when there is a high probability that much of the gain in test scores is the result of highly specific transfer from materials and training in the nursery programme that closely resemble those used in the test. For example, the writer has noticed that in one pre-school programme, some of the nursery materials consisted of some of the identical equipment used in the Stanford-Binet IQ test, and IQ gains resulting from children's spending several weeks in the programme were based on pre- and post-training with the Stanford-Binet! Such unwitting self-deception must be guarded against in evaluating the effects of pre-school programmes.

The most important evidence for the efficacy of such programmes, of course, will be based on the child's performance in the elementary grades, especially his progress in reading. Probably the most significant predictor of satisfactory progress in the educational programme, as it now exists in the public schools, is reading ability. If a child can surmount the reading hurdle successfully, the prognosis for satisfactory educational progress is generally good. It is also at this early point in the educative process—the introduction of reading—that so many culturally disadvantaged children meet a stumbling block, and head down the demoralizing path of educational retardation. Pre-school programmes for the disadvantaged should concentrate, as does Bereiter's, on the development of cognitive skills basic to reading. In many cases this will probably require a greater attention to the development of perceptual-discriminative skills than is found in the Bereiter programme.

The motivational aspects of reading and reading-readiness are much less clear, but most teachers who are experienced with the disadvantaged believe there are social-class differences among children's attitudes towards reading that affect their desire to learn to read. The best guess is that this motivational component of reading has its origin in early parent-child interaction in reading situations. Social-class differences in this respect apparently are enormous. Can anything be done about it?

This brings us to the question of parent involvement in intervention programmes. Unfortunately, it has been the common experience that low socio-economic-status parents are difficult to change with respect to child-rearing practices. If these parents are not reached long before their children are four or five years of age, much valuable time is lost in terms of the development of the child's educational potential. The child will come to Head Start or to kindergarten without ever having looked at a book, without ever having been read to, and without ever having seen an older child or adult engaged in the act of reading. Some unknown, but possibly large proportion of the determinants of reading failure among low socio-economic-status children may be attributable directly to this set of conditions. Since it is unlikely that the majority of mothers of the most severely disadvantaged children can be reached by any feasible means that could create lasting changes in their mode of child-rearing, we should look elsewhere for practicable means of bringing appropriate influences to bear on culturally disadvantaged children early in their development.

One possible approach would be to require junior and senior high school girls to work with culturally disadvantaged children between six months and four years of age. It would be regarded as a practical course in the psychology of motherhood for all school girls, especially those from a low socio-economic-status background extending from about the 8th or 9th grade through the 12th. Each girl would spend at least an hour a day with a child, either in a nursery or in the child's own home. Instruction and supervision would, of course, accompany the girls' activities in working with young children. Much of the activity would consist of types of play thought to promote cognitive development. Children would, for example, be read to regularly from about one year of age. There should be sufficient consistency of the relationship between the child and the student for emotional rapport to develop. In many cases, of course, low socio-economic-status high school girls will have to be taught and coached in detail about how to interact with infants and children in ways that promote cognitive development. They must be made to realize that these activities are probably the major hope for realizing the educational potential of low socio-economic-status children. An experiment essentially very much like this was carried out on a small scale by Skeels and Dye (1939) some twenty-five years ago, with extremely encouraging results, substantiated by follow-ups over a twenty-five-year period (Skeels, 1966). Such a programme on a large scale would, of course, constitute a major educational undertaking, involving considerable expenditure of funds for additional personnel, facilities, and efforts to gain widespread public acceptance. It could first be tried experimentally on a modest scale to test its feasibility.

Finally, it must be emphasized that all educators who have worked with the disadvantaged are agreed that pre-school intervention without adequate follow-up in the first years of elementary school is inadequate, because the culturally disadvantaged child does not go home after school, as does the middle-class child, to what is essentially a tutorial situation. Middle-class parents take a greater interest in their children's school work and offer them more help than do low socio-economic-status parents. The educational system should make some provision for the lower-class child's opportunity for a tutorial relationship with an older child or an adult, at least throughout the elementary grades.

We are gradually having to face the fact that, in order to break the cycle of poverty and cultural deprivation, the public school will have to assume for culturally disadvantaged children more of the responsibilities of good child-rearing—responsibilities universally regarded among the middle-class as belonging wholly to the child's own parents. The brutal fact is that for culturally disadvantaged children, these responsibilities are not being met, for whatever reason. Whether or not the public school system should intervene where educationally important environmental lacks exist is, of course, strictly speaking, not a psychological or scientific question, but one of social policy.

References

Bayley, N. (1965). "Comparisons of mental and motor test scores for ages 1-15 months by sex, birth order, race, geographical location, and education of parents," *Child Developm.*, 36, pp. 379-411.

Bereiter, C. (1965). "Academic instruction and preschool children." In: *Language Programs for the Disadvantaged*. National Council of Teachers of English, pp. 195-203.

Bereiter, C. and Engelmann, S. (1966). *Teaching Disadvantaged Children in the Preschool*. Englewood Cliffs, New Jersey: Prentice-Hall.

Bernstein, B. (1961). "Social structure, language and learning," *Educ. Res.*, 3, pp. 163-76.

Bloom, B. S. (1964). *Stability and Change in Human Characteristics*. New York: Wiley.

Burt, C. (1937). *The Backward Child*. London: University of London Press.

Burt, C. (1955). "The evidence for the concept of intelligence," *Brit. J. Educ. Psychol.*, 25, pp. 158-77.

Burt, C. (1957). "The distribution of intelligence," *Brit. J. Psychol.*, 48, pp. 161-75.

Burt, C. (1958). "The inheritance of mental ability," *Amer. Psychol.*, 13, pp. 1-15.

Burt, C. (1961). "Intelligence and social mobility," *Brit. J. Stat. Psychol.*, 14, pp. 3-24.

Burt, C. (1963). "Is intelligence distributed normally?", *Brit. J. Stat. Psychol.*, 16, pp. 175-90.

Burt, C. (1966). "The genetic determination of differences in intelligence: A study of monozygotic twins reared together and apart," *Brit. J. Psychol.*, 57, pp. 137-53.

Burt, C. and Howard, Margaret. (1956). "The multifactorial theory of inheritance and its application to intelligence," *Brit. J. Stat. Psychol.*, 9, pp. 95-131.

Carter, C. O. (1962). *Human Heredity*. Baltimore: Penguin Books.

Corah, N. L., *et al.* (1965). "Effects of perinatal anoxia after seven years," *Psychol. Monogr.*, 79, Whole No. 596.

Deutsch, M. (1962). "Social and psychological perspective for the facilitation of the development of the preschool child." Prepared for the Arden House Conf. on Pre-School Enrichment of Socially Disadvantaged Children. (mimeo.)

Dreger, R. M. and Miller, K. S. (1960). "Comparative psychological studies of Negroes and whites in the United States," *Psycholo. Bull.*, 57, pp. 361-402.

Eichenwald, H. (1966). "Mental retardation," *Science*, 153, pp. 1,290-6.

Ellis, H. R., ed. (1963). *Handbook of Mental Deficiency*. New York: McGraw-Hill.

Entwisle, Doris R. (1966). *Word associations of Young Children*. Baltimore: John Hopkins Press.

Erlenmeyer-Kimling, L. and Jarvik, L. F. (1963). "Genetics and intelligence: a review," *Science*, 142, pp. 1,477-9.

Frost, J. L. and Hawkes, G. R. (1966). *The disadvantaged Child*. New York: Houghton Mifflin.

Graham, Frances K. (1962). "Development three years after perinatal anoxia and other potentially damaging newborn experiences," *Psychol. Monogr.*, 1962, 76, Whole No. 522.

Gray, Susan W. and Klaus, R. A. (1965). "An experimental preschool program for culturally deprived children." Reprint from *Child Developm.*, 36, pp. 887-98.

Hess, R. D. and Shipman, V. "Early blocks to children's learning," *Children*, 12, pp. 189-94.

Honzik, Marjorie P. (1957). "Developmental studies of parent-child resemblance in intelligence," *Child Developm.*, 28, pp. 215-28.

Huntley, R. M. C. (1966). "Heritability of intelligence." In: Meade, J. E. and Parkes, A. S., eds. *Genetic and Environmental Factors in Human Ability*. Edinburgh: Oliver & Boyd, pp. 201-18.

Jensen, A. R. (1961). "Learning abilities in Mexican-American and Anglo-American children," *Calif. J. Educ. Res.*, 12, pp. 147-59.

Jensen, A. R. (1963). "Learning abilities in retarded, average, and gifted children," *Merrill-Palmer Quart.*, 9, pp. 123-40. [Reprinted in: DeCecco, John P., ed.

(1964). *Educational Technology: Readings in Programmed Instruction*. New York: Holt, Rinehart and Winston, Inc.]

Jensen, A. R. (1965). "Rote learning in retarded adults and normal children," *Amer. J. Ment. Defic.*, 69, pp. 828-34.

Jensen, A. R. (1966). "Verbal mediation and education and educational potential," *Psychol. in the Schools*, 3, pp. 99-109.

Jensen, A. R. (1966). "Social class and perceptual learning," *Mental Hygiene*, 50, pp. 226-39.

Jensen, A. R. (1967). "Estimation of the limits of heritability of traits by comparison of monozygotic and dizygotic twins," *Proc. Nat. Acad. Sci.*, 157.

Jensen, A. R. (1968). "Social class, race, and genetics: implications for education," *Amer. Educ. Res. J.*, 1968, in press.

Jensen, A. R. (—). "Social class and verbal learning." In: Deutsch, M., Jensen, A. R. and Katz, I., eds. *Social Class, Race and Psychological Development*. New York: Holt, Rinehart and Winston (in press).

Jensen, A. R. and Rohwer, W. D., Jr. (1963). "Verbal mediation in paired-associate and serial learning," *J. Verb. Learn, Verb. Behav.*, 1, pp. 346-52.

Jensen, A. R. and Rohwer, W. D., Jr. (1965). "Syntactical mediation of serial and paired-associate learning as a function of age," *Child Developm.*, 36 pp. 601-8.

John, Vera P. (1962). "The intellectual development of slum children." Paper presented at American Ortho-psychiatric Association, 1962.

Kennedy, W. A., Van De Riet, V. and White, J. C. (1963). "A normative sample of intelligence and achievement of Negro elementary school children in the South eastern United States," *Monogr. Soc. Res. Child Developm.*, 28, No. 6.

McCarthy, Dorothea. (1946). "Language development in children." In: Carmichael, L., ed. *Manual of Child Psychology*. New York: Wiley, pp. 467-581.

McGurk, F. C. J. (1956). "A scientist's report on race differences." Originally printed in *U.S. News & World Report*, 21 Sept. 1956. Reprinted in: Humphrey, H. H., ed. (1964). *School Desegregation: Documents and Commentaries*. New York: Thomas Y. Crowell Co., 1964.

Osler, Sonia F. and Cooke, R. E. (1965). *The Biological Basis of Mental Retardation*. Baltimore: John Hopkins Press.

Pasamanick, B. and Knobloch, Hilda. (1966). "Retrospective studies on the epidemiology of reproductive casualty: old and new," *Merrill-Palmer Quart.*, 12, pp. 7-26.

Pearson, K. (1903). "On the inheritance of the mental and moral characters in man, and its comparison with the inheritance of physical characters," *J. Anthrop. Inst.*, 33, pp. 179-237.

Rapier, Jacqueline L. (1966). "The learning abilities of normal and retarded children as a function of social class." Unpublished doctoral dissertation. University of California, Berkeley, 1966.

Shuey, Audrey M. (1966). *The Testing of Negro Intelligence*. (2nd ed.) New York: Social Science Press.

Skeels, H. M. (1966). "Adult status of children with contrasting early life experiences: a follow-up study," *Child Developm. Monogr.*, 31, No. 3, Serial No. 105.

Skeels, H. M. and Dye, H. B. (1939). "A study of the effects of differential stimulation on mentally retarded children," *Proceedings & Addresses of the American Association on Mental Deficiency*, 44, pp. 114-36.

Skodak, Marie and Skeels, H. M. (1949). "A final follow-up study of one hundred adopted children," *J. Genet. Psychol.*, 75, pp. 85-125.

Tyler, Leona E. (1965). *The Psychology of Human Differences*. New York: Appleton-Century-Crofts.

Zigler, E. (1967). "Familial mental retardation: a continuing dilemma," *Science*, 155, pp. 292-8.

Cultural Influences in Reading

Jensen—Questions for Discussion

Jensen states that once the threshold of adequate environment is attained, practically all the variability in children's I.Q.s will be determined by genetic factors. What is the implication in this fact for the education of the disadvantaged? How does Jensen define the terms "Intelligence," "Learning Ability," and Educability?" What is Jensen's explanation for the fact that minority groups' measured I.Q.'s are below that of Caucasians of European origin? Can the experimental deficiencies discussed by Jensen be readily overcome?

Dina Feitelson

Teaching Reading to Culturally Disadvantaged Children

Any successful teaching method will eventually be the outcome of an interaction between two main factors: the subject matter and the pupils. In the teaching of reading it seems evident that the considerations of subject matter will have to do with the specific linguistic qualities of the language being taught as well as with the visual features of the script in which that language is written.

The second factor influencing the approach to the teaching task is the students. With them one has to consider age, sex, previous experience with the subject to be taught, mental ability, motivation, interest, general range of knowledge, among other things. With first graders, it is clear that the students would be more or less the same age and of both sexes. But with regard to previous experience, acquired knowledge and the various aspects of cognitive and affective development, it is now generally accepted that pupils from different cultural backgrounds will differ greatly. Consequently it would seem that methods of teaching should be developed to suit the special characteristics of the pupils for whom they are intended. Yet, the basic problem of adapting teaching procedures to the special personal characteristics of culturally disadvantaged students does not seem to have gone beyond fairly general proposals (Bloom, 1965). There seems no doubt that more knowledge about selected characteristics of the culturally disadvantaged school entrant would make it possible to structure teaching approaches suited to his special needs. The needed adaptive process reaches far deeper

From Dina Feitelson, "Teaching Reading to Culturally Disadvantaged Children," *The Reading Teacher* 22, no. 1 (October 1968): 55-61. Reprinted with permission of Dina Feitelson and the International Reading Association.

than the mere provision of appropriate backgrounds in story content and accompanying illustrations. Naturally, a discussion of the general problems encountered by culturally disadvantaged children in school is much beyond the scope of this article, which will be limited to problems related to the learning of reading.

The factual material on which the following observations and suggestings are based was collected in Israel between the early 1950's and the present day. In the years following the mass immigration to Israel, school failure was rampant among first graders whose parents had immigrated to Israel from Middle Eastern countries (Dror, 1963). Most studies indicate that the problems faced by Middle Eastern children in the setting of the Israeli school system are fairly typical of the problems faced by children of various cultural subgroups in different parts of the world, and also in the large urban centers of the United States (Feitelson, 1964).

Learning Problems and Solutions

Lack of Adequate Motor Skills

The early home environment of the culturally disadvantaged child typically lacks certain types of manipulative play and work materials usually found in middle class homes such as crayons, paper, scissors, paste, play dough, and other commercial mechanical and manipulative toys. Presumably, children who use toys of these kinds will develop deftness and coordination in the use of their hands. For many years, in Israel at least, school entrants were expected to be able to copy words and even short phrases from their very first day in school. Students who had had no chance to develop these skills sufficiently in their home environment were thus often exposed right from the beginning to repeated frustrating experiences of failure. Recognizing the importance of writing is a valuable reinforcement in learning to read. The solution is not to postpone writing for these children but to introduce it in slow, easily manageable stages so that the possibility of experiencing failure would be minimized.

Cognitive Unpreparedness

Many and various construction toys and, more especially, the various form boards and puzzles found among the toys of middle class children seem to develop a series of skills essential to the successful acquisition of reading. Using the simplest kind of form board, one in which a triangle, square, circle, and hexagon have to be removed and put back in their correct positions, the young child learns to perform an act of abstract reasoning based on visual clues which he had perceived, compared, and differentiated successfully. The more difficult the puzzles the child solves, the more highly developed the series of skills becomes. Similar skills are developed by the presence and use of picture books. When learning to read, the child is called upon to observe minute printed symbols, compare them to his previous experiences, perceive similarities and differences and base overt acts only on the results of his abstract reasoning process. Obviously, the more experience he has had in comparable situations, the more he will be likely to succeed, since many components of reading readiness consist essentially of the ability to observe, compare, and perceive pertinent differences of printed symbols.

The question now arises: To what extent are children who have not been exposed sufficiently to play materials of the kinds described handicapped when trying to learn to read? There can be little doubt that their visual discrimination skills in regard to small, and perhaps insignificant, details will be less developed than those of children who had ample experience with certain play and printed materials. Moreover, it would seem that the absence of these types of play activities will result in less opportunity to transfer experience obtained in one situation to other situations. When it is known in advance that the student who is about to learn reading has poorly developed perceptual habits, the teacher should make sure that differences such as those between printed symbols are pointed out to him and elaborated upon at each stage. Furthermore, it would be useless or even harmful to introduce many symbols at any one time since there would be little hope that the student would be able to distinguish between them, or remember them. Slow sequential introduction of the symbols accompanied by sufficient exercises to enable him to absorb them would seem a much more hopeful approach. Actually, this is but an illustration of the more general principle proposed by Ausubel that learning is facilitated by use of sequentially organized, structural material (Ausubel, 1963). What is perhaps of greatest interest in this approach is its provision for overcoming insufficient readiness, not by going back and building readiness before actual teaching can be started, but by modifying the teaching techniques in such a way that the insufficient readiness can be overcome and the pupil left with a sense of achievement without having been exposed to the possibility of failure.

Linguistic Deficiency

Because the problem of language inadequacy in culturally disadvantaged students has been dealt with extensively in educational literature, it will be referred to only briefly here. The studies of Bernstein (1964) and Deutsch (1964) have shown that there is a great difference between the style of language interaction used in different types of families. According to Bernstein's terminology, the child in the middle and upper-class home is typically exposed to an "elaborate" language code, whereas the child in the culturally disadvantaged home has much less language experience and it is of a different kind. Deutsch (1964) points out that the culturally disadvantaged child has a much poorer command of his mother tongue, and many words and language forms usually known to six-year-olds are foreign to him. If the reading materials used in the initial teaching stage do not take this deficiency into account, some children will be unable to derive meaning from the passages they are "reading," and reading might well become a meaningless, mechanical, and essentially frustrating task. Fortunately, because this problem has been recognized, language difficulty is sometimes considered in reading materials prepared for culturally disadvantaged students. Still it should be recognized that the language deficiency evidenced by many of these children is one of quality as well as of quantity. Vocabulary control alone will not be sufficient to overcome the potential difficulties. Care must be taken that in story content, length and complexity of sentence structure and usage of special language forms, the reading material is within the grasp of the student population for whom it is intended.

Affective Difficulties

It is often mentioned that, in general, the attention span of culturally disadvantaged students tends to be short and their ability to concentrate poor. A teaching method which relies mainly on short periods of concentrated learning might prove more useful, at least in the initial stages, than one which has to be sustained by prolonged individual effort on the part of the students.

A second obstacle to successful involvement with a prolonged learning task is the inability of many culturally disadvantaged pupils to defer gratification. In an attempt to overcome this problem, reading matter could be handed out in single pages or leaflets (and accumulated in a binder) rather than exposing the beginning reader to the whole primer or preprimer in which the unlearned portion is always in somewhat menacing evidence. The accumulated pages are of material read and thus become evidence of knowledge acquired rather than of hurdles still to be overcome. An abstract and long-range goal—the ability to read, which necessitates an extended arduous learning task—is transformed in this case into a series of small efforts easily undertaken, each of which culminates in the reception of new and varied materials.

It is hoped that such accumulating evidence of achievement ultimately will affect the child's opinion of himself since a low opinion of his own abilities or poor self-confidence is another factor which often proves a handicap to good school attainment by culturally disadvantaged students. Experience in Israel would tend to show that, when compared to typical middle-class children, culturally disadvantaged school entrants might not be as self-confident, but they have not reached the stages of crippling self-doubt found so often among culturally disadvantaged pupils at a later stage in their school careers. Thus, at this stage, instilling self-confidence means mainly the forestalling any possible experiences of failure. One way to achieve this in the teaching of reading would be by structuring the whole teaching process as a sequence of well-defined learning stages through which the child would proceed at his own rate. In this case the student would never be confronted with reading materials which contained symbols not studied before.

Another aspect of pupil attitude mentioned in descriptions of culturally disadvantaged children is their inability to deal with failure. As long as the teaching of reading is considered as an unstructured process and is thought of mainly as taking place by means of diversified activities, there seems little danger that six-year-olds will be greatly aware of differences in their rate of progress. But once the teaching of reading is structured in any way, pupils often become very sensitive to their own progress as comparisons are made. Inevitably a sense of failure will evolve in those pupils who are still laboring at stages through which many of their classmates have already passed.

If lack of self-confidence and inability to tolerate failure are two of the major threats to success in learning to read by culturally disadvantaged first graders, one possible way to overcome these problems might be by the prevention of any experience of failure. This could be achieved by two means. First, it is recommended that the structure of the teaching materials be programmed into a series of sequential stages in which the student would proceed to a new stage only after having mastered the previous one. Second, it is suggested that the rate of progress through the brief period of the sequential changes be kept uniform and be adapted to the rate appropriate for the slower pupils. The argument in favor of such a course of action is that while it might result in slowing down the faster pupils by a number of weeks, this price would seem well worth it if it meant a real reduction in the number of pupils who would eventually develop serious reading problems, which would in the long run, cost the school system an incredibly great effort.

Actually proceeding at one rate for all the students would greatly facilitate the effectual carrying out of one of the earlier recommendations, namely that learning can best proceed by way of repeated short periods of concentrated teaching. Interest and effort can often be stimulated more easily in a group situation than when the teacher is confronted by a single student. Moreover, the teacher can devote more effort to the creative presentation of new material when she has to do it only once than when she knows in advance that she will have to repeat her performance again and again. Individual teaching quite often has a fragmenting effect on the teacher's efforts, and the teaching situation to which the single child will be exposed might prove much less enthralling than when she is able to concentrate her full effort to one instance only.

Unavailability of Help During the Learning Period

While much attention has been paid to the role of the home in furthering reading readiness, less thought seems to have been devoted to the role of the home while learning is already in progress. It would seem that in this respect the student from the culturally deprived home is at a grave disadvantage. It might well be that the apparent inability of culturally disadvantaged children to transfer learning experiences, in reading at least, is not a result of any actual difference, but only a direct outcome of the unavailability of direct help at certain crucial stages of the learning process. Observation of the teaching of reading in the regular classroom setting in Israel revealed that many teachers seemed to depend to a great extent on knowledge which their pupils had supposedly acquired by themselves. When, for example, the combination of consonants with a specific vowel had been taught a few times, it was often assumed that the pupils would now be able to deal successfully with all further combinations of consonants with that particular vowel. Many talks with parents in school-oriented homes seem to leave no doubt that in cases like this, the teaching task is often completed in the home. Actually it might not necessarily be the parents themselves who provided this kind of help, but siblings, relatives, or nursemaids. What appears in school as ability to generalize might in actual fact be the outcome of direct teaching which goes on unknown to the school.

If, because of inability or simple lack of direct help at critical stages, the culturally disadvantaged first grader is generally not able to avail himself of this kind of knowledge, teachers will have to reckon with this fact in subsequent instruction. If cultural deprivation means, among other things, that there is no hope for any additional enriching or reinforcing in the student's home and if the student will not acquire any knowledge beyond that taught in class, it would mean that this teaching must be as complete and all-encompassing as possible.

Conclusions

Assuming that any teaching approach has to rely on two main factors: subject matter and pupil characteristics, some of the implications of the second factor in the teaching of reading have been discussed. When dealing with a fundamental educational problem like the teaching of reading to culturally disadvantaged school entrants, it might prove beneficial to try to break down the basic problem into a series of sub-problems which could be dealt with on a more direct level. Such an analysis might allow the seeking out and testing of specific solutions for each of the separate sub-problems as a means of solving the whole problem.

It should be remembered that the analysis which has been undertaken here was meant to serve as a model for the general approach advocated. It is not assumed that the problems which have been discussed are the only problems faced by culturally disadvantaged school entrants when learning to read. Nor is it implied that the suggestions for corrective measures are the only ways in which each of the problems can be approached, or in every instance even an especially good way. It so happened that in particular circumstances these problems appeared especially relevant and that these circumstances evoked certain solutions rather than others.

References

Ausubel, P. O. A teaching strategy for culturally deprived pupils: cognitive and motivational consideration, *School Review*, 1963, *71*.

Bernstein, B. Elaborated and restricted codes: their social origins and some consequences. *American Anthropologist*, 1964, *66*, (6).

Bloom, B. S., Davis, A., and Hess, R. *Compensatory education for cultural deprivation*. New York: Holt, Rinehart and Winston, 1965.

Deutsch, M. *The role of social class in language development and cognition*. New York: Institute for Developmental Studies, 1964. (*mimeo*)

Dror, R. Educational research in Israel. Vol. 13, *Studies in education. Scripta hierasolymitana*. Jerusalem: Magnes Press, The Hebrew University, 1963.

Feitelson, Dina. *Causes of scholastic failure among first graders*. Jerusalem: Kirjat Sefer, 1964. (Hebrew)

Feitelson, Dina. Structuring the teaching of reading in accordance with considerations of language specifications. *Elementary English*, 1965.

Gibson, J. J., and Osser, H. A. Possible effect of learning to write on learning to read. *A basic research program on reading*. Ithaca, New York: Cornell University, 1963.

Moore, O. K. Orthographic symbols and the pre-school child: a new approach. New educational ideas. *Second Minnesota Conference on Gifted Children*, 1961.

Cultural Influences in Reading

Feitelson — Questions for Discussion

How do Feitelson's recommendations for building self-confidence in children with poor self-concepts differ from those often recommended by authorities in this field? What possible solutions might one offer for the problem of unavailability of help during the learning period as discussed by Feitelson? Do you agree with Feitelson's recommended approach for study of the problem of the disadvantaged? Do you agree with Feitelson's statement that the adaptation of teaching procedures to the special personal characteristics of culturally-disadvantaged students does not seem to have gone beyond fairly general proposals?

Alwin B. Coleman

The Disadvantaged Child Who Is
Successful in School

For the past several years we have been concerned about our public school dropouts, and we have expended considerable energy and time trying to find a solution to this problem. We have attacked the problem from various vantage points hoping to find convergence in our findings, some overlap in the results from these different approaches to the problem. Certain factors seemed to recur in case after case, making it possible to characterize the dropout. For example, he was usually a poor reader.[1] The probability was high that his home environment was fragmented or mixed.[2] He almost certainly came from the lowest socio-economic group in America.[3]

This characterization led us to relate dropping out to social class. But I should like to suggest that school success and dropout are not class phenomena but rather are contingent upon certain parental school-reinforcement behaviors.

It seemed to be a large step forward to be able to characterize the typical dropout, to be aware of those factors whose presence in the

From Alvin B. Coleman, "The Disadvantaged Child Who Is Successful in School," *The Educational Forum*, November 1969, pp. 95-97. Reprinted by permission of the author and Kappa Delta Pi, An Honor Society in Education. Copyright © 1969 by Kappa Delta Pi.

[1]Robert J. Havighurst, Paul Hoover Bowman, Gordon P. Liddle, Charles V. Matthews, James V. Pierce, *Growing Up In River City* (New York: John Wiley & Sons, 1962), p. 62.

[2]Frank Riessman, *The Culturally Deprived Child* (New York: Harper & Row, 1962), p. 48.

[3]Robert D. Strom, "Family Influence on School Failure," in Joe L. Frost and Glenn R. Hawkes (eds.), *The Disadvantaged Child, Issues and Innovations* (Boston: Houghton Mifflin Company, 1966), p. 379.

school dropout were highly probable, because if we were able to identify the potential dropout, we could help him to develop more satisfactorily in the school environment and hence ultimately prevent his dropping out. However, I noted in my studies that some candidates for early school exodus, belonging to the lower working class with all of the "earmarks" of a dropout, failed to drop out. This led me to ask the following questions:

1. Why is it that even though the vast majority of our public school dropouts come from the lower working class many youth belonging to this social class do *not* drop out and are in fact recognized as successful students?

2. What makes for the success of certain lower working class children in school in comparison with their social class peers?

3. Do their parents exercise school-reinforcement behaviors similar to those employed by parents whose children are very likely to be successful in school, such as upper middle class parents?

4. Are the characteristics of their families similar to those of the upper middle class?

5. Do these children express certain attitudes and behaviors which are similar to those of successful upper middle class students?

Since the literature suggests that certain parental attitudes and behaviors contribute to the success of a child's performance in school,[4] my approach to the problem has been to study the attitudes and behaviors of representative samples of lower working and upper middle class parents of successful children.[5]

The results of this approach permit us to identify certain behaviors held in common by parents of successful children regardless of class. They also make it possible to hypothesize as to the type of home en-

---

[4]The following sources are examples: Richard Hamilton Berg, "Mothers' Attitudes on Child Rearing and Family Life Compared for Achieving and Underachieving Elementary School Children," Unpublished doctoral dissertation, University of Southern California (1963).

J. E. Floud, A. H. Halsey, and F. M. Martin, *Social Class and Opportunity* (Melbourne, London, Toronto: Wm. Heinemann Ltd., 1956), pp. 92-94. Also: Joseph Allan Kahl, "Educational and Occupational Aspiration of 'Common Man' Boys," *Harvard Educational Review,* 23:183-203 (1953).

F. V. Mannino, "Family Factors Related to School Persistence," *Journal of Educational Sociology,* 35:194 (1962).

Elizabeth F. Wheeler, "Social Class Differences in Maternal Expectations and Perceptions of School, Prior to School Entrance of First Child," Unpublished doctoral dissertation, Northwestern University (1965).

[5]Alwin B. Coleman, *School-Related Attitudes and Behaviors of Parents of Achieving Adolescents.* U. S. Office of Education: Cooperative Research Branch Project No. 5-8401-2-12-1 (Ann Arbor: The University of Michigan, 1966).

vironment that is necessary to the success of the lower working class child in school.

It was found that the parents in both social classes exercised the same or similar control techniques with respect to the child's behavior, and an item analysis identified the following specific behaviors held in common: Channels of communication between parent and child were kept open and operative. Mutual respect, reliance, and trust existed between parent and child. Parental assistance was received by the child whenever it was requested and whenever the parent perceived that assistance as being necessary to the child's welfare. Parents utilized encouragement and praise rather than disparaging remarks and blame when dealing with their children. Both groups of parents threatened punishment and resorted to it when misbehavior occurred.

Family characteristics were similar for the two social class groups. These lower working class families were relatively small and closely approximated the average family size of the upper middle class families. There was a high intact family ratio, dropout incidence among siblings was low, and some college enrollment occurred among other siblings.

There were similarities in the attitudes and behaviors expressed by the two sets of children. Both groups pursued hobbies and enjoyed reading. Both groups displayed self-confidence when faced with mental and physical tasks. Both had close friends and got along well with their peers.

On the basis of the data derived from this study, I shall now attempt to postulate the type of home environment that seems to be necessary to the success of the lower working class child in school.

There exists in this home a feeling of mutual respect between the parents and the child, a condition which is built and established through conscious parental effort. There is an atmosphere characterized by help-fulness, stimulation, reward, and freedom together with parental concern and guidance for the child. Parental assistance is always available but is given only when required. Parents overtly encourage the child to do well in school, to read, to have hobbies, and to make friends. Stimulation is also provided by way of conversations between the parents and the child. Parents of successful children reward their children for accomplishment, and usually the reward is praise. The child is allowed a good deal of freedom in managing his own affairs, in his conversations with his parents, and with regard to the points of view he chooses to defend and to maintain. The parents are interested and involved in his immediate life and require that he meet certain obligations to them, such as keeping them informed of his whereabouts and of his out-of-school activities, and by insisting on certain standards of behavior. Punishments are not of a physical nature and do not interfere with the prevailing positive atmosphere of the home or the feeling of mutual respect which has been generated between the child and his parents.

It would seem that families of successful children, regardless of class, are similar in character, and that these children tend to express similar attitudes and behaviors both in school and outside of school.

Cultural Influences in Reading

Coleman — Questions for Discussion

Do you think Coleman's list of the factors related to success in the disadvantaged child is complete? What other factors might one consider? Can the factors enumerated as prerequisites to success in school be built into a family that does not initially possess them? Can the problems encountered by children who come from homes that do not possess the characteristics enumerated here be made up for at school?

CHAPTER TEN

Linguistic-Psycholinguistic Implications for Reading

Most reading teachers have heard a lot, but often understood very little, about the relationship between linguistics and the teaching of reading. The articles in this chapter were selected because the editor believes they will, if carefully read, give the average teacher a much better knowledge of the relationship between linguistics and reading. They should also help reading teachers put some of the linguist's research into practical application.

The first article by Rose-Marie Weber was chosen because it gives the reader what might be termed a "mini-course" in linguistics. It is rather long and the student new to linguistics will need to read it very carefully. It does, however, contain a great deal of useful information for the reading teacher.

The article by Kenneth S. Goodman on the subject of comprehension-centered reading should be of value in helping reading teachers understand the relationship between comprehension and oral reading. As you read this article, be sure to consider the practical application of the information presented by Goodman.

The last article by Frank Smith and Kenneth S. Goodman cautions reading teachers to beware of "psycholinguistic materials." Be sure to note their reasoning and also note whether or not the same line of thought might be applied to other terms and materials.

Rose-Marie Weber

Linguistics and Reading

This paper surveys the principles and findings from the field of linguistics that have been brought to bear on questions dealing with learning to read, the analysis of the reading process, and the sources of reading failure. It is intended to guide the reader through the significant areas in the literature and to note the specific works that have explored them.

The first section presents the trends in the rapidly changing field of linguistics that are reflected in the literature. The second goes on to describe the rationale for the "linguistic method," a proposal for teaching reading that has been widely adopted, but which represents only one approach that might be derived from linguistics. The following two sections deal, on the other hand, with areas that have only distant implications for classroom practice, but which can contribute to greater understanding of how the reading process is learned and carried out: the language competence of beginning readers and the relationship between spoken and written language. The next section gives examples of how such linguistic considerations have been applied in analyzing the process of reading and learning to read. The following section deals with regional and social variation in the English spoken by American

From Rose-Marie Weber, "Linguistics and Reading," *ERIC Clearinghouse for Linguistics,* May 1970, pp. 1-29. Reprinted by permission of the author.

This publication was prepared pursuant to a contract with the Office of Education, U.S. Department of Health, Education and Welfare. Contractors undertaking such projects under Government sponsorship are encouraged to express freely their judgment in professional and technical matters. Points of view or opinions do not, therefore, necessarily represent official Office of Education position or policy.

children and in fact touches on all the topics treated in earlier sections: the relation between spoken and written English, the possible effects of mismatch between the two on learning to read, and suggestions for educational practice to deal with these problems. The final section discusses these same points for children who speak other languages.

These are the topics that have been discussed in a rather diverse literature. It is obvious that they do not exhaust the areas that could be examined with profit from the linguist's point of view.

1. The Linguistic Perspective on Reading

The relevance of linguistics to the teaching of reading is not at all direct. But because reading involves the use of language, linguistics offers an approach to understanding the nature of reading that can ultimately contribute to a rationale for educational practice. Two main lines of relevance are clear. The first deals with the relationship between a speaker's knowledge of his language and his ability to read. When linguists describe the intricacies of English grammar, phonology, and the lexicon, their goal is to characterize the knowledge that a speaker must have in order to speak and understand English. They can therefore contribute to understanding how people read by describing the linguistic knowledge that a speaker must have in order to understand written English. The second line of relevance deals with the special knowledge that a speaker must acquire in order to do this. That is, linguists can help to determine the magnitude of the task of learning to read by describing the characteristics of the written language and its relation to the spoken language, taking geographical and social variation in the spoken variety into account.

The literature on the application of linguistics to reading reflects the two approaches to the study of language that have dominated American linguistics. The structuralist approach has dealt for the most part with describing the relationship between sound and spelling while the generative approach has dealt with the larger problem of relating a speaker's knowledge of his language to his ability to read. The structuralists, among them Leonard Bloomfield and Charles C. Fries, were the first to address themselves to reading. Their primary aim in describing languages has been to capture the regularities in the sounds and sentences that they observe in speech. In relating linguistics and reading they analyze the relationship between sound and spelling in English and insist that mastering the correspondences is the main task in learning to read. Like many reading specialists, they concentrate on letters, significant sounds, and words as the prime units in reading.

More recent work relating linguistics and reading has been influenced by transformational-generative linguists, especially Noam Chomsky and Morris Halle, in part by way of their impact on the psychology of language. Their concern to make explicit all the knowledge of a language that a speaker brings to understanding even simple sentences is particularly significant for reading. It has lead to an emphasis on reading as an active process of reconstructing the message set out by the writer while matching sounds and letters plays a relatively minor part, even among beginning readers. Generative linguists have also analyzed the relation between sound and spelling in English. But they are more concerned than structuralists with the problem of specifying the relationship between a speaker's internalized rules for forming sentences and his ability to read. These different perspectives on reading do not necessarily conflict; it would seem that the generativist view has emphasized the linguistic competence that the new reader brings to the task while the structuralist view has emphasized what he must learn.

For the most part, the implications of linguistics for reading have been discussed with respect to beginning instruction on the one hand and to the analysis of highly fluent reading on the other.

Bloomfield (1961), Hall (1961), Soffietti (1955), and Smith (1963, 1968) present the structuralist perspective; Fries (1963) places it in the larger context of American reading instruction. Lefevre (1964) sketches English from a structural stance, but takes the sentence as the significant unit in reading.

Goodman and Goodman (1967) and Broz and Hayes (1966) give annotated bibliographies on the structuralist influence. Carroll (1964) discusses its relevance to the psychology of learning to read. Wardhaugh (1969) examines the implications of the generative approach in detail, contrasting it to the structural. Various papers in Goodman and Fleming (1969), Walden (1969), Singer and Ruddell (1970) and Levin and Williams (1970) reflect the influence of generative theory.

2. The Linguistic Method

The so-called linguistic method has grown out of proposals made by several structural linguists to improve reading instruction. They outlined what they saw as the implications of linguistics for initial reading instruction because they were dissatisfied not only with widely used instructional materials, but also with the assumptions about language that they were based on. They stressed that the English writing system was basically a representation of the phonology of the spoken language rather than the other way around. Since other aspects of language, the grammar and the lexicon, were largely the same in speech as in writing, they insisted that the central task in learning to read was to master the correspondences between the writing and the phonology. They maintained that the beginning reader must go from the printed page to sound before he can understand a word, although they recognized that the highly fluent reader shortcuts this process drastically.

Bloomfield and Fries, who prepared introductory materials, objected to instruction by whole words that were chosen without concern for their spelling because it obscured the systematic correspondences between speech and writing. On the other hand, they objected to traditional phonics instruction because it led to cutting up the speech stream, distorting individual sounds, and having to reintegrate the sounds into recognizable words. They also pointed out that phonics deals largely with individual letters and so fails to show much of the systematic correspondence between patterns of letters and sounds. They therefore proposed to teach the regular correspondences between sounds and letters, and particularly between sounds and letter patterns, in the context of whole words. Clearly this methodological proposal and the programs that have grown from it do not inevitably follow from linguists' observations of the English writing system and its relationship to the spoken language. Since other approaches to teaching the correspondences are possible, many linguists object to the term "linguistic method" to describe this one. Nevertheless, it has turned out to be at least as effective as any other for teaching children to read.

The structuralists' rationale has also influenced the preparation of English materials for children who speak another language. The materials, which the children are to read only after they have mastered the sentences orally, are controlled not only for sound-letter correspondences but also for sound contrasts and grammatical structures that may present particular problems in learning English, especially for children who speak Spanish.

Wardhaugh (1969), Olsen (1968), and Hull (1965) compare and critically review linguistic methods. Dykstra (1968) and other studies compare their effectiveness to that of other materials. Robinett (1965) outlines the working premises underlying materials for Spanish speakers.

3. The Spoken Language of Six-Year-Olds

Since reading includes the use of language, it is important to consider the linguistic competence that illiterate six-year-olds bring to the task of learning to read. Examining the system that children must control in order to speak and to comprehend speech can further our understanding of what is involved in the comprehension process. It can also clarify what they must learn to control in order to comprehend the special case of language in print. Furthermore, studying spoken language can test the assumptions that underlie instructional materials with regard to children's linguistic abilities.

All in all the spoken language of children when they are taught to read has not been studied in substantial detail. It is obvious that they have passed well beyond the stage of short, "telegraphic" sentences and that, in fact, they seldom produce sentences that would not be acceptable in adult speech. On the other hand, they do not have the full flexibility of adults in their range of vocabulary or grammatical rules. Therefore at times the literature emphasizes their sophistication and other times their immaturities.

3.1. Phonology

By the time children reach school, they control word and sentence stress, intonation, timing, and the refinements of vowel and consonant articulation with great skill. This remark is equally applicable to children who speak a nonstandard variety of the language; they just have a slightly different system from children who speak the standard. Immaturities such as a "weak" /r/ at the beginning of words do not seem to create immediate difficulties in understanding or in matching sounds and letter patterns. Some persistent immaturities may be symptomatic of deepseated difficulties that may affect overall capacity for learning to read, but the source of reading difficulty cannot be simply attributed to poor articulation.

When compared to adult speech, the speech of six-year-olds by and large reflects the same system of contrasting vowels and consonants and the same distribution of sounds within words. It also shows the same phenomena at word boundaries, e.g., an expected /y/ immediately following a /t/ is pronounced /š/, as in *Can't you see?* But the child and adult systems are not entirely identical. One important difference is that children have not yet had the opportunity to learn some of the more abstract phonological relationships in the language. They hardly control any groups of multisyllabic words such as *geography/geographic* or *electric/electricity/electrician* which by their stress shifts and sound alternations exemplify important aspects of English phonological structure. These relationships emerge only with the acquisition of complex, often bookish, words. Another difference between children's and adults' speech is that children do not control the range of styles that adults do. Children's speech is most like the casual speech of adults, in which *sand* rhymes with *man* and *led her* with *better*. Instructional materials, on the other hand, are based on more formal pronunciation. In practice children seem to have little trouble adjusting their pronunciation to clear, formal style for those first steps of reading when every word in a sentence is pronounced individually.

3.2. Lexicon

Even though six-year-olds come to school with an extensive vocabulary, this is the aspect of their language that will most obviously expand with maturity. Most of the studies on children's vocabularies have concentrated on their size. These are subject to methodological problems, one of the most severe having to do with the word as a basic unit. For instance, *walk/walked/walks* may be counted as variants of the same word, but what about *teach/taught* or *break/broken?* Should *call up* be considered one word or two words? If two words, should *up* be counted the same word as in *He ran up the hill?* For this and other reasons, estimates of the size of first-graders' vocabularies vary from as low as 5,000 to as high as 24,000 words.

The relative frequency of words has also been studied for young readers in light of the relationship between high frequency and ease in comprehension. But the significance of frequency in learning to identify words at the beginning stages of learning to read is not clear and is complicated by the irregularity of sound-letter correspondences in very frequent words such as *some, have,* and *from.* Little work has gone beyond the facts of frequency to explore children's reference systems, or the relationship of items to each other, such as *tree, bush, branch, pine,* or selectional restrictions exemplified by the use of *roast* with *meat* but not with *bread.*

Although the lexicon is often separated from grammar in many discussions, it is important to note that learning new lexical items involves learning how they can be used in sentences. In other words, the learner's grammar grows as his vocabulary grows. But knowing a word's grammatical characteristics tends to lag behind knowing the reference of the word. For instance, although first graders show that they know what *promise* means in a sentence like *He promised to listen,* in a sentence like *Jack promised Mary to sing,* they may identify Mary as the one who will sing.

3.3. Grammar

It is evident that children know many of the rules for forming English sentences by the time they enter first grade. They show nearly complete mastery over inflections, only occasionally producing forms like *tooths* or *grewed*. They use a wide range of sentence types that show control not only of basic sentence structures but also of many other derivative structures. For instance, the *-ing* forms of verbs occur in the speech of first graders as the object of a verb, as in *She does the cooking*, or the object of a preposition, as in *This is for cooking*, or as an adjectival complement, as in *I see the cowboy cooking*. On the other hand, the *-ing* form in subject position, as in *Cooking is hard*, does not show up in their speech although they seem to understand it with no trouble. This is the sort of refinement that emerges in children's syntax as they mature. Other developments include learning the grammatical characteristics of both old and new words in their growing vocabulary. For instance, *ask* takes both *to* and *that* complements, as in *She asked him to leave* and *She asked that he leave,* while *want* takes only *to*, as in *She wanted him to leave*, but not **She wanted that he leave*. The more formal *She asked that he leave* exemplifies another aspect of children's grammatical development, the emergence of constructions restricted to formal and written usage.

The grammatical development of children during the school years remains to be examined in close detail. It has been shown, however, that sentences in standard textbooks do not display the variety of structures that children use in their spontaneous speech.

McCarthy (1954) surveys language development through the school years. Ruddell (1970), Fleming (1968) and papers in Walden (1969) review recent research on it with respect to reading. Templin (1957) reports on pronunciation and Lobdell (1965) discusses vocabulary lists. Strickland (1962) analyzes grammatical development in the elementary grades from the structural viewpoint, and Loban (1963) and O'Donnell *et al.* (1967) from the transformational viewpoint. Menyuk (1969) reports on experimental research based on transformational-generative theory.

4. The Relationship Between Spoken and Written English

Much of the literature on linguistics and the teaching of reading makes the point that writing is simply a representation of speech. This is an overstatement that perhaps succeeds in dampening the notion that writing is somehow the more genuine form of language. But it obscures the fact that as soon as a language is set to paper, even for the first time, it takes on a life somewhat independent of its spoken counterpart. By examining the relationship between the spoken and written forms of the language, linguists can in the long run contribute to assessing the learning task that is involved in becoming literate. But educators as well as linguists themselves cannot assume that systematic correspondences described on paper necessarily reflect generalities in the mind of a highly literate person or that these correspondences should in any way be explicitly taught. Linguists' descriptions are a long way from being applicable to educational goals.

Studies on the relationship between spoken and written English have been based for the most part on the competence of an idealized formally educated adult. How learning to read and write affects children's spoken language or, on the other hand, how development in the spoken language through the years affects their reading and writing has hardly been studied.

4.1. Spelling

English spelling is often viewed as a rather inexact representation of the significant sounds, or phonemes, of the language. A good deal of recent research on English phonology and the writing system, however, has shown that this notion obscures much of the regular correspondence between them. The refined view requires recognizing systematic relationships between writing and levels of linguistic organization other than surface sounds.

It is first important to note that the writing system shows patterning that is independent of the spoken language. It is obvious that there are many units of more than one letter. Moreover, position in the word conditions the occurrence of some letters, e.g., *i* and *u* in digraphs hardly ever occur finally in words and are replaced by *y* and *w*, thus *maid* but *may* and *proud* but *prow; dge* does not correspond to /ǰ/ at the beginning of words, while *gh* corresponds to /g/ and never to /f/ in the same position. Finally, English spelling is particularly notable for the pervasiveness of markers, letters that do not themselves correspond to sound units, but indicate the particular correspondence of other letters. For instance, final -*e* marks the "long" *a* in *state* and in *stage* the "soft" *g* as well. (In at least one analysis of English phonology, these have a place in the phonology and are not just markers in the spelling.)

The necessity for recognizing the relationship between spelling and "deeper" levels of the language than surface sounds rests on the frequent occurrence of morphemes—roots, prefixes, suffixes, and simple words—

that are pronounced differently in different environments but in each instance are spelled the same. For example, *can* usually corresponds to /kIn/ in *He can make it,* but to /kæn/ *I know he can; -ed* corresponds to /t/, /d/ or /Id/ in the large majority verbs, e.g., *walked, staggered,* and *bolted; geograph-* corresponds to /ǰi əg ræf-/in *geographic* but to /ǰi ág rəf-/ in *geography,* while similar patterning can be seen in *geolog-, geometr-, biograph-* and *photograph.* In these and thousands of other words in the language, spelling represents the morphemes or meaning-bearing elements consistently, in spite of differences in pronunciation, either under different grammatical conditions or across dialect boundaries. Linguists do not agree on precisely how this regularity should be described in relation to the spoken language because of different theoretical approaches.

4.2 Other Features

The writing system reflects various aspects of the grammar of English that are only indirectly related to phonology, if at all. For instance, the question mark at the end of a sentence corresponds to the structural feature of being a question rather than to a rising intonation pattern. It marks both the feature and the intonation in questions of the form *Do you see the horse?* but the structural feature only in *Where's the horse?* which is ordinarily said with a falling intonation.

The grammar of written English itself differs from that of spoken English in various ways that are not always obvious. Certain types of structures, e.g., *The horse went galloping, galloping, galloping; Down came the sled; Having arrived safely, he was exhausted; My father, who loved cars, washed his every Sunday,* are generally restricted to the written form, while others, such as *He sort of tried; Won't drink his milk; Under the bed is safe,* are generally restricted to the spoken form. Furthermore, written English tends to be far more precise and less repetitive than spoken English. Rather formal speech, when transcribed into writing, must be edited before it projects the same high degree of formality as the spoken version. Although differences in grammar and vocabulary may be minor within a given sentence, through longer passages they accumulate to make written and spoken English appreciably different.

The coherency of longer passages and the relations among the sentences that contribute to this coherency have hardly been studied from the viewpoint of linguistics. The structure of written discourse, however, may demand more of the child learning to read than is generally supposed.

Gleason (1961) and Joos (1960) discuss the relationship between spoken language and writing systems in general. Francis (1958) presents a useful analysis of the English writing system, including punctuation. Hanna *et al.* (1966) and Higginbottom (1962) deal with extensive data. Weir and Venezky (1968) and Venezky (1967, 1970) develop a detailed framework for analyzing the system with special emphasis on spelling-to-sound, i.e., reading, rules. Reed (1966, 1968) and Smith (1968) apply their analysis to dialectal data. Halle (1969), Noam Chomsky (1970), and Carol Chomsky (1970) discuss writing in relation to the theory of generative-transformationalist phonology. Wardhaugh (1968, 1969) compares approaches to describing speech-spelling relations. Berdiansky *et al.* (1969) give spelling-to-sound rules for words found in children's vocabularies. Gleason (1965) notes differences between spoken and written English in grammar and discourse.

5. The Psycholinguistics of Reading

As a person reads, he uses language in a special way. Linguistics does not offer a way of analyzing what he is doing, however, since it deals primarily with the structure of linguistic systems in and of themselves. The discipline which does take the analysis of the reading process within its domain is psycholinguistics, which combines the viewpoints of both psychology and linguistics. In practice, this field has brought the theory and findings of linguistics to bear on questions dealing with how people learn, remember, understand, and produce language. The contributions to reading research can be seen in papers by linguists, psychologists, and educators that focus on the psychology of the reading process with linguistic considerations in the foreground. Such studies are well represented in Goodman (1968), Goodman and Fleming (1969), Singer and Ruddell (1970) and Levin and Williams (1970). An especially useful technique for examining linguistic aspects of the reading process is the analysis of oral reading errors, both in naturalistic and experimental settings (Goodman 1969; Kolers 1970).

Linguists have brought up many questions and suggestions about how children should be taught to read, how they learn, and how fluent readers handle print with such ease. But their suggestions require empirical validation which linguistics as a field does not provide. The following sections illustrate various considerations about reading and learning to read that derive in part from linguists' views on language.

5.1 Learning the Writing System

Sound segments in English are closely represented by letters while at the same time morphemes are generally represented by the same string of letters, even though their pronunciation may change in different contexts. The implications of this type of correspondence system for learning to read and for fluent reading skill have been examined time and again. Linguists have tended to take the point of view that learning the correspondences explicitly—either in patterns or individually—should facilitate transfer to new words and so should form the basis of early reading instruction. Research has provided some support for this viewpoint, but no particular method has proved to be most effective.

Even though children may receive rather intensive training in sound-letter correspondences, many details of the correspondence system are not included in the instruction. Furthermore, the consistent representation of morphemes in different contexts is generally ignored. The details seem to gain rule-like status in the competence of maturing reading, nevertheless, as in the pronunciation of final -a as /ə/ in *America, rubella, harmonica*, or the alternations in *music/musician* or *electric/electrician*. Children seem able to infer regularity between speech and writing, even though the data on which they base their inferences appear only haphazardly in what they read. The process may well be similar to the way they acquire language as toddlers. In the past, much of the concern about instruction on decoding has dealt with how early and how intense it should be. Given the recent descriptions of the deeper regularity in the sound-spelling system, the concern may shift toward the content of instruction and especially toward facilitating children's own inferential strategies for discovering the less obvious regularities.

Materials for teaching sound-letter correspondences are reviewed with reference to experimental evidence in Desberg and Berdiansky (1968). Carol Chomsky (1970) speculates on learning more abstract spelling regularities.

5.2 Intonational Features of Beginning Reading

When a child first learns to read aloud, his performance is slow, disconnected, and sometimes strained. If it is remarkably choppy, he may be regarded as a poor reader who has trouble understanding much of what he mouths. Some observers may suppose that he sounds like a poor reader because he is one; others may suppose that he is a poor reader in part because he distorts the message so badly that he does not grasp the grammatical relations among the words.

Several features distinguish his reading from his ordinary speech. First of all, the words are distinctly separated from one another, while in speech they are smoothly linked. Ordinarily, for instance, the first two words of *He's your new teacher* rhyme with *seizure,* but in early reading they are separated. Secondly, each word receives a stress equal to all the other words in the sentence, while in speech different words receive different degrees of stress, depending on their grammatical function. *In a flash* is ordinarily said with the same stress pattern as *unabashed,* but in beginning reading it has the same pattern as *John needs cash.* The heavy stresses in turn affect the quality of the vowels that are usually weakly stressed so that in beginning reading the vowels in *an, to,* and *them* are said with the same vowel quality as in *ant, two,* and *send.*

But another dimension of the speech signal, the relative levels of pitch, indicate that choppy readers do not lose "sentence sense" after all. Even the poorest oral reader almost always pronounces each successive word of a sentence on a pitch contour that signals "more to come" until the last word in the sentence, where the pitch contour signals "end of sentence." In spite of the distortion, even beginning readers show that they recognize the boundaries of sentences.

Other features that can be heard among beginning readers are slowness, overloudness, oversoftness, a narrow pitch range, and a wide pitch range imitating adults, isn't-this-an-exciting-story style. The source of the various features is not clear. Some may be a necessary part of learning to read, perhaps aggravated by teaching words in lists and fostered by the notion that you should sound different when you read from when you talk. Their effect is not clear, either. The rate may be so slow that the reader may forget the earlier part of a sentence or passage. But, after all, ungraceful reading may be only a superficial aspect of reading skill that has little to do with deriving meaning from print.

Lefevre (1964) and Pival and Faust (1965) are among those who have suggested the detrimental effects of distorted intonational features on sentence comprehension.

5.3. Syllabification

Instruction in the middle grades often includes exercises in dividing words into syllables, either as a strategy for analyzing long words or as a writing convention for keeping right-hand margins even. The instruction seems to be based on the assumption that counting the number of syllables in a word and drawing the boundaries between them is a simple matter. Any extended practice in syllabifying words, however, turns up several problems.

First of all, syllabification in speech and writing must be distinguished for at least some details. For instance, the rule for dividing a word between double consonants, as in *fun-ny* and *rab-bit* does not apply to speech, i.e., /fəni/ and /ræbIt/, since the double letters do not correspond to double sounds.

Secondly, although the number of syllables in a long word may be phonetically clear, where one syllable ends and another begins is not. The medial consonant sounds in words like *rabbit* and *robot*, for example, cannot be unequivocally assigned to one vowel or the other. Structural characteristics of the language have been selected to guide the division of words into syllables. One basic phonological principle is that syllables should be divided according to the distribution of vowels in monosyllabic words. Therefore, *rabbit* would be divided /ræb-It/ because no words end with the vowel /æ/ in English; it is always followed by a consonant. The principle is irrelevant for *robot*, however, since /o/ can appear both finally or preceding a consonant, as in *row* /ro/ and *robe*/rob/. A morphological principle, that words should be divided at morpheme boundaries, is often applied to word division, e.g., *beast-ly* and *hot-house*. But sometimes it conflicts with a phonological principle. For instance, on morphological grounds *fiddler* might be divided *fiddl-er*/fIdl-ər/ but no English monosyllabic words end in a vowel plus /dl/.

Some sort of practice in dividing words into syllables might be useful for breaking down complex words. But instruction in analyzing such words should not be based on the premise that there is a "correct" way of dividing each and every long English word into syllables.

Wardhaugh (1966) discusses problems in the description of English syllabic structure. Shuy (1969) suggests a set of rules to guide syllabic division.

5.4 The Place of Grammar

More and more evidence has been accumulating to reject the notion that reading is simply sequential word recognition. Part of the evidence comes from considering the role of grammar in the reading process. Even as they first learn to read children seem to use their knowledge of grammar in a way similar to when they listen to spoken language. Their speech shows that they have flexible control over the grammatical system. In bringing it to bear on reading, they demonstrate not only that they understand sentences by virtue of it, but also that they actively use it to anticipate what will follow in a sentence.

Most of the evidence for children's use of grammar in their reading strategy comes from the analysis of their oral reading errors. A comparison of their performance on words in lists with the same words in passages shows that the context of the passage provides cues that contribute to their identifying more words successfully. On the other hand, they will sometimes miss or omit familiar words in the context of passages. For instance, they will miss a word like *help* in the sentence *He can help Sam.* But what they substitute will be a word that almost invariably conforms to the preceding grammatical context of the sentence, namely, a verb like *hear* or *hop,* but not *hot* or *her.* Furthermore, even first graders will as a rule correct errors that result in a sentence that is not grammatical, e.g., **He can hop Sam.*

Clay (1968), Weber (1970), Beaver (1968) and various studies from Goodman and his associates (e.g., Burke and Goodman 1970) describe children's errors with respect to grammatical structure. MacKinnon (1959) provides many examples. Lefevre (1968) stresses the sentence as the basic meaning unit in reading. Kolers (1970) and Ryan and Semmel (1969) emphasize the role of grammar in their description of reading as a constructive cognitive process.

5.5 Grammar and Comprehension

Reading specialists have tended to slight the significance of grammatical structure in their descriptions of the reading process. Recently, however, linguists' emphasis on analyzing what a person must know in order to understand sentences has contributed to giving the comprehension of grammatical structures a central place in the process. All in all, the psychological processes by which people understand speech or writing are still far from clear, but the broad relations between grammatical structure and overall comprehension have received some attention.

For instance, the effect on comprehension of making materials grammatically similar to the speech of the children who read them has been examined. Their comprehension scores are higher on passages written in surface grammar patterns that appear frequently in their speech than on passages written in patterns that appear infrequently.

Recent work on readability, that is, on developing measures that will predict the relative ease of comprehension of a passage, has also given certain grammatical indicators primary emphasis.

Wardhaugh (1969), Ruddell (1969) and Bormuth (1969) bring recent linguistic theory to bear on their discussions of reading comprehension. Ruddell (1965), Nurss (1968) and Tatham (1970) have studied children's comprehension of grammatically controlled materials. Bormuth (1966) has refined readability measures with grammatical variables.

6. Variation in English

An important aspect of linguistic inquiry is the study of variation within a language and its relationship to factors outside linguistic structure. It is convenient to talk about English as though everyone — including children — always used the identical phonological system, the same rules for forming sentences, and the same vocabulary for talking about the same things. Most treatments of language with reference to reading avoid dealing with the range of variation within English, or else mention only those differences which have traditionally been stigmatized as nonstandard. Linguists, it should be added, mention variation more often than they actually study it, partially because it brings up enormous complexities and requires special methodological techniques.

The uniform spelling system and traditions of non-fiction writing in English tend to mask the differences in grammar, pronunciation, and vocabulary that turn up every day. Writing usually comes to mind when people discuss English and, as in other speech communities, they think of the written form as the model for the spoken. When they do notice differences they often consider them unfortunate deviations from the norm and tend to deal with them categorically: she *never* pronounces *l*'s or he *always* says *ain't*. But it should be noted any speaker's abilities can be seen as a coherent system without reference to a standard. Furthermore, each speaker's use of his language shows some variability under different conditions, e.g., the person who says /wɔ/ for *wall* in *They built a high wall* may well pronounce the /l/ before a vowel, as in *a high wall around there*.

Three types of variation can be distinguished in spoken English. First, there is variation by region. Second, there is variation by the social identity of the speaker. Third, there is variation by factors in the speaker's immediate social situation such as the setting, the person he is speaking to, and his topic. Within American English, then, there are regional dialects, social dialects, and styles, but they are not entirely independent. Casual style, for instance, often shows more regional characteristics than formal style. For the most part, materials for the teaching of reading have not taken such variation into account, nor has the teacher-training curriculum. On the other hand, it is not altogether clear what sorts of accommodations to such variation might be made in order to teach reading effectively.

6.1 Regional Dialects

In the United States, regional dialects differ only somewhat in vocabulary, e.g., *tennis shoes* vs. *sneakers,* and even less in grammar, e.g., *dived* vs. *dove*. For the most part they differ in the quality, number and distribution of vowels and the closely related status of /r/. Most materials designed to teach systematic sound-letter correspondences present fourteen vowel types as well as /r/ in words like *shore* and *short*, as though all American children come to school using that precise set of distinctive sounds. Although this "General American" may not accurately describe the speech of many children, it is not clear that adjustments to regional American dialects in teaching materials would facilitate learning to read. Perhaps an introduction to the main corespondences is all that is useful for working out efficient reading strategies. Detailed rules limited to a particular dialect may not be worth learning as special correspondences, even to the children who speak that dialect, especially because other cues, such as grammar and the meaning of the passage, may sufficiently complement the information provided through a set of general correspondence rules.

If a particular regional dialect turns out to have a slightly different relationship to the spelling system than the "General American" presented in educational materials, the differences may show up precisely when the teacher's point is to show consistency, that is, in words that are supposed to rhyme or to differ by only a final consonant. Examples of dialect characteristics that involve shifts from the normalized correspondence system are given below. It should be noted, however, that a phonetic characteristic of a given dialect does not necessarily require such a shift. For instance, the pronounciation of /au/ as in *out* and *owl* beginning more like *apple* or *air* rather than *arm* is a noticeable trait in some regions. But it presents no problem because wherever the spellings *ou* and *ow* correspond to /au/, speakers consistently use the regional version.

Regional variations from the sound letter system described in educational materals include the following types:

(1)   Some contrasts described in materials are not maintained in speech. West of the Mississippi, few speakers contrast /a/ with /ɔ/ in words like *stock/stalk, log/dog.*

(2)   Some contrasts described in materials are not maintained in given positions relative to other sounds in speech. While some speakers do maintain a contrast between /æ/ɛ/e/ before /r/ as in *very/vary, fairy/ ferry* or *marry/merry/Mary* as described in materials, others do not.

(3)   Some contrasts are not mentioned in materials, nor are they reflected in traditional spelling. For instance, in some parts of the East, the following pairs do not rhyme: *dad/bad; has/jazz; can(run)/(tin)can.*

(4)   Some contrasts in given positions relative to other sounds are not mentioned in materials; they may be reflected in spelling. For instance, in parts of the South the distinction between /o/ and /ɔ/ before /r/ — which may be pronounced as a vowel — is maintained, so that *wore/war, four/for* contrast.

(5)   The basic sound system may be the same as the one represented in the educational materials, but the distribution of sounds in words may

differ. Although speakers may contrast /a/ and /ɔ/ in *frog/log/dog/hog* or /I/ and /ɛ/ in *wet/bit/get*, the exact words in which these sounds occur may differ from area to area.

In the case of types (1) and (2), instructional materials may uselessly provide practice on differences. In the case of (3), (4), and (5), materials may insist on rhymes while students themselves can hear differences.

6.2 Social Dialects

Within a geographical area there is variation from speaker to speaker that depends on such factors as a speaker's age, sex, level of education, and occupation. The linguistic features that distinguish speakers of low and high social and economic standing are very slight compared to the features that they share. But it is the speech of high status speakers that has been established and maintained as standard English. Standard speech is most closely reflected in writing; features that are marked as non-standard in speech are automatically excluded from nonfiction writing. For children who come to school speaking a nonstandard dialect, then, there is a greater gap between what they ordinarily say and what they read than there is for their standard-speaking age-mates. This is not to suggest that they suffer from a language deficit, but that their system of rules for forming sentences differs in details.

The variety of nonstandard speech that has been examined most closely in relation to standard English is that spoken by many black children throughout the United States. The phonological system of this variety differs from the General American Standard in ways outlined above for the regional dialects. Specifically, several vowels merge, /r/ /l/ are not consistently pronounced in post-vocalic position, nor are certain consonants at the ends of words or in particular clusters. In ordinary speech, then, speakers do not distinguish *tin/ten, oil/all, fault/fought, fine/find* or *pass/past.* An important qualification is that sometimes speakers do distinguish them. Final consonants are apt to be pronounced, for instance, when they are followed by a word beginning with a vowel. But by and large this dialect is noticeable in its tendency for the spoken word to have fewer segments than the written words has letters. What learning problem this creates is not altogether clear.

On the grammatical level there are parallel sorts of omissions relative to the standard that in some cases coincide with the omission of consonants. Like the /t/ and /d/ in *find* and *past,* the past tense endings /t/ and /d/ on verbs such as *fined* and *passed* are often omitted. The *-s* endings for plurality and possession in nouns *(dogs, dog's)* and for person in verbs *(dries)* are also dropped, as are forms of the verb *to be* under certain conditions. Here again, from the point of view of the speaker, printed English is overwritten. Still other grammatical constructions widen the distance from the standard for instance, *It ain't nobody there* in contrast to *There's nobody there* or *There isn't anybody there.* Some of the features in the dialect, like this one, are peculiar to it; others, including many of the phonological features, are shared with other dialects. All in all, they constitute a significant number of systematic differences from the standard that are disregarded in teaching and testing materials.

In learning to read, a child who speaks a nonstandard variety of English faces several special problems. More than other young readers, he has to calibrate what he reads with what he already knows how to say. After all, this in and of itself may not be a very difficult job; a child's abilities to learn a new language or regional dialect are well known. On the other hand, the task of learning a new variety of the language may be great enough to interfere with learning to read. A further problem is that without an understanding that speaking and reading the standard are distinctly different, the teacher may count dialect differences as reading errors. For instance, if a child says "hisself" for *himself* or "brung" for *brought*, he will be penalized as though he had said "hammer" for one and "bright" for the other. Still another problem has basically no relevance to the specifics of the reading task. Some teachers place such strong negative value on nonstandard English that it biases their judgments of a child's capacity to learn to read or to use his language effectively.

6.3. Style

Another dimension of variation depends on factors in the immediate situation. Adults control a range of styles from casual to formal which show differences in pronunciation, grammatical structure, and vocabulary choice. Compare *Won't make it; He won't make it; He will not succeed.* Learning the styles and when to use them continues into adulthood; becoming literate is only one aspect of the process. The more formal speech styles are influenced by the written variety and are to some extent maintained by it. People will use their most formal pronunciation, for instance, when they read aloud.

Six-year-olds have little stylistic variation in their speech. Their pronunciation is generally like the casual style of adults, with perhaps a few alterations like *Put them away/Put 'em away.* Perhaps it is in reading that some children first put the /t/ on *don't* or make a contrast between the /t/ and /d/ in *Betty/ready.* Acquiring more formal pronunciation seems to be a necessary process in cutting up the flow of speech to match written words.

Gleason (1965) discusses the several dimensions of variation in English. McDavid (1958) and Shuy (1967) survey regional dialects. Reed (1966, 1969) and Smith (1968) consider dialectal variation and Fasold (1969) considers social variation in their analyses of the relationship between speech and writing. Baratz and Shuy (1969), Aarons *et al.* (1969), Horn (1970) and Figurel (1970) gather papers on reading with respect to social dialects. McDavid (1967) provides a checklist of features. Goodman (1965), Labov (1967, 1970) and Stewart (1969) deal with potential sources of reading difficulty for blacks, McDavid (1970) for whites. Serwer (1969) argues for using the experience method with children who speak nonstandard English, Goodman (1965) for letting them read standard material in their own dialect, and Stewart (1969) for preparing materials in dialect. Labov (1965) deals with the emergence of standard English in the school years.

7. Reading English as a Second Language

The special problem of the child who speaks a nonstandard dialect of English is that there is less correspondence between what he says and what he reads than there is for other children. The problem for the child who does not speak English at all is that there is no obvious systematic correspondence between his spoken language and written English. In learning to read English, then, the child who is monolingual in another language must learn the language as well as reading skills.

One reasonable approach to teaching such children to read English is to separate the tasks: First of all, teach the children to speak English and then teach them to read the English that they have learned. In practice, this approach has been implemented in two ways. One is by providing the children with a good deal of experience in speaking English for as much as a year or two before reading instruction begins. Another is by teaching the children to speak English in carefully controlled materials and at each step having them learn to read what they have just learned to say and understand.

Another way of separating the reading from the language learning task is to teach the children to read in their native tongue first, even though the ultimate goal may be to teach them to master English reading and writing. There is some evidence that this approach has long-term benefits. It gives children immediate skills that are transferred to reading the second language with more success than those taught to read the second language directly. Furthermore, it affirms the value of the child's native tongue by giving it a place in the curriculum.

Although it is reasonable to separate learning a language from learning to read, it clearly is not always necessary. Given their capacity for language learning, many children are able to integrate the two tasks so that within a year they are as competent in reading as native speakers. These are among the variables related to language that may play a part in determining a child's success: the similarity between English and his native tongue (Spanish is structurally closer to English than Navajo is); the proportion of other children in the class who are native speakers of English; the opportunity for the child to use English outside class, especially with other children; the value that they or their parents place on learning English.

Rosen and Ortego (1969) provide an annotated bibliography on reading in a second language. Sayville (1970), Young (1970) and papers in Aarons *et al.* discuss the problems of various groups of American children who do not speak English. Robinett (1965) provides a rationale for materials.

References

Aarons, Alfred C., Gordon, Barbara Y., and Stewart, William A., eds. 1969. Linguistic-cultural differences and American education. *Florida FL Reporter* 7, No. 1.

Baratz, Joan C. and Shuy, Roger W., eds. 1969. *Teaching black children to read.* Washington: Center for Applied Linguistics.

Beaver, Joseph C. 1968. Transformational grammar and the teaching of reading. *Research on the Teaching of English* 2.161-71.

Berdiansky, Betty, Cronnell, Bruce, and Koehler, John, Jr. 1969. *Spelling-sound relations and primary form-class descriptions for speech-comprehension vocabularies of 6-9 year olds.* Inglewood, California: Southwest Regional Laboratory.

Bloomfield, Leonard. 1961. Teaching children to read. In *Let's read* by Leonard Bloomfield and Clarence L. Barnhart, pp. 19-42. Detroit: Wayne State University Press. (An expanded version of Linguistics and reading, Elementary English Review 19. 125-30; 183-86, 1942.)

Bormuth, John R. 1966. Readability: a new approach. *Reading Research Quarterly* 1.79-132.
————— 1969. An operational definition of comprehension instruction. In *Psycholinguistics and the teaching of reading,* ed. Kenneth S. Goodman and James T. Fleming, pp. 48-60. Newark, Delaware: International Reading Association.

Broz, James, Jr., and Hayes, Alfred S. 1966. *Linguistics and reading: a selective annotated bibliography for teachers of reading.* Washington: Center for Applied Linguistics.

Burke, Carolyn L. and Goodman, Kenneth S. 1970. When a child reads: a psycholinguistic analysis. *Elementary English* 47.121-29.

Carroll, John B. 1964. The analysis of reading instruction: perspectives from psychology and linguistics. *Theories of Learning and Instruction,* ed. Ernest R. Hilgard, pp. 336-53. Sixty-third Yearbook of the National Society for the Study of Education, Part I.

Chomsky, Carol. 1970. Reading, writing, and phonology. *Harvard Educational Review* 40.287-309.

Chomsky, Noam. 1970. Phonology and reading, In *Basic studies on reading,* ed. Harry Levin and Joanna P. Williams. New York: Basic Books.

Clay, Marie M. 1968. A syntactic analysis of reading errors. *Journal of Verbal Learning and Verbal Behavior* 7.434-38.

Desberg, Peter and Berdiansky, Betty. 1968. *Word attack skills: review of the literature*. Inglewood, California: Southwest Regional Laboratory.

Dykstra, Robert. 1968. Summary of the second grade phase of the Cooperative Research Program in Primary Reading Instruction. *Reading Research Quarterly* 4.49-70.

Fasold, Ralph. 1969. Orthography in reading materials for Black English speaking children. In *Teaching black children to read*, ed. Joan C. Baratz and Roger W. Shuy, pp. 68-91. Washington: Center for Applied Linguistics.

Figurel, J. Allen, ed. 1970. *Reading goals for the disadvantaged*. Newark, Delaware: International Reading Association.

Fleming, James T. 1968. Oral language and beginning reading: another look. *The Reading Teacher* 22.24-29.

Francis, W. Nelson. 1958. *The Structure of American English*. New York: Ronald Press.

Fries, Charles C. 1963. *Linguistics and reading*. New York: Holt, Rinehart and Winston.

Gleason, H. A., Jr., 1961. *An introduction to descriptive linguistics*. New York: Holt, Rinehart, Winston.

_____. 1965. *Linguistics and English grammar*. New York: Holt, Rinehart, Winston.

Goodman, Kenneth S. 1965. Dialect barriers to reading comprehension. *Elementary English* 42.853-60. (Reprinted in Baratz and Shuy, pp. 14-28, 1969, and in *Dimensions of dialect*, ed. Eldonna L. Evertts, pp. 39-46, 1967. Champaign, Illinois: National Council of Teachers of English.)

_____. ed. 1968. *The psycholinguistic nature of the reading process*. Detroit: Wayne State University Press.

_____. 1969. Analysis of oral reading miscues: applied psycholinguistics. *Reading Research Quarterly* 5.9-30.

_____ and Fleming, James T., eds. 1969. *Psycholinguistics and the teaching of reading*. Newark, Delaware: International Reading Association.

Goodman, Yetta M. and Goodman, Kenneth S. 1967. *Linguistics and the teaching of reading: an annotated bibliography*. I[nternational] R[eading] A[ssociation] Annotated Bibliography 12.

Hall, Robert A., Jr. 1961. *Sound and spelling in English*. Philadelphia: Chilton.

Halle, Morris. 1969. Some thoughts on spelling. In *Psycholinguistics and the teaching of reading*, ed. Kenneth S. Goodman and James T. Fleming, pp. 17-24. Newark, Delaware: International Reading Association.

Hanna, Paul A. *et al.* 1966. *Phoneme-grapheme correspondences as cues to spelling improvement*. Washington: United States Government Printing Office.

Higgenbottom, Eleanor M. 1962. A study of the representation of English vowel phonemes in the orthography. *Language and Speech* 5.67-117.

Horn, Thomas D., ed. 1970. *Reading for the disadvantaged*. New York: Harcourt, Brace and World.

Hull, Louise. 1965. Linguistic reading in the first grade. *Elementary English* 42. 883-88.

Joos, Martin. 1960. Review of *Regularized English* by Axel Wijk. *Language* 36.250-62.

Kolers, Paul A. 1970. Three stages of reading. In *Basic studies on reading*, ed. Harry Levin and Joanna P. Williams. New York: Basic Books.

Labov, William. 1965. Stages in the acquisition of standard English. In *Social dialects and language learning*, ed. Roger W. Shuy, pp. 77-103. Champaign, Illinois: National Council of Teachers of English.

_____. 1967. Some sources of reading problems for Negro speakers of non-standard English. In *New directions in elementary English*, ed. Alexander Frazier, pp. 140-167. Champaign, Illinois: National Council of Teachers of English. (Reprinted with revisions in Baratz and Shuy, pp. 29-67, 1969.)

_____. 1970. Language characteristics of specific groups: blacks. In *Reading for the disadvantaged*, ed. Thomas D. Horn, pp. 139-156. New York: Harcourt, Brace and World.

Lefevre, Carl A. 1964. *Linguistics and the teaching of reading*. New York: McGraw-Hill.

_____. 1968. The simplistic standard word-perception theory of reading. *Elementary English* 45.349-53.

Levin, Harry and Williams, Joanna P., eds. 1970. *Basic studies on reading*. New York: Basic Books.

Loban, Walter. 1963. *The language of elementary school children*. Champaign, Illinois: National Council of Teachers of English.

Lobdell, Lawrence O. 1965. Let's update the word lists. *Elementary English* 42.156-58.

MacKinnon, A. R. 1959. *How do children learn to read?* Vancouver: Copp Clark.

McCarthy, Dorothea A. 1954. Language development in children. In *Manual of child psychology*, ed. Leonard Carmichael, pp. 492-630. New York: Wiley.

McDavid, Raven I. 1958. The dialects of American English. In *The Structure of American English* by W. Nelson Francis, pp. 480-543. New York: Ronald Press.

_____. 1967. A checklist of significant features for discriminating social dialects. In *Dimensions of dialect*, ed. Eldonna L. Evertts, pp. 7-10. Champaign, Illinois: National Council of Teachers of English.

_____. 1970. Language characteristics of specific groups: native whites. In *Reading for the disadvantaged*, ed. Thomas D. Horn, pp. 135-139. New York: Harcourt, Brace and World.

Menyuk, Paula. 1969. *Sentences children use*. Cambridge, Massachusetts: M.I.T. Press.

Nurss, Joanne R. 1968. Children's reading: syntactic structure and comprehension difficulty. In *Proceedings of the International Reading Association 12*, ed. J. Allen Figurel, pp. 571-75. Newark, Delaware: International Reading Association.

O'Donnell, Roy C., Griffin, William J., and Norris, Raymond C. 1967. *Syntax of kindergarten and elementary school children: a transformational analysis*. Champaign, Illinois: National Council of Teachers of English.

Olsen, Hans C. 1968. Linguistics and materials for beginning reading instruction. In *The psycholinguistic nature of the reading process*, ed. Kenneth S. Goodman, pp. 270-287. Detroit: Wayne State University Press.

Pival, Jean and Faust, George. 1965. Toward improved reading instruction: a discussion of variation in pronunciation with weak stress. *Elementary English* 42.861-865.

Reed, David W. 1966. A theory of language, speech, and writing. *Highlights of the pre-convention institutes: linguistics and reading*, ed. Leonard Courtney, pp. 4-25. Newark, Delaware: International Reading Association. (Reprinted in Ruddell and Singer, 1970, pp. 219-238. The first part originally appeared in *Elementary English* 42. 845-51, 1965.)

_____. 1969. Linguistics and literacy. *Georgetown University Monograph Series on Languages and Linguistics* 22.93-103.

Robinett, Ralph F. 1965. A linguistic approach to beginning reading for bilingual children. In *First grade reading programs, Perspectives in Reading 5*, ed. James F. Kerfoot, Newark, Delaware: International Reading Association.

Rosen, Carl L. and Ortego, Philip D. 1969. *Issues in language and reading instruction of Spanish-speaking children: an annotated bibliography*. Newark, Delaware: International Reading Association.

Ruddell, Robert B. 1965. Effect of the similarity of oral and written patterns of language structure on reading comprehension. *Elementary English* 42.403-10.

_____. 1969. Psycholinguistic implications for a systems of communication model. In *Psycholinguistics and the teaching of reading*, ed. Kenneth S. Goodman and James T. Fleming, pp. 61-78. Newark, Delaware: International Reading Association. (Reprinted in Ruddell and Singer, 1970.)

_____. 1970. Language acquisition and the reading process. In *Theoretical models and processes of reading*, ed. Harry Singer and Robert B. Ruddell, pp. 1-19. Newark, Delaware: International Reading Association.

Sayville, Muriel R. 1970. Language and the disadvantaged. In *Reading for the disadvantaged*, ed. Thomas D. Horn, pp. 115-34. Newark, Delaware: International Reading Association.

Serwer, Blanche L. 1969. Linguistic support for a method of teaching beginning reading to black children. *Reading Research Quarterly* 4.449-67.

Shuy, Roger W. 1967. *Discovering American dialects*. Champaign, Illinois: National Council of Teachers of English.

_____. 1969. Some language and culture differences in a theory of reading. In *Psycholinguistics and the teaching of reading*, ed. Kenneth S. Goodman and James T. Fleming, pp. 34-47. Newark, Delaware: International Reading Association.

Singer, Harry and Ruddell, Robert B., eds. 1970. *Theoretical models and processes of reading*. Newark, Delaware: International Reading Association.

Smith, Henry Lee, Jr. 1963. Review of *Let's Read*, by Leonard Bloomfield and Clarence L. Barnhart. *Language* 39.67-78.

_____. 1968. *English morphophonics: implications for the teaching of literacy*. New York State English Council Monograph 10.

Soffietti, James B. 1955. Why children fail to read: a linguistic analysis. *Harvard Educational Review* 25.63-84.

Stewart, William A. 1969. On the use of Negro dialect in the teaching of reading. In *Teaching black children to read*, ed. Joan C. Baratz and Roger W. Shuy, pp. 156-219. Washington: Center for Applied Linguistics.

Strickland, Ruth G. 1962. *The language of elementary school children: its relationship to the language of reading textbooks and the quality of reading of selected school children*. Indiana University Bulletin of the School of Education 38.

Tatham, Susan Masland. 1970. Reading comprehension of materials written with select oral language patterns: a study at grades two and four. *Reading Research Quarterly* 5.402-26.

Templin, Mildred. 1957. *Certain language skills in children*. University of Minnesota Institute of Child Welfare Monograph 26.

Venezky, Richard L. 1967. English orthography: its graphical structure and its relation to sound. *Reading Research Quarterly* 2.75-106.

_____. 1970. Regularity in reading and spelling. In *Basic studies on reading*, ed. Harry Levin and Joanna P. Williams. New York: Basic Books.

Walden, James, ed. 1969. *Oral language and reading*. Champaign, Illinois: National Council of Teachers of English.

Wardhaugh, Ronald. 1966. Syl-lab-i-ca-tion. *Elementary English* 43. 785-88.

_____. 1968. Linguistic insights into the reading process. *Language Learning* 18.235-252.

_____. 1969. *Reading: a linguistic perspective*. New York: Harcourt Brace.

Weber, Rose-Marie. 1970. First graders' use of grammatical context in reading. In *Basic studies on reading*, ed. Harry Levin and Joanna P. Williams. New York, Basic Books.

Weir, Ruth H. and Venezky, Richard L. 1968. Spelling-to-sound patterns. In *The psycholinguistic nature of the reading process*, ed. Kenneth S. Goodman, pp. 185-199. Detroit: Wayne State University Press.

Young, Robert W. 1970. Language characteristics of specific groups: American Indians. In *Reading for the disadvantaged*, ed. Thomas D. Horn, pp. 161-66. Newark: International Reading Association.

Linguistic-Psycholinguistic Implications for Reading

Weber—Question for Discussion

How would you define each of the following approaches to the study of language—the structuralist approach, the generative approach and the transformational approach? Is there such a thing as "a linguistic method?" What is the meaning of the terms "phonology," "lexicon," and "grammar?" In what ways do spoken and written English differ? What is the meaning of the term "psycholinguistics?" What implications might variations in regional and social dialects have for the classroom teacher of reading?

Kenneth S. Goodman

Comprehension-Centered Reading

Reading is a process by which a person reconstructs a message encoded graphically by a writer. Like all language activities, reading has as its central purpose, effective communication of meaning. In the full sense, comprehension is the only objective of the reader. To the extent that he has this end continuously in view he is reading; to the extent that he loses comprehension as a goal he is doing something other than reading: saying sounds, naming words, manipulating language. This alone would be enough to justify the claim that instruction in reading must center on comprehension.

But there is an even more basic reason why reading instruction must be comprehension centered. Language does not exist apart from its relationship to meaning. Now this meaning is not a property of language— the sounds or ink blotches have no intrinsic meaning. Meaning is supplied by the reader himself as he processes the symbolic system of language. As a user of the language he relates language sequences to experiences and conceptual structures. He cannot get the message unless he can process the language. But neither can he process the language unless he has the relevant experiential-conceptual background to bring to the particular task. I can't read a technical treatise on nuclear physics: I'm disadvantaged; I lack the background. But I do well at reading even highly technical material where I have strong interests and relevant cognitive structures. Meaning, in short, is both output and input, in the reading process. Unless the teaching of reading is comprehension centered the

From Kenneth S. Goodman, "Comprehension-Centered Reading," Claremont Reading Conference, *Reading Conference Yearbook* 34 (1970): 125-35. Reprinted by permission of the author and the editor of the *Yearbook*.

very nature of the task is changed from reading to something other than reading.

That's my basic message. The rest of my discussion will be (1) an attempt to support this view, and (2) an attempt to explore its implications.

Building Reading Instruction
on a Sound Theoretical Base

My view of reading instruction I must warn you is built on a strong theoretical base which has been continually tempered by plunging it into the reality of real people reading real language.

I am convinced that, to build effective reading methods and materials, we must (a) understand the reading process (b) know what it is that proficient readers do (c) get clear in our minds what reading is for (d) understand how people become proficient readers: that is, how reading is learned.

My research has been devoted to describing what readers do when they read material new to themselves and deriving from that a theory and model of the reading process which in turn can be applied back to predicting, categorizing, and describing what people do when they read. I am fully aware that each day thousands of teachers are confronted with millions of learners who must be taught *now* and that the educational assembly line cannot be shut down until basic knowledge is available on which instruction must be based. But I am convinced that the quest for that basic knowledge must be pursued.

The alternatives are visible in the old and new solutions to the reading dilemma in current vogue.

At the risk of setting up straw men I'd like to characterize these approaches.

(a)   There's the *butterfly collector* approach. Most relatively effective reading teachers and clinicians are butterfly collectors. They have large collections of bits and pieces, and gimmicks that work with some children some time. And every so often they add a new butterfly to the collection making a mental note as they do so that one day they must organize that collection. But they never do and they are unable to build on knowledge or put it in a form that can be transmitted to others.

(b)   Some solutions to the reading problem are neat, sequential, behaviorally stated *stairways to nowhere*. Assumptions are made about what readers must do or know or existing materials are searched for bits and pieces and gimmicks and these are stated as behavioral objectives. Early results with such approaches are always impressive since (1) the readers already could do a lot of the things they're taught and (2) evaluation is through tests composed of items that are just like the instructional materials. But the stairways never get the learner to that glorious behavioral valhalla in the sky because to complete the stairway the entire reading process would have to be understood and that process would have to be amenable to sequencing into neat behavioral steps. And it is not so amenable.

(c)   Other programs are derived from diligent and rigorous *trial and error*. Try method A, book A, system A against method B, book B, system B, discard the poor and use the better. Then proceed with C, D, etc. Or keep changing your procedures until you get better results. While the latter is practical advice for a teacher the teacher will certainly need some criteria for determining how to change. How long would we have waited for a cure to polio if we were depending on testing any proffered method against any other or making sporadic and intuitive modifications in existing treatments? How in fact can you achieve major innovations in solving any problems through trial and error, however rigorous?

(d)   A rather homey solution to the reading problem is one I call the *chicken soup approach*. Phonics is liberally served up to all like chicken soup on the assumption that it might help and it couldn't hurt. Unfortunately it can hurt some learners.

(e)   Finally there is the *systems approach,* recommended as a solution for everything (so why not reading). If we are confused let's organize our confusion systematically. This approach was pioneered by the Department of Defense (affectionately known as the DOD) and has demonstrated its utility in the solution of such problems as the Viet-Nam war. In the aero-space industry problems are solved through systems approaches at no more than three to ten times their original projected cost. There is however an adage which has found its way into even the Pentagon: Garbage in, garbage out. Reading problems will apparently not be solved simply by broadening the scope of the DOD and renaming it the Department of Education and Defense (DEAD).

Fortunately many children have the internal resources to surmount all obstacles we place in their way and to learn to read anyway. For this fact we should be grateful though it confuses research since children can apparently learn in spite of their instruction rather than because of it.

The Reading Process

There *is* a process of reading with certain essential characteristics regardless of the nature of what is being read or even the language and orthography in which it is printed.

Reading, like listening, *is* a receptive psycholinguistic process. Language in its graphic form is the starting point. The reader brings to the text his knowledge of the language. As he reads there is an interaction between language and thought processes such that the reader moves from a language encoding of meaning to meaning itself.

Though the sensory modality involved is visual, the reading process is only incidentally visual since even what the reader thinks he sees at any point is only partly what he sees and partly what he expects to see. On the basis of the language structures he controls, the reader is constantly predicting what he will see. He samples from the available cues of the graphic display using language strategies he has developed to select only those cues which carry the most information. He arrives at hypothetical, tentative choices (guesses), as he reads, checking them against his predictions and the grammatical and semantic constraints of which he is aware. Then he needs only enough subsequent information to confirm or disconfirm his prediction.

Reading printed words then is a spiral of predict, sample, select, guess, and confirm activities. The reader has strategies for these activities. *The proficient reader uses the least amount of information to make the best possible first guesses.* He also has an effective set of strategies for checking the validity of his guesses. Simply, he asks himself whether (a) they produce language structures as he knows them and (b) they make sense. Finally he has a set of strategies for correcting when he realizes that he has been unsuccessful.

Reading is *not* an exact precise process of identifying each letter and then each word and then each sequence. Such a process would be not only inefficient since all information need not be processed, but it would be ineffective as well, because readers would be distracted by the excess of graphic and phonic information and would be less able to integrate it with the syntactic and semantic information they must process to deal with the text as language.

No single cue or system of cues in fact is useful in reading unless it is processed in its relationship to all other cues in a natural language setting. Language is *not* a salami which can be sliced as thin as one wishes with each slice retaining all the essential qualities of the whole. When language is broken into sounds, letters, words, or even phrases what results is something other than language. Language must be understood *in process* as it stands in relationship to its use. It must have structure and there must be meaning for it to be language.

A word needs to be said about context in reading. There are in reality two contexts: one is syntactic, the language structure. The other is semantic: the meaning or message. These are interdependent. In fact it is not possible to have meaning without grammer; but readers use both contexts. Let us remember that the reader is not ultimately concerned with naming, recognizing, or identifying words but that his concern is comprehension. Reading programs have been word centered for too long. The reader does not use context simply to identify words, rather he uses all cues in relationship to all others to reconstruct the message.

The Reader as a
User of Language

Because reading instruction was disconnected from its language base for so long the most important resource children bring to the task of learning to read has been underestimated or ignored. That resource is their highly developed language competence. Beginners in reading are already highly skilled in using language. They are able to communicate their needs, thoughts, and reactions to the world to others by encoding them in language and producing speech. They are able to understand messages from others by processing the surface phonological structures of speech, inducing the underlying language structures and reconstructing the meaning.

Any limitations on the child's ability to function as a listener in his own community are experiential and conceptual and not primarily linguistic.

All of this is of enormous use to the beginner reader. His task is to learn to induce the underlying language structures from *written* language. As long as he is confronted with graphic material which is real and meaningful (as opposed to fragmentary, artificial, and/or non-sensical) he can utilize his language competence. If however the meanings require more semantic input than he can provide then the task becomes nonsense for him. He must in fact be able to know whether the message he is reconstructing makes sense.

To give the child beginning to learn to read his native language full credit we must differentiate between language competence and language performance. Too many studies of child language have equated the two assuming that what children *do* in language is the same as what they are capable of doing. That can be put another way; we have confused behavior with the competence that underlies it and makes it possible. In studying vocabulary, for example, we have assumed that we could judge its breadth by listing the words used by a child in a given situation. Vocabulary however is highly contingent on a particular individual's interest *in,* background *for,* and willingness *to discuss,* a particular topic under particular circumstances. We have been quite willing to accept the conclusion that boys are less competent linguistically than girls at school and pre-school ages because in fact girls perform better on typical research tasks. It is at least as likely however that under different conditions that favor boys they would perform better than girls.

We must learn to relate linguistic performance to a theoretical understanding of language competence in order to interpret the former and gain insight into the latter.

Frequently we interpret particular language performance as indicative of lack of competence where in fact it indicates quite the opposite.

The pre-schooler who says "I taked it" is showing mastery of a basic pattern for indicating past tense, not sloppy speech. Similarly, the beginning reader who reads *home* for *house* in *The dog had a new warm house*, is showing a high degree of reading competence, not a lack of word recognition. A child who says *horse* for *house* in the same sentence is not showing a lack of phonics generalizations so much as he is some difficulty in using them in language context. A key to his competence will be whether he corrects if his reading is not comprehensible.

The goal of reading instruction is not to change reading behavior but to expand the reader's competence in comprehending written language. Behavior, at best, is a shadow image of that competence.

Perception as it functions in language is very much misunderstood. Every language user learns two things as he learns the language: (1) What to pay attention to (2) What not to pay attention to.

Each language uses only a small number of the ways that sounds may differ as significant distinctive features. The user of language must learn to note those significant features. If he did not also learn to ignore non-significant differences he would be constantly distracted. The unitary symbols of any language are perceptual rather than real units. Features may vary widely within the units but language users will ignore the differences. But minor differences *across* the boundaries must be noted. This is true for written as well as oral language. A reader comes to treat *A* and *H* as different though they are very similar and A *a* a d *a* as the same though they are very different.

We tend to treat performance on "auditory discrimination" tests as indicative of linguistic incompetence when it really shows how well the child has learned to screen out differences not significant in his own speech (pin, pen for example).

Speakers of low-status dialects are repeatedly misjudged as linguistically deficient by teachers and researchers because their language behavior does not match an expectation model. But difference and deficiency are not the same. All children, normal in the broadest sense of the word, have a high degree of language competence to bring to learning to read.

The Purposes of Reading

There is a romance that surrounds the purposes of reading that obscures its most vital functions and exaggerates others.

Written language develops in human societies when they become so complex that communication must be carried on over time and space and not merely on a face-to-face basis. Writers may seek to communicate messages to people whose ears they can not reach. They may preserve messages for the later use of others as well as themselves.

The basic reason for existence of competence in written language in an individual in a literate society is to cope with the everyday experiences in his culture which employ written language. He must read signs, follow written directions, fill out forms, read his mail.

Written language is the basic (though not exclusive) medium of literature. But one can function in literate society without reading literature. Minimal functioning with no reading competence at all is much harder.

Putting the purposes of reading in proper perspective it would appear that instruction should be built around what I choose to call situational reading, the kind that is so universal in a literate society that it is incidental to life itself. Situational reading, by virtue of its constant impingement on the life of children is self motivating. Many an American five year old can recognize five kinds of peanut butter and twice that many cereals by their labels. Four year olds quickly learn to know which door says "Men" and which one says "Ladies."

Once it is learned, reading can, of course, be used in pleasure seeking activities as in the reading of comic books or other literary works.

It may even be used in learning. But I must point out that in situational reading the meanings are either well defined by the situational contexts or within the conceptual grasp of the learner because they relate to recurrent experiences. Both the reading of literature and reading to learn move out and away from the learner and his immediate world.

Language grows in direct proportion to the experiences and conceptual growth of the learner. But there are limits on the leaps he can make. To gain new knowledge or concepts in reading requires considerable relevant semantic input. Bormuth's work indicates that unless a reader can score fairly well on a comprehension test over material *before* he reads it he will learn little from the reading.

Particularly in the elementary years, where skill in using written language lags well behind oral language competence, reading to learn has severe limitations. That suggests that reading should support or even follow learning in school rather than become its basic medium. A defensible cycle would be first to do, then to discuss, then to read, and then to write.

Text books are, by design, difficult reading tasks. They deal with many concepts unlikely to be known to the learners; the lower the level the more superficial they are likely to be. That doesn't necessarily reduce the comprehension problem since instead of treating a few topics in depth they treat many, bouncing along without developing any semantic context well enough to give the struggling reader much to go on. Many teachers have the mistaken notion that the text book's function is to teach *for* them and that each child should be able to read and learn from a text written for use at his grade level.

If the focus is kept clearly on comprehension teachers can sense some of the inherent difficulties children encounter in reading school texts. Particularly teachers will need to realize that vocabulary, in and of itself, is seldom the key problem but that the profusion of new concepts, the special ways that language is used, the reading tasks that are particular to each area of study are all major sources of problems.

Vocabulary can develop, in any useful sense, only in close relationship to experiences and concepts. It is the ideas that need introduction before reading. New vocabulary is only of value as it is needed to cope with those ideas.

Even the grammar of language used in mathematics texts, science texts, and social studies books varies. Though all are rooted in the same grammatical system the special uses of language in each field require structures which may be unique to the field or uncommon in other areas. Conditional statements in mathematics involve rather unusual structures somewhat different than conditional statements in science.

Recipes are special language forms which require special strategies to adequately comprehend and use them.

Even the reading of literature requires strategies for dealing with language that has special characteristics. In the situational language which is basic, the reader can depend on it to be predictable. Writers of literature tend to avoid common predictable structures, forms, and vocabulary and to seek novel and hence unpredictable ones. Further, each writer establishes a style of language all his own. The language of Hemingway is not that of Steinbeck.

If learners are to develop the competence to comprehend a wide range of reading materials they must then develop general reading competence to handle other kinds of language. They will also have to see purposes for themselves to make the development of such competencies necessary.

Intrinsic motivation in reading is simply a matter of wanting to get the meaning. That is true whether the form is a sign on a wall, a set of directions for assembling a model airplane, a comic strip, a chapter in a text or a short story.

Motivation which is extrinsic, such as grades, rewards, punishments, may lead to acceptable behavior which does not in fact represent the underlying reading competencies sought. Too many readers can answer questions acceptably over reading materials they do not comprehend. If so they have learned not to read but to behave acceptably.

Teaching and Learning Reading

It should be apparent that I am advocating organizing reading instruction totally around advancing comprehension. Each instructional activity should in fact be screened on the basis of whether it contributes to comprehension. Any skills or strategies should be developed within the quest for meaning in which the reader should be continuously engaged.

Relevancy is not a vague proposition in selecting reading materials. Since meaning is both input and output in reading, materials must be closely related to the background, interests, and experiences of particular learners.

To be comprehensible the language *at every stage of instruction* must be real language which is natural to the learners.

With the focus on meaning pupils will be able to move toward the integrated use of all cue systems in reading.

Throughout this discussion reference has been made to comprehension strategies. Strategies are general patterns readers develop for utilizing the varied kinds of cues available to them in reading print. The term "skills" has come to mean an isolated, or isolatable, bit of knowledge or technique which a reader uses. Such a term is inappropriate for describing what a proficient reader does (hence what a pupil must learn to do) since no such skill could be used invariantly in dealing with *actual* written language. In fact the reader's strategies must be flexible enough to allow for the changing relative importance of cues and cue systems in relationship to each other in given tasks.

In reading a recipe, for example, the difference between *2t baking powder* and *2T baking powder*, is the difference between success and failure of the recipe's use. But a cook who understands the function of baking powder and who is experienced would recognize the improbability of a reading error almost immediately. Semantic input serves, then, as a safeguard on graphic or phonic miscuing.

It is only when the focus is on comprehension that the relative importance of cues becomes clear and useful strategies may emerge.

Readers need a set of initial strategies for coping with varied reading tasks. They need a set of related, but somewhat different strategies for testing the acceptability of their reading as they proceed. And they need still another set of strategies for correcting and recovering meaning when they recognize that they have miscued.

Some strategies will be general for all reading tasks. Others will be utilized for special kinds of reading.

Uses and Misuses of Reading

With the focus on comprehension certain key misconceptions about the uses of reading become apparent.

The "By the third grade" myth is very popularly subscribed to. Many teachers believe that if a child can't read "by the third grade" he is doomed to school failure. This belief comes from a strong tendency to make written language the main medium of instruction much too early and much too completely. No child can read and comprehend material that assumes concepts and experiences that he hasn't had. When this is compounded by a limited control over the reading process (as compared to listening) he is very much at a disadvantage. Reading to learn must be used much more carefully at all levels of instruction. It will be most successful after initial learning has taken place.

Many secondary teachers use a "here, read and learn" approach. They assume that the text is the teacher, that the pupil is fully able to learn through reading and that their own role is to test, evaluate and grade. Such a view is untenable. The text can be a component in the learning process only if it is used in relationship to experience and oral language. Further, the teachers must work with their pupils on developing and extending their comprehension strategies to deal with the texts.

Particularly, teachers must ask themselves how much semantic input is necessary to make it possible for the reader to produce semantic output from a reading assignment. The answer to that inquiry will suggest how the pupils may be prepared for the task as well as whether the task is fundamentally appropriate or inappropriate.

Both the acquisition of the reading process and the effective use of that process depend on the reader and his teachers seeing comprehension as the continuous objective at all times.

Linguistic-Psycholinguistic Implications for Reading

Goodman — Questions for Discussion

Do you agree with Goodman's criteria for building effective methods and materials? Would you add or delete any criteria? In what way might many reading programs need to be modified to make them conform to the pattern suggested by Goodman? What are the implications from this article for teachers of science and/or social studies? Do you believe that articles of this nature have had substantial influence on the development of new reading methods and materials in the past few years?

Frank Smith
Kenneth S. Goodman

On the Psycholinguistic Method of Teaching Reading

Our concern is with an imaginary monster—the "psycholinguistic method." At the time of this writing, it is as mythical a beast as the phoenix, the unicorn, or the hippogriff. But we have no confidence that in the near future this monster will not show its face upon the earth. In fact, we would put such a method into the same category as female presidents of the United States—a logical possibility that happens only temporarily to be an empty set.

We must declare our interest. Each of us is responsible for a book about reading that has the word "psycholinguistic" in its title (1, 2), and we are both anxious not to have the term associated with a particular instructional dogma. To be blunt, we regard the development of "psycholinguistic materials" as a distinct threat, not just to us but to the entire educational community. Already we think we detect perturbations in the publishing underworld indicating that a new vogue word is about to be launched into reading pedagogy. Therefore we have decided on this pre-emptive strike. Our objective is to destroy the phoenix of "psycholinguistic instruction" before it can arise from the methodological ashes of the 1960's, although our expectation of success is slight. Our numbers are small, and we have nothing but reason on our side.

The value of psycholinguistics lies in the insights it can provide into the reading process and the process of learning to read. As such,

From Frank Smith and Kenneth S. Goodman, "On the Psycholinguistic Method of Teaching Reading," *Elementary School Journal* 71 (January 1971): 177-81. Reprinted by permission of the authors and The University of Chicago Press. Copyright © 1971 by The University of Chicago Press. This article also appears in *Psycholinguistics and Reading* by Frank Smith (Holt, Rinehart and Winston, 1972).

a "psycholinguistic approach" to reading would be the very antithesis of a set of instructional materials. As we shall argue, psycholinguistic analysis formally confirms what we have all known intuitively for years— that the key factors of reading lie in the child and his interaction with information-providing adults, rather than in the particular materials used. Materials most compatible with such interaction are those that interfere the least with natural language functioning.

Obviously we write with some feeling. This would not be the first time that the reputable name of a scientific discipline had been used with marginal justification as a label for classroom fads. The new science of psycholinguistics has much to offer the study of reading, and its contribution could be sullied by the first comer to attach its name to a souped-up package of classroom impedimenta.

Psycholinguistics, as its name suggests, lies at an intersection of psychology and linguistics. As an independent discipline, it is about fifteen years old. Its central task, according to Miller, is to describe the psychological processes that go on when people use language (3, 4). From linguistics, the new science derives insights about the system that is language—about the competence that individuals acquire when they become fluent users of their language. Some of these insights are incompatible with hypotheses about language-learning that psychologists have held for decades.

Linguistic analysis, for example, shows that it would be impossible for a child to learn to speak simply by imitating adult sentences. The number of sentences possible in a language is infinite—at least a hundred billion billion different grammatical twenty-word sentences could be constructed, and practically every utterance we make or hear is unique. Therefore language must be a system, a set of rules that is capable of generating an infinite number of sentences.

We are all capable of learning what these rules are, because we are all capable of distinguishing acceptable from unacceptable grammatical constructions in our language (even if our own individual grammars vary a little from one person to another). The rules must be learned; they cannot be taught, partly because no one can say what they are.

Not even linguists can describe with any adequacy the rules by which grammatical and ungrammatical sentences can be distinguished; if linguists could, we would have computers that could converse and translate with the facility of human beings.

Linguistic analysis also shows that language has two levels—a surface structure—that is, the sounds or written representation of language—and a deep structure—that is, meaning. These two levels of language are related in a complex way through the system of rules that is grammar, or syntax. Without these rules we could never understand a sentence because the meaning of a sentence is given not by the individual words, but by the manner in which the words interact with each other. (If it were not for syntax, "man bites dog" would mean the same as "dog bites man" and a Maltese cross would be indistinguishable from a cross Maltese.)

Psychology contributes insights about how language must be learned and used. Psychology shows that there are severe perceptual limitations on the amount of acoustic (or visual) "surface structure" that we can process to comprehend language. Psychology shows that our working memory is so constrained that we could not possibly comprehend speech or writing if we analyzed individual words. Psychology also provides a wealth of data about human learning, showing, for example, that negative information can be as valuable as positive information. It can be just as instructional to be wrong as to be right, although all too frequently we are conditioned to avoid the "error" of our ways. Psychological studies show that all human beings have preferred strategies that use a small and apparently innate range of capacities for acquiring new knowledge. These studies also show that learning is rarely the result of a passive exposure to "instruction" but rather the result of an active search for specific kinds of information, which is another reason why rules can be learned but not taught.

At the intersection of these areas of psychology and linguistics lies the growing and fascinating field of psycholinguistics. Already there is an imposing body of knowledge about how fluent language-users construct and perceive sentences. Psycholinguistic research confirms, for example, the linguistic insight that language is processed at deep structure levels. We remember meanings, not individual words. We distinguish elements and relationships that are not actually represented in the surface structure but are constructed from the meanings that we derive from the hidden deep structure.

Some of the most exciting advances made by psycholinguists have been in their studies of how children acquire the rules of adult language (2). Studies show that these rules are developed rapidly between the ages of eighteen months and four years, and appear to follow a similar pattern of development in all children. This pattern, so systematic and invariant, is nothing like a miniature or deformed version of adult language. This fact had led to the suggestion that children have an innate predisposition for discovering the rules of language. The view is supported by the fact that no one can verbalize these rules to tell them to a child.

Insights of the kind found in linguistics and psychology appear to be leading to a profound review of long-held beliefs about reading and how it is learned. It is becoming clear that reading is not a process of combining individual letters into words, and strings of words into sentences, from which meanings spring automatically. Rather the evidence is that the deep-level process of identifying meaning either precedes or makes unnecessary the process of identifying individual words.

Psycholinguistic techniques are beginning to be applied directly to the study of learning to read. They show that the type of information a child requires is not best presented in the form of stereotyped classroom or textbook rules and exercises. Rather, a child appears to need to be exposed to a wide range of choices so that he can detect the significant elements of written language. Experiments have shown that even beginning readers look for and use orthographic, syntactic, and semantic redundancy in written language—but whoever thinks of trying to "teach" a child about that? The child learning to read, like the child learning to speak, seems to need the opportunity to examine a large sample of language, to generate hypotheses about the regularities underlying it, and to test and modify these hypotheses on the basis of feedback that is appropriate to the unspoken rules that he happens to be testing (5, 6).

None of this can, to our mind, be formalized in a prescribed sequence of behaviorally stated objectives embalmed in a set of instructional materials, programmed or otherwise. The child is already programmed to learn to read. He needs written language that is both interesting and comprehensible, and teachers who understand language-learning and who appreciate his competence as a language-learner.

The value of psycholinguistics, we are firmly convinced, lies in the new understanding it can give us all—researchers and practitioners —about the reading process and learning to read. If we were given to slogans, we might well be among the first to assert (with the publishers and the publicists) that this is the dawn of the psycholinguistic era in reading instruction. But we appeal for caution for two reasons. First, because the discipline of psycholinguistics is new, especially in its application to reading. It is far too early to derive rigid practical conclusions from the data that have been collected. But second, because, as we have already asserted, the data clearly indicate that the "revolution" that psycholinguistics might create in reading pedagogy lies in a richer understanding of what the child is trying to accomplish and of his superb intellectual equipment.

We do not deny that there might be a psycholinguistic approach, or attitude, toward reading. In such an approach, the adjective "psycholinguistic" would be synonymous with "objective," "analytical," or "scientific." But in phrases such as "psycholinguistic primer" or "psycholinguistic kit" the adjective would be devoid of meaning.

Nor do we deny that materials for reading instruction could be improved both in their construction and use by the insightful application of psycholinguistic knowledge. Enlightened teachers do not need to wait for new materials. They can make much more effective use of existing materials simply by viewing the reading process as one in which the developing reader functions as a user of language. It may well be that such teachers will find themselves rejecting large portions of the materials and the accompanying guide books as inappropriate, unsound, and even destructive.

We stated earlier that our fears about the misuse of the word "psycholinguistic" were based on precedent. We are thinking of what has already happened to one half of the psycholinguistic partnership.

The study of reading was advanced significantly when linguists turned their attention to the subject. They contributed a number of profound and important insights that continue to serve the discriminating reading researcher and the teacher. But the name of linguistics also became associated with a particular clutch of instructional materials and that is a different kettle of fish. The attachment of the label "linguistic" to reading materials had two disadvantages. The first disadvantage was that any material or procedure that could be associated with the label gained a spurious authority, as if anything that bore the trademark "linguistic" carried a scientific seal of quality. The second disadvantage was that the word "linguistics," and the science itself, became devalued in many circles because of a kind of Gresham's Law that operates among instructional materials.

We shall not speculate about reasons why no instructional materials have ever been characterized as the "psychological" method for teaching reading, although such a label would seem to be as justified as "linguistic." Whatever the reasons for the inhibitions about using the world "psychological," they do not appear to apply to "psycholinguistic," which is gaining growing prominence in the promotional literature of the education industry.

Our plea is simply that the term be used with respect.

Some teachers who read our arguments may still look forward to a psycholinguistic basal reading program. These teachers may believe that useful knowledge can come to reading teachers only in the form of a textbook series or a kit, ready for immediate application with no prior training. In fact, knowledge, however valid, can usefully influence reading instruction only if teachers have grasped its nature. When teachers understand the relevance of psycholinguistic theory and research, they will see reading materials in their true perspective.

References

1. K. S. Goodman (editor). *The Psycholinguistic Nature of the Reading Process.* Detroit: Wayne State University Press, 1968.
2. F. Smith, *Understanding Reading: A Psycholinguistic Analysis of Reading and Learning To Read.* New York: Holt, Rinehart and Winston, 1971.
3. G. A. Miller. "The Psycholinguists," *Encounter, 23* (July, 1964), 29–37.
4. G. A. Miller. "Some Preliminaries to Psycholinguistics," *American Psychologist, 20* (January, 1965), 15–20.
5. K. S. Goodman and C. Burke. "Study of Children's Behavior while Reading Orally." Final Report. United States Office of Education Project S425, 1968.
6. K. S. Goodman and C. Burke. "Study of Oral Reading Miscues That Result in Grammatical Retransformation." Final Report. United States Office of Education Project 7-E-219, 1969.

Linguistic-Psycholinguistic Implications for Reading

Smith and Goodman — Questions for Discussion

Are you familiar with any commercially-prepared materials that are advertised as being psycholinguistic in nature? What does the term "psycholinguistics" really mean? Why do Smith and Goodman stress the point that we should not attempt to develop materials that represent the "psycholinguistic method?" From the authors' explanation of the value of the study of psycholinguistics, what are the practical implications for the first grade teacher? Based on the Smith-Goodman explanation of the meaning and value of psycholinguistics, what might be one of the most serious criticisms of some of our presently used materials?

CHAPTER ELEVEN

Physical and Psychological Limits of the Reading Skills

Perhaps no issue other than amount and type of phonics instruction has stirred such controversy in the field of reading as that of the physical and psychological limits of the reading skills. The purpose in choosing the two articles for this chapter is to present the reader with a review of many years of research as well as to present the view of one of many persons who believe that the research in this field may have been somewhat misleading. The research is very conclusive, especially concerning the physical limitations of the eye. Yet, so many reputable people have claimed to read in excess of the apparent limitations that no clear-cut conclusion exists even now. No doubt a great deal of the problem lies in the semantics involved in our definition of reading itself, and for that reason one needs to study the problem even more carefully in order to analyze the merits of both sides of the issues involved.

The article by G. Harry McLaughlin presents a brief review of some of the research and writing, which points to some very severe limitations on reading speed imposed by the physical capabilities of the eye. McLaughlin stresses the point that, although this research is apparently accurate, there are other important factors involved. He also mentions some rather informal research that he has done which adds credence to his argument that much higher speeds than those often reported are perhaps possible. If McLaughlin's argument is correct, then there are certainly some interesting implications for the teacher of both developmental reading and the teachers of speed reading courses. For example, a number of the machines presently being sold as aids to the development of reading speed must certainly be detrimental to the reading patterns of students with high potential for what he terms "parallel processing."

The article by Paul A. Witty is an example of this great scholar's ability to gather the facts and present an unbiased interpretation of their meaning. Witty discusses the phenomenal claims of students who have completed speed reading courses and points out that his own research does not support the validity of such claims. He does, however, state that some reputable scholars have been able to reach reading speeds well beyond those thought possible from a physical point of view. He stresses the fact that even these claims are for reading speeds well below those often reported by the promoters of speed reading courses.

As you read these articles you may wish to compare the research results presented with the claims of some commonly advertised speed reading courses with which you are familiar. You may also wish to consider the following questions: To what extent does our definition of reading influence the research results reported? What method of measuring comprehension is used by most teachers in speed reading programs? Would "parallel processing" account for the tremendous speeds reported by the marketers of certain speed reading courses? What factors other than speed should be considered in developing one's ability to read?

G. Harry McLaughlin*

Reading at "Impossible" Speeds

The educational publisher was not impressed. "It is all very well for your subject to deal with a book at 10,000 words per minute, but how much can she get out of it?"

"The rough gist. What is really surprising is that she can take in any information at all at that speed," I replied.

"That's not good enough for me. I have to know not only exactly what the writer says, but how he says it. In the publishing trade we must evaluate both content and style. You can't do that by speed reading."

"How then," I countered, "do you read?"

"Oh, I just look down the center of the page—but my normal rate is only 1,500 words a minute."

The Problem

In a widely-quoted paper Spache insisted: "It is impossible to read faster than 800 to 900 words per minute" (*22*). I cannot accept this dictum, because I have met so many people capable of speed reading— defined as "gaining meaning from the printed page while inspecting more than 1200 words a minute" (*21*). Although speed readers sometimes try to go too fast for their powers of comprehension, Neisser (*14*, p. 137)

From G. Harry McLaughlin, "Reading at 'Impossible' Speeds," *Journal of Reading* 12, no. 6 (March 1969): 449-54, 502-10. Reprinted with permission of G. Harry McLaughlin and the International Reading Association.

*With technical notes by Henry O'Beirne, Institute of Bio-Medical Electronics, University of Toronto.

is surely correct when he remarks, "Rapid reading represents an achievement as impossible in theory as it is commonplace in practice." Obviously, some new theory must be devised to account for the phenomenon of speed reading. That is the problem I shall attempt to solve below.

But first we must search for the false assumption in current theorizing which leads even such an eminent teacher as Earl Taylor(24, p. 41) to write off speed reading as a "fad," stigmatizing the claims of its "promulgators" as "absurd."

Spache's paper provides a convenient starting point for our search. According to a selected bibliography on speed reading published by the IRA(2), Spache, "in an attempt to scientifically validate" the claims made by Reading Dynamics, Inc., "found" that speed reading is physiologically impossible. This suggests that Spache's paper was based upon original empirical investigation. That was not the case. Spache simply quoted other researchers' data on the time required for the shortest effective fixation in reading (166 milliseconds), the time required for the saccade to the next fixation (33 milliseconds), and "the maximum number of words that the eye can possibly see with a single fixation during continuous reading (probably 2.5 to 3 words." Thus, it appears, we can see only three words every fifth of a second, and because there are 300 such intervals in a minute, we can see only 3 x 300 = 900 words per minute. This must be the upper limit because it is difficult to sustain the rate of five fixations a second.

As Spache himself observes, his dictum hinges on the definition of "reading." He interprets the term "in the common understanding of reading most of the words on a page." As this interpretation of reading itself contains the term which was to be defined, let us suppose that reading requires the establishment of the meaning of each word. It is now possible to "prove," by an argument parallel to Spache's, that reading at more than 300 words a minute is impossible. In a recent series of experiments(15) subjects searched through a list of words, each three to six letters long, in order to find one which denoted an animal. All that the subjects had to do was establish enough of the word's meaning to determine whether is belonged to the target class. Yet, even with practice, scanning rates hardly exceeded five words per second, i.e. 5 x 60 = 300 words per minute.

In fact, it became apparent later in Spache's paper that he identifies reading with having every word in clear vision. He mentions Walton and "a number of European and American researchers" who have shown that "at reading distance only words within a span of one inch (2.5 or 3 words) are seen with greater than 50 per cent acuity." Because visual acuity depends upon a multitude of variables such as time and intensity of stimulus presentation(7), it is not certain that published acuity figures, obtained by having subjects inspect stimuli isolated in space and time, are applicable to the reading process. But even if they are, why must we accept the assumption that a reader makes no use of his peripheral vision, that is, of what he can see with 50 percent acuity or less?

The best Spache can do to justify this assumption is to cite investigations showing that ordinary readers do not use peripheral vision. They limit their attention to a maximum of three words per fixation, which is equivalent to processing a maximum of 900 words per minute, as shown above.

Now we can discern the shortcoming of Spache's argument. It is circular. It amounts simply to this: "If reading is defined as seeing every word with greater than 50 percent acuity, nobody can read more than 900 words a minute, because nobody can read more than 900 words a minute in the sense defined." In short, this is not an argument but a fiat telling us how we must use the word "reading." Of course anyone is entitled to define the term in whatever way he wishes, but surely in ordinary usage reading means acquiring the intended meaning from printed or written symbols. Whether this process *necessarily* requires seeing every word with greater than 50 percent acuity is a matter for empirical investigation. The fact that the normal reader fixates every single word one after the other is as irrelevant as the fact that in the Dark Ages a normal reader always moved his lips. What we have to do is discover whether a reader can spot enough cues to determine the meaning of words seen with peripheral vision.

There is evidence in the opthalmological literature that peripheral vision is a good deal more useful than certain reading experts would have us believe. For instance, it has been demonstrated that letters presented in the far periphery can be resolved(18); there are classic studies which show that when a nonsense word is fixated at the center, letters in the periphery are often recognized more easily than the central ones(6); it has also been found that any reduction of the number of words visible in peripheral vision increases errors in word recognition(16). Furthermore eye-movement studies, such as those reported by Yarbus(25), show that when people inspect pictures their saccadic movements are nearly always made to points of maximum information value, and that the points fixated are much more often than not those which were in the extreme periphery of vision during the previous fixation, yet saccadic movement is so swift and accurate that the position of each fixation must have been decided (unconsciously of course) with great exactness during the preceding fixation.(10).

You, dear reader, can check for yourself that you can read a good deal more at a glance than some experts would allow. All you need is a camera shutter, set to give an exposure of 250 milliseconds, mounted in a piece of cardboard so that you cannot see anything else when you hold the shutter to your eye. Seat yourself comfortably with a book open on your lap, aim the shutter, then press the release. After two or three practice trials you will find that you can see at least five words every time. If the illumination is suitable you may find that you do just as well with even shorter exposures. But even at 300 milliseconds you would have had time only for a single fixation.

I tried this demonstration with a subject whom I will call M, for reasons of professional discretion. M lays no claim to extraordinary reading speeds; indeed she regards herself as irremediably the slowest reader I ever married. Nevertheless, at only her ninth trial, she correctly reported seeing not only a two-inch long sentence "It went on and on forever" but also the word "beautiful." This is significant, because the reported items occurred on two separate lines.

Some Clues

That was one clue to what is probably the secret of the speed reader. As the informal exploratory investigation reported below will suggest, speed readers appear to use their peripheral vision not only to examine the words on either side of each fixation point but also to inspect the lines above and below.

It was my aim to find a subject who could read at 10,000 words a minute. I reasoned that a subject absorbing information at that rate could not possibly be merely skimming. Notice that I am distinguishing between speed reading—which I take to include any technique of dealing with more than 1,200 words a minute—and skimming, by which I mean absorbing information only from what is clearly seen on one line at each fixation. In other words, a skimmer uses the technique of ordinary reading, by definition, but a speed reader could well use a different technique. Therefore we may take it that a skimmer cannot inspect more than 900 words a minute, though these 900 may be distributed, in groups of three, through a much greater quantity of material. However, I challenge anybody to produce a coherent account of any material looking at 300 groups of three words spaced out more or less randomly among 10,000.

I found four subjects who believed that they could attain the 10,000 words-a-minute target, but only one actually managed it.

Subject X was a boy aged 15 with an IQ of 165. Master X had completed a rapid reading course three months previously and his record showed that he had read several paperbacks at the target speed with full comprehension as measured by true-false questions. I was rather suspicious of this measure of comprehension, because I have found that after speed-reading material I usually do well on test questions which I could not have answered from previous knowledge—yet I cannot recall the material I am supposed to have read unless I am prompted by the reminders contained in the questions themselves. Therefore, all the subjects in this study were tested by asking them to give an unaided recall of the test material. The recall was recorded on a dictating machine and later transcribed.

One of the reading materials was a detective novel, each page of which had been photographed as a frame of a film strip that was back-projected on to a translucent screen six feet away from the subject's eyes, so that the image subtended the same angle as an octavo volume at normal reading distance. The subject was given a remote control button so that he could advance the film to the next page within 100 milliseconds. Master X read the story at 5,000 words a minute but his recall was too garbled to be acceptable.

Subject J was a young lady with a doctorate who teaches at the University of Toronto. She had no special training in rapid reading. Her recalls were ample and coherent, but she absorbed very little when dealing with more than 1,200 words per minute.

Subject K was a university student of theology who gives public demonstrations for Reading Dynamics, Inc. He is a fluent verbalizer, so that he may give the impression that he has understood reading material better than is actually the case. He dealt with about 5,000 words per minute and could make reasonably adequate recalls even though he, like other subjects, was not permitted to make the overviews before and after reading which are called for by the Dynamics system. Unfortunately, he could not be tested on the projected material because he had been conditioned to pace himself by looking above his fingertip as he made it snake down the page, and the screen was too far away to permit this. Nevertheless, by using an electro-oculograph (a very sensitive device for continuous eye-movement recording, described below in Professor O'Beirne's technical note) we were able to establish that Mr. K, like other subjects, made quite ordinary fixations lasting from 200 to 400 milliseconds. The only difference between his technique and that of a normal reader was that after fixation he would make a saccade to the point his finger had just reached.

The last subject, Miss L, was a university graduate with an IQ of 140. Miss L believes that she was never taught to read. At the age of three she watched while her five-year-old sister laboriously deciphered the words of a reader, probably by some phonic system. Little Miss L learned the words by heart and thus, she claims, came to associate word shapes directly with their meanings. Her colleagues at the firm where she worked as a scientific editor told me that she usually read at "phenomenal" speed.

Miss L had finished a speed reading course six months before she acted as a subject. She maintained that the course had been of no value, but, according to the records which she had compiled herself, her rate had gradually increased until she was dealing with novels and light non-fiction at 16,000 words per minute with complete comprehension as measured by true-false questions.

In the laboratory Miss L read Evelyn Waugh's *A Handful of Dust* at 10,000 words-a-minute. The electro-oculograph showed she was making an average of five fixations scattered over each page, so she was not skimming. When she was half way through I asked her for a recall. Perhaps the best way of assessing this recall is to compare it with a published summary of the plot(*12*). The relevant portion of this summary can be analyzed into 24 main points. Miss L recalled a number of details but only six of the main points. She did not mention the most crucial point of all, namely that the heroine was having a love affair.

(Although I shall continue to use the more or less meaningless measure of words dealt with per minute, the foregoing observation suggests a much more valid measure of reading efficiency, namely the number of essential propositions recalled after a standard period of reading, say five minutes. This measure allows for the fact that material with few crucial points, such as a dime novel, should be easier to read at speed than material stating many essential propositions, such as a textbook. The measure also avoids the disadvantage of comprehension questions referred to above. Judging what is or is not an essential point is, of course, no more arbitrary than deciding what is or is not a fair comprehension question.)

As nobody was available who could better Miss L's performance, she became the principal subject. Miss L read the projected material at an average of 3,500 words a minute. At this slower speed she gave a much more satisfactory recall, although she again missed a central point. By this time we had come to the conclusion that the projection situation, or the material, or both imposed great difficulties upon a subject. The reason for using the projector was that it obviated parallax errors when using an eye camera mounted on the subject's head. As explained in detail in Professor O'Beirne's technical note, this camera simultaneously photographed both a spot of light reflected from the eye, and the material which the subject was reading. This apparatus appears to have been used only once before to plot the eye movements of a speed reader(8): in that study the subject was found to deal with 10,000 words a minute by moving her eyes down the center of one page and *up* the center of the next page.

As for Miss L, she typically read a page of 260 words in 14 fixations distributed in a rough zig-zag down the page. Sometimes her gaze moved back up the page to make a flattened loop: she explained that she did this when she wished to see the same area twice. Electro-oculograms show that Miss L made similar eye-movements when reading from the printed page.

The photographic record shows that most of the fixations lasted 250 milliseconds and appeared steady. It may therefore be that what Smith believed to be microfixations making up each fixation in reading (19) may be attributed to errors inherent in his system of recording. He photographed corneal reflections with a camera mounted on the chair in which the subject was held by restraining devices. Only when the film was developed did he match the recorded eye-spot against the material which the subject had read. Although our subjects were restrained, they were able to make minute head movements so the eye-spot appears to move from frame to frame, but this is shown to be artifactual, because the projected material makes a corresponding shift, whereas Smith's method permits no such check.

For one study Miss L read a publisher's proof of a book which was not available in Canada at the time(3). The quality of her performance may be gauged from a crucial part of her recall of the entire book, the 223 pages of which she read at rates varying between 1,200 and 9,000 words per minute, averaging 3,750 words per minute. A summary of each relevant page is followed by the corresponding extract, italicized, from Miss L's recall.

p. 99 Holden Britwell tells a British Cabinet meeting that he will resign the post of Foreign Secretary. The Prime Minister mumbles that he is "terribly, terribly sorry." Two young ministers suggest Sebastian Fleming as a replacement.

Holden resigns. He seems to have seen the Prime Minister and he resigns. They discuss putting the man Sebastian in his place. The Prime Minister is very upset about it all.

p. 100   The Prime Minister gives a cryptic reply to his juniors.

(Nothing)

p. 101   Holden walks past the Downing Street house he will soon have to leave.

Holden resigns. He is leaving the house.

p. 102   Holden returns and is given a letter.

He is sent a note ...

p. 103   The letter is from Morton. Holden remembers that this Foreign Office once piloted him around Washington. Morton's letter requests an interview. He is shown in and asks: "Do you know about the American plot to overthrow the Indian Government?"

(The note is) ... from a Washington press aide whom he remembers as once showing him around Washington, that he would like to see him. So he sees him. He says: "Did you know there is a plot in Washington to overthrow the government in Delhi in India?"

p. 104   Holden says he knows of this plot only because the Prime Minister told him. It would be a betrayal of trust if he tried to foil the plot by publicizing it.

He says he won't do anything about it.

p. 105   Holden advises Morton to keep silent too, remarking that a Civil Servant is not responsible for policy.

He is only doing his job.

p. 106   Morton replies: "We hanged quite a lot of people at Nuremburg who said that."

That statement came out at Nuremberg.

It is instructive to see how Miss L divided up the time which she spent on this passage. She had been reading a not overexciting chapter at her average speed when she encountered the critical incident on page 99. Her behavior on this occasion was unique. She made four fixations, returned to the top of the page, read at her average speed for five seconds, paused for another second, then read the page again for the period shown in the accompanying table. Notice how Miss L's speed varied with the information content of each page. However, the electro-oculographic records show that she maintained her typical eye-movement patterns throughout, and did not resort to normal reading or skimming.

TABLE 1

Analysis of Subject L's Reading Time on a Critical Incident

Page Number	Words on Page	Number of Fixations	Fixations and Saccades	Sweep to Next Page
99	243	49	12.2 secs.	0.5 secs.
100	55	5	1.2	0.05
101	221	18	4.8	0.6
102	259	21	4.4	0.05
103	217	39	9.8	0.4
104	278	35	7.8	0.05
105	272	27	6.5	0.4
106	33	4	1.0	0.05

Variations in reading rate are not always correlated with information content. On one occasion Miss L read an article in *Scientific Amer-*

ican at 3,450 words a minute. She could recall only one significant point: actually it was the crux of the article, but it was contained in a paragraph buried midway down the final column and was not alluded to in the introductory matter or anywhere else in the article, yet her eye movements preserved exactly the same pattern throughout the entire reading.

The Solution: Parallel Processing

From these exploratory studies, several conclusions can be tentatively drawn. How far they can be generalized is a matter for further investigation.

(1) *Speed reading has strictly limited usefulness.* The technique is useful in that it enables a reader to locate important information, especially in material that contains a lot of redundancies. However, a speed reader may miss a vital point and thus fail to make sense of the whole. Reading at very high speed appears to be more useful for deciding that certain stretches of writing may be ignored than for gleaning what is contained in the more informative sections. These must either be read more slowly or re-examined in a post-reading overview.

The apparently more astounding speed reading performances are not so convincing when an unaided recall is carefully compared with the material read. It will often be found that part of the recall is confused. An example of this occurred when Miss L identified Morton as a press aide: actually his job is never stated precisely, but his name occurs twice in conjunction with that of embassy press secretary. Sometimes parts of a recall are mere fabrication.

(2) *A speed reader's behavior is similar in nearly all respects to that of a normal reader.* Both make fixations of similar duration. The reason for this doubtless lies in the fact that the reticular formation appears to act as a gate to the brain: in any case there is a minimum time required to switch attention from one input to another. For auditory stimuli this has been found to be about 168 milliseconds(*17*). This is fascinatingly close to Spache's figure of 166 milliseconds for the minimum useful fixation in reading.

Furthermore, a speed reader's fixations do not appear to differ in nature from those of a normal reader. Nonetheless it is not an unreasonable conjecture that normal readers, unlike speed readers, make microsaccades during each fixation. Microsaccades are eye movements which occur involuntarily to correct for the slow, tiny drifts of up to five minutes of arc which occur during prolonged fixation. Usually microsaccades do not occur until a fixation has continued for at least 200 milliseconds. If one did occur during the normal reading fixation this would be disadvantageous because, as several recent quantitative studies have shown (e.g. *26*) even the smallest involuntary eye movement is accompanied by a decrement in visual threshold and acuity for 50 milliseconds before and after the start of the movement. Unfortunately, this conjecture cannot yet be tested. The techniques available for measuring the large saccadic movements necessary in reading are still not sufficiently sensitive to detect microsaccades.

Speed readers do not differ from normal fast readers with regard to subvocalization. As Edfeldt has shown in a brilliant but too little known monograph(*5*), subvocalizing occurs whenever a reader, however good, slows down to study a difficult passage: evidently, among efficient readers at least, subvocalization is an effect not the cause of slow reading.

It has been suggested that speed readers may rely on eidetic imagery (*1*). Certainly this is not the case with Miss L. When viewing a complex picture through the camera shutter she needed several 250 millisecond views to make it out, her account of what she saw becoming more accurate at each trial.

(3) *The only essential objective difference between speed readers and other people is in their eye movement patterns.* A normal reader or skimmer reads along a printed line; a speed reader follows a straight or zig-zag path, often moving from right to left and sometimes even going up the page. It is interesting to note that photographs of the eye movements of an eight-year-old boy prodigy showing just such ragged patterns were published in 1937, long before the current speed reading "fad" arose. The caption is as follows:

> "When his eye movements were photographed, he was in the ninth grade but was carrying tenth-grade mathematics successfully. His eye movements have been photographed thirteen different times, and all the records are somewhat similar to those shown . . . He reads backwards as well as forward, evidencing few of the characteristics usually associated with the . . . reading process. The rate of . . . reading has varied from 646.15 words per minute to 2,202.53 words per minute. During one period of photography lasting 44.91 seconds he averaged 853.71 words per minute with 100 per cent comprehension. At another time, for 9.8 seconds he averaged 1,989.79 words per minute, with excellent comprehension. He evidently has an unusually large macular area which enables him to read with what has been termed a 'photographic eye'."

Considering that no evidence for a "photographic eye" has been discovered elsewhere, it may be that the subject's important characteristic was one evinced by our own subjects, namely high intelligence. It is perhaps noteworthy that the photographs were published by Taylor (*23*, p. 115), though I fail to see any mention of this prodigy in his more recent book(*24*).

Certainly the speed reader's tendency to inspect material in topsy-turvy fashion demands an explanation. The reason for this behavior, I submit, is that the speed reader sees a jumble of words at each fixation, so a bit more disorder makes very little difference.

I must admit to having saved two important pieces of evidence for this denouement. One is that every speed reader I have met claimed to see more than one line at a time. "I read in globs." "I see a bubble of words." Those are the phrases they use to describe their subjective experience. The other bit of evidence bears out these subjective reports. When Miss L looked at a book, not on sale in Canada at the time[20], through the camera shutter, she reported up to seven words or phrases occurring as far as ten lines apart: she could not make sense of these items because she was reporting words scattered within a circular area up to two inches in diameter.

It may be that she recognized a great many more items at each fixation but was unable to report them because of the notorious fact that the human immediate memory cannot retain more than seven plus or minus two disconnected items[13]. Of course, the items occurring in a randomly selected area of type must appear disconnected, because they can only be parts of several different grammatical clauses. At the next fixation more items will be recognized, and if any one of them can be combined grammatically with any item already held in the immediate memory, then it is probable that such a combination will be made and retained, still as a single memorized item. It is difficult to explain the comprehension of ordinary written or spoken discourse except by such a process of combining related items. However, an ordinary reader or a listener tries to complete only one sentence at a time. The speed reader, in contrast, is attempting to combine parts of up to seven or so different sentences. Often he will fail in the attempt because the sentences are too complex or his fixations are unsuitably located. On the other hand the redundancy of the English language will often enable the speed reader to think for himself of those parts of a sentence which he has missed. As Neisser so nicely puts it, "Reading is externally guided thinking," [14, p. 136].

This may be called the theory of parallel processing, because it suggests that seven or so different sentences can be built up at the same time in a reader's mind, just as parallel electric circuits within a single computer can perform different tasks simultaneously. Support for the theory is provided by the fact that, with training, it appears to be no great strain for a human being to search for even hundreds of items simultaneously, as do the employees of a news-clipping agency when looking for references to their clients.

If the theory is correct then certain important implications follow: (1) It is probably fruitless to try to make a speed reader of someone who lacks high verbal intelligence. On the other hand it would seem to call for little more visual skill than the ability to relax so that the span of apprehension is not narrowed, just as the skilled driver relaxes and uses his peripheral vision, whereas a learner is so tense that he sees only what is straight ahead.

(2) It may be that by training children to read line by line with "good" directional attack, we are forcing them to limit their span of apprehension, thereby preventing them from becoming speed readers, and thus severely restricting their flexibility at one end of the range.

(3) Anyone who wishes to acquire the skill of speed reading should concentrate on acquiring mental schemes for organizing items of information, and should avoid the expensive training devices which are claimed to promote rapid reading. Although they have motivational value, like any unfamiliar toy, they nearly all tend to narrow the student's attention to a single line or, more often, to part of a single line. To forestall any controversy this remark might otherwise arouse, I should point out that the promulgators of speed reading are not the only ones whose vested interests may prompt them to express wishful thinking as if it were fact.

(4) Speed reading is as impossible as . . . going to the moon.

Acknowledgments

This investigation was supported by a grant from the Center for Continuing Education, York University. The projection apparatus was loaned by the Psychology Department and Psychological Services of York University. The experiments were carried out at the Institute of Bio-medical Electronics, University of Toronto. I sincerely thank all these institutions for their co-operation, although, of course, none of them are in any way responsible for the opinions expressed in this paper. I am particularly grateful to Professor O'Beirne for giving up time at many week ends to operate the recording apparatus belonging to the Institute of Bio-medical Electronics.

Technical Notes

The Electro-Oculograph (EOG)

The human eyeball appears to be charged electrically so that the retina is more negative than the cornea. By placing bipolar electrodes on the temples, it is possible to detect these charges and to use them for measuring horizontal eye movements(4). Thus, for example, when the eyes turn to the right, the electrode on the right temple becomes more positive and the left electrode becomes more negative. The potential change is reasonably proportional to angular movement of the eyeball. When the electrodes are connected to a suitable chart recorder, a graph showing horizontal eye movements plotted against time is obtained.

Similarly, by placing bipolar electrodes just above and below one eye, it is possible to measure vertical eye movements. However, the vertical recording usually contains more noise and artifacts than the horizontal recording. A blink causes a strong vertical artifact, and the sensitivity is dependent somewhat on the height of opening of the eyelids. The timing information is, of course, still accurate.

We obtained very clear records by using Beckmann bipotential skin electrodes, which are silver/silver chloride electrodes with a special electrolyte gel. Each three-electrode assembly has a positive electrode, a negative electrode and a ground electrode. Each electrode assembly was coupled through a 980A coupler and 481B preamplifier into a Beckmann Offner type S-II Dynograph.

The overall system, as used, has the following characteristics:
Deflection sensitivity: 1 cm = 10 microvolts.
3db Bandpass: 0.16 to 150 Hertz.
Common mode rejection (60 Hertz): 112 db.
Input impedance: 2 megohms.
Chart speed: 5cm/sec.

The Eye-Marker Camera

The eye-marker camera, designed by Mackworth and Llewellyn-Thomas(11, 9) makes it possible to record the actual point of fixation within a scene.

An 8 mm electrically-driven movie camera is mounted on a close-fitting helmet worn by the subject. The camera records two superimposed images; the scene observed by the wearer, which changes as he moves his head, and a bright marker spot which shows the point of actual eye fixation within the scene. The bright marker spot is a magnified image of a small light bulb, reflected in the cornea of the left eye, and picked up by the head camera through a periscope and a system of prisms and lenses. This reflection moves as the eye moves, and within about ± 15 degrees horizontally and ± 10 degrees vertically, its deflections correlate well with those of the eye. Thus the spot can be superimposed on the scene and adjusted to show the paths of the eye movements and the actual position of each fixation, with a long-term accuracy of some 2 degrees.

Some of the timing information is lost, because the camera speed of 10 frames per second, while fast enough to insure that *all* fixations are recorded, is not fast enough to allow timing the beginning and end of a movement. Thus it is not possible to measure the velocity or acceleration of a saccade, and the length of a fixation can be estimated only to the nearest 100 milliseconds.

The eye-marker camera has a parallax error, due to the subject's eye and the camera lens being separated by about 6 inches. This error is increased at close viewing distances; thus it is not practical for the subject to read a book at the normal distance.

References

1. Adams, R. Buchanan. "The Phenomenon of Supernormal Reading Ability." *Twelfth Yearbook of the National Reading Conference,* 1963.

2. Berger, Allen. *Speed Reading.* International Reading Association, 1967.

3. Clark, William. *Special Relationship.* London: William Heinemann, 1968.

4. Davson, H. *The Eye.* Academic Press, 1962. Vol. 3, pp. 67-71.

5. Edfeldt, Ake W. *Silent Speech and Silent Reading.* Chicago: University of Chicago Press, 1960.

6. leGrand, Yves. *Form and Space Vision.* Bloomington: Indiana University Press, 1967.

7. Lit, Alfred. "Visual Acuity," in P. R. Farnsworth and others (Eds.), *Annual Review of Psychology,* 1968.

8. Llewellyn-Thomas, Edward. "Eye Movements in Speed Reading," in Russell G. Stauffer (Eds.), *Speed Reading: Practices and Procedures, Forty-fourth Annual Education Conference at the University of Delaware,* 1962, pp. 104-114.

9. Llewellyn-Thomas, Edward. "Movements of the Eye," *Scientific American,* 219 (August, 1968), 88-95.

10. Llewellyn-Thomas, Edward, and Henry O'Beirne. "Curvature in the Saccadic Movement," *Archives of Ophthalmology,* 77 (January 1967), 105-109.

11. Mackworth, Norman H. and Edward Llewellyn-Thomas, "Head-mounted Eye-marker Camera," *Journal of the Optical Society of America,* 52 (June 1962), 713-716.

12. Magill, Frank N. *Masterpieces of World Literature in Digest Form: First Series.* Harper and Row, 1952, pp. 350f.

13. Miller, George A. "The Magical Number Seven, Plus or Minus Two: Some Limits on Our Capacity for Processing Information," *Psychological Review,* 63 (1956), 81-97.

14. Neisser, Ulric. *Cognitive Psychology.* Appleton-Century-Crofts, 1967.

15. Neisser, Ulric, and H. K. Beller. "Searching through Word Lists," *British Journal of Psychology,* 56 (1965), 349-358.

16. Poulton, E. L. "Peripheral Vision, Refractoriness and Eye Movements in Fast Oral Reading," *British Journal of Psychology,* 53 (1962), 409-419.

17. Reid, Ian E., and Robert M. W. Travers. "Time Required to Switch Attention," *American Educational Research Journal,* 5 (1968), 203-211.

18. Saugstad, P., and I. Lie. "Training of Peripheral Visual Acuity," *Scandinavian Journal of Psychology,* 5 (1964), 218-224.

19. Smith, Donald E. P. "Micro-movements, Discrimination Learning and Self-instruction," *Thirteenth Yearbook of the National Reading Conference,* (1964), 146-149.

20. Smith, Lee. *The Last Day the Dogbushes Bloomed.* Harper and Row, 1968.

21. Smith, Peter B. "Eye Movements and Rapid Reading Reconsidered," *Fourteenth Yearbook of the National Reading Conference,* 1964.

22. Spache, George D. "Is This a Break-through in Reading?" *The Reading Teacher,* 15 (January 1962), 258-263.

23. Taylor, Earl A. *Controlled Reading.* University of Chicago Press, 1937.

24. Taylor, Earl A. *The Fundamental Reading Skill.* Springfield, Ill.: Charles C. Thomas (2nd edn.), 1966.

25. Yarbus, Alfred I. *Eye Movements and Vision.* New York: Plenum, 1967.

26. Zuber, B. L., and L. Stark. "Saccadic Suppression: Evaluation of Visual Threshold Associated with Saccadic Eye Movements," *Experimental Neurology,* 16 (1966), 65-79.

Physical and Psychological Limits of the Reading Skills

McLaughlin—Questions for Discussion

What is "parallel processing"? What does McLaughlin believe are the most serious limiting factors in speed reading? How does McLaughlin's apparent definition of reading differ from that of Spache, whom he quotes? Is McLaughlin really in serious disagreement with most university researchers? Does McLaughlin believe that the methods taught in commercially-operated speed reading courses are effective?

Paul A. Witty

Rate of Reading — A Crucial Issue

Scarcely a week goes by without reports being published about companies or individuals that offer courses with a guarantee to improve the student's reading rate and comprehension. Some agencies state that the student will attain such rates as 1500 or 3000 words per minute on completion of a short course. One organization guarantees to enable the student to triple his reading efficiency in an eight-week course. And rates of reading 20,000 to 40,000 words per minute are reported for individuals who have taken courses. For example, in the *Chicago Tribune*, June 28, 1968, the spectacular improvement of a 14-year-old boy was cited. This boy "topped his class with a reading achievement of 20,000 words a minute and a 65 per cent comprehension. Before he started the course, Ken had read 197 words a minute with 45 per cent comprehension."

In an issue of the *Green Bay Press-Gazette*, the story of a fifteen-year-old girl was presented. It was stated that, according to her teacher, this girl read "at a rate of 50,000 words a minute with nearly 100 per cent comprehension, while adult readers average 300 words a minute at 60 per cent or less comprehension."

During the past few years, claims for phenomenally rapid rates of reading have repeatedly appeared in current publications. For example, in the *Wall Street Journal,* September 27, 1967, it is noted by Ira West that:

From Paul A. Witty, "Rate of Reading—A Crucial Issue," *Journal of Reading* 13, no. 2 (November 1969): 102-6, 154-63. Reprinted with permission of Paul A. Witty and the International Reading Association.

... Evelyn Wood, ... who founded the chain of speed-reading schools in Washington, D.C. in 1959, argues that even though the average person reads at a rate of about 250 words a minute, maximum reading speed limits don't exist. Mrs. Wood claims that some people can read more than 40,000 words a minute — a speed that would enable them to knock off *Gone With the Wind* in 12 minutes.

A Brief Background

Interest in increasing speed of reading was evident in the professional literature as early as the period 1920-1930 when studies showed the possibilities of improving speed of reading in relatively short periods of time with gains in comprehension.(24) For example, as early as 1921, John A. O'Brien described the efficiency of a reading improvement program for pupils in grades 3-8.(7) During a short training period, he succeeded in eliciting a 56 per cent gain in speed of reading and a small gain, too, in comprehension.

From 1925-1930, attempts were made to improve rate and comprehension in college classes. In the writer's college courses in educational psychology, the students attempt to improve their rate and comprehension in reading. Each student arranged to spend several 30-minute periods every week in reading rapidly supplementary materials in addition to the textbook. After every practice period, he made a summary or outline of the materials read. He was encouraged also to do extensive reading in the areas of his interests and to improve his rate and comprehension in reading different kinds of subject matter. Leisure reading was also emphasized and attention was given to the development of vocabulary and concepts. Records were kept by each student of the amount and nature of his reading.

The results of tests, given at the beginning and at the end of the semester, were compared. Most of the students showed marked improvement in reading materials in the area of educational psychology. The average increase in rate was about 50 per cent during the single semester. Comprehension, too, was favorably affected as indicated by subjective evaluation of the summaries made by students and by short objective tests. Although these gains were considered important, it was recognized that the program emphasized the reading of materials in only one field. It was suggested, therefore, that the program be continued and expanded during the second semester to stress reading improvement in other areas and to provide more adequately for individual differences in interests and needs. At the end of the second semester, the students gave evidence of further gains in reading proficiency. These efforts suggested the possibility of the college student improving greatly his rate and comprehension in reading various types of materials and led to later development, by the writer, of more comprehensive reading programs for high school as well as for college students.(25)

Development of Devices for Controlling Rate of Reading

Knowledge concerning the possibility of making improvement in speed of reading was widely disseminated during the period 1930-1940. Attention to the success, in the armed forces, of identifying rapidly moving planes and warships intensified interest in cultivating rapid recognition of printed materials. Gradually, commercial companies made available devices for studying and controlling eye movement. In efforts to control eye movement, simple flash cards were replaced by other tachistoscopic devices of varying degrees of complexity. One of the most widely known was the metronoscope, a complex triple-shuttered device, which exposes successively three segments of a line of large print.(18)

Interest in the conditioning or control of eye movement resulted in the making of many other tachistoscopic devices such as the *Reading Accelerator*, the *Reading Rate Controller*, the *Flashmeter*, and the *Rate Reader*. For example, the *Reading Accelerator* is a device by which the speed of reading a page in a book is controlled by a shutter which is lowered mechanically to expose successive lines of print on each page. The *Flashmeter* is another instrument by which different kinds of materials may be exposed upon a screen at varying speeds. Films, too, have been designed to encourage the student to increase his speed of reading.

The use of instruments became a feature of many "accelerated reading programs." In 1951, George S. Speer emphasized the current demand for such programs and stated:

Accelerated reading, using a variety of instruments, has as its main emphasis the development of more rapid and efficient reading, while at the same time effective comprehension or understanding is retained. (16)

Speer pointed to the gradual development of reading instruments and concluded:

All of the instructional technics have demonstrated their value at all
grade and age levels above the seventh grade.... The successes, however, have encouraged many teachers to extend the work to lower grade
levels. *(16)*

"Accelerated reading programs" proved particularly attractive to
adult groups. In *Business Week*, April 5, 1952, it was reported that a
program of reading improvement, utilizing facilities in the University
of Pittsburgh, resulted in attracting various groups of business men to
its courses. Similarly, *The Foundation for Better Reading* in Chicago
also attracted groups of business men. In New York City, the *Reading
Laboratory* provided a program for workers in the Mutual Life Insur-
ance Company. In *Business Week*, April 5, 1952, the president of
Reading Laboratory is quoted as follows:

Some clients begin reading at from 150 to 200 words a minute; others
can do as well as 300 to 500 words. The average is about 250. With individual equipment, each can work at his own rate toward the goal of
650-700 words a minute. Some of the pupils go way beyond that. A
Chicago lawyer set a Foundation record of 3,750 words.

The foregoing "record" seems a very modest claim in terms of the
current reports of reading rates of 40,000 or more words per minute.

For a time, machines and devices were somewhat widely used
and enthusiastic reports were made about them. To be sure, there were
some skeptics and an occasional article cast doubt on their value. Such
an attitude was expressed in an article by George Manolakes.*(5)* The
subjects for the investigation were officers in the Marine Corps supply
schools who were divided into an experimental and a control group.
"The variable element within their instruction was the exclusion of
tachistoscopic training from the program of the experimental group, and
the extension of instruction in vocabulary and comprehension skills."*(5)*

The investigator reports that significant differences were not found
between the groups in "the reduction of the number of fixations, the
increase of the span of recognition, the reduction of regressive movements, or reduction of the duration of fixations."*(5)* There was a significant difference, however, in reading rate at the conclusion of the
training program but this difference favored the experimental group.

Doubts were also expressed by Eloise B. Cason in an earlier investigation. Cason studied four groups of third grade children. One
group was provided specially prepared materials. A second group received a type of training in which the metronoscope had an important
place. Two control groups read materials they chose from the library.
Cason concluded:

In the groups studied, and under the conditions of the experiment, the measurements made did not show that any clear-cut gains were produced in the reading process by the reading programs stressing the mechanics of reading that were not secured by free library reading. *(1)*

Somewhat similar findings were reported by F. L. Westover. College students who did not use a metronoscopic device did fully as well as a group using the device. *(23)*

From the experimental work, A. I. Gates concluded in 1947:

In general, the elaborate mechanical devices should be regarded as last resorts to be used when other methods have failed or when there are some tangible reasons for selecting them at an earlier stage. *(2)*

We have seen the results of studies which have led authorities in reading to question the use of mechanical instruments, particularly in the elementary school. The situation is similar for high school and college students. It is often pointed out that at the more advanced levels, pupils may derive some value from the enhanced interest resulting from the introduction of pacing devices. That such devices are necessary for conducting a successful program has yet to be demonstrated.

Miles Tinker reviewed studies on the use of pacing devices and concluded:

The improvement obtained by eye-movement training, with or without elaborate apparatus, is no greater than that resulting from motivated reading alone . . . The use of pacing devices too often tends toward overemphasis on the mechanics of reading to the sacrifice of adequate attention to the more important processes of perception, apprehension, and assimilation. This mechanical training may result in a decrease in flexibility and adaptability of reading habits. The tachistoscope is without value for increasing speed of reading. The money spent on the tachistoscope and rate controller devices might be better used for books and other supplies. *(19)* See also *(20)*

A detailed analysis of studies led George D. Spache to similar conclusions. *(15)*

Methods Employed in
Reading Improvement Programs

In the experiments of research students, it is generally held that eye movements in efficient reading tend to be horizontal (word-by-word or line-by-line). A novel method, described by Ira West (22), which is employed by Evelyn Wood and her associates "is designed to replace the average person's word-by-word, line-by-line reading pattern."

> The method . . . is to expand the student's reading vision so his eye sees large areas of print and to require him to read a printed page at such a high speed that he breaks the habit of "subvocalizing," or hearing every word mentally. (22)

In this approach:

> A student is taught to move a finger down a page in rapid, zig-zag patterns and force his eyes to keep pace by taking in large groups of words at a glance. . . . This technique . . . enables graduates to read at least 1000 to 3000 words a minute without skipping or skimming. (22)

A clear description of the improvement of reading by the Wood approach is found in Russell G. Stauffer's account of the introduction of this procedure at the University of Delaware.(17) Stauffer, himself, took the course. He states that he "checked in at an initial rate of about 750 words per minute and checked out reading *Exodus* at about 5000 words per minute." Stauffer discusses carefully certain features of the approach and reports that in a similar class later set up for his colleagues, "the men progressed at varying rates; three of them did unusually well, attaining rates of 4000-5000 words per minute reading fiction and rates of about 2500-3000 words per minute reading nonfiction." It should be noted that the rates of reading attained by these scholarly and intelligent men were not the fantastically high rates sometimes cited in magazine articles.

Another method used in speed reading courses combines vertical and horizontal methods of instruction. Florence Schale believes that:

> . . . Skimming is a vertical skill in which the eyes of the student move rapidly down a page. . . . The first and lowest level the writer terms "exclusively skimming," such as locating a word in a dictionary . . .
>
> The second phase, "inclusive skimming," may accompany surveying or overviewing written materials. With practice on somewhat familiar materials, a student may need to read only the first sentence of each paragraph and skim the rest of the supporting details for key words. He may be able to infer the less important details clustered about these nucleus words and thereby grasp inclusive meaning.(10)

The combination of horizontal (line-for-line) reading and "inclusive skimming," is referred to as the Reinforced Reading "Or Alert" Method. Seven steps in this method are described by Schale:

O–verview (Read first and last paragraphs. Guess about the story)

R–ead at predetermined rate (e.g.,) (250 words per minute)

A–nswer questions (70% comprehension is adequate, but 80% is desired)

L–ocate mistakes by going back to look within the story

E–xamine causes of mistakes

R–eread story at same rate (250 wpm)

T–ransfer mastery of story at 250 wpm to next article. (*11*)

Schale states that "as a result of using a combination of 'inclusive skimming' and line-for-line horizontal reading in the 2R or Reinforced Method, average adult and student rates consistently have been over 2000 words per minute with better than 70 per cent comprehension . . ."(10) Schale also cites gains made by fifth-grade pupils "while using the 2R (Reinforced Reading) method" and concludes that "more work in improving rates of reading at the intermediate and above levels needs to be done."(*11*)

Eye Movements and Reading

Are the claims of proponents for special approaches such as the Wood method of reading down the page at phenomenal rates substantiated by investigations? George D. Spache(*14*) cites data compiled by L. C. Gilbert (*4*) which "confirm that the shortest possible fixation in reading two or three words is at least 1/5 to 1/4 of a second." Spache continues:

> . . . assuming that the reader can recognize and comprehend the maximum span of three words per fixation, and that there are *no* regressions, the line of ten words is read in .66 of a second, or at a rate of approximately fifteen words per second or nine hundred words per minute. Any speed greater than this involves omitting lines, the technique recognized by most authorities as skimming, not "reading." It is apparent that the upper speeds suggested as feasible in these various newspaper articles are not possible in the act of reading as here defined, but must be characteristic of such performances as skimming or scanning, in which relatively large portions of the reading material are skipped. (*14*)

In an article which appeared in March, 1969, G. Harry McLaughlin(*6*) points out that Spache "identifies reading as 'having every word in clear vision.'" Thus, it would appear "that we can see only three words every fifth of a second" or about 900 words per minute. These words "are seen with greater than 50 per cent acuity" according to Spache. McLaughlin suggests "that speed reading may be explained by parallel processing, that is by simultaneously decoding fragments of several sentences seen in peripheral vision" defined as what can be seen "with 50 per cent acuity or less."

Perhaps the clearest evidence of the need for questioning the phenominal results obtained by the "vertical" method of reading instruction is in the study of George D. Spache who states:

> It is interesting to note that according to this author's knowledge, students trained at the Reading Dynamics Institute usually refuse to answer questions on the material they have read.... Thus, to our knowledge, no scientific test of the improved comprehension claimed to result from this special training has previously been available....
>
> To secure such data, we began a year ago the collection of records of the eye movements of students before and after their training by instructors of the Institute. These graphs were recorded on the latest eye-movement camera, the Reading Eye. Two kinds of records were obtained, one in the act of reading one of the test selections which are supplied for use with the camera; and second, the act of skimming the pages of a book. Comprehension checks by true-false questions acompanied both types of reading. Inspection of these graphs reveals the following:
> 1.   As a result of the special training these students showed a small average gain in rate, approximately 20 to 25 per cent in various groups.
> 2.   In the test selections no students showed exceptional speeds of reading, the average for various groups falling in the 400-600 words per minute category. The fastest rate recorded was about 900 words per minute.
> 3.   In the skimming records various groups covered 1800-2400 words per minute.
> 4.   Comprehension in the test selections was normal (70 per cent or better) before and after training. The gain in comprehension after training averaged less than 5 per cent.
> 5.   Comprehension in skimming was weak, averaging about 50 per cent after training.
> ... The eye-movement records cited earlier again refute the belief that the students of the Institute succeed in reading large portions of the page at a single fixation. (*14*)

Moreover, it has been shown that speed reading does not eliminate subvocalization. Other reports from reading clinics confirm previously cited studies. For example, Helen M. Robinson and Helen K. Smith write:

> ... It is rare, however, that a student learns to read easy material more rapidly than a thousand words a minute. Even doubling or trebling one's speed of reading easy material with an accompanying proportionate increase in study-type rate results in ease and comfort in reading for pleasure which in turn tends to increase rate in accord with the indi-

vidual's general tempo. There is no magic about the techniques used. The major teaching procedure involves high motivation and continuous encouragement. . . . (9)

The foregoing reports concerning rate of reading are in accord with results obtained in our studies of high school and college students in the Psycho-Educational Clinic at Northwestern University. Rare indeed was the student who obtained a higher rate than 800-900 words per minute during courses designed to improve reading rate and comprehension. However, the average student did improve greatly in reading the types of materials introduced. For example, for 180 students:

> The average rate (for relatively easy materials) at the beginning of the program was 272 words per minute. After the program was completed, the students read the same type of materials at an average rate of 474 words per minute. (26)

Moreover, the students learned to "skim" some materials, to read others carefully in terms of certain purposes, and to apply study skills intensively in others. It was recognized that different rates of reading should be anticipated as students read different kinds of materials for different purposes. Accordingly, rate of reading was not looked upon as a single ability which characterized all of a pupil's reading, but as an aggregate of different rates.

As J. Harlan Shores has indicated:

> Fast readers are the good readers when reading some kinds of materials for some purposes. When reading other kinds of materials for other purposes, there is no relationship between speed of reading and ability to comprehend. . . .
>
> Inasmuch as there are different relationships between rate and comprehension when rate is measured as an original reading time and when rate is measured to include rereading and question-answering time, it is important to define what is meant by reading rate. This finding also suggests that authorities in the field of reading would do well to attempt to standardize a practice for measuring reading rate. . . . (12)

Inadequacies in Measures of Reading Rate and Comprehension

In the foregoing studies a crucial question arises: What is meant by reading rate and reading comprehension? Miles A. Tinker states:

The two aspects of reading which have received the most attention are speed and comprehension. Various tests have been devised to test either the speed or the comprehension factor. The content and structure of these tests would seem to indicate that there exists little agreement among authors concerning the most adequate method of measuring either speed or comprehension.(*21*)

One of the most obvious limitations in standardized tests of reading comprehension is the fact that they are often "timed." Ralph C. Preston and Morton Botel attempted to check the hypothesis that "when reading comprehension is tested under 'untimed' conditions, rate and quality of reading are unrelated." They utilized 32 students in a class at the University of Pennsylvania.

> ... The correlation of rate and *timed* comprehension yields the statisti-
> cally significant coefficient of .48. The correlation between rate and
> untimed comprehension yields the coefficient of .20 — not statistically
> significant. Since untimed comprehension is the "purer" comprehension
> score, we conclude there was little relationship between rate and com-
> prehension. It is clear that the usual procedure for measuring compre-
> hension is untenable.... (*8*)

It seems from studies such as Preston's and Botel's that faulty or inadequate testing procedures have led to the invalid conclusion that reading rate and comprehension are closely associated. Several other studies support this criticism. For example, J. Harlan Shores and Kenneth L. Husbands obtained data upon the reading of pupils in grades four through six. They "found that comprehension depended less upon speed than upon intelligence, purposes of the reading, difficulty of the material read, opportunities for verifying questions of comprehension, and the continuity of the text."(*13*)

We have indicated some limitations in standardized tests. The possibilities for error in the approaches used to measure rate and comprehension in some reading improvement programs are even greater. Many reports of reading improvement tell one simply that a particular individual may have started with a rate, for example, of 200 words per minute with 45 per cent comprehension, and that at the completion of a course, his reading rate was 20,000 words per minute with 65 per cent comprehension. Moreover, only one type of material may have been used in the tests. It is frequently assumed that the gains made with the limited training materials will transfer to other kinds of reading. Occasionally, in reports of reading improvement, one finds an account in which the student's gains are given for reading three or more types of materials. However, one seldom finds even in these cases much information about the difficulty of the various samples.

It is clear that different concepts of the reading process are held by proponents for diverse approaches. The inadequacy of current practices in estimating speed and comprehension is conspicuous when one defines effective reading as a process of getting meaning from printed or written symbols and when one stresses the fact that reading is a two-way process involving each individual and his reaction to the materials. Moreover, when one recognizes that reading is both oral and silent in nature, the process of measurement becomes more complicated. It is to be hoped that the future will bring the development of new and more comprehensive tests of reading ability and progress. Until testing is improved, many reports of gains will continue to be crude estimates at best, and oversimplified and misleading at worst.

Summary, Comments, and Recommendations

In this paper, the writer has presented representative studies of rate and comprehension by scholars in an effort to determine the validity of claims concerning approaches which result in phenomenally high rates of reading, such as 40,000 words per minute. He also presented conclusions from reviews of studies by reading specialists. And he indicated briefly some of the results of investigations extending from the period of the twenties to the present time. In the early studies it was clearly shown that the reading rates of children, youth, and adults could be greatly improved in periods of a few weeks to a single semester. Speed gains were usually reported through the use of standard tests and through less formal estimates of reading rate and comprehension.

A period followed in which machines and devices were recommended for fostering improvement in reading rate and comprehension. Repeatedly, studies showed that equally satisfactory results could be obtained in programs which did not employ pacing devices as in those which did.

The writer discussed investigations concerning the maximum rates of reading various kinds of materials. Again and again, reading authorities concluded that silent reading rates above 800 or 900 words per minute were largely manifestations of various kinds of skimming. Moreover, the assumption that there exists a "general" rate of reading which can be greatly accelerated by practice was questioned. Studies showed that good readers learn to read different kinds of materials at different rates according to their needs and purposes. Investigators reported that fast readers are good readers of some kinds of materials read for certain purposes. But with other kinds of materials read for other purposes, there was no relationship between reading speed and comprehension. Thus, it became clear that reading rate and comprehension are not always closely related.

On the basis of eye-movement records, the claim was questioned that students can be trained to read large portions of a page at a single fixation. Moreover, the value of fantastically high rates of reading was also questioned since it was held that as rates of reading increased, more and more materials were skipped.

Scholars frequently stressed the inadequacy of current tests and emphasized the need for more comprehensive procedures for evaluation that would include tests of reading different kinds of materials as well as records of the amount and nature of the pupil's reading experience. It was pointed out that not only testing, but procedures of instruction also need to be vastly modified and extended.

The writer would like to point out that in the voluminous literature on courses in "reading improvement," far too much emphasis appears to be given to rapid reading rather than to the other very important aspects of the reading process.[1] Moreover, he feels that methods of instruction and eye-movements are accorded too much importance. It is unfortunate, too, that skimming is often equated with reading.

The foregoing statements reflect the writer's belief that eye-movements play only a minor role in effective reading. "We read with the back of the head as well as the front" is a statement sometimes made to indicate that reading is a two-way process involving the material read and the individual. His "response in reading" is a most important aspect of the process.

The writer believes also that skills such as critical reading should be given greater attention in reading improvement programs. Studies have shown repeatedly that relatively few pupils, and adults too, read critically. Too often they accept without question the printed page, failing to examine the authenticity and accuracy of presentations. One needs only to examine the character of the tests used in reading improvement courses to realize that primary attention is given to factors other

---

[1]After this manuscript was presented, the writer obtained a reprint of Stanford E. Taylor's relevant and highly significant study entitled "An Evaluation of Forty-One Who Had Recently Completed the 'Reading Dynamics' Program," from the *Eleventh Yearbook of the National Reading Conference.*

than critical response in reading. Moreover, one will usually look in vain in such programs for materials and procedures to foster problem solving and thinking about the importance of the presentations or of the ideas to be gained from the reading. Seldom is the student encouraged to find solutions to problems in novel, imaginative, and creative ways.

In the accounts of reading improvement programs, consideration is rarely given to the role of oral reading and various forms of creative expression. The writer is not suggesting that oral reading be made the primary objective of programs. But it is a skill that merits a place in comprehensive programs of reading instruction. So, too, should provisions be made for sharing the results of reading with other students.

Reading improvement programs should recognize also the importance of relating the outcomes of reading to other aspects of communication such as skills in listening, speaking, and writing. The time used in reading improvement programs is often so little as to permit emphasis only upon a few skills. But why should one skill, speed of reading, receive the lion's share of the time?

Perhaps an effective antidote to speed reading programs lies in shifting the emphasis from a concern for eye movements and the results of specific methods to an approach which stresses creative thinking, problem solving, and greater flexibility in applying reading skills.

Despite the fact that many reading improvement programs are characterized by marked limitations, there are other programs, especially in secondary schools and colleges, in which emphasis is placed upon flexibility in applying reading skills and upon adjusting reading rates to varied purposes and needs, as well as upon the development of more adequate vocabulary and concepts in various fields. Skill in skimming of diverse kinds of materials for varied purposes is also stressed. In such programs, improvement in rate is often great. Thus, studies show that pupils have been able to increase, during a single semester, their rates for reading different types of materials fifty per cent or more and, at the same time, to have made gains in comprehension. Such gains in reading are of vast importance to the student and citizen in an era, such as the present time, which is characterized by a widespread "explosion" of information related to our unparalleled, rapid developments in science and other fields. Because of these facts, we should look upon efforts to improve reading speed as an important aspect of developmental reading, a skill to be emphasized particularly in the education of young people and adults.

The writer believes that, at the elementary school level, relatively little emphasis should be placed upon speed reading. Instead, attention should be directed to the cultivation of essential habits and skills and to wide reading designed to satisfy interests and needs. Of course, pupils will be given encouragement and guidance in reading more rapidly and in adapting rates to different purposes. But the objective of developmental reading instruction will be to help pupils enjoy the act of reading and the results. They will enjoy the act of reading when they have acquired the essential habits and skills in silent and oral reading. And they will enjoy the results of reading when they are offered the opportunity to read widely in accord with their varied interests and needs. Thus, developmental reading programs should be planned and offered in the elementary school. In all reading programs, attention should be given not only to individual differences, but also to interest and the enjoyment of reading.

When such a developmental approach is widely followed, far-reaching benefits will accrue in the lives of the pupils. As Mortimer J. Adler is quoted in the *Journal of Reading*, February, 1968:

> In the case of good books, the point is not to see how many of them you can get through, but rather how many can get through to you.

Bibliography

1. Cason, Eloise B. *Mechanical Methods for Increasing the Speed of Reading.* New York: Teachers College, Columbia University, 1943.

2. Edfeldt, Ake W. *Silent Speech and Silent Reading.* Chicago: University of Chicago Press, 1960.

3. Gates, Arthur I. *The Improvement of Reading.* New York: The Macmillan Company, 1947.

4. Gilbert, Luther C. "Speed of Processing Visual Stimuli and Its Relation to Reading," *Journal of Education Psychology, 55* (Feb. 1959).

5. Manolakes, George. "The Effects of Tachistoscopic Training in an Adult Reading Program," *Journal of Applied Psychology, 36* (Dec. 1952).

6. McLaughlin, G. Harry. "Reading at 'Impossible' Speeds," *Journal of Reading, 12* (March, 1969).

7. O'Brien, John A. *Silent Reading.* New York: The Macmillan Company, 1921.

8. Preston, Ralph C., and Morton Botel. "Reading Comprehension Tested Under Timed and Untimed Conditions," *School and Society, 74* (August 4, 1951).

9. Robinson, Helen M., and Helen K. Smith. "Rate Problems in the Reading Clinic," *The Reading Teacher, 15* (May, 1962).

10. Schale, Florence. "Vertical Methods of Increasing Rates of Comprehension," *Journal of Reading, 8* (April, 1965).

11. Schale, Florence. "Can Fifth-Grade Pupils Benefit from an Adult Rapid Reading Method?" *Multidisciplinary Aspects of College-Adult Reading.* Seventeenth Yearbook of the National Reading Conference, edited by George B. Schick and Merrill M. May, 1968. Distributed by the National Reading Conference, Inc., Reading Center, Marquette University, Milwaukee, Wisconsin.

12. Shores, J. Harlan. "Dimensions of Reading Speed and Comprehension," *Elementary English, 45* (Jan. 1968).

13. Shores, J. Harlan, and Kenneth L. Husbands. "Are Fast Readers the Best Readers?" *Elementary English, 27* (Jan. 1950). Quote from A. I. Gates, *Teaching Reading* (What Research Says to the Teacher). Washington, D.C.: National Education Association (June, 1953).

14. Spache, George D. "Is This a Breakthrough in Reading?" *The Reading Teacher, 15* (Jan. 1962).

15. Spache, George D. "Rate of Reading—The Machine Approach," *Toward Better Reading.* Champaign, Illinois: Garrard Publishing Company, 1963.

16. Speer, George S. "Using Mechanical Devices Can Increase Speed of Reading." *The Nation's Schools, 48* (Oct. 1951).

17. Stauffer, Russell G. "Speed Reading at the University of Delaware," *Speed Reading: Practices and Procedures,* Vol. 10 Proceedings of the 44th Annual Education Conference held at the University of Delaware, March 2, 3, 1962. Compiled and edited by Russell G. Stauffer, The Reading-Study Center, School of Education, University of Delaware, Newark, Delaware, 1963.

18. Taylor, Earl A. *The Fundamental Reading Skill.* Springfield, Illinois: Charles C. Thomas (2nd edn.), 1966.

19. Tinker, Miles A. "Devices to Improve Speed of Reading," *The Education Digest, 33* (Sept. 1967). Reported from *The Reading Teacher, 20* (April, 1967).

20. Tinker, Miles A. "Recent Studies of Eye-Movements in Reading," *Psychological Bulletin, 55* (July, 1968).

21. Tinker, Miles A. "Speed Versus Comprehension in Reading as Affected by Level of Difficulty," *Journal of Educational Psychology, 30* (Feb. 1939).

22. West, Ira. "Evelyn Wood Schools' Speed-Reading Claims Spark a Controversy," *The Wall Street Journal* (Sept. 27, 1967).

23. Westover, F. L. *Controlled Eye Movements Versus Practice Exercises in Reading: A Comparison of Methods of Improving Speed and Comprehension.* New York: Teachers College, Columbia University, 1946.

24. Witty, Paul A. "Evaluation of Methods and Devices to Improve Reading Rate and Comprehension," *Elementary English, 31* (May, 1954).

25. Witty, Paul A. "The Improvement of Reading Abilities," *Adult Reading,* Fifty-Fifth Yearbook, National Society for the Study of Education, Part II, Chapter I. Chicago: University of Chicago Press, 1956.

26. Witty, Paul A., Theodore Stolarz, and William Cooper. "Some Results of a Remedial Reading Program for College Students," *School and Society, 76* (Dec. 13, 1952).

Physical and Psychological Limits of the Reading Skills

Witty — Questions for Discussion

Are claims of speed up to 40,000 WPM ever reported by university researchers? What are the most serious factors limiting reading speed? Does any research verify the usefulness of the zigzag vertical sweep method of reading? What are some of the reasons for the serious discrepancies in results reported by various promoters and researchers? Does research support evidence for the usefulness of certain mechanical devices to increase reading rate?

CHAPTER TWELVE

Dyslexia

Perhaps any respectable book of readings on the psychology of reading should have a chapter on dyslexia. However, before one can begin to write about this malady, he must first of all know what it is. This, it seems, is where the problem begins. Just what is dyslexia? Is there a definite set of symptoms that would enable the trained observer to say, "This child definitely has dyslexia"? Do people in the medical profession use the term in the same way as it is used by people working in the various fields of education? Can dyslexia be "cured"? A number of books and articles have been devoted to answering these as well as other questions concerning this elusive malady; however, the editor must confess that these too have only added to his bewilderment.

The articles chosen for this chapter illustrate the state of confusion in which we find ourselves in attempting to define the term and describe its symptoms. The first article by Richard B. Adams illustrates the author's attempt to define the term, and the second article by William L. Rutherford will test your DQ (Dyslexia Quotient) after you feel you are well-versed on the subject. If, after reading both articles, you feel a little confused about the whole thing, then perhaps you should congratulate yourself for no longer being among those who can easily diagnose the dyslexic child.

'The time has come,' the Walrus said,
  'To talk of many things:
Of shoes—and ships—and sealing wax—
  Of cabbages—and—kings—
And why the sea is boiling hot—
  And whether pigs have wings.'

"When I use a word," Humpty Dumpty
said in rather a scornful tone, "it means
just what I choose it to mean—neither
more nor less."

"The question is," said Alice, "whether
you can make words mean so many
different things."

"The question is," said Humpty Dumpty,
"which is to be master—that's all."

343

Richard B. Adams

Dyslexia: A Discussion of Its Definition

If man is master of his own inventions then he is free to manage the meaning of his words to suit his own conventions. But sometimes a word gets born which, rather than live as servant to man, moves out in life like a Frankenstein monster wreaking havoc in the discourse of sensible men. *Dyslexia is such a word.* Its meaning is obscure and it has divided the efforts of professional men when collaboration would have been the better course. The quest to realize a fully literate society, no longer allows for the luxuries of divided effort. The definition problem has gotten so bad that it must be made clear that the polyphony of semantics was not meant to be carried on according to a private tune. To continue a musical analogy, the field of learning disabilities could benefit if the song of semantics were sung as a chorale in which every singer knows not only the harmony, but the meaning of the words as well. The time, then, has come for us to pause amidst our dialogue and examine this monster word *dyslexia* and tame its meaning.

Webster advises that the word is of Greek parentage formed by the uniting of *dys* (meaning hard or ill) with *lexis* (meaning speech or word). Altering *lexis* to *lexia* denotes "a specified type of incapacity to read." (Webster's New International Dictionary, 1961) So we know that dyslexia speaks to the matter of reading difficulty, a specified type. Webster, however, only begs the question: What *type* of reading difficulty is dyslexia reserved to specify? For the answer to that question we must

From Richard B. Adams, "Dyslexia: A Discussion of Its Definition," *Journal of Learning Disabilities* 2 (December 1969): 616-26. Reprinted by permission of the author and the journal.

look elsewhere. Specialized dictionaries should clear up the question of specificity.

> "dyslexia: *noun*, impairment of the ability to read, or to understand what one reads silently or aloud, independent of any speech defect.— Distinguished from alexia, a type of visual aphasia" (English and English, 1958).

This definition isn't too much help. Aside from telling us that a speech defect is not involved, it tells nothing whatever about the nature or character of the *impairment*. However, since dyslexia is to be distinguished from alexia, perhaps there are some inferences we can draw by looking into the definition of alexia and decide what dyslexia is *not*.

> "alexia: *noun*, a form of sensory aphasia characterized by loss of ability to read written or printed language despite unimpairment of vision or intelligence.—Synonyms: visual aphasia, word blindness (preferred).— Compare strephosymbolia" (English and English, 1958, p. 22).

We are told dyslexia is *NOT* a form of visual aphasia. Furthermore, dyslexia is an *impairment* while alexia is a *loss* of the ability to read. The ability to read is presumed; dyslexia *impairs* or diminishes the ability making the act increasingly hard or difficult while alexia *eliminates* the ability altogether. The difference, then, between alexia and dyslexia is only a matter of *degree*. Now we are getting someplace.

But, we still don't know what it *is* which distinguishes the *degree of difference* between alexia and dyslexia.

Since *visual aphasia* is a synonym for alexia, let us check the entry under *aphasia* for a clue.

> "The term (aphasia) is highly general and tends to be loosely used, but authorities insist on restriction to cases resulting from brain lesion" (English and English, 1958, p. 36).

That helps a great deal. By reasoning *a priori* we can now say that the distinguishing characteristic between alexia and dyslexia is the presence or absence of a brain lesion; with dyslexia there is no structural fault in the brain.

However, we still do not know the specifics underlying the reading *impairment* in dyslexia. What is its nature or character? Let us consult another authority.

> "dyslexia. 1. An inability to read understandingly due to a central lesion.
> 2. A condition in which reading is possible, but is attended with fatigue

and disagreeable sensations" (Dorland's Illustrated Medical Dictionary, 1957).

The distinction (a lesion) between alexia and dyslexia does not seem to apply. Now we know how Alice felt when she called Humpty Dumpty's cravat a belt. She couldn't tell where his neck ended and his waist began.

We have yet to determine what type of reading difficulty dyslexia is reserved to specify. Let us consult one more dictionary.

"dyslexia. Distorted speech; the ability to read may be intact, but there is little or no understanding of what is read" (Psychiatric Dictionary, 1960).

Distorted *speech!?* The ability *intact!?* Let this be a lesson; dictionaries have their place but their dismembered light is much too feeble to illuminate shadowy shades of meaning. Perhaps an understanding of dyslexia will come into focus if we look at it within the framework of a larger context.

"The primary sensory systems concerned with language perception and development are the auditory, visual, and tactile-kinesthetic (proprioceptive). Language perception and cognition are defined as the ability to correctly process, pattern, and retain (recognize, interpret, assimilate, and store) for memory recall the information provided by the sensory systems. Difficulty in perception and cognition in these sensory systems results in language disability in intellectually normal children. The following diagram suggests a theoretical outline of the most obvious language disabilities:

Language Disabilities

The etiology of these disabilities is not known. Until the etiology is clearly understood, we should assume these to be developmental in origin with a disturbance in neuropsychological function at the cortical level.

These are not brain damaged children, they are not mentally retarded, and emotional problems are not the basis of the language disability" (Waites, 1966, p. 9).

This authority is providing some structure. Nevertheless, earlier he said, "Visual imperception seems to be the most common difficulty in the form of specific dyslexia (specific language disability)" (Waites, 1966, p. 5). But later on he says, "Specific dyslexia is defined as an inborn language disability of central origin with disorders in reading, writing, spelling and sometimes verbal expression" (Waites, 1966, p. 10). This authority's argument appears flawed by the introduction of a contradition. On page 9 he asks us to assume the language disabilities in his diagram *be developmental in origin*. On page 10 he defines specific dyslexia as an *inborn language disability*. Is it possible for an inborn disability to be developmental in origin? Logic dictates not. If a disability is *inborn* its origins are in the genetic material of the germ plasm. Furthermore, we are not instructed how *specific* dyslexia is different from the plain old garden-variety *dyslexia*.

Let us turn to another definition:

"Dyslexia is a syndrome characterized by a decreased ability to learn to read properly, even though the intelligence may be normal or superior. This unusual condition is functional, and in a high percentage correctable in contra-distinction to alexia" (Park, 1955, p. 71).

This definition is interesting for two reasons. First, it introduces the notion that dyslexia is a *syndrome*. Secondly, it restricts the definition to the ability to *learn* to read. Since we have been preoccupied from the outset with the *nature or character* of the impairment in dyslexia, and in view of the pregnant use of the terms *syndrome* and *learn* in the above definition, perhaps a closer look at Dr. Park's study will be instructive.

The study was conducted on 198 dyslexic subjects ranging in ages from 7 to 22 years with a mean age of 10 years 10½ months. No subject had a history of brain injury; the lowest I.Q. in the subject population was 85 — the mean I.Q. was 105. The I.Q.'s were measured by the WISC. Reading ability was measured by the California and Progressive Achievement Test; reading retardation was defined by the discrepancy between the expected reading score for the subjects' chronological age and the obtained score on the test.

Blood cell determinations and basal metabolic rates were studied. The erythrocyte count, the total leucocyte count, and the ratio between neutrophils and lymphrocytes were calculated. Dr. Park and his colleagues undertook this study because the incidence of dyslexia is 4 to 1 in favor of males over females, a fact they interpreted to suggest that a hormonal imbalance may be a factor associated with dyslexia.

The erythrocyte counts were within normal limits suggesting no anemia was present in the subjects. The data on the circulating leucocytes indicated that leucopenia was present in the average dyslexic child. Because of the leucopenia they observed an absolute decrease in the number of the total circulating neutrophils in addition to a disturbed ratio between the number of neutrophils and leucocytes. Thirty-seven per cent of the subjects had a low basal metabolism.

Between the ages of 13 and 14 years their subjects' data on the neutrophils, lymphocytes, and leucocytes abruptly approached standard values. The biological significance of these differences occurring near the age of puberty called into question the implications of gonadal functions. Also, they speculated that leucopenia and neutropenia may assume an important role.

They conclude their study with the following observations.

"There are probably many complexly interrelated determinants in dyslexia, such as hormonal imbalances, functional cerebral defects, thwarting of the sublimation of the aggressive drive, disturbances in the interpersonal relationships, especially in the family climate, lack of motivation, and perhaps many unknown factors, which should prevent the assignment of any single causative factor. But, it is generally recognized and the extensive clinical experience of the Dyslexia Institute Staff indicates that a factor of stress or tension is present in almost all patients with reading difficulties. It is also evident, on the basis of the literature reviewed, that the factor of stress or tension would be manifested in a number of patients, if not all, by a change in the white blood cell picture ... So, in some individuals their resultant "physiological compensatory response" to stress and any other influence is a factor in the etiology of dyslexia, and in some dyslexics the effects of an abnormal autonomic-pituitary-ardrenal-thyroid (gonad) function on the white blood in response to stress is found. These symptoms merely occur simultaneously, and form only a part of the complex physiological manifestations found in the dyslexic child" (Park, 1955, pp. 83-4).

So, the Walrus's advice was prophetic. The talk is now of many things: of blood, and stress, of cerebral defects and of metabolic swings. Let us push on.

"The psychophysiological sources of reading retardation can be divided into five categories: general debility, sensory defects, intellectual defects, brain injury, and idiopathic or specific reading disability. Overlap and multiple conjunctions of causes are common ... specific reading disability (is) also known as congenital word blindness, primary reading retardation, and developmental dyslexia. The adjective *specific* calls attention both to the circumscribed nature of the disability and to our ignorance of its cause. Operationally, specific reading disability may be defined as the failure to learn to read with normal proficiency despite conventional instruction, a culturally adequate home, proper motivation, intact senses, normal intelligence, and freedom from gross neurologic defect" (Eisenberg, 1966, pp. 359-360).

We now have an operational definition. We also have an admission of ignorance as to its cause. Note, too, "the failure to *learn* to read . . ." A consensus is emerging; let us hear from another authority.

"As noted in the Preface, the short and simple expression *reading disability* has been used in the title of this book. In more exact terminology, the word *specific* is placed before *reading disability* to indicate a differentiation from lack of reading due to absence of education. Furthermore, it implies that the learning problem is specific to the language area and does not extend into other fields such as science and mathematics. A broader and perhaps better designation — namely, *specific language disability* — often referred to as *S. L. D.,* is gaining in favor, but the short expression *reading disability* remains as a convenient term in common usage.

Concerning developmental dyslexia, the word *dyslexia* comes from Greek *dys* plus *lexis*. *Dys* means hard, bad or difficult; *lexis* pertains to words or to the vocabulary of a language as distinguished from its grammar. *Dyslexia*, then, is the ideal word to describe specific reading disability, but it was used in the earlier descriptions of language disturbances to apply to reading disturbances due to organic brain pathology. However, when the qualifying word *developmental* is used, we rule out brain injury and bring in the concept of developmental lag. Therefore, *developmental dyslexia* is the best term for the language disability dealt with in this book. In the test, *specific reading disability, innate dyslexia, strephosymbolia,* and even *word-blindness* will appear in context with the immediate topic under discussion but as synonyms for *developmental dyslexia*" (Thompson, 1966).

An entanglement of synonyms is perhaps obscuring our path.

"Our Foundation has coined the word *eulexia* to commemorate the occasion. This means *good reading*, in contrast to *dyslexia*, the term often used as an erudite description of the *reading disability* which accompanied the introduction of the configurational or look-and-guess system of teaching reading, — the system imposed on our schools by the educational hierarchy forty years ago, which has proved as ruinous in practice as it was unsound in theory. The symptoms of dyslexia are so closely associated with look-and-guess instruction that with the disappearance of the latter, dyslexia should soon fade away, except in the rare case of congenital, physical or mental defects" (Reading Reform News, 1967, p. 1).

An interesting point — dyslexia fading away. Despite the pejorative reference to the look-and-say method of teaching a reading vocabulary, the implication is provocative. The Reading Reform Foundation will have us think that if our schools return to instructional practices of the good old days when "look-and phonetically sound out the letters-then say the word" characterized the reading lesson, reading disabilities will dissolve under the solvent of better teaching methods. They acknowledge, however, that teaching phonics is not sufficient for the dyslexic child, the rare case of "congenital, physical or mental defects." They do not, however, define the limits of *rare*. Let us, therefore, pursue their point further and tease out a figure which is representative of the number of children who are dyslexic. I use *tease* advisedly. We want to uncover a figure which is acceptable to the proponents of both the phonics *and* the look-and-say teaching methods.

"...the results of a study of 478 first-grade pupils is reported. An average of 14.48% dyslexia was found, which increased to 15.36% when dsylexias were included which were accompanied by slight mental weakness" (Bernaldo de Quiros and Della Cella, 1959).

This data is reported from two cities in Argentina, Sante Fe and Rosario. The language in Argentina is of course Spanish, a language in which the phoneme-grapheme relationship is regular. Hence, there is no controversy in Argentina regarding phonics versus look-and-say methods of teaching reading. The proponents of the phonics method should accept this data because the Argentine child learns to read—or fails to learn—under the system of phonics. The proponents of the look-and-say method should also accept this data because they claim the good teacher uses phonics in teaching "word attack skills." It follows that by focusing on the number of dyslexics in a country whose orthography, unlike English, behaves reliably according to phonetic rules, we can leap-frog the "phonics versus look-and-say" teaching controversy and remain aloof to the claims and counter-claims of the warring groups.

Still, we must not be guilty of generalizing from one particular.

"A study of 2000 school children at the end of the second grade showed 78% relatively free from reading disabilities; 18% had moderately severe and 4% had severe dyslexia" (Schenk-Danzinger, 1961).

This data comes from Vienna, Austria. The German orthography, like Spanish, is obedient to phonetic rules.

It is difficult to understand the vigor of the special pleading for the phonics system in the face of data like this. Perhaps they just want to argue "why the sea is boiling hot—and whether pigs have wings."

But let us return to the main problem. We were talking about dyslexia and trying to get a better understanding of what it is all about. Our survey has left us in Vienna. Let us gather up our thoughts and travel to Copenhagen.

"...I shall first endeavor to define congenital word-blindness in the medical sense. The term is to be understood to signify a defective capacity for acquiring, at the normal time, a proficiency in reading and writing corresponding to average performance; the deficiency is dependent on constitutional factors (heredity), is often accompanied by difficulties with other symbols (numbers, musical notation, etc.), it exists in the the absence of intellectual defect or of defects of the sense organs which might retard the normal accomplishment of these skills, and in the absence of past or present appreciable inhibitory influences in the internal and external environment.

The definition has to be descriptive since one does not have one single symptom nor one straightforward objective finding on which to base the diagnosis. On this point there is no difference from the kind of delimitation one is obliged to adopt with other psychic disorders, where a descriptive definition has to be used and is fully adequate both for practical diagnosis and for detailed scientific study. With regard to the definition of congenital word-blindness just given, it should be stressed that one must distinguish between primary and secondary forms of dyslexia, but I shall return to this point a little later.

It should, furthermore, be mentioned that the term *congenital word-blindness* is used synonymously with constitutional dyslexia, or just *dyslexia*. In cases of acquired disturbances of language function (aphasia), *alexia* refers to the partial or complete loss of the ability to read, due to disease. Likewise, the term *agraphia* is applied to an acquired impairment of the ability to write (words as well as letters). Similarly, in regard to congenital word-blindness one can speak of *dyslexia* as referring specially to difficulties in reading, and of *dysgraphia* as referring to constitutionally determined difficulties in writing. As already mentioned, the term dyslexia is often used in such a way as to cover difficulties in both reading and writing in congenital word-blindness (the word "constitutional" being omitted) — but this is not wholly correct. Just as "word-blindness," strictly speaking, refers only to the defect of reading, but is used in everyday speech to include all the symbol disturbances which occur in this condition, so can dyslexia be used to designate the whole disorder.

The decisive points in the medical view of word-blindness as a specific abnormality are:
1) the difficulties in reading and writing persist into adult life in nearly all cases, in spite of special teaching,
2) the faulty performance in reading and writing has a certain characteristic quality; although no single symptom is so absolutely characteristic that the condition can be diagnosed from it alone, various errors occur so frequently that the condition thereby acquires a particular quality (rotation of certain letters, reversals, confusion between and disfigurement of various letters),
3) the familial incidence of word-blindness is strong evidence of the constitutional factor's importance,
4) the difficulties in reading and writing are not isolated symptoms, but appear side by side with other symbol defects (numbers, musical notation, morse, stenography and so on)" (Hermann, 1959).

Note carefully the point Hermann made. The term dyslexia can stand alone and "be used to designate the whole disorder" a disorder which is "dependent on constitutional factors (heredity) . . ." He is opting for a genetic factor as a single cause. You will remember Dr. Park (1955) cautioned us that "there were probably many complexly interrelated determinants in dyslexia . . . which should prevent the assignment of any single causative factor." The question posed by Alexander Pope in his Moral Essays is relevant here; just who *shall* decide when doctors disagree?

Let us move on and consult another authority.

"In recent years the term *dyslexic* has been applied to children of normal intelligence with marked specific disability in reading. Apparently this term has been adopted in order to indicate that these cases are comparable with those of *alexia* produced by cortical injury. For reasons described in chapter v, this hypothesis cannot at present be accepted. Therefore the term *dyslexic* will not be employed in this book" (Vernon, 1958, p. 3).

And in chapter five we find the following sentence.

"We may state categorically that no child exhibiting reading disability should be stigmatized as suffering from an irremediable defect labelled *congenital word-blindness...*" (Vernon, 1958, p. 115).

There's no equivocating in those words. And it's not difficult to figure out to whom they are directed. When the doctors disagree do you count the votes? Vote counting may lead to good government but it will surely lead to bad science.

Let's pause for a moment and consider our progress. A while ago it looked as if a consensus was going to emerge from the fog. Instead of consensus we've encountered conflict. And the fog is just as thick. Perhaps the problem is that the materials we're consulting are somewhat dated. If wisdom is standing on the shoulders of your predecessor, let us look at some fairly current definitions.

"I define dyslexia very literally as an impairment of the ability to read or a reading disability. This is the definition given in *Webster's Unabridged* and *Gould's Medical Dictionary*.

To me, this includes reading disabilities of all kinds regardless of the etiology or pathophysiological mechanisms involved. It is a generic term. Those who have a reading disability need to be examined carefully and the reading disability described in terms of etiology and pathophysiology.

I feel quite strongly against the use of dyslexia to describe some specific disease syndrome with a describable etiology or pathophysiology. This offends my semantic dignity, as well as being contrary to my training and clinical habits" (Bering, personal communication to the author).

Dyslexia a generic term. But do not use the term to "describe some specific disease syndrome with a describable etiology or pathophysiology." I will leave it to the reader to decide why this offends his semantic dignity. Is it because dyslexia eludes a "describable etiology or pathophysiology;" Or is it because he objects to the notion of dyslexia being a disease?

"I suggest that if the word dyslexia, *a disturbance of the ability to read* can be useful as an euphemism for all forms of illiteracy, i.e., 'a melange of the educationally inadequate, the intellectually deficient, the emotionally disturbed, the infirm of purpose and the genuine dyslexics'— Critchley; then use the word in this generic sense. True developmental dyslexia can be considered as a subcategory with its basic manifestations as determined by present diagnostic methods" (Williams, personal communication to the author).

Another vote for the generic. But note the qualification "if." And, how will we know "true" dyslexia from "false" dyslexia? What are "present diagnostic methods?"

"The term *Dyslexia* to me is a vague, non-specific, confused waste basket. When I use the term, I have in mind the condition which affects a

354 Richard B. Adams

significant group of our school age population. The individuals described as having dyslexia are those individuals who have an inability to use written language at a level related to their intellectual capacity in the absence of some clearly identifiable interferring causative factor" (Davies, personal communication to the author).

The generic votes are piling up. Note the qualifier "at a level related to their intellectual capacity in the absence of some clearly identifiable interfering causative factor." We'll hear more about that later.

"Dyslexia is inability to learn to read when exposed to an educational program in which most pupils successfully learn to read. It is a symptom common to many poorly defined and overlapping conditions: *Mental retardation, brain dysfunction, cultural deprivation, specific learning disability, language impairment,* etc. It seems likely that it may be caused by either a biologically abnormal brain, inadequate environmental programming of the brain, or to a combination of brain abnormality and inadequate programming. For this reason it seems unwise to include qualifications such as *due to abnormal neurologic function* or *not accounted for by low intelligence or emotional problems* or *despite a normal home environment* to any definition.

Current knowledge would indicate that neurologic, socio-cultural, emotional, intellectual and motivational factors all are interwoven in children who fail to learn to read, and the definition should not be conditional on the apparent presence or absence of any of these factors" (North, personal communication to the author).

Is this a generic definition? Or is it a *retrospective* definition? That is, the child is dyslexic when he has been taught yet failed to learn. If a child has been taught *and* learns could he have been dyslexic? How will the kindergarten or first grade teacher spot the dyslexics among her charges? Does the educational program *develop* dyslexia in the same way chemicals develop a picture on a photographic plate?

"Dyslexia to me means simply *an inability to read* and like any other symptom of higher nervous system function has a different diagnosis. First, there is the acquired lesion in the left posterior hemisphere of an adult in which a previously acquired reading ability is lost. This, of course, is not the type of dyslexia used by educators and psychologists in describing the elementary school child who demonstrates difficulty in acquiring reading skills. An arbitrary dividing line must be drawn, I think, necessarily in order to distinguish a group with enough difficulty to warrant specal investigation. This group has been defined elsewhere as reading two grades below expected for his chronologic age. Immediately, there will be some overlap with children with real reading disability and those who are commonly termed *late bloomers.* After this group has been collected, one will find those with deficient intelligence, auditory and visual problems, emotional problems, those of insufficient motivation, those who have been denied adequate opportunity to learn and finally, a group of idiopathic nature. Many investigators seem to regard the latter group, the idiopathic group, as *specific dyslexics* or *developmental dyslexics* and have centered their research and therapeutic efforts on these.

I suppose then a definition of dyslexia would depend upon what group of reading disabilities one chooses to work with. If we may be assured that the mentally retarded, those with visual and auditory complaints and those of poor emotional matrix are being discovered and are adequately cared for, then we may concentrate definition of specific reading disability or dyslexia to exclude these; however, if the reading disability as found in the school, is not now being broken down into those with visual problems, etc., then we should use a larger definition of dyslexia or reading disability. I would personally think a definition to include a large population of reading disabilities would be the most appropriate keeping in mind that there is an idiopathic group which may require additional remedial techniques" (Capistrant, personal communication to the author).

If the first paragraph gave it to us the second paragraph took it away: note the "if . . . however . . . if."

"In the very broadest sense of the word, *Dyslexia means difficulty in reading,* which theoretically could extend from attempting to read under inadequate light to specific cerebral defects associated with inability to interpret visual symbols. A comprehensive classification of the dyslexias must be agreed upon and should, where possible, be based on the causative factors rather than performance ability alone. The latter is currently important in programming the educational drills and remedial exercises in the sphere of the educator or educational psychologist. To analyze the results of therapy with meaningful reference, however, necessitates relating accomplishments to causative pathology" (Keeney, personal communication to the author).*

For the "causative factors" see his discussion in the manuscript. The integrated organization of his manuscript militated against citing the "causative factors" without doing violence to their meaning as imbedded

---

*The author is indebted to Dr. Keeney for generously giving his time to prepare his 10 page manuscript which "carries much of the highlight" of the "Conference Dyslexia" held at the Willis Eye Hospital and Research Institute in November 1966. Dr. Keeney was Chairman of that Conference. The quotation is taken from page one of the manuscript.

in their original context. I hesitate to attempt a summary of his "causative factors" for the same reason as well as for reasons of space limitations. Suffice to say that his definition is of the generic variety but turns on "causative factors" and "performance ability."

"Dyslexia is the inability to integrate auditory and visual linguistic symbols in proper spacial position and time sequence. The term *dyslexia* carries the medical diagnosis of minimal cerebral dysfunction. This inability is manifested when the child cannot associate the speech symbols he has learned to receive and express during his preschool years with the representative visual symbols he must learn during his initial school years.

Dyslexia is only one area of symbolic learning disabilities. The inability to associate and integrate symbols manifested through a required specificity of response is to be found in arithmetic (dyscalculia), spelling, writing (dysgraphia), telling time, reading maps, blueprints and even the world of silent language which exists in all inter-personal relationships" (DeWitt, personal communication to the author).

That is not a generic definition. I will leave it to the reader to decide if it is an operational definition or a "process" definition, or both.

"The diagnostic evaluation of children with learning problems must be made as operational as possible. The label to be attached is less helpful than one would like in light of the confusion with which it may be applied. The term *dyslexia* may be variously applied to the child with difficulties in learning to read on the basis of the following syndromes: pure visual-perceptual difficulties with or without motor disabilities, auditory channel disabilities with or without motor disabilities or combinations of all. Further, the difficulty in learning to read may or may not be associated with difficulties in learning other concepts involved in arithmetic and other school work. It is suggested that emphasis should be placed upon describing the levels of performance of the relatively broad pre-requisite behaviors in the various channels that may be used for teaching. One may indeed find that visual perceptual difficulties are relatively poor as opposed to the other channels available and level of performance can, in addition, be rated on a quantitative continuum of increasing complexity. The child's perceptual profile, defined in terms of the specific behaviors required for learning would thus operationally define his disabilities and strengths. It is suggested therefore that testing of these children be an actual probe of the qualitative and quantitative levels of the individual child.

A further aspect of probing must relate to the variable of previous teaching techniques used. The conditions under which teaching has gone on is a very important variable in determining the present level of performance in toto as well as in various channels. The child from a relatively confused home environment is peculiarly susceptible to failure in meeting developmental expectations in the area of language. His present level of performance must be further probed. One might teach him the materials involved by explicit concern with the process of programming and the reinforcements useful in this particular child.

It is suggested that the diagnostic evaluation be on an operational description of the child's level of performance in various broad categories of function such as visual, auditory, kinesthetic, etc. In addition to the concern with present levels of performance, one should attempt to define the rate with which these levels can be modified under relatively optimal conditions which involve diagnostic teaching on a short term basis. One can then provide an operational description that is explicitly relevant to the processes and conditions under which remediation may be provided" (Ozer, personal communication to the author).

So there you have them. Each is fairly current. Some are more open than others. Which single one will work best?

Dyslexia

Adams—Questions for Discussion

Is there any general agreement among the various professional groups on the meaning of dyslexia? Is there general agreement within certain professional groups on the meaning of dyslexia? What is your perception of the relationship among the following terms: dyslexia, alexia, specific dyslexia, disgraphia, and aphasia? How do you suppose the subjects chosen by Dr. Park for his study were diagnosed? Do you feel that Adams's article was written to make the confusion over the term appear worse than it really is, or is he simply presenting the facts?

William L. Rutherford

What Is Your DQ (Dyslexia Quotient)?

Apparently we are in the midst of a new wave of interest in dyslexia. Verification of this contention may be found in the increased number of professional articles and speeches on this topic. Among parents there also seems to be a new awareness of dyslexia. Accompanying this resurgence of concern with dyslexia is the expected number of questions, debates, and uncertainties.

Some of the questions about "specific" or "developmental dyslexia" that are asked most frequently are handled here with no promise to resolve all the debate and uncertainties surrounding the topic generally.

In keeping with good test procedures, the reader is asked to respond to all the following questions before referring to any of the answers.

Questions

1. Dyslexia has a genetic etiology?
2. Only persons with average and above average IQ are affected by dyslexia?
3. Reading and spelling are the only skills impaired by dyslexia?
4. In countries where there is a consistency between the sounds and symbols of the language, dyslexics are unknown?

From William L. Rutherford, "What Is Your D.Q. (Dyslexia Quotient)?" *The Reading Teacher* 25 (December 1971): 262-66. Reprinted with permission of William L. Rutherford and the International Reading Association.

5. There is a constellation of behaviors and characteristics that is unique to dyslexics?

6. Which of the following characteristics are common to dyslexia? (This does not infer a cause and effect relationship, only that they are or are not usually present.)
   a. Poor auditory discrimination.
   b. Poor visual discrimination.
   c. Weakness in translation of sounds into symbols.
   d. Gross motor difficulties.
   e. Excessive letter reversals and inversions.
   f. Right-left disorientation.
   g. Difficulty in generalizing from word to concept.
   h. Faulty memory of sequences.
   i. Speech disorders.
   j. Spatial disabilities.
   k. Faulty cerebral dominance.

7. For all practical purposes the dyslexic child is doomed to educational failure?

Answers

1. True. Most authorities (Rabinovitch, 1968; Critchley, 1964; Bender, 1968; Nicholls, 1968; Orton, 1968) seem to feel that dyslexia is genetically rather than environmentally determined. Within this framework there is still much variance of opinion. For instance, some maintain dyslexia is a neurologic or brain dysfunction (Rabinovitch, 1968; Nicholls, 1968; Johnson and Myklebust, 1967) or a maturational lag (Orton, 1968; De Hirsch, 1968; Thompson, 1966) that may be genetically determined. Still others postulate brain damage as a possible cause (Cruickshank, 1968; Money, 1962), or they avoid specification of cause (Eisenberg, 1962; Harris, 1963).

2. False. This answer tends to fly in the face of most opinions on this question. Johnson and Myklebust (1967) and Nicholls (1968) along with others have stated that typically the dyslexic has an IQ of average or above. Nevertheless, Critchley (1964) points out that since dyslexia is genetically determined, there is no reason why it should not occur in children with subnormal intelligence.

Perhaps the association of dyslexia and average or high IQ is due to the fact that the reading problems of low IQ children are attributed to their intelligence without looking for other possible causes. When able children have reading problems, causes such as dyslexia are often sought out and assigned.

3. False. Dyslexia may adversely affect arithmetic as well as reading and spelling in the opinion of Critchley (1968) and Rabinovitch (1968). Spontaneous writing and writing to dictation are usually faulty also, according to Blau, *et al.* (1969), Critchley (1964), and Johnson and Myklebust (1967). Ability to copy printed material is more likely to be satisfactory.

4. False. Critchley (1968) cites known dyslexics from a number of countries as evidence that neither race nor national origin nor language influences dyslexia. Dyslexics are found among many races and in countries even where there is great regularity between the sounds and symbols of the language. Money (1962) contends that the child who cannot remember sounds and symbols is not aided by their regularity.

5. False. Money (1962) states that "No one has as yet uncovered any tell-tale sign or group of signs that are exclusive to the syndrome of specific dyslexia and are not found in other conditions of reading retardation." There are certain signs that are common in cases of dyslexia (see #7), but they are also found in non-dyslexics, so they cannot be relied on as diagnostic signals. Rarely is dyslexia found in isolation (Johnson and Myklebust, 1967).

6. a and b. The majority of the opinions (and evidence) indicates that visual and auditory discrimination weaknesses are not influential factors in dyslexia. A notable exception to this position is that of Johnson and Myklebust (1967), who feel that dyslexics can be divided into two categories — visual and auditory — by their weaknesses in one of the two areas.

c. Difficulty in translating sounds into symbols poses serious problems for the dyslexic in the opinion of virtually everyone who writes on this topic.

d. Dyslexics are not likely to have gross motor difficulties, and if they do, it is not relevant to the reading disability (Rabinovitch, 1968). Poor manual dexterity is fairly common, however (Johnson and Myklebust, 1967; Critchley, 1964).

e. Reversals and inversions are common among beginners in reading and writing, but most authorities feel that dyslexics persist in this for a longer period of time and do it with greater regularity. On this point it should be recognized that reversals are associated with reading level rather than chronological age. Therefore, until dyslexics read beyond the beginning level, regardless of their age, a certain amount of reversing should be accepted as normal.

f. The significance of right-left disorientation is not clearly established in the literature. Benton (1962) writes that "both Harris and I have found the incidence of right-left disorientation to be only slightly higher in dyslexics than in normal readers." On the other hand, Critchley (1964) and Blau, *et al.* (1969) have observed confusion of left and right in many dyslexics, and Johnson and Myklebust (1967) report that "a number of investigators noted left-right disorientation." (You may count your answer correct regardless of how you responded.)

g. Inability to generalize from word to concept seems to be one of the three most limiting features of dyslexia. Translation from sound to symbol (c) and faulty memory of sequences (h) are the other two traits that are particularly handicapping to dyslexics.

i. Zangwill (1962), Critchley (1964), and Vernon (1968) all call attention to speech disorders in the dyslexic. Others mention slow development of speech. In the opinion of De Hirsch (1968), dyslexics frequently have difficulty with all verbal symbols, spoken, written, or printed.

j. Up-down confusion, inability to give directions or to read and draw maps, charts, and dimensional plans, and poor placement of digits in math problems are just a few of the spatial difficulties Johnson and Myklebust (1967), Critchley (1964), and others have found to be common among dyslexics.

k. Faulty cerebral dominance has for years been one of the prominent theories for explaining dyslexia. Cerebral dominance was mentioned as the cause of poor speech in the late 1800's. More recently (1930's) and with much greater attention, Orton associated faulty dominance with strephosymbolia—a term later supplanted by dsylexia. Yet, the evidence to support this theory is still sketchy.

Writing about the relation of dyslexia to cerebral dominance, Zangwill (1962) agreed that an appreciable proportion of dyslexics have poorly developed laterality. But he goes on to make the following statements:

> It is surely more fruitful to ask whether forms of reading backwardness exist in which anomalies of laterality are especially prominent. If any such be found, it can then be asked whether there are any associated disabilities which might suggest delayed or incomplete maturation of cerebral function. In this way, one or more syndromes might be defined which might permit of explanation in terms of failure to establish normal cerebral dominance.

The fact that many ill-lateralized children have no reading problems must also be considered, says Zangwill.

Regarding dominance and dyslexia, Hardy (1962) makes the following comments:

> It seems entirely reasonable that this is what is involved in much of dyslexia — not just a twisting of orthographic details because of some lack of cerebral dominance, and not necessarily anything to do with a focal lack of tissue; but an inadequacy in the reinforcing mechanisms, which make processing, pattern-formation, and retention possible and productive.

Quite obviously the final judgment on the relationship between dyslexia and faulty cerebral dominance is yet to be made. While the jury is still out, the warning issued by Money (1962, p. 28) is worthy of serious consideration — "Scientifically speaking, it is far too premature to be applying hypotheses of cerebral dominance to methods of treatment."

7.   False. While it is true that many dyslexics do suffer educational failure, there are a number of examples in the literature of dyslexics who have succeeded educationally and socially. However, if a dyslexic is to avoid becoming an educational casualty, De Hirsch (1968) and Rabinovitch (1968) agree that he must have long-term and intensive treatment beginning as early as possible in his school career. Without this, Rabinovitch feels that children with severe dyslexia will do well to attain a fifth or sixth grade reading level. Money (1962) is more optimistic. He feels that a dyslexic with a high IQ can readily reach a level average for his age in reading with proper remediation. If dyslexics are doomed to the educational failure, it is because the educational system has failed them.

The test you have just taken consisted of seven questions with a total of seventeen responses required. Allowing five points per response, a perfect score would be eighty-five. What is your DQ?

References

Bender, Lauretta. "Part Two: Neuropsychiatric Disturbances." *Dyslexia Diagnosis and Treatment of Reading Disorders.* Eds. A. Keeney and V. Keeney. St. Louis: The C. V. Mosby Company, 1968, pp. 42-48.

Benton, Arthur L. "Dyslexia in Relation to Form Perception and Directional Sense." *Reading Disability: Progress and Research Needs in Dyslexia.* Ed. J. Money. Baltimore: Johns Hopkins Press, 1962, pp. 81-102.

Blau, Harold, et al. "Developmental Dyslexia and Its Remediation." *The Reading Teacher* (April 1969), 649-53, 669.

Critchley, Macdonald. *Developmental Dyslexia.* London: William Heinemann Medical Books Limited, 1964.

Critchley, Macdonald. "Isolation of the Specific Dyslexic," and "Part One: Minor Neurologic Defects in Developmental Dyslexia." *Dyslexia Diagnosis and Treatment of Reading Disorders.* Ed. A. Keeney and V. Keeney. St. Louis: The C. V. Mosby Company, 1968, pp. 17-20, 38-41.

Cruickshank, William M. "The Problem of Delayed Recognition and Its Correction." *Dyslexia Diagnosis and Treatment of Reading Disorders.* Eds. A. Keeney and V. Keeney. St. Louis: The C. V. Mosby Company, 1968, pp. 84-89.

De Hirsch, Katrina. "Specific Dyslexia or Strephosymbolia." *Children with Reading Problems.* Ed. G. Natchez. New York: Basic Books, Inc., 1968, pp. 97-113.

Eisenberg, Leon. "Introduction." *Reading Disability: Progress and Research Needs in Dyslexia.* Ed. J. Money. Baltimore: Johns Hopkins Press, 1962, pp. 3-7.

Hardy, William C. "Dyslexia in Relation to Language Acquisition and Concept Formation." *Reading Disability: Progress and Research Needs in Dyslexia.* Ed. J. Money. Baltimore: Johns Hopkins Press, 1962, pp. 171-77.

Harris, Albert. "The Diagnosis of Reading Disabilities." *Readings on Reading Instruction.* Ed. A. Harris. New York: David McKay, 1963, pp. 129-133.

Johnson, Doris J. and Helmer R. Myklebust. *Learning Disabilities Educational Principles and Practices.* New York: Grune and Stratton, 1967.

Money, John. "Dyslexia: A Postconference Review." *Reading Disability: Progress and Research Needs in Dyslexia.* Ed. J. Money. Baltimore: Johns Hopkins Press, 1962, pp. 9-33.

Nicholls, John V. "Part Three: Ophthalmic Disturbances." *Dyslexia Diagnosis and Treatment of Reading Disorders.* Eds. A. Keeney and V. Keeney. St. Louis: The C. V. Mosby Co., 1968, pp. 49-52.

Orton, June L. "Part Two: Treatment Needs of the Child with Developmental Dyslexia." *Dyslexia Diagnosis and Treatment of Reading Disorders.* Eds. A. Keeney and V. Keeney. St. Louis: The C. V. Mosby Company, 1968, pp. 131-36.

Rabinovitch, Ralph D. "Reading Problems in Children: Definitions and Classifications." *Dyslexia Diagnosis and Treatment of Reading Disorders.* Eds. A. Keeney and V. Keeney. St. Louis: The C. V. Mosby Company, 1968, pp. 1-10.

Thompson, Lloyd J. *Reading Disability Developmental Dyslexia.* Springfield, Ill.: Charles C. Thomas, 1966.

Vernon, Magdalen D. "Specific Dyslexia." *Children with Reading Problems.* Ed. G. Natchez. New York: Basic Books, Inc., 1968, pp. 114-21.

Zangwill, O. L. "Dyslexia In Relation to Cerebral Dominance." *Reading Disability: Progress and Research Needs in Dyslexia.* Ed. J. Money. Baltimore: Johns Hopkins Press, 1962, pp. 103-13.

CHAPTER THIRTEEN

Other Important Factors That Affect Reading

The articles in this chapter were chosen because they represent, in the editor's opinion, several other extremely important factors in the teaching of reading. Some of the editor's own research bears out the conclusions stated by Robert E. Martin. The factors presented by no stretch of the imagination are all of the important ones that contribute to the successful teaching of reading. They are, however, so important that the beginning or practicing teacher or the administrator should be cognizant of them. Furthermore, the concepts and suggestions are of such a concrete nature that they should provide some excellent guidelines for the improvement of presently existing reading programs.

In the first article Jerry G. Keshian describes a study designed to determine whether or not there were certain social, emotional, physical, and environmental characteristics and experiences which were common to children who were successful readers. Keshian answers a number of important questions such as the following: What factors contribute to success in reading? Does success in reading come as a result of one important factor, or is it the result of a number of combined factors?

Robert E. Martin's article emphasizes the importance of building a reading program that encourages children to *want* to read. He says that children cannot be forced to read certain materials that do not necessarily appeal to them and then be expected to enjoy reading. Martin stresses the fact that research studies as well as good common sense have shown many commonly used practices to be highly unsuccessful, but still we continue to use these methods which have met with past failure. Martin lists a number of practices which, if conscientiously used, would almost certainly guarantee success in building lifetime readers.

Jerry G. Keshian

The Characteristics and Experiences of Children Who Learn to Read Successfully

Purpose of the Investigation

This study was conducted in order to discover if there were certain identifiable social, emotional, physical and environmental characteristics and experiences which were common to children who were successful readers.

General Plan of the Investigation

The outline for the study was patterned after the research of Helen Mansfield Robinson, Professor of Education at the University of Chicago. Her study, *Why Pupils Fail in Reading*,[1] was published in 1946 and was a very substantial contribution to the reading field. This study, using a positive approach, might also be called *Why Children Succeed in Reading*.

All of the children in the fifth grades in three schools, each in a different community and each representative of a different socio-economic level, were administered reading and intelligence tests. The schools fell into a low, middle, and high socio-economic level according to the cri-

From Jerry G. Keshian, "The Characteristics and Experiences of Children Who Learn to Read Successfully," *Elementary English* 40, no. 6 (October 1963): 615-16, 652. Copyright © 1963 by the National Council of Teachers of English. Reprinted by permission of the publisher and Jerry G. Keshian.

[1]Helen Mansfield Robinson, *Why Pupils Fail in Reading* Chicago: University of Chicago Press, 1946.

teria set up by Professor Lloyd Warner in his widely used text, *Social Class Status in America.*[2]

Four hundred and six children were tested, and 362 were found to be reading at or above their mental age. This was determined by taking the scores on the intelligence test and if the reading age was equal to or above the mental age, the child was called a successful reader, so far as this study was concerned. The scores in each school were then divided into three intelligence classifications, low, average, and high. They were then further divided into two groups, boys and girls. Twenty-four children were selected from each school by sampling procedure, for intensive and systematic study, using the case study method. The total number of children in the research was 72.

Each of the 72 children was administered two tests of personality: the *Aspects of Personality,* and the *California Test of Personality.* The *Brace Motor Ability Test* was given in order to collect data on physical ability. Environmental and social information was taken from the pupil questionnaire form, and from the case study interview form. In addition to the information being written up in a narrative case study format, tables were constructed summarizing the data.

What did the data reveal? What were some of the characteristics and experiences of these 72 children, selected at random from among 362 fifth-grade children who were all successful readers?

Characteristics and Experiences of 72 Fifth-Grade Children Who Were Successful Readers

An analysis of the data indicated that:
1.   The range in reading ability was very great. There were seven children who were reading just at their mental age, while there were eleven children who were reading two years or more above their mental age.
2.   The distribution of the more successful readers among the three communities was fairly even. There was no apparent relationship between reading success and socio-economic level. (This finding supports that of Ladd[3] who found a lack of significant relationship between social characteristics and reading ability.)

---

[2]Lloyd Warner, Meeker, Marcher and Eels, *Social Class Status in America* New York: American Book-Straford Press, Inc., 1949.

[3]Margaret Ladd, "The Relation of Social, Economic and Personal Characteristics to Reading Ability," *Teachers College Contributions to Education*, No. 582. New York: Bureau of Publications, Columbia University, 1933.

3. The children were well-adjusted in terms of personality. Test data indicated that the median score for total adjustment for girls was at the 70th percentile, while it was at the 60th percentile for the boys. However, when a test of Chi-square was used, neither scores were significant at the .05 level. Thus it could not be assumed that these children were better adjusted than the population. Interview data supported the findings of the test data.

4. The parents of these children encouraged them to read. They provided stimulation to read by giving books for gifts, taking their children to the library, and by reading themselves. This latter point is quite significant in the light of what we know about parents' reading habits. In an exploratory investigation of teachers' reading values, Professor Alvina Burrows of New York University found that a child has about one chance in five of seeing his parents reading books daily.[4]

5. The parents indicated their strong interest in their children's school work. Examples of this interest was their attendance and participation in PTA work and other school functions.

6. The formal education of the parents was above that of the population. According to the Statistical Abstract of the United States[5] only six per cent of the population 25 years of age and over had four or more years of college. In this study the median for number of years of schooling for fathers was 16. Here again was demonstrated what we have known for a long time—that formal education is a major correlate of reading.

7. All of the children were read to by their parents on a regular sustained basis, throughout their early childhood.

8. General health of the youngsters was excellent. Little time was lost due to illnesses of long duration. No relationship was present between height and reading success and weight and reading success.

9. The children walked and talked at about the same time as the children in the population. Also reading success was not related to the child's relative position among siblings.

10. Most of the children owned their own library cards, and made use of them. This was in spite of the comparative inaccessibility of the public libraries to their homes.

11. The families were strong units—they did things together such as attending athletic events, going to movies, and working at hobbies. The writer suggests that this might be a very important factor in building a strong emotional basis for reading success.

---

[4]Alvina T. Burrows, *Teachers' Reading Values—An Exploratory Investigation* New York: New York University, 1957.

[5]United States Bureau of the Census, *Statistical Abstracts of the United States 1954* Washington: Government Printing Office, 1954.

12. Twelve per cent of the children had memberships in book clubs, and 76 per cent had their own subscription to a magazine.

13. These children came from homes where there was a great variety of reading materials. The parents subscribed to more magazines and read more newspapers than did the population.

Conclusions

Several conclusions may be drawn as a result of the analysis of the data. These are:

1. Though the children were well-adjusted both socially and emotionally, they did not fall within any well-defined personality pattern. These children were in a broad range of personality adjustment, with only average adjustment in certain areas of personality and excellent adjustment in some other areas of personality.

2. Reading success appears to be the result of many factors, some of which apparently lie beyond the control of some individuals with whom the child comes into contact.

3. Factors operating singly, such as a lack of reading materials in the home, do not in themselves prevent a child from becoming a successful reader. Rather, a whole range of characteristics and environmental factors appearing in combination, enable a child to achieve success in reading.

Other Important Factors That Affect Reading

Keshian—Questions for Discussion

Can the factors identified here as being important in contributing to successful readers be changed in homes where these factors do not exist? Can the public schools provide a compensatory program for those students whose home environment is not conducive to later reading success? Would the results of this study apply to children in any section of the country and at any age-grade level? What are the implications gained from this study for early childhood education programs? What further research would be helpful, based on the information presented here?

Robert E. Martin

Too Much Teaching; Too Little Reading

Are Americans improving their reading habits? Optimistic reports are pointing to dramatic increases in published materials of all kinds. This seems to indicate that we are becoming a nation of more literate, better informed and increasingly discerning readers. But seldom does any one raise such basic questions as: What percentage of our population are readers? Just whom are we talking about when we say more people are reading more? How many more people, how much more, and what are they reading?

Over the years, I have visited thousands of classrooms in the United States as well as in some ten foreign countries. I have spent and am spending a considerable amount of my time in these visitations, observing classroom procedures and talking with teachers and boys and girls. Quite frankly, I haven't seen, nor do I now see, much interest being generated in reading and very little enthusiasm being exhibited by the kids for the kind of reading that goes on in the classroom. On the contrary, there is a good deal of evidence of a widespread dislike for involvement in any activity which requires reading. Many of our boys and girls associate reading with required tasks, often unpleasant. They view it as a subject to be taught and learned by means of specified material (the same for all) in labeled groups which, by this very fact, testifies to the degree of goodness, brightness, and worthiness of the individual.

From Robert E. Martin, "Too Much Teaching; Too Little Reading," *New York State Education* 56 (May 1969): 22-23, 34-35. Reprinted by permission of the author and the publisher.

Reading has become (Has it not always been?) a subject matter field. The traditional myth that the best readers become the best individuals persists and persists and persists despite evidence to the contrary. What evidence do we have that our best readers are our most worthy human beings, our most successful people, our greatest contributors to community, national, or world welfare or, for that matter, that they excel in any of the societal values with which we equate our educational goals? About all we can predict from reading ability is ability to read and perhaps success in school, as measured by grades and marks, which are closely correlated with reading.

It is not my purpose to disparage reading but somehow to make a fervent plea to put it in its proper perspective. I see no special virtue in reading early. I can easily visualize a five-year-old or a six-year-old or even a seven-year-old living a full, exciting and interesting life, growing, developing, and even learning successfully before he has accomplished the symbolic skills which we call reading, assuming of course that unrealistic expectations of his parents and teachers do not impinge inordinately upon him. Nor do I see any special virtue or even any great advantage in being able to read fast except perhaps in most unusual circumstances.

Reading is important; no doubt about it. It is so important that we can't afford to continue to deprive our young people of its benefits, its rewards, its joys and the downright fun that can be derived from it. But we can't afford to go on teaching children that it is painful, punishing, boring, and fraught with the risks of failure and the damage to feelings of adequacy and self-worthiness. We can't afford to protect them from the enormously wide range of written communication by so restricting their diets that they equate reading with such works as *Dick and Jane, Alice in Wonderland, The Swiss Family Robinson, Little Women, Silas Marner, Julius Caesar,* "To a Waterfowl," or with any such narrow menu arbitrarily labeled "literature," "classics," or "the tried and the true" by the so called "authorities in the field." These are only examples of the kind of diet we afford them. Anything that doesn't fit the pattern or doesn't live up to certain agreed-upon criteria or has not somehow met the test of time is deemed not really respectable.

Leland Jacobs in his essay "Give Children Literature" makes the point that much of the children's literary heritage is old, classical adult material. He cites as an example the poem "The Children's Hour," the title of which is quite misleading since it is not about children, but concerns "the reminiscences of an old man looking back upon the joys of having children in his household." As another example, he cites a classic usually given in the fourth grade, "Little Boy Blue." Rather than being *for* a child, it is *about* a child, describing the emotion of an adult who has lost a child.

Let's face it! Many of our kids today are just not interested in such literary fare. (If my memory serves me at all, neither were the kids of yesterday.) Somehow or other, poor old Silas Marner just doesn't swing for today's young people, and King Arthur can't compete with Mike Hammer, James Bond, or Batman.

In the past ten years or so, schools in their concern for this problem have been spending more and more for library materials. Almost all new elementary schools include a library and full or part-time librarians. But the fact is that too often the library is still viewed as the repository for books, with the librarian as custodian. It is still a general practice that each class have its weekly library period, during which the kids file in, select some book within the allotted time, and file back to their room, thus fulfilling another of the academic rituals. The next week, they repeat the process, returning their books to check out another. Recently I have been questioning boys and girls about their selections and, according to the response I get, many of them don't read the books they select. They merely fulfill the requirement of the weekly library period, which becomes year after year as routine as the traditional toileting period.

The crucial problem is not lack of materials. The reason that more young people are not reading is that they just aren't interested. Somehow, with all our emphasis upon the teaching of reading, we are building negative attitudes about reading and conditioning children against it. Smith and Dechant, in discussing the influence of interest on reading (*Psychology in Teaching Reading*), indicate that to an extent the child's interest pattern will be influenced by his special fitness for it and they conclude that lack of interest may be a prime cause of poor reading. In Paul Witty's study of 100 poor readers at Northwestern University Laboratory School, he showed that 82 had little interest in reading and over half of these (43) actually disliked to read. He found few reasons other than lack of interest for the poor reading.

All kinds of evidence shows that the key to this whole problem is tied closely to bad attitudes consistently reinforced by failing experiences and discouragement. Dan W. Dodson, director of the Center for Human Relations and Community Studies at New York University, in a paper presented at the Sixteenth Annual Reading Conference of Lehigh University, sums it up by saying, "Teachers do pretty well with children who come to school highly motivated, but fall flat on their faces when they are expected to do the motivation."

John Holt, author of *How Children Fail*, cites what he considers to be the underlying causes of the bad attitudes engendered by common classroom practices:

"From the very beginning of school we make books and reading a constant source of possible failure and public humiliation. When children are little we make them read aloud, before the teacher and other children, so that we can be sure they 'know' all the words they are reading. This means that when they don't know a word, they are going to make a mistake, right in front of everyone. . . .

"Before long many children associate books and reading with mistakes, real or feared, and penalities and humiliation. . . . If books cause them humiliation and pain, they are likely to decide that the safest thing to do is to leave books alone."

His studies have also convinced him that it is not only the poor readers and the unable who reject reading. He writes, "After a while it became clear that many of the very bright kids, from highly literate and even literary backgrounds, read very few books and deeply dislike reading."

Roma Gans, in a survey of the research in reading for 1967, makes the following observation regarding reading practices:

"The topic of negative effects of pressures on slow learners to meet grade level achievements has been worn threadbare. Many studies of predelinquents and delinquents reveal children's frustrations over work too difficult for them, their discouragement over failure, and ultimately their dropping out to save further embarrassment. No summation of researches is needed to carry this point."

The most astonishing phenomenon of all is that, although this situation we are in is so apparent and has been discussed for such a long time, it doesn't fundamentally affect our practices. We continue to use the same old failing methods and, because of our concerns, increase the amount and intensity of the bad methods and thus intensify the failures inherent in the method. Kids become more discouraged, boredom grows, negative attitudes mount and we succeed only in convincing more children that reading is not for them.

Teachers are notoriously afraid of change. Why fear change? We have so little to lose. We could hardly do worse and the chances of finding better ways are great. We need professional, creative teachers who are willing to innovate, to try something different. We need professionals who have enough insight to recognize the sorry plight we are in and the conviction and the confidence in their own skills as teachers to lose their insecurities and fears of going "out on a limb" or of "being different." These teachers must above all like to read themselves. Amy Elizabeth Jensen describes the qualities needed to inspire children to read, qualities that create an atmosphere conducive to building positive attitudes:

". . . one who knows books and has a contagious delight in them, who knows boys and girls are individuals with many sided interests and enthusiasms, and who knows how to set the stage to bring books and boys and girls together."

These teachers need to be free to take some positive action in terms of helping all children to have successful and rewarding experiences with reading and of protecting them from the experiences that have proved so harmful and defeating to the basic purposes of all reading programs. Let me submit for consideration some suggestions in the form of "do's" and "don'ts."

Some Do's:

1. Spend a lot of time reading to kids. Read to them what is exciting, fun, and enjoyable for you regardless of its "grade-placement." I am convinced that interest is not very "grade-placeable." Here is a sampling of a few things I found most successful with kids I worked with in elementary classrooms all the way from fourth to eighth grade. Short stories: Ring Lardner's "Haircut" and "Alibi Ike;" the stories by H. H. Munro (Saki); Jack London's "To Start a Fire;" almost anything by O. Henry; Richard Connell's "Most Dangerous Game;" Hemingway's "The Killers." Poetry: Robinston's "Richard Corey" and "Miniver Cheevey;" Frost's "The Mending Wall" and "Birches;" Wordsworth's "We Are Seven." Plays (especially if you have a flair for dramatization): *Life With Father; Arsenic and Old Lace; Harvey; You Can't Take it With You; Don't Drink the Water.*

There is a whole world of exciting detective stories, mysteries, fantasies, and adventures, as well as absorbing and stimulating biography, travel, humor and nonsense, science and science fiction, hundreds of which are written for children. I'm not recommending my own "tossed salad." My only point is to be sure that whatever you read to them, you yourself really enjoy, and that you be sensitive enough to recognize whether or not they get a kick out of it. Give some real status to reading. Make it a priority, not simply a Friday afternoon routine or reward.

2. Build up a good lively classroom reading center from every available source—school libraries, public libraries, home libraries or wherever — with a wide range of interests and reading levels. Keep that reading center renewed and alive. Include current magazines, newspapers, and comics (if you dare). Get the books off the shelves and into the children's hands and desks and homes. Keep books well displayed, available, and moving.

3. Give children plenty of time to read when they want to read. If you're wondering where the time is coming from, I have a couple of good suggestions. You might eliminate the textbook reading classes.

Admit it! You're possibly as bored with this deadening activity as they are and for years have been questioning, at least subconsciously, its limited value. If you need more time (and I believe you will), take a good hard look at some of the ways kids are now using their time. You may decide that some of the busy work is not as fruitful as you thought it might be, or that the time spent in writing and memorizing spelling lists is not of such importance that it couldn't be cut—maybe by as much as one-half.

4. Give the kids ample opportunity to show and talk about and discuss with others what they're reading, but be sure it's 100 percent voluntary and not required. This gives them a chance to perform in an actual audience situation in which they can really contribute something.

5. In such areas as science and social studies, minimize the dependence on *the* textbook. Here, too, is an abundance of beautiful, interesting, exciting, and available material on all levels of reading ability in every area included in your course of study. Given the motivation, the freedom, and the help in discovering these materials, the kids will surprise you with their ability to develop some honest-to-goodness research techniques. You may even find an improvement in their much deplored "study habits."

6. Get rid of the library *period*. Work closely with the librarian. Enlist her help in planning both with you and the children in a continuous use of this facility whenever and in whatever way it is needed. If she is a trained librarian and worth her salt, chances are she'll be an invaluable resource, your avid supporter, the children's good friend and a reading consultant. She will also be flattered that you regard her as a professional educator rather than the "custodian of the books."

Some Don'ts:

1. Don't be too concerned with grade placement of reading materials. Reading achievement scores are not always reliable. We have no tests which determine how well or at what level a person can read when his interest is high. On the other hand, many of the most capable readers enjoy reading some of the highly interesting and entertaining books written for the lower grades, such as the Dr. Suess books and many others.

2. Don't require reports, either oral or written. You'll be hard put to find enough time to schedule the kids who can hardly wait to share their reading with the others.

3. Don't dissect, test, reward or punish. Reading itself has enough intrinsic value. Don't give stars or points or hold competitions. There is

certainly no need to reward the already over-compensated high achievers or heap more discouragement and failure on the unable.

4. Don't become discouraged. Be patient. Wait for them. They won't get interested in reading all at once. Too many of them for too long have been thoroughly conditioned against reading. If you get even half of them reading a little more on their own, you can consider yourself eminently successful, and if you persist, the non-reader rather than the reader will become the exception.

5. Don't be too concerned with trying to raise the level of their reading tastes. Experience shows that as one reads more and more he becomes increasingly selective in his diet. Your first concern is building positive attitudes toward reading, no matter what, and developing a permanent interest in reading.

6. Don't do much recommending. For quite obvious reasons, children suspect the teacher's recommendations and usually look upon them with disfavor.

What I propose is not a panacea for all of our reading ills, nor would I wish it to be regarded as a prescription. It is an idea, a process that has been tried by some teachers and found quite successful. It's neither new nor revolutionary nor particularly original. It should be comparatively easy to initiate, and it won't cost a lot of money. If it would reduce the tremendous and current outlay for textbooks, workbooks, and expensive commercial gimmicks, there would be a great deal more funds available for enriching our libraries. How many good, attractive, interesting paperbacks could you buy to replace the 30 copies of the *one* sixth grade reading text and the 30 copies of the *one* accompanying workbook?

As Roma Gans said in her study:

"Studies portraying children's feelings and attitudes which influence their success in reading and in other learning should have ceased startling us years ago. However, it is imperative that today we say, 'Let's do something about policies and practices that actually destroy children.' "

Other Important Factors That Affect Reading

Martin—Questions for Discussion

Do we really know how to make children enjoy reading? Can children be *made* to enjoy reading? What are some ways with which we can "give some real status to reading"? Could Martin's suggestions be implemented by the average classroom teacher?

CHAPTER FOURTEEN

Some Promising Techniques

The articles in this chapter were chosen because they are representative of the many new and exciting things that are happening in the field of reading. This is, by no stretch of the imagination a comprehensive coverage of this subject. The reader will note that much of what is mentioned here is not entirely new but is often an assemblage of various parts of already-known facts and techniques into something considerably more useful than the individual components themselves.

In the article by Harold and Harriet Blau an interesting technique for teaching words is described. Their approach is similar to the original Fernald-Keller method; however, in using this method the visual modality is bypassed. Blau and Blau believe that the Visual-Auditory-Kinesthetic-Tactile approach often has been successful because it enabled the child to make use of the auditory, kinesthetic, and tactile approaches even though vision also was used. They believe, in other words, that children were successful with this approach *despite* the emphasis on the visual modality and not because of it. They present an interesting description of its use as well as a discussion of actual students with whom it has been most successful.

The article by James Gardner and Grayce Ransom is a report of a pilot project to develop a counseling procedure that would be directly relevant to the student's learning problems and to systemize these procedures so that they could be used effectively by school personnel. Research indicates that approximately 75 percent of the children who need remedial reading also have some type of social or emotional problem. Since this is the case, one cannot expect a remedial reading program to be successful unless it provides for children's affective as well as cognitive needs. As Gardner and Ransom indicate, few teachers have adequate training in counseling techniques; therefore, there is a need for specific procedures which can be used by school counselors and remedial reading teachers. The authors present an excellent description of their procedure that is structured and precise enough to be clearly understandable.

The last article by R. G. Heckelman explains the "Neurological Impress Method" of remedial reading instruction developed and researched by him. The method sounds so simple that it is hard to believe it could really work. However, in this article as well as in others Heckelman presents some statistical proof of the effectiveness of this procedure. If Heckelman's method can be used by others with similar results, then there are some tremendous possibilities for the use of this method by semi-professional personnel having only a minimal amount of training.

Harold Blau and Harriet Blau

A Theory of Learning to Read

Customarily, the approved and almost universally recommended technique for dealing with the problems of the severely handicapped reader is the careful and consistent use of all sensory modalities, with special attention given to strengthening the visual modality, commonly acknowledged to be, most often, the weak link. This multi-sensory approach is termed VAKT or the Visual-Auditory-Kinesthetic-Tactile method. This article reports on a new and interesting alternative in which the visual modality is deliberately suppressed or blocked, initially at least, instead of being reinforced. The basic theory involved is that, in some cases, learning, and especially learning to read, may be literally cut off or short-circuited by the visual modality rather than merely obstructed.

One of the most frequently expressed attitudes toward non-readers may be summed up as follows: he can say the words; why can't he read them?

It now appears possible that reading teachers may offer with assurance a specific answer, rather than a generalized and more or less descriptive diagnosis, such as those listed by Bateman (1965). This answer would seem to be that individuals who have learned to speak adequately, but who have not learned to read adequately, have achieved one and not the other, because there was

1. no interference or short-circuiting from the visual modality or input system in the *learning of speech*, and

---

From Harold and Harriet Blau, "A Theory of Learning to Read," *The Reading Teacher* 22, no. 2 (November 1968): 126-29, 144. Reprinted with permission of Harold and Harriet Blau and the International Reading Association.

2. maximum destructive interference from the visual modality or input system in the *learning of reading.*

The necessary corollary is that visual input, rather than requiring reinforcement, must be blocked off. Certain students must literally be blindfolded, in other words, at certain stages in the remediation process if they are to learn to read. As indicated, this is quite opposed to most current theoretical formulations and most suggested remediation also. Children with learning disorders, including reading, Bateman points out, have probably been given as many special names as has any type of exceptional child: specific language disability, brain-injured, perceptually handicapped, dyslexic, neurologically involved, educationally retarded, word blind, strephosymbolic, hyperkinetic, aphasic, dysgraphic, interjacent, and so forth. But, most, if not all, of these diagnostic appellations fall short with respect to one criterion, substantial differentiation in treatment. In almost every case, whatever the theoretical beginning, whatever name is used to describe the difficulty the end point tends to be what may be called the doctrine of combined modalities, or, as indicated, a form of VAKT.

A key aspect of this method, also called the Fernald-Keller method, is presented as follows (Cooper, 1965, P. 3): "During Stage 1, the child makes use of several aids to learning. First, the word has meaning. . . . Second, the child *sees* (author's emphasis) the word written by the teacher, he *sees* it as he traces, he *sees* it as he writes, and he *sees* it in final typed form. . . . When all modalities of learning are used, the child should learn."

This article would suggest that in any group which it characterized as recognizing very few words at sight, many, if not most, of those who learn by this method, VAKT, do so *despite* the emphasis on the visual modality and not because of it, and then only because of their own and their teacher's persistence. In an article on psychoneurological disturbances, Myklebust (1964, P. 357), makes the point that the "psychoneurosensory" systems can and sometimes do function "semi-independently," so that children "with minimal brain damage" are reported to have serious difficulties "when the learning task entails interrelated functions, such as both auditory and visual learning. . . . These children may learn what the letters look like but find it exceedingly difficult to learn what they sound like or the opposite. When presented with one aspect of the word, the visual, they cannot normally convert it to the auditory. . . . Apparently, when two or more types of information are delivered to the brain simultaneously, a breakdown in neurological processes occurs. The clinical manifestations are confusion, poor recall, random movements, disturbed attention, and occasionally even seizures."

It appears possible, therefore, that to avoid such difficulties, and not only in the minimally handicapped, the conflicting modality could be blocked off with constructive results at strategic stages in the learning process. Such is the purpose of this proposed *Non-Visual* AKT method. The visual modality was identified as the critical one because, in all the cases involved, speech had developed in an acceptable fashion, suggesting that the auditory input system was working properly.

Non-Visual AKT differs from VAKT in several ways, and variations of Non-V AKT are possible too. Primarily, however, the child is blindfolded or closes his eyes, and the word to be learned is traced on his back. As the teacher traces the word, she spells it aloud, letter by letter. Often, the second or third time around, the student can identify the letters being traced and he too spells out the word. Usually (until the student becomes too advanced for this), three-dimensional letters, arranged to spell out the word, are placed before the student and, still blindfolded, he traces these with his fingertips as he feels the letters being traced on his back. The letters are then scrambled, and still blindfolded, the student arranges the letters in the proper sequence. The blindfold is then removed, the student sees what he has done (often his first experience with coherent sequencing) and writes the word on paper, or at the board, and then on a file card for future review.

Inasmuch as the student can often learn by this method to spell words a few years above his reading level, words to be learned may be selected from his class spelling list, offering an opportunity for quick success in at least one academic area. Words excerpted from the child's own dictated story, from an old text, from current reading material, or according to a carefully structured phonic sequence may also be used.

In general, once a word has been mastered by the "Non-V" method, it seems to be handled by the student with complete normalcy. Also, a learning factor seems to mature or to be matured and word recognition, spelling, and reading comprehension improve at a considerably faster rate than would be expected from the limited number of words taught.

It is interesting to note that subsequent to its independent development by the authors, a similar technique was reported from England. Called "haptic training," it was being used to teach geometric forms, but not words (Tansley, 1967).

Parenthetically, it should be noted that Non-V AKT does not seem to require the teacher's personal attention. An aide seems to do very well. It may also be possible to send it home for use there, not only to speed up learning, but also to restore something like the normal child-parent helping relationship which is usually nonexistent or badly distorted.

Current cases are illustrated by the case of Jay. A fourth grade student in a large, highly rated suburban school system, he was initially referred to the special reading teacher for help in March, 1966. At that time he scored 1.5 on the *Gates Primary Paragraph Test.* He was eight years and six months old at the time of testing, a premature child of normal intelligence, but with serious difficulties in visual perception, in behavior, and to a degree in the motor area, in fact with some presumption of brain damage. He scored on the five-year-old level in several sections of the *Frostig Test of Visual Perception.*

As late as May he was still confusing *say* for *saw, who* for *how,* etc., and when confronted with the word "my" in a "Grab" game, remarked that he had never seen that word before. He managed, in early June, to score 2.4 on an alternate form of the Gates, but his spelling skills continued non-existent. Asked about them, his teacher of that year remarked succinctly, "Yes, he could spell—*the.*"

In October, 1966, when work was resumed, one of his more difficult spelling words, *ought,* was taught experimentally by the Non-Visual method. He learned it, remembered it two days later (and eight weeks later) and demanded to know why this method had not been invented the preceding year. His class spelling test of the following week demonstated a marked change:

1. one
2. anyone
3. mong (mountain)
4. excuse
5. ink
6. bottom
7. prought (president)
8. insahtam (instead)
9. sonsw (straight)
10. horn

All of the words spelled correctly had been taught during the week by the Non-V method. The spelling of the other words which were taught by the usual classroom techniques serve as an indication of his characteristic difficulties.

Jay continued to gain. After six weeks he scored 2.8 on a Gates test, an Advanced Primary this time, of word recognition and paragraph reading respectively, and by the middle of May was up to 3.8 on an alternate form of the *Gates Advanced Paragraph Test.*

In December of 1967, a fifth grader, he read many more books than were required by classroom assignments—mostly on a fourth grade level—and often scored very well on classroom spelling tests, occasionally achieving a 100 per cent score on lists of twenty-five words. Of these, usually no more than from three to five words needed to be taught via an abbreviated form of AKT.

Others with whom the technique has been used since October 1966 have benefited in various ways. One student, over forty, has gone from a third grade level to a level of "normal" adult competence.

Work with brain-injured children has very clearly demonstrated (Cruickshank, et. al., 1961) the value of environments in which auditory and visual stimuli are much modified. In view of all of the foregoing, it is conceivable that a still greater degree of differentiation, and success, may be possible.

In any case, it is a speculative but persuasive thought that there may be a number of children, especially in the early grades, classified as reluctant or non-learners, who really suffer from a kind of modality conflict and for whom instruction centering around modality blocking may be required prior to or at least simultaneous with any other program for the amelioration of their difficulties.

References

Bateman, Barbara. An educator's view of a diagnostic approach to learning. In J. Hellmuth (Ed.) *Learning disorders I*. Seattle: Special Child Publications of the Seguin School, 1965. Pp. 171-196.

Cooper, J. L. An adaptation of the Fernald-Keller approach to teaching an initial reading vocabulary to children with severe reading disabilities. *Bulletin of the University of Connecticut Reading-Study Center, 1965*. (mimeo)

Cruickshank, W., Bentzen, F., Ratzeburg, F., and Farmhauser, M. *A teaching method for brain-injured and hyperactive children*. Syracuse: Syracuse University Press, 1961.

_____. *Gates reading tests*. New York: Columbia University, 1956.

Myklebust, H. R. Psychoneurological disturbances in childhood. *Rehabilitation Literature, 1964*, 25 (12).

Tansley, A. E. *Reading and remedial reading*. New York: Humanities Press, 1967. P. 14.

Some Promising Techniques

Blau and Blau — Questions for Discussion

Why do Blau and Blau believe that the visual modality should be blocked off for some children? Would this method apply to nearly all children who are retarded readers? If not, then how could one identify children who might benefit from the nonvisual AKT method described here? What implications are contained within this article for further research?

James Gardner and Grayce Ransom

Academic Reorientation: A Counseling Approach to Remedial Readers

The emotional components of reading problems, both as causal factors and as corollaries of the disability, have been widely recognized. The educational treatment of choice for remedial readers* is to attempt to provide specialized reading instruction either in special classes or special schools. The psychological treatment of choice is not as clear-cut. A review of standard references in the fields of remedial education (Bond and Tinker, 1957; Harris, 1961; Kephart, 1960; Money, 1962; Money 1966) and psychotherapy (Dittman, 1966; Ford and Urban, 1963; Munroe, 1955; Urban and Lord, 1967) failed to unearth a single reference to any specifically named types of psychological counseling with remedial students. Since the number of remedial students unfortunately appears to be on the increase, and since psychological counseling techniques seem to many educators to be useful adjunctive procedures in the remediation of such students, it would appear desirable, from the standpoint of increased effectiveness, to attempt to develop a counseling procedure specifically focused on the student and the learning problems. Further, in light of the continuing shortage of trained psychotherapists, it would seem highly desirable to develop specific procedures which could be used under appropriate supervision by school counselors and remedial reading teachers.

From James Gardner and Grayce Ransom, "Academic Reorientation: A Counseling Approach to Remedial Readers," *The Reading Teacher* 21, no. 6 (March 1968): 529-36, 540. Reprinted with permission of James Gardner, Grayce Ransom, and the International Reading Association.

*By general definition, a "remedial reader" is a student of at least average intelligence whose reading skills are two or more years below his level of intellectual functioning.

The Project

This paper reports the initial findings of a pilot project with remedial readers in which an attempt has been made to develop a counseling procedure which would be directly relevant to the student's school learning problems. Further, an attempt has been made to systematize the elements in the procedure felt to be effective, in order that school personnel may begin to use the procedure. This counseling procedure has been termed "academic reorientation" in order to specify its general goal, that is, attitude and behavior change on the part of the remedial student vis-a-vis school. The term also serves to differentiate this counseling procedure from the more in-depth psychodynamic techniques.

The essence of the "academic reorientation" technique is a broadly conceived behavior modification program. There are two basic premises: 1] that remedial students manifest more avoidance behaviors in the school situation than do nonremedial students and that these responses are more prolonged or intense, and 2] that the pattern of these avoidance behaviors must be altered in a positive direction before effective skill remediation can begin.

In many cases, it appears that the student's avoidance behaviors are a function of a combination of high anxiety regarding the failure-associated school learning tasks and simple low motivation due to nonreinforcement in the reading area. Unfortunately, such avoidance patterns generally serve to maintain, and often increase, the student's academic difficulties. Thus, the alteration of such patterns is a primary goal of academic reorientation.

Subjects

To date, sixteen male students (S's) have participated in academic reorientation counseling at the University of Southern California NCL-USC Reading School. Three additional groups of six S's per group have been seen at the Reading Clinic of the Barstow Unified School District, Barstow, California. The counselor for each group was a remedial reading teacher. The teachers are under the general direction of the Director of the Barstow Reading Clinic, and under the supervision of the senior author. The Barstow groups were initiated after the basic academic reorientation formula had been developed at the USC Reading School. This represented an attempt to assess the feasibility of training reading teachers or school counselors in the approach. The reading teachers felt that it provided them with much greater understanding of the nature of their students' learning problems and thus helped them toward more effective teaching procedures.

S's were chosen for participation on the basis of the school faculty's rating of them as chronic, "hard core" learning problems. Most of these *S's* had appeared to be benefiting very little from the educational program of the school, which specializes in remedial reading problems. The *S's* manifested a variety of avoidance patterns ranging from frank negativism to excessive daydreaming to highly disruptive behavior.

Procedures

The academic reorientation procedure involved first meeting with the *S's* in small groups of three or four with the only basis for grouping being age (under twelve or over twelve) and administrative convenience. Following several group sessions, *S's* were seen individually by the counselor (*C*) in sessions of approximately twenty minutes duration and on a once per week basis. Three *S's* were seen for only six sessions (summer school); eight *S's* were seen for about one semester (fifteen to twenty sessions); and five *S's* were seen for a full academic year (approximately forty sessions).

Academic reorientation tends to be more verbal than most traditional counseling procedures with children. In general, *C* tends to impart much information of a specific nature about school, *S*, and *S's* relationship to teachers. Because of this highly verbal aspect, the academic reorientation procedures as set forth below have not, in the initial experimentation, been found to be very useful with children younger than about nine years of age. It has been suggested that the academic reorientation procedures might be usefully employed with children younger than nine using doll play situations. This seems likely and experimentation in this area is anticipated.

The academic reorientation approach consists of several features. Although these features are listed below in discrete, step-by-step fashion for explanatory purposes, they are not so used in practice. In practice, the various features are emphasized to varying degrees to suit the needs of the various *S's* though all of the features are always used with each *S*. One other point should be made before amplifying the steps of this procedure. The academic reorientation procedure appears to be most effective when used in an extremely redundant manner. That is, it seems most effective to work through the various features with any given *S* many, many times. Going through the steps once, or even twice, with an *S* *can not be assumed to have had effect*. It appears that some remedial students manifest such intense and well-developed avoidance techniques that they also effectively block out or distort their conversation with *C*.

The primary features of the academic reorientation counseling technique are:

1.   Providing *S* with an adequate rationale for his learning problem.

Virtually all remedial students manifest a strong underlying fear that they are mentally retarded or have some unusual type of brain problem. Consequently, it appears to be extremely useful to move at once against such attitudes and to begin assisting *S* in restructuring his perception of himself as a student. First, *C* attempts to ascertain *S's* own unique and idiosyncratic rationalization for his learning problems. These tend to be rationalizations which mask or avoid the more anxiety-provoking thought that *S* may not be as bright as his peers. It has seemed useful and effective for *C,* in the first or second session with *S*, to point out in a matter-of-fact way that most students who do not read well think that they are not as bright as their classmates and to go on from there to open a discussion regarding *S's* feelings about his intelligence. In such a discussion, *C* is usually dealing from strength inasmuch as he has the weight of the authority of various intelligence test scores which he can use with discretion. He can also point to the fact that there are special classes for mentally retarded youngsters and that *S* is not in such a class. It also seems helpful to stress various intelligent behaviors which *S* manifests by knowing the rules of complicated games such as Monopoly, baseball, and football; being able to ride a ten-speed bike; and so on.

Following this direct move against the assumed underlying fear of mental slowness, *C* then begins to work with *S* in developing a more accurate description of his learning problem. In many instances, certain types of sensorimotor problems may have been associated with the learning difficulties. In such cases, it is undesirable to go into a complicated explanation of neuromuscular development and its relation to reading acquisition. A simplified explanation seems effective. For example, it appears more meaningful to explain a child's visual-perceptual difficulties as one of "eye muscle immaturity" than as one of "minimal cerebral dysfunction". If there were many transfers of school in the early grades or other major emotional adjustments which the child had to make in these grades, it appears useful for *C* to cite these as known factors which can impair the learning process. In fact, *C* should explain *in detail* just how these factors attenuate skill acquisition and how a gradual vicious cycle of frustration and avoidance and further lack of skill acquisition could be initiated.

To summarize this point, it appears that most remedial S's hold major misconceptions of how their learning problem developed. It appears very important that C disabuse S of such notions when they are incorrect. To do this requires replacing the erroneous conception with a more valid one.

2.   Providing social reinforcement of S for positive statements about school.

Following a verbal conditioning model which suggests that altering an individual's verbalizations may lead to alterations in other types of behavior (Krasner, 1958), C "reinforces" S's positive statements about school and teachers by heightened interest, smiles, and over-all attention to S whenever S manifests such statements.

3.   Helping S learn basic discriminations about his own behavior.

C attempts to help S to begin discriminating when and under what circumstances he tends to manifest certain types of behavior. Specifically, C points out S's avoidance patterns and relates them to school-related stimuli which seem to elicit them. C obtains this information from his own observations of S in the learning situation if this is possible, as well as from teacher observations and S's statements. In the latter instance, a very useful procedure seems to be direct situational reenactment. Here, C asks S to be himself and act as nearly as possible just as he usually does in class. C then plays the part of the teacher or tutor and observes S's responses carefully. It seems useful at this point to ask S what he usually does under these circumstances. C must attempt to get a conception of precisely what it is that S does. It seems important to work this out rather thoroughly for not only does each S appear to have some very unique responses, but this step is closely related to the following two steps.

4.   Teaching S the aversive consequences involved in the continued use of the avoidance patterns.

At this point, C attempts to dramatize the aversive long-range consequences by tying them more closely to S's behavior in the immediate situation. Most remedial students have been told countless times the impact that their lack of reading skills is likely to have on job procurement. This would appear to be an aversive consequence to most adults but it seems rarely to have the desired effect of motivating the remedial student. In the present approach, C attempts to relate specific behaviors on the part of S to rather immediate aversive consequences. For example, C might suggest the following to an S who tends to avoid school stimuli by the heavy use of daydreaming. "You look out the window because you feel you are not a good reader. But now you are in a practice situation, with reading material that you know you can handle. But you have the *habit* of looking out the window. You must break that habit. It will cause nothing but trouble, for you look out the window and you miss the word. When you miss the word, you fall behind and lose your place. When this happens, you start foundering around, getting scared, thinking you are stupid, and getting mad at yourself and the teacher and the book. These are the things that happen when you start to look out the window." This variation on the "for the want of a nail a battle was lost" theme enables *C* to link meaningful aversive consequences with *S's* actual responses in the class situation.

5.   Developing alternative modes of responding.

After *S* begins to discriminate his particular type of avoidance response in the learning situation and after the aversive consequences of such behaviors are detailed, *C* then begins to offer *S* alternative modes of responding. This may be done in a number of ways. *C* may, for example, reverse the roles and play the part of *S,* using all of *S's* avoidance behaviors. *C* then might ask *S* to suggest other ways the situation might be handled. *C* might also use verbal directives, simply suggesting that *S* attempt certain responses instead of others. There it is extremely helpful for *C* to review these directives with *S's* teacher whenever possible, in order that the teacher can be aware of what types of behavior *S* is attempting to develop and can be alert to reinforce *S's* initial efforts.

6.   Labeling the feelings.

It is assumed that most remedial students begin experiencing school learning difficulty at a relatively young age. Consequently, the ability of most of these students to discriminate their emotional states as they are associated with any particular person or activity is at best at a very rudimentary level at a time when they are beginning to experience much pressure and general unpleasantness in the school situation. A large portion of these unlabeled feelings involves dread or anxiety connected with reading. Other unlabeled feelings which seem to be commonly associated with school and academic learning by remedial *S's* are those of frustration and anger. It appears that in many instances feelings of both anxiety and anger begin to be elicited as *S* approaches or is pressured into the reading situation. In many instances, it seems that these feelings may act as cues for the initiation of the avoidance responses. It seems useful, therefore, to help *S* label these feelings. That is, *S* is assisted in discriminating his internal events (feelings) just as he is in discriminating his external events (avoidance responses). An important point here is that, when *C* first begins such internal discrimination training, *S* seems to have little or no idea of how he feels in the reading situation. A useful approach here appears to be one in which

C requests *S* to read to him. *C* then stops *S* at some point in the reading, usually when *S* is blocking on a word or otherwise manifesting signs of anxiety or anger, and asks *S* how he is feeling *right now*. Many *S's* will report feeling "funny." These feelings generally turn out to be feelings of fear and anger. The attaching of verbal labels to these "funny" (unspecific and unlabeled) feelings appears to enable *S* to dissipate some of the anxiety through talk as well as to begin the fundamental discrimination process involving making the connection between the reading situation, the "funny" feelings, and the avoidance behaviors. This particular aspect of academic reorientation is closely akin to "insight" in psychotherapy. The primary difference is that here the insight is focused on the school learning situation.

7.   Attitude of the counselor.

Implied but unstated in all of the above procedures is a basic counseling attitude of positive regard for the worth and dignity of the student as a person, and a fundamental sense of expectancy that the student can and will overcome his academic problems. In brief, *C* has to believe that *S* is worth all the fuss and bother of special educational programs and academic reorientation counseling. *C* then has to show this belief to *S* in word and deed. This essential feeling on the part of *C* is felt to be a vitally necessary, though not sufficient, aspect of academic reorientation.

8.   Working with the teacher.

In addition to the academic reorientation counseling sessions, *C* met weekly with the school staff. In the meetings with the teachers, classroom "programs" were developed for each *S's* idiosyncratic needs. These programs were largely based on information developed in the counseling sessions regarding the manner in which *S* perceived himself, his rationale for his school difficulties, and his unique avoidance patterns in the learning situation. This aspect of the procedure appeared to be quite important inasmuch as the classroom teacher could be apprised of a particular *S's* attempts to alter a given pattern of maladaptive behavior and thereby provide immediate reinforcement for *S* as he moved toward developing more positive responses in the classroom setting.

Results and Conclusions

The results of this exploratory project were considered encouraging by all concerned. Fourteen of the sixteen *S's* manifested marked attitude changes toward school, according to the school staff. One *S* dropped out of school part way through the semester due to emotional and situational problems well beyond those with which this procedure or this school is equipped to cope. As a group, these fourteen *S's* appeared to have become more cooperative and achievement-oriented while manifesting a concomitant reduction in avoidance patterns. The change in attitudes in turn opened the way for better achievement in reading skills emphasized in the school.

These initial findings indicate that the possibility of a systematic "academic reorientation" of remedial students has sufficient potential to be worth a continuation and expansion of clinical and research efforts.

Several additional comments are relevant at this point. First, the possibility of a "Hawthorne effect" must be considered—that is, change alone as being helpful for these *S's*. This does not seem likely. These *S's* have had many procedures "tried out" on them at one time or another over the years and there have been many school and teacher changes, pep talks, admonitions, and exhortations. These previous efforts had not resulted in any noticeable behavioral changes in the classroom situation on the part of the students.

Second, the present eight stage procedure is clearly a "shotgun" approach to the problem. This is primarily because it is not yet possible to more clearly delineate the various weights to assign the various aspects. In fact, it seems that these aspects must be emphasized or deemphasized according to the needs of the particular student, though it does appear that it is necessary to cover all of the aspects of the procedure.

Third, the personality of the counselor is always a variable in counseling and it is difficult to separate what portion of the positive (or negative) results in counseling are because of personality factors of the counselor and what part are the result of technical factors inherent in the procedure. The design of the present study was clearly inadequate to tease out such a complex counselor variable and some type of yoked-control procedure or large scale study would be necessary in this regard. However, it should be noted that the senior author has had considerable experience in counseling relationships with remedial students, and only with the gradual systematization of techniques now presented as the academic reorientation procedure has it appeared that counseling had a more direct and positive relationship to the student's classroom behavior.

Fourth, it is clear that a counselor attempting to employ the academic reorientation procedures must be alert and opportunistic. This approach appears, however, to be relatively easily mastered by reading teachers and school counselors. Those who have tried the procedures experimentally report that it feels natural and, in fact, is not unlike some of their usual informal procedures for dealing with remedial students. Most of those who have attempted the technique state that they like its structure and specificity. They also seem to have come to a better appreciation of the great redundancy which seems necessary to use with remedial students. That is, going through the aspects of the technique once cannot be assumed to have sufficiently clarified the student's behavior and feelings. It seems necessary to work through the various aspects several times, emphasizing those aspects which are most relevant for the given student.

Fifth, the academic reorientation procedure is definitely *not* intended as a substitute for more intensive and far-reaching counseling procedures when such are necessary. In fact, our initial experience suggests that the academic reorientation procedures can be carried on simultaneously with an *S* being involved in a more intensive psychotherapeutic program without attenuation of either procedure. This is because the academic reorientation procedure is so specific to the school learning problem.

Sixth, in any case, one of the primary implications of these initial results is that it appears that remedial students can be significantly helped through activist counseling procedures based specifically around the learning problem. A second major implication is that these procedures can apparently be quickly mastered and effectively used by school counselors and reading teachers and do not necessarily have to be employed only by trained psychotherapists.

References

Bond, G. L., and Tinker, M. A. *Reading difficulties, their diagnosis and correction.* New York: Appleton-Century-Crofts, 1957.

Dittman, A. *Annual review of psychology.* Vol. 17, 1966. S 1-78.

Ford, D., and Urban, H. *Systems of psychotherapy.* New York: Wiley, 1963.

Harris, A. J. *How to increase reading ability.* New York: McKay, 1961.

Heilman, A. W. *Principles and practices of teaching reading.* Columbus, Ohio: Merrill, 1961.

Kephart, N. C. *The slow learner in the classroom.* Columbus, Ohio: Merrill, 1960.

Krasner, L. Studies of the conditioning of verbal behavior. *Psychological Bulletin,* 1958, 55, 148-170.

Money, J. (Ed) *Reading disability.* Baltimore: Johns Hopkins Press, 1962.

Money, J. (Ed) *The disabled reader.* Baltimore: Johns Hopkins Press, 1966.

Munroe, Ruth. *Schools of psychoanalytic thought.* New York: Dryden Press, 1955.

Urban, H., and Lord, D. *Annual review of psychology.* Vol. 18, 1967, 333-372.

Some Promising Techniques

Gardner and Ransom — Questions for Discussion

What do the authors mean by the term "academic reorientation"? How can one measure or recognize avoidance behaviors? Would the explanation given by the authors be adequate for a remedial reading teacher to begin academic reorientation on his own without any further training? Could this type of procedure be built into or should it precede the regular remedial program?

R. G. Heckelman

Using the Neurological-Impress Remedial-Reading Technique

One of the most economical and time-saving methods for working with children who need remedial-reading instruction is the neurological impress method (NIM).

The simplicity of this method often makes people doubt its efficacy. However, experimentation has shown that it is an effective program of remedial reading for many children and often the method of choice. One of the added advantages of using this approach is the ease of use for both instructor and student and the low cost factor. Also, if a child does not respond to this particular type of program after four hours of instruction, there is a strong possibility that it is not the method of choice to be used with this child and some other system of instruction should be tried in its place.

I carried out the original experiment with the NIM in 1961 in the Merced County schools.[1] Twenty-four students took part. The students were selected from grades six through ten. They showed a mean reading gain of 2.2 on the Gilmore Oral Reading Test. The longest period of instruction received by any student was seven and one half hours.

From R. G. Heckelman, "Using the Neurological-Impress Remedial-Reading Technique," *Academic Therapy Quarterly* I (Summer 1966): 235-39. Reprinted by permission of the author and the journal.

[1] R. G. Heckelman, "Report on Neurological Impress Method," (Merced, Calif.: Merced County Schools, 1961). (Unpublished.)

A second pilot project in a Sonoma County school was carried out in 1963 by C. Gardner, using six students.[2] After six weeks of instruction with the NIM (each child received ten minutes of instruction daily—a total of five hours), the students showed a growth of 1.6 years.

In 1965, Gardner reports another experiment.[3] Three groups were used, consisting of twenty children each, from grades five through eight. Gains were significant and were maintained over a period of time. The Hawthorne effect was discounted.

In essence, the NIM is a procedure which calls for a multisensory approach in remedial reading. It is most effective when it is employed in a one-to-one relationship, although it can be used in a group setting where earphones are employed by the students and the teacher speaks into a mike while the reading material is projected.

The individual method consists of the instructor and the student meeting for approximately fifteen minutes a day in consecutive daily sessions for a total period of time ranging from eight to twelve hours. If this method is proving effective there is often a sharp rise in achievement at about the eighth hour of instruction.

The child is seated slightly in front of the instructor so that the instructor's voice is close to the child's ear. From the very first session the instructors and the students read the same material out loud together. It is generally advisable in the beginning sessions for the instructor to read a little louder and slightly faster than the student. There is some beginning difficulty at times. The student complains about not being able to keep up with the instructor, but the student is urged to continue nevertheless and forget about the mistakes he is making. Also, the instructor may have to slow down slightly to a more comfortable speed for the student. By rereading the initial lines or paragraphs several times together before going on to new reading material, this discomfort on the part of the student is quickly overcome. The practice of rereading lines, paragraphs, and pages over and over is not advised for those students who take off rather rapidly with the NIM. However with children who have audio-interpretive problems this method may have to be prolonged and augmented if the NIM is to be used successfully. In the initial sessions, the paragraphs or sentences are repeated several times

---

[2]Charles E. Gardner, "Sonoma County Schools Office Research Project," (Santa Rosa, Calif.: Sonoma County Schools, 1963). (Unpublished.)

[3]Charles E. Gardner, "Experimental Use of the Impress Method of Reading Habilitation," *Cooperative Reading Project No. S-167* (Washington, D.C.: U.S. Office of Education, 1965).

until a normal fluid reading pattern is established. In most cases two to three minutes of repetitious patterning is sufficient.

Very little preliminary instruction is given to the student before the reading starts. He is told not to think of reading since we are training him to slide his eyes across the paper. The teacher says that he is not at all concerned with what the child does in terms of reading. At no time is any correction done with the child. When the instructor and the student read together, his finger simultaneously under the spoken words in a smooth, continuous fashion at precisely the same speed and with the same flow as his verbal reading. If desired, the student may later take over this function, alternating with the teacher in the use of the finger, the teacher may reach out and place his hand on the student's finger and guide it to a smooth flowing movement. Particular attention should be paid to the ends of the line where the finger should be made to move rapidly back to where the new line begins. It is a common habit for people not to move their fingers back rapidly enough. This can be likened to the speed of the typewriter carriage returning to position at the end of a line.

Teachers should be watched during their first sessions of using this method to see if they are able to synchronize their voices with their fingers. Many teachers have difficulty in doing this and they are not always aware that their voices and fingers are not operating together. Good readers tend to look ahead and run their fingers ahead of the place where their voices are. For the purpose of the NIM it is absolutely essential that the finger movements, voice, and words all be synchronized, because many children do not read well due to a malfunctioning of the eye movements.

At no time during the reading instructions does the instructor interrogate the student or resort to any type of testing to determine whether the student is mastering the words, either for word recognition or for reading comprehension. The major concern is with the style of reading rather than with reading accuracy.

This reading technique should be considered a part of an audio-neural-conditioning process whereby the incorrect reading habits of the child are suppressed and then replaced with correct, fluid reading habits. By the time most children reach remedial-reading teachers, they have accumulated many incorrect reading habits and eye movements and have lost all confidence. These conditions combine to produce inefficient reading patterns. They are apt to read word by word, and often this is accompanied by the body rocking back and forth as they try to force assimilation of each word as it comes along.

One of the most important aspects of the NIM—as far as the instructor is concerned—is to forget conventional approaches to the teaching of reading and think more in terms of a child being exposed to correct reading processes. Even after the reading has speeded up considerably and functional reading has improved by several grade levels, if the instructor were to test he would probably find that word recognition was improving on a slower rate pattern. It appears to lag behind the functional reading process by a year to a year and one half. Once the child has begun to read in newspapers and magazines at home on a voluntary basis and has gained confidence in reading, he makes rapid strides. The word-recognition ability increases gradually after the NIM training period is over.

As mentioned earlier, if a child does have difficulty using the NIM and does not respond rapidly and easily within four hours, a changeover to kinesthetic or motor methods we have termed "echoing" may be indicated. Echoing is a supplemental technique used throughout the NIM at the discretion of the instructor. Its most intensive use should be with children who have marked auditory-discrimination problems. In these special cases it may be noted that the child also has difficulty in verbal expression. In "echoing" the child is asked to repeat phrases and sentences, and it is often found that he has great difficulty in repeating these accurately. To care for this auditory problem, much time is spent in reading sections of words. For example: The boy went *down the street*. The teacher would say, "Down the street," and the child would repeat it rather rapidly, duplicating the teacher's voice. Then the teacher would say, "The boy went down the street," rapidly in a conversational tone. The child would repeat the entire sentence. After this is repeated accurately several times, the words are shown to the child as they are written and he returns to reading along with the teacher, "The boy went down the street," in the normal conversational tone. The use of echoing is almost equal to the time that he spent in the normal NIM unison reading for these special cases.

When group techniques are employed, the main disadvantage to the instructor is that of using up materials rapidly. Filmstrips have been found to be beneficial. The opaque projector can also be used, as can other projectors using plastic transparencies. Group techniques will not work unless the instructor uses a microphone and each child has a head set to pick up the instructor's voice. Without earphones, the children hear each other's mistakes, become disorganized, and lose the effect of the method.

Pacing is another extremely important aspect of the NIM, both in the individual and in the group setting. Pacing means that the material read should be periodically speeded up and the student is literally dragged to higher rates of speed in the reading process. This is done only for a few minutes at a time but probably should become a part of every reading instructional session. After two or more hours of instruction, reading may at times be speeded up to the fastest speed at which the instructor can read out loud without discomfort. There are cases where eventually words cannot be read clearly due to the tremendous speeds that are obtained by the student and the instructor.

Another important aspect of the NIM—either group or individual —is the material used. It is suggested that the starting material should be on a level slightly lower than the child is presently able to handle adequately. The most common mistake in using the NIM is to spend too much time at the lower levels of the child's reading ability. For example: in a twelve-hour session for a child of average intelligence in the eighth grade, he would be started at first- or second-grade reading level, and by the end of the second hour be at the third-grade reading level. At the end of the sixth hour, he would probably be at the fifth- or sixth-grade level and by the time he has finished the twelve hours he might possibly be as high as the seventh- or eighth-grade level on reading exposure. It is not important whether he has learned from this material or not. Overexposure to difficult words is far better than underexposure. One of the reasons for the success of the NIM seems to be due to the enormous exposure students have to words. During an ordinary session of NIM reading lasting fifteen minutes, the child may be exposed to as many as two thousand words. It is not uncommon to cover ten to twenty pages of reading material in one session when using the elementary books. Too little exposure is more harmful than too much. There have been no instances reported where excessive exposure to difficult words has been harmful to any child.

Care must be taken that teachers do not try to push children beyond their intelligence-expectancy grade level in using the NIM. For example, if a child has approximately 100 I.Q. and is in the fifth grade, we would normally assume that he would read up to the fifth-grade level. Many times this grade level can be achieved within eight to twelve hours using the NIM if the child has started at the third-grade level. If you continue on with the NIM after expectancy has been achieved, very little additional gain is to be expected. Another example is a fifth-grade child with an 80 I.Q., who reads at second-grade level. He is brought up to his expectancy level which is the third grade. For a teacher to attempt to continue to advance him to yet higher levels would be unrealistic. However, if the teacher wishes to spend three or four hours of instructional time experimenting to make sure the child has reached his optimum level, this may well be justified. It will not harm the child if the teacher does not begin to pressure the child for results beyond his capacity.

In several cases where the NIM has been considered inffective, an evaluation has disclosed that the expectancy level of the child was achieved rather rapidly and the instructors had been frustrated in efforts to push them past normal limits. No learning technique can create capacity, it can only expand learning to capacity. Another complaint voiced by those trying this method for the first time is that it went rapidly for a brief time and then had no further effect. Apparently it is difficult for teachers to realize that children can move up through the grade levels of reading as rapidly as they do using this method. The fact that a child might conceivably advance one grade level for every two hours of instruction seems so unbelievable that most tradition-oriented teachers assume that after two hours the growth process has hardly begun. Yet herein lies the key to the NIM's effect. It is the rapid upward gain achieved by forced exposure to greatly expanded quantities of written material that underlies the method, plus a forced efficiency in moving through and speeding up reading heretofore bogged down in a dozen or so faulty habits. The adage that the proof of the pudding lies in the eating can be paraphrased. The proof of a process lies in the reading. Objective studies have furnished this proof.

Some Promising Techniques

Heckelman—Questions for Discussion

Why is this technique called the "Neurological Impress Method"? Why might this technique be especially useful for teacher aids or other untrained personnel? What are some problems that a teacher untrained in this technique may encounter? In what ways is this technique contrary to the methods that many remedial reading teachers have learned?

CHAPTER FIFTEEN

Theories of Reading and Learning

As pointed out in the preface, the purpose of this book of readings is to bring together some of the best, most recent, and most usable research and writing in the psychology and pedagogy of teaching reading; however, one must realize that theory cannot be ignored. All original research stems from some theory, and without that theory there would be no meaningful research.

Many reading specialists feel that up to this point we merely have been groping in the dark in terms of developing materials and techniques for the teaching of reading. They believe that, until a suitable working model of the reading process is developed, we cannot really develop materials and/or techniques on a scientific basis. All attempts without a working model would be somewhat similar to a medical doctor giving a patient a sample of every kind of medicine in the pharmacy in the hope that one would eventually cure the patient's ills.

The article by Harry Singer presents several theoretical models of reading. Singer, who was a student of the late Harry Holmes, describes the substrata-factor theory developed by Holmes and himself, and he also presents an excellent discussion of cognitive, language, and reading development.

The brief but excellent article by Morris L. Bigge has been included in this book for the purpose of outlining various concepts from ten important theories of learning. The student should find this brief outline useful in determining how his ideas, as well as those of others, compare with commonly recognized theories of learning. This outline should also be beneficial as a reference or beginning point in doing further research in the various learning theories.

Harry Singer

Theoretical Models of Reading

Abstract

Several theoretical models of reading are examined in detail and reviewed. The models utilize and depict interrelationships among cognitive and linguistic systems as they function in reading performance. The development of cognition, language and reading ability is also reviewed.

Theoretical models of reading are currently being used implicitly and explicitly in research and in teaching to explain the processes of decoding, comprehending, and encoding of printed messages. Several of these models have been selected for critical review in this paper. In addition to use of such criteria as heuristic value and empirical support, these models will also be evaluated from a developmental point of view. Since these models primarily utilize and depict interrelationships among cognitive and linguistic systems as they function in reading performance, this review will begin with a summary of the development of cognition, language, and reading ability.

Cognitive Development

A major theory of cognitive development has been formulated by Piaget (Piaget, 1937; Inhelder and Piaget, 1958; Inhelder, 1963; Flavell,

From Harry Singer, "Theoretical Models of Reading," *Journal of Communication* 19 (June 1969): 134-56. Reprinted by permission of the author and the journal.

1963). He uses two mental processes to explain how information is incorporated into the individual's mental repertoire and how new mental structures are formed. When the individual is confronted by new information derived from his action on objects, he "assimilates" or interprets this information according to "schemas" or mental structures that have been formed out of interactions of the child and his environment. When new information departs too much from existing schemas—if the difficulty level of the information is not too great—the individual tends to resolve the discrepancy by the process of accommodation or the formation of a new schema and thus achieves a stage of equilibrium again. These mental processes operate not only in relation to tangible objects, but also in interaction with oral and printed language. However, the level of thought that the child can attain in these interactions is dependent upon his stage of mental development.

Piaget has posited four cumulative stages of cognitive development. In the first stage from about birth to age 2 the child adapts to his environment through sensori-motor rather than through symbolic means. The child's mental activity during this stage consists of establishing relationships between sensory experience and action by physically manipulating the world. The child's sensori-motor actions on objects thus results in knowledge of perceptual invariants of his environment. If the appropriate linguistic forms are associated with these perceptual invariants and the child is normal, he begins to use these linguistic forms to identify objects and to represent his actions on them.

From approximately age 2 to 4, the individual goes through the second major stage of development in which he rapidly learns to represent objects by symbolic means. For example, fifty percent of children age 2 can identify common objects, such as a cup and parts of a doll's body, and can repeat two numbers. At age 4, they can repeat a 9 to 10 word sentence, name a variety of objects, and answer some simple questions, such as "why do we have a house." During this stage, the child learns to represent his world symbolically. He has acquired knowledge of spatial, temporal, and causal relationships among the perceptual invariants of his environment, and use of movables appear in his speech at this time.

In the third stage from about age 4 to 7, the child is going through the initial stages of logical thought. He can group objects into classes by noting similarities and differences. He can also form the superordinate concept of "fruit" for relating "orange" and "apple." Through social reinforcement, he has intuitively learned and uses the grammar of the language spoken in his environment. He has also acquired a vocabulary of about 2,500 to 7,500 words and has learned the physical relationships of time, space, and has some idea of causality; but his causal reasoning is dependent upon his perceptions and is often erroneous because his attention is attracted by irrelevant or insufficient attributes. For example, he concludes that a tall, thin jar contains more liquid than a broad, shallow container, even though he has seen the liquid poured from one vessel into the other.

Beginning about age 7, the child develops the capability of carrying out logical operations, which means he can internalize actions that represent physical objects and relationships. For example, the child can use his imagination to mentally reverse actions: you break a candy bar in half and he can mentally put the parts together. He can also transform and manipulate sentences. Such operations reflect the freeing of thought and language from dependence upon sensation and perception. But, during this stage the child's mental operations can only be applied to concrete or physical situations.

About age 11 to 15, an individual attains the fourth and mature stage of mental development in which he can imagine possible and potential relationships and think in terms of formal propositions. His thinking is freed from dependence on directly experienced events. Conditional, suppositional, and hypothetical statements are likely to begin to appear in the individual's language. But not all adults reach this ability to soar into the abstract and those who do can regress to more immature modes of thought.

Although the sequence of these stages of cognitive development are presumably the same for all individuals, concepts or basic means of representing experience can vary from individual to individual. In responding to words, either orally or graphically presented, concepts may be evoked.[1] Whether or not an individual comprehends a message then is a function in part of the degree to which the concepts transmitted by the sender are congruent with the concepts elicited in the receiver of the message.

However, as individuals mature, their concepts tend to become more congruent. With increased range of experience, an individual's concepts broaden, become clearer, and hierarchically organized. They also change from egocentric to conventionalized significance. As the concepts of individuals become consistent with the concepts of their culture, they can and do communicate more effectively and efficiently (Russell, 1956; Bruner and Olver, 1963; Singer, 1964).

---

[1]The same word, for example, "apple," may be a label for a particular object, or a name for a concept or set of interrelated attributes, such as color, shape, size, etc. (Osgood, 1956; Singer, 1956a).

Children whose experience is more limited and who have less verbal interchange with adults are less likely to attain the information, linguistic forms, and syntax for organizing and communicating new experiences. Because of some gaps in the materials or content of their thinking, they might not be able to communicate effectively in certain content areas, even though they have the requisite general mental capabilities (Gagné, 1966).

Thus, the level of thought and the variety of an individual's ideas are a function of his stage of cognitive development and his interaction with his environment. These interactions operate in oral as well as in written communication and underlie his general language development.

Language Development

The child's language development is slow at first and then accelerates. At age 12 months, the average child can say two words (Bayley, 1949). The gradient of vocabulary development remains low from age one to two as the child continues to learn the perceptual invariants of his environment. During the next four years, the vocabulary gradient accelerates as the child goes from a vocabulary of approximately 100 to 2,500 words. By age 6, he uses all parts of speech and has unconsciously learned and intuitively uses the rules of grammar in expressing his ideas and manipulating his vocabulary into a variety of utterances (Smith, 1926; McCarthy, 1946; Noel, 1953; Ervin and Miller, 1963). He can communicate effectively with his peers and with adults provided that the intended meaning of the communication does not exceed his mental capabilities (Strickland, 1962). Indeed, upon entrance to school, the average child has learned through various processes, such as conditioning, shaping of utterances, echoes of heard speech, unconscious acquisition of the transformation rules of grammar, and through identification with language models to speak whatever sound system, vocabulary, and grammar are characteristics of his home and neighborhood (Noel, 1953). The child is then ready to transfer his oral language system to learning how to read and in responding to printed material.

Oral language continues to develop through the elementary school years. In a longitudinal study of a representative sample of 237 pupils, Loban (1963) analyzed the characteristics of oral language development, using a standardized interview and a set of six pictures to elicit language responses. Loban applied a recently devised method of analysis for recording and quantifying these responses. The method consists of dividing speech into phonological units (utterances between initial and terminal junctures), communication units (usually independent clauses with their modifiers) and mazes ("tangles of language"). Recording these, Loban discovered that linguistic fluency increases each year. After the third grade, there was a general decrease in incidence of mazes and in number of words per maze; consequently, there was improvement in coherence of speech. Improvement in effectiveness and control of language was not attained through changes in pattern of communication unit, but by degree of flexibility, expansion, and elaboration of elements within the pattern. Children who are more proficient in oral language use a greater degree of subordination, are more sensitive to conventions of language, score higher on vocabulary and intelligence tests, and perform better in reading and writing. Although those who are less proficient in language tend to improve throughout the grades, the gap between the most and least proficient tends to widen.

In a study similar to Loban's, but using a cross-sectional rather than a longitudinal design, Strickland (1962) also found significant relationships throughout the grades between structure of oral language and reading ability. At the second grade, the superior readers used greater sentence length. At the sixth grade level, those who were high in oral and silent reading used in their oral language greater sentence length, made more use of movables and subordination, had fewer short utterances, and used more common linguistic patterns. In oral reading, the better readers were freer of errors of substitution, repetitions, hesitations, mispronunciations, insertions, refusals and self-corrections. They were more fluent and used more appropriate phrasing and intonation.

In an interesting linguistic analysis of basal reading textbooks, Strickland (1962) found that language patterns increased from a few common ones in primary grades to many patterns in grade six, but not in a systematic manner. There was some expansion in elaboration from grade to grade and movables (expressions of time, place, manner, purpose, and cause) began to appear from grade 2 on. However, there was no clear arrangement for subordination and the sentence structure patterns appeared to be used randomly with no attempt to gain mastery through repetition. Whether control of sentence structure as vocabulary is controlled in basal readers would help or not, she pointed out, was unknown.

Following up Strickland's research, Ruddell (1965a) tested and confirmed the hypothesis, at the fourth grade level, that greater correspondence between the structure of oral language and reading paragraphs would improve comprehension as assessed by the cloze test. Then, drawing on the theory of transfer of learning that similarity between oral language pattern and reading pattern of instruction would aid in rate of achievement in word recognition and reading comprehension, Ruddell (1965b) undertook a training study at the first grade level, in which he compared the achievement of pupils taught by basal versus programed instructional material. The programed material had a high consistency of correspondence in grapheme-phoneme relationships whereas the basal reader did not. Instruction of half of each of these groups was supplemented by use of materials designed to improve their language development with respect to certain aspects of morphemes and syntax. He found that the supplement to a program of instruction which had a high degree of phoneme-grapheme correspondence as compared with basal reader instruction, whether supplemented or not, tended to result in better achievement in word recognition and reading comprehension. He also discovered that the degree of control over certain aspects of the morphological and syntactical language systems at the beginning of first grade is predictive of reading achievement at the end of grade one. Ruddell concluded that degree and control of language ability are significant components in learning to read, particularly when they reinforce a program that stresses grapheme-phoneme correspondence.

Reading Development

An average child's receptive, mediational, storage, and oral subsystems for processing and responding to spoken language are fairly well developed before he systematically starts to form his subsystems for decoding, comprehending, and encoding responses to printed language. Consequently, the popular strategy in teaching the child to read is to have him learn to reconstruct printed messages into spoken language through use of vocal, subvocal, or even inner speech so that he can then comprehend printed messages with his subsystems for spoken language. In the process, intermodal communication subsystems between auditory and visual systems are developed which are necessary for transfer of meaning from one modality to the other (Holmes, 1957).

Individuals taught through an oral method might continue to subvocalize or use inner speech when reading silently (Edfeldt, 1960), but they can learn on their own or be taught through sensory feedback mechanisms to suppress subvocalization (Hardyck, Petrinovich, and Ellsworth, 1966). Although a non-oral method of instruction could be used to teach children to read silently from the very beginning of reading instruction (Buswell, 1945), formation of oral reconstruction or at least recoding subsystems are necessary for oral reading. However, a reader who has attained maturity in both oral and silent reading has not only developed subsystems for both of these types of reading but can minimize or suppress his oral reconstruction and recoding subsystems when reading silently. He also learns to reorganize his mental organization as he shifts from one reading task or purpose to another (Holmes, 1960; Singer, 1965a, 1965c, 1965f, 1967).

Peripherally and centrally determined changes in eye-movement behavior accompany development in reading (Laycock, 1966). By grade 9, the average individual has attained maturity in functional oculomotor efficiency and accuracy in targeting familiar printed stimuli in reading (Gilbert, 1953). At first grade level, eye-movement behavior on primary grade material consists of two fixations per word, each lasting about seven-tenths of a second, and one regression or backward eye-movement about once for every two words. As children learn to perceive words, associate meaning to them, process information, and formulate appropriate responses, their eye-movement behavior also tends to improve. At the college level, eye-movement behavior is more rhythmic (one regression for every two lines of print), broader in span of perception (one and one-fourth words per fixation), and relatively rapid in pause duration (one quarter second per fixation). The developmental curve of span and pause duration in reading is relatively steep in grades 1-4, tends to level off from grades 5-10, has another upward spurt at grade 10, and then levels off again, but rhythmic growth continues all the way to college (Buswell, 1922).

As individuals progress through the grades, perceptual processes tend to decrease in relative importance while meaning factors tend to increase. Systematic changes also occur in general mental organization of factors underlying speed and power of reading (Holmes, 1954, 1961; Holmes and Singer, 1964, 1966; Singer, 1964, 1965d).

Theoretical Models of Reading

Several models, varying in heuristic value and empirical testing, have been formulated to define, depict, and explain the structure and functioning of subsystems that underlie performance in reading. Four of these models have been selected for presentation.

The first model is simple because it uses extremely broad categories and minimizes the use of hypothetical constructs. This model is implicit in Carroll's (1964) definition of reading:

"We can define reading ultimately as the activity of reconstructing (overtly or covertly) a reasonable spoken message from a printed text and making meaning responses to the reconstructed message that would parallel those that would be made to the spoken message." (p. 62)

He defines the responses made by the listener to a spoken sentence in the following way:

"A sentence is a series of discriminative stimuli, learned by the speaker of a language, which in effect 'program' the mediating responses of the hearer in such a way that certain constructions are put on the sentence and corresponding responses are evoked in the hearer." (p. 61)

Figure 1 systematically depicts his model. The input stimulus is on the left. The individual then internally orally reconstructs the message and to this orally reconstructed message gives whatever meaning responses he would give to the identical spoken message. The meaning responses to the spoken message consist of mediating responses whose sequence is determined by the orally reconstructed message.

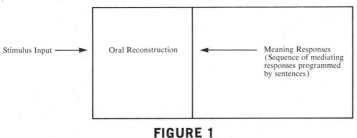

FIGURE 1

Carroll's Implicit Model of Reading

A more explicit model composed of three simultaneous systems has been postulated by Goodman (1966) for comprehending printed messages. He defines reading in the following way:

"Let's start with the simple statement that through reading the reader acquires meaning from written language. This means that the reader goes from written language, visually perceived, toward a reconstruction of a message which had been encoded in written language by the writer. In a basic sense, the extent to which his reconstructed message agrees with the writer's intended message is the extent to which he has comprehended." (p. 188)

"To reconstruct the message, the reader must decode from language. This means that he must know and use the language in pretty much the same way that the writer knows and uses it. It also means that he must have sufficient experience and conceptual development so that the message will be comprehensible to him. The process of reading comprehension differs from the process of listening comprehension only in the form of the perceptual input. The latter works from aural input; the former from visual input." (p. 188)

The three decoding systems in his model, shown in Figure 2, are: (1) the graphophonic, (2) syntactic cues, and (3) the semantic system. The graphophonic system refers to the perception of printed cues, such

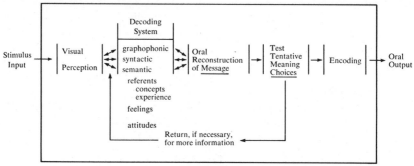

FIGURE 2
Goodman's Implicit Model of Reading

as letters, words, and punctuation marks, and to the utilization of knowledge of spelling sound patterns. The syntactic cues system consists of knowledge of sentence patterns, pattern markers, usually suffixes, that signal information or redundantly confirm the use of a word, function words that point to meaning bearing elements, punctuation marks that partly replace suprasegmental phonemes. The semantic system consists of concepts, information, and other experiences elicited by the message. These three systems work together to reconstruct the message, which leads to tentative meaning choices that are then tested and, if necessary, modified by going back to get more information. The receiver of the message will understand it to the extent that (a) the reconstructed message is in agreement with message of the sender and (b) the receiver shares concepts and experiences with the sender of the message. The message as understood by the receiver can then be encoded for oral output.

A systems of communication model has been constructed by Ruddell (1967). This model, shown in Figure 3, consists of four dynamically interacting levels:

(1) Auditory and visual input systems, (2) a surface structure level, containing graphemic, phonemic, morphemic systems, and their interrelationships; (3) a structural and semantic level, incorporating a syntactical system, short term memory, transformational and rewrite rules, and a mental dictionary; and (4) a deep structure level, consisting of

SYSTEMS OF COMMUNICATION MODEL

SURFACE STRUCTURE —————| STRUCTURAL AND SEMANTIC READINGS |————— DEEP STRUCTURE

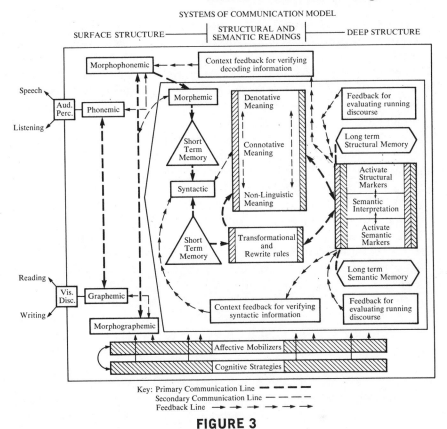

Key: Primary Communication Line ▬ ▬ ▬ ▬
Secondary Communication Line ─ ─ ─ ─
Feedback Line →▬ →▬ →▬ →▬ →▬

FIGURE 3

Ruddell's Systems of Communication Model

semantic interpretation, structural and semantic markers, and long term memory. Structural and semantic markers, generated by the semantic interpretation system which integrates structural and semantic components of a sentence, operate in feedback lines and are stored in long term memory. Three other systems complete the model: (1) affective mobilizers, representing individual interests and values, enter into the goal-setting and evaluating phases of communication, (2) cognitive strategies, interacting with affective mobilizers, influence the organization and reorganization of components for decoding, processing, and encoding information, and (3) context feedback lines for verifying decoding and syntax, and for evaluating discourse.

The operation of the model can be explained by tracing the act of reading from the surface to the deep structure level through one of many possible sequences for perceiving, decoding, structural and semantic processing, interpreting, feeding back, and storing information: stimuli, input through the visual system, initiate the process of decoding. In accordance with the individual's objective and cognitive strategy, knowlelge of the language code and one or more subsystems are mobilized to decode the message. If utilization of phoneme-grapheme relationships does not succeed in decoding the message, sound-spelling clues at the morphographemic and morphophonemic levels may become involved. Also, other systems, such as context feedback from the deep structure level may influence the decoding process. More advanced readers can minimize this surface level of decoding and maximize a more meaningful response by proceeding more directly to a morphemic level.

At the next level, the syntactical system, cued in part by variations in pitch, stress, and juncture within the sentence, is involved in determining the structure of the sentence. For example, different concepts are called forth from the sentence, "They are frying chickens," when the sentence structure is shifted as implied by the questions, "What are they doing," and "What kind of chickens are they?" Information on the structure of the sentence is stored in short-term memory and then transformational and rewrite rules operate on the structure of the sentence to reduce it to its most basic form, e.g., sentences in the passive negative are changed to the active affirmative. Next, meanings for the various morphemes are selected from denotative, connotative, and non-linguistic components of the individual's mental dictionary.

Structural and semantic processing of the sentence are then interpreted and integrated in the semantic interpretation system. Generated by the semantic interpretation system, structural and semantic markers narrow possible semantic alternatives and identify classes of meaning, respectively. For example, "the" is a structural marker which cues and delimits the following noun and "male" is a semantic marker for the class of words, such as *man, boy, father, son*. These markers are then stored in long-term memory and are used in generating sentences during recall. Thus the model can be used to trace through the systems and interacting processes of decoding and comprehending oral and printed language. Proceeding through the model in the reverse direction, the systems and processes resulting in the encoding of speech and writing can be explained.

Statistically-determined models of reading have been constructed at the college (Holmes, 1954), high school (Holmes and Singer, 1961, 1966) and elementary levels (Singer, 1960, 1962, 1965). These models were constructed by use of substrata analysis, which extends the Wherry-Doolittle multiple correlation selection technique to successive levels of analysis. The Wherry-Doolittle technique analytically selects and deter-

mines weights for a minimum set of variables in a regression equation
that will tend to predict a maximum degree of variance in a criterion.

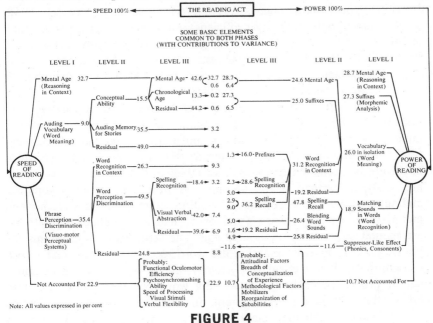

FIGURE 4

Flow Chart to Show the Results of the Substrata Analysis
of Speed and Power of Reading at the Fourth Grade Level

This statistical procedure, described in detail elsewhere (Holmes, 1954;
Holmes and Singer, 1966; Singer, 1965e), was applied to a matrix of 36
variables that had been administered to an average sample of fourth
graders. Since the variables had been determined by previous research
or had been postulated from theoretical formulations to be predictors
of speed or power of reading, substrata analysis resulted in the parsi-
monious structure shown in the model in Figure 4. Adjacent to each
predictor is its percent contribution to the variance of a criterion, speed
or power of reading, or subcriterion, such as vocabulary in isolation or
word recognition in context.

The model reveals that four systems, inferred from predictors
selected for the multiple regression equations, accounted for 89 percent
of the variance in Power of Reading, and three systems accounted for
77 percent of the variance in Speed of Reading. (Only the Test names
of the predictors are shown in the model; system names are given in
parentheses in the text.) The remaining variance must be attributable

to other variables that were not included in the study, such as personality (Athey, 1965), attitudes and values (Athey and Holmes, 1967), biological support systems (Davis, 1963, 1964), flexibility (Laycock, 1958, 1966), functional oculomotor efficiency and speed of processing visual stimuli (Gilbert, 1953, 1959). Since general reading ability was assessed by the Gates Reading Survey subtests, "Level of Comprehension" and "Speed," the structure of the model depicted in Figure 4 is delimited to the domains assessed by these variables.

On the left side of the model are the three broadly categorized systems for Speed of Reading: mental age (reasoning in context), auding vocabulary (word meaning), and phrase perception discrimination (visuo-motor perceptual systems). Except for mental age which could not be predicted from other variables in the matrix, these systems are analyzed further at the second and third levels. Subsystems for auding vocabulary are conceptual ability (conceptual subsystem) and auding memory for stories (memory); underlying conceptual ability are mental age and chronological age. The sequence of subsystems for phrase perception discrimination are word recognition in context (word recognition and syntactical subsystems), and word perception discrimination (visual perception); underlying word perception discrimination are spelling recognition (subsystems for spelling, including sequencing and phoneme-grapheme relationships) and visual verbal abstraction (subsystem for perceiving and abstracting recurring groups or letters). "Residual" refers to unaccounted variance, attributable to variables not included in the construction of the model.

On the right side of the model are the four systems for Power of Reading: mental age (reasoning in context), suffixes (morphemic analysis), vocabulary in isolation (word meaning) and matching sounds in words (word recognition, which includes decoding subsystems such as phonemics). The systems for word meaning and word recognition are analyzed further. Subsystems for vocabulary in isolation are mental age (reasoning in context), suffixes (morphemic analysis) and word recognition in context (word recognition and syntax). Underlying word recognition in context are the subsystems of prefixes (morphemic analysis) and spelling recognition and recall (spelling subsystems, including sequencing and phoneme-grapheme relationships). Matching word sounds breaks down into spelling recall and blending word sounds (integrating phoneme-graphemic relationships).[2]

---

[2]The figures in the center columns are estimates of contributions of second and third level subsystems to the variance of speed and power of reading, computed by multiplying percent contributions across a sequence of subsystems in a particular system (Holmes, 1965).

Thus, the model indicates that silent reading ability is divisible into two major interrelated components, speed and power of reading. Underlying each of these components is a complexly interwoven hierarchy of predictors which represent systems and subsystems that can be mobilizedt for attaining speed and power of reading. It can be inferred from the model that in changing from one task to another in reading, for example, from speed to power of reading, an individual reorganizes his set of systems and subsystems from one that emphasized his visuo-motor perceptual system to one that stressed his morphemic and word recognition systems, in addition to word meaning and reasoning in context.

The model may be read in various other ways to determine how an individual might organize his subskills, ideas, and capacities to solve a problem in reading. For example, spelling recognition together with prefixes and spelling recall (Figure 4, right hand side, Level III), enter into the constellation of subabilities that could be mobilized for solving a problem in Word Recognition in Context. The subsystems of word recognition in context, plus suffixes and mental age, could then be organized for associating meaning to Vocabulary in Isolation. Finally, on the highest level, vocabulary in isolation could be integrated with suffixes, mental age, and matching sounds in words to culminate in a combination of systems for attaining Power of Reading. Again, starting with spelling recognition, a set of systems for achieving Speed of Reading can similarly be worked out. Thus, as an individual reads, he is continuously organizing and reorganizing his systems and subsystems according to his changing purposes and the demands of the reading material.

Discussion of the Models

Two of the four models have been explicitly formulated and therefore only these two models can be compared and critically evaluated. The other two, Carroll's and Goodman's, taken as examples of implicit models, are consequently less detailed and therefore not comparable, but nevertheless have certain general features which can be discussed in relation to Ruddell's and Singer's models.

Both Carroll and Goodman postulate that oral reconstruction of printed material necessarily occurs in the process of reading, presumably in both oral and silent reading. Ruddell (1967) agrees with Edfeldt (1960) that some oral component, subvocalization or inner speech, albeit at a minimal level, accompanies the process of reading. But, Singer, adducing other evidence (Hardyck, *et al.*, 1966), takes the position that when an advanced reader is reading familiar material rapidly, he can suppress or not activate at least part of it, if not his entire, oral system. Therefore, the difference among the models in regard to oral reconstruction may be a function of the type of reading. For slow, analytical or study type of reading, oral reconstruction may be a part of the process, but for rapid, skimming type of reading, oral reconstruction may be suppressed or not mobilized. If empirical testing finds that this hypothesis is tenable, then a model of reading would have to depict an oral reconstruction system that is activated or suppressed according to the maturity level of the reader and his purpose in reading.

Feedback lines from the comprehension stage of the model back to the decoding or surface level are explicit in Goodman's and Ruddell's models. Such lines are implicit in Singer's model. Indeed the central hypothesis of the substrata-factor theory of reading postulates that there is a dynamic interrelation among systems and subsystems. Also, predictors which identify them are, in fact, statistically associated with each other. However, it must also be postulated that if some systems or subsystems are suppressed when others are mobilized or activated for a particular reading task, then feedback lines would be necessary for facilitory and for inhibitory functions.

Different procedures were used in constructing the models. For example, Ruddell reviewed and attempted on a *logical* basis to interrelate psycholinguistic research in defining and organizing his model, while Singer selected his variables from a comprehensive review of research in reading and then used statistical procedures in constructing his model. Nevertheless, there is considerable overlap in the models, which becomes apparent when comparing the models system by system. Broadly categorized, the four systems for Power of Reading in Singer's model are word recognition, word meaning, morphemic analysis, and reasoning in reading. In addition, a visuo-motor perceptual system, but not morphemic analysis nor word recognition, accounted for individual differences in Speed of Reading. Word recognition and word meaning appear to be similar to Goodman's graphophonic, syntactic, and semantic systems for decoding and to Ruddell's phonemic, graphemic, morphemic and syntactic systems, plus feedback from the deep structure level to the decoding level. Word meaning consists of knowledge of vocabulary and conceptual ability and, in general, what Russell (1956) has labeled as "materials of thinking" (percepts, images, concepts, information, and feeling tone). Morphemic analysis consists of ability to analyze words into their meaning components and through this process arrive at the meaning of words. Word meaning and morphemic analysis appear to be functionally equivalent to Ruddell's mental dictionary and morphemic system and to Goodman's semantic system. Reasoning in context includes cognitive processes and strategies for inferring, interpreting, integrating, and conceptualizing ideas, which seem to be comparable to the semantic interpretations and cognitive strategies of Ruddell's model and might include at least part of the system for transforming and rewriting sentences. At least part of the visuo-motor system perceptual system would probably correspond to Ruddell's and Goodman's visual perception system. Both Singer and Ruddell accept evidence and include in their models systems of values, attitudes and interests which can influence a system or even the entire operation of their models. Singer also includes in his model a biological support system which physiologically affects the functioning of the reading process.

In contrast, Singer's model does not contain certain subsystems found in Ruddell's model. Missing are structural and semantic markers and storage systems for classifying sentences and semantic aspects of words. Nor does Singer's model identify transformational and rewrite rules and syntactical systems as such. While Ruddell's model is intended for all four aspects of communication, Singer's is limited to the particular criterion used, speed or power of reading, and to the particular grade level at which the model was constructed.

From the cursory review above of certain aspects of development, the conclusion can be supported that qualitative and quantitative changes occur in the interrelated areas of cognition, language, and reading performance. Consequently, a series of models is necessary in order to explain and predict reading performance throughout the educational continuum. Indeed, Singer (1964, 1965d) found that qualitative and/or quantitative changes do occur in the organization of systems and subsystems that accompany development in speed and power of reading.

Summary and Conclusion

Four models, representing the structure and functioning of systems in reading performance, were explained, compared, and critically evaluated. The models did not agree on the necessity of oral reconstruction of printed material in silent reading. However, three of the models were similar, particularly in the systems mobilized for decoding purposes.

In an attempt to integrate these models, which are somewhat similar, the following description of the reading act was formulated: Oral reading is a process of utilizing oculomotor and visual processes for perceiving and transforming printed stimuli through a decoding phase, consisting of reasoning, word meaning, morphemic, word recognition and syntactic systems, into mental representations. In the process, the reader mobilizes his knowledge of the language code and syntactic cues to reconstruct and to transform these representatives into simpler sentence structures whenever possible. He then responds to the reconstructed or transformed message with materials of thinking, such as concepts, images, information, and feeling tones retrieved from his memory storage systems, and with appropriate thought processes and cognitive strategies. The structural and semantic aspects of the sentence are then interpreted, tested for meaning, and, if necessary, feedback impulses are sent to systems closer to the surface structure level to modify the processing and output of one or more systems or to reorganize the systems employed for the particular reading task.

Structural and semantic markers, generated by the interpretation system, are stored in long term memory. These markers can be utilized for regenerating and encoding stored meanings into oral output. The mobilization and organization of responses to the message, evaluation of and feelings aroused by the message, and emphases given to encoded messages through choice of words as well as through such suprasegmental phonemes as pitch, stress, and juncture, are a function, in part, of the reader's attitudes, needs, and values. The person's style of reading is also a function of his biological subsystems.

For other types of reading, such as rapid reading, a general reorganization of systems and subsystems mobilized for the reading task occurs. In silent reading, oral reconstruction and encoding systems may be suppressed, particularly as the individual matures in reading to the level where he has formed and gained control over feedback mechanisms for suppressing these components of reading (Singer, 1967). Such suppression is more likely to occur when the individual's purpose is to read rapidly and the demands and difficulty level of the material for the individual are not high.

All of the models need to be put to empirical and statistical tests to determine whether they can explain and predict reading behavior. Evidence from statistically determined models of reading and from a cursory review of development of language, cognition, and reading suggest that a series of models is necessary to account for quantitative and qualitative changes in systems and subsystems associated with improvement in reading achievement as individuals progress through school. Also, the models will, of course, have to be up-dated as new concepts are formulated. Already such concepts as perceptual scanning (Geyer, 1966) and linguistic form (Reed, 1965) may have to be incorporated into the models.

None of the models has yet been used for experimental purposes, but one of them was used for clinical diagnosis and evaluation (Singer, 1965b). However, these as well as other models, such as one that has been designed for developing conceptual responses in the initial stages of reading (Singer, 1966; Singer, Balow, and Dahms, 1968) and one that has been hierarchically structured (Gagné, 1965), need to be experimentally tested and evaluated (Singer, 1968). Through such means, it would be possible to determine empirically the heuristic and explanatory value of models that are currently being used explicitly or implicitly in teaching and in research.

References

Athey, Irene J. *Reading-Personality Patterns at the Junior High School Level.* Doctoral dissertation. Berkeley: University of California, 1965.

Athey, Irene J. and Holmes, Jack A. *Reading Success and a Personality Value-Systems Syndrome: A Thirty-year THEN and NOW Study at the Junior High School Level.* Final Report, Contract No. S-248; Bureau of Research No. 5-8027-2-12-1, Washington, D.C.: Office of Education, U.S. Department of Health, Education, and Welfare, 1967.

Bayley, Nancy. "Consistency and Variability in the Growth of Intelligence from Birth to Eighteen Years." *Journal of Genetic Psychology* 75: 165-96, 1949.

Bruner, J. and Olver, Rose. "Development of Equivalence Transformations in Children." *Monographs of the Society for Research in Child Development* 28: 125-43, 1963.

Buswell, Guy T. *Fundamental Reading Habits: A Study of Their Development.* Chicago: University of Chicago Press, 1922.

_____. *Non-oral Reading—A Study of Its Use in the Chicago Public Schools.* Chicago: University of Chicago Press, 1945.

Carroll, John B. *Language and Thought.* Englewood Cliffs, N.J.: Prentice-Hall, 1964.

Davis, Frank R., Jr. *Speed of Reading and Rate of Recovery in Certain Physiological Subsystems.* Berkeley: University of California, 1963.

_____. "The Substrata-Factor Theory of Reading: Human Physiology as a Factor in Reading." *Improvement of Reading Through Classroom Practice.* International Reading Association Conference Proceedings, Vol. 9, 1964. (Edited by J. Allen Figurel.) Newark, Del.: International Reading Association, 1964. p. 292-96.

Edfeldt, Ake W. *Silent Speech and Silent Reading.* Chicago: University of Chicago Press, 1960.

Ervin, Susan M. and Miller, W. R. "Language Development." *Sixty-second Yearbook of the National Society for the Study of Education, Part I.* Chicago: University of Chicago Press, 1963, p. 108-43.

Flavell, John H. *The Developmental Psychology of Jean Piaget.* Princeton, N.J.: Van Nostrand, 1963.

Gagné, Robert. *The Conditions of Learning.* New York: Holt, 1965.

Geyer, John J. *Perceptual Systems in Reading: The Prediction of a Temporal Eye-Voice Span Constant.* Final Report, Contract No. O. E. 5-10-362. Cooperative Research Program, Washington, D.C.: Office of Education, U.S. Dept. of Health, Education, and Welfare, 1966.

Gilbert, L. C. "Functional Motor Efficiency of the Eyes and Its Relation to Reading." *University of California Publications in Education* 2: 159-232, 1953.

_____. "Speed of Processing Visual Stimuli and Its Relation to Reading." *Journal of Educational Psychology* 55: 8-14, 1959.

Goodman, Kenneth S. "A Psycholinguistic View of Reading Comprehension." *New Frontiers in College-Adult Reading.* (Edited by George B. Schick and Merrill M. May.) Fifteenth Yearbook of the National Reading Conference, Milwaukee, Wisc.: The National Reading Conference, 1966, p. 188-96.

Hardyck, C., Petrinovich, L., and Ellsworth, D. "Feedback of Speech Muscle Activity During Silent Reading: Rapid Extinction." *Science* 154: 1467-68, 1966.

Holmes, Jack A. "Factors Underlying Major Reading Disabilities at the College Level." *Genetic Psychology Monographs* 49: 3-95, 1954.

_____. "The Brain and the Reading Process." *Reading is Creative Living.* Twenty-second Yearbook of the Claremont Reading Conference, Claremont, Calif.: Curriculum Laboratory, 1957. p. 49-67.

_____. "The Substrata-Factor Theory of Reading: Some New Experimental Evidence." *New Frontiers in Reading.* International Reading Association Conference Proceedings, Vol. 5, 1960. (Edited by J. Allen Figurel.) New York: Scholastic Magazines, 1960. p. 115-21.

_____. "Personality Characteristics of the Disabled Reader." *Journal of Developmental Reading* 4: 111-22, 1961.

_____. "Basic Assumptions Underlying the Substrata-Factor Theory." *Reading Research Quarterly* 1: 5-28, 1965.

Holmes, Jack A., and Singer, Harry. *The Substrata-Factor Theory: The Substrata Factor Differences Underlying Reading Ability in Known Groups.* Final report, Contracts 538 and 538A, Office of Education, U.S. Department of Health, Education, and Welfare, Washington, D.C.: 1961.

_____. "Theoretical Models and Trends Toward More Basic Research in Reading." *Review of Educational Research* 34: 127-55, 1964.

_____. *Speed and Power in Reading in High School.* Office of Education, U.S. Department of Health, Education, and Welfare. A publication of the Bureau of Educational Research and Development. Washington, D.C.: U.S. Government Printing Office, 1966.

Inhelder, Bärbel. "Criteria of the Stages of Mental Development." *Psychological Studies of Human Development.* (Edited by R. Kuhlen and G. J. Thomson.) Second Edition, New York: Appleton-Century-Crofts, 1963. p. 28-48.

Inhelder, Bärbel and Piaget, Jean. *The Growth of Logical Thinking from Childhood to Adolescence.* New York: Basic Books, 1958.

Laycock, Frank. "Flexibility in Reading Rate and Einstellung." *Perceptual and Motor Skills* 8: 123-29, 1958.

_____. "Conceptual and Personality Factors Underlying Flexibility in Speed of Reading." *New Frontiers in College-Adult Reading.* (Edited by George B. Schick and Merrill M. May.) Fifteenth Yearbook of the National Reading Conference, Milwaukee, Wisc.: The National Reading Conference, 1966. p. 140-46.

Loban, Walter D. *The Language of Elementary School Children.* Champaign, Ill.: National Council of Teachers of English, 1963.

McCarthy, Dorothea. "Language Development in Children." *Manual of Child Psychology.* (Edited by Leonard Carmichael.) New York: John Wiley, 1964. p. 476-581.

Noel, Doris L. "A Comparative Study of the Relationship Between the Quality of the Child's Language Usage and the Quality and Type of Language Used in the Home." *Journal of Educational Research* 47: 161-67, 1953.

Osgood, Charles E. *Method and Theory in Experimental Psychology.* New York: Oxford University Press, 1956.

Piaget, Jean. "Principal Factors Determining Intellectual Evolution From Childhood to Adult Life." *Factors Determining Human Behavior.* Harvard Tercentenary

Conference of Arts and Sciences, Cambridge, Mass.: Harvard University, 1937. p. 32-48.

Reed, David W. "A Theory of Language, Speech and Writing." *Elementary English* 42: 845-51, 1965.

Ruddell, Robert B. "The Effect of the Similarity of Oral and Written Patterns of Language Structure on Reading Comprehension." *Elementary English* 32: 403-10, 1965.

_____. *The Effect of Four Programs of Reading Instruction With Varying Emphasis on the Regularity of Grapheme-Phoneme Correspondences and the Relation of Language Structure to Meaning on Achievement in First Grade Reading.* Cooperative Research Project No. 2699, U. S. Office of Education. Berkeley, California: University of California, 1965. (Multilith)

_____. *Linguistics and Language Learning.* Redwood City, Calif.: Bay Region Instruction Television for Education, 1967.

Russell, David B. *Children's Thinking.* New York: Ginn, 1956.

Singer, Harry. Conceptual Ability in the Substrata-Factor Theory of Reading. Doctoral dissertation. Berkeley: University of California, 1960.

_____. "Substrata-Factor Theory of Reading: Theoretical Design for Teaching Reading." *Challenge and Experiment in Reading.* International Reading Association Proceedings, Vol. 7, 1962. (Edited by J. Allen Figurel.) New York: Scholastic Magazines, 1962. p. 226-32.

_____. "Substrata-Factor Patterns Accompanying Development in Power of Reading, Elementary Through College Level." *The Philosophical and Sociological Bases of Reading.* (Edited by Eric Thurston and Lawrence Hafner.) Fourteenth Yearbook of the National Reading Conference, Milwaukee, Wisc.: The National Reading Conference, 1965. p. 41-56.

_____. "Conceptualizations in Learning to Read." *New Frontiers in College-Adult Reading.* (Edited by George B. Schick and Merrill M. May.) Fifteenth Yearbook of the National Reading Conference, Milwaukee, Wisc.: The National Reading Conference, 1966. p. 116-32.

_____. "Substrata-Factor Evaluation of a Precocious Reader." *The Reading Teacher* 18: 288-96, 1965.

_____. "A Theory of Human Learning for Teaching Reading: A Discussion of Professor Arthur Staast's 'Integrated Functional Learning Theory for Reading'." *Use of Theoretical Models in Research.* (Edited by Albert J. Kingston.) Newark, Del.: International Reading Association, 1965. p. 68-73.

_____. *Substrata-Factor Reorganization Accompanying Development in Speed and Power of Reading.* Final report, Project No. 2011, U.S. Office of Education, Washington, D.C.: 1965.

_____. "Symposium on the Substrata-Factor Theory of Reading: Research and Evaluation of Critiques." *Reading and Inquiry.* International Reading Association Proceedings, Vol. 10, 1965 (Edited by J. Alden Figurel.) Newark, Del.: International Reading Association, 1965. p. 325-31.

_____. "An Instructional Strategy for Developing Conceptual Responses in Reading Readiness." *Vistas in Reading*, II, Part I. International Reading Association Proceedings, Vol. 11, 1966. (Edited by J. Allen Figurel.) Newark, Del.: International Reading Association, 1966. p. 425-31.

_____. "Developmental Changes in the Subsystems of Reading and Listening." *Paper Abstracts.* (Edited by Ellis B. Page.) Washington, D.C.: American Educational Research Association, 1967. p. 127.

_____. "Stimulus Models for Teaching Reading." *Proceedings of the Fifth Annual Conference of the United Kingdom Reading Association*, Edinburgh, Scotland: 1968.

Singer, Harry; Balow, Irving H.; and Dahms, Patricia. "A Continuum of Teaching Strategies for Developing Reading Readiness at the Kindergarten Level." *Forging Ahead in Reading.* International Reading Association Proceedings, Vol. 12,

1968. (Edited by J. Allen Figurel.) Newark, Del.: International Reading Association, 1968. p. 463-68.

Smith, Medorah E. "An Investigation of the Development of the Sentence and the Extent of Vocabulary in Young Children." *University of Iowa Studies of Child Welfare* 3: No. 5, 1926.

Strickland, Ruth B. *The Language of Elementary School Children: Its Relationship to the Language of Reading Textbooks and the Quality of Reading of Selected Children.* Bulletin of the School of Education, Indiana University 38: 1-131, 1962.

Theories of Reading and Learning

Singer — Questions for Discussion

Of what practical value is a theory of reading? In what respects do the models presented by Singer agree? In what respects do they disagree? Do you believe that we are "groping in the dark" with our presently used methods and materials of reading instruction? Which of the models presented could possibly be of greatest value in guiding the development of diagnostic instruments?

Morris L. Bigge

Theories of Learning

Since ancient times, most civilized societies have developed and, to some degree, tested theories about how man learns. As each new theory has gained support, it has seldom displaced its predecessors but merely competed with them. For this reason, the educational philosophies and practices of many teachers may include ideas from a variety of learning theories, some of which are basically contradictory in nature.

Each theory of learning is linked to a conception of the basic nature of man: In basic moral inclination, is he innately good, is he evil, or is he neutral? Then, in relation to his environment, is he active, passive, or interactive? Each of the different conceptions has its adherents, and each has its own approach to learning.

The accompanying chart outlines the concepts involved in ten major learning theories (Column I) either prevalent in today's schools or advocated by leading psychologists. Reinforcement and conditioning (No. 7), especially as represented by B. F. Skinner's "operant conditioning" and the cognitive-field theory (No. 10), first advanced by Kurt Lewin but refined by contemporary psychologists, are two leading contenders in the present scene.

Teachers may find this chart useful in thinking through and noting possible inconsistencies in their own educational outlook and how their outlook agrees or disagrees with that of their school administration. Although some of the theories have roots that go back to antiquity, they all still exert influence in presentday schools.

Each theory has its unique approach to education. However, some of them have enough in common to justify grouping them in families. Thus, in a more general sense, there are only five basic outlooks in regard to learning—the three families plus theories 3 and 4.

From Morris L. Bigge, "Theories of Learning," *Today's Education: NEA Journal* 55, no. 3 (March 1966): 18-19. Reprinted by permission of the author and the journal.

REPRESENTATIVE THEORIES OF LEARNING

	I Theory of Learning	II Psychological System or Outlook	III Assumption Concerning the Basic Moral and Psychological Nature of Man
MIND SUBSTANCE FAMILY	1. Theistic mental discipline	faculty psychology	bad-active mind substance continues active until curbed
	2. Humanistic mental discipline	classicism	neutral-active mind substance to be developed through exercise
	3. Natural unfoldment	romantic naturalism	good-active natural personality to unfold
	4. Apperception or Herbartionism	structuralism	neutral-passive mind composed of active mental states or ideas
CONDITIONING THEORIES OF STIMULUS- RESPONSE (S-R) ASSOCIATIONISTIC FAMILY	5. S-R bond	connectionism	neutral-passive or reactive organism with many potential S-R connections
	6. Conditioning (with no reinforcement	behaviorism	neutral-passive or reactive organism with innate reflexive drives and emotions
	7. Reinforcement and conditioning	reinforcement	neutral-passive organism with innate reflexes and needs with their drive stimuli
COGNITIVE THEORIES OF GESTALT-FIELD FAMILY	8. Insight	Gestalt psychology	naturally-active being whose activity follows psychological laws of organization
	9. Goal insight	configurationalism	neutral-interactive purposive individual in sequential relationships with environment
	10. Cognitive-field	field psychology or relativism	neutral-interactive purposive person in simultaneous mutual interaction with environment, including other persons

IV	V	VI	VII
Basis for Transfer of Learning	**Main Emphasis in Teaching**	**Key Persons**	**Contemporary Exponents**
exercised faculties, automatic transfer	exercise of faculties — the "muscles" of the mind	St. Augustine, John Calvin, J. Edwards	many Hebraic-Christian fundamentalists
cultivated mind or intellect	training of intrinsic mental power	Plato, Aristotle	M. J. Adler, St. John's College
recapitulation of racial history, no transfer needed	negative or permissive education	J. J. Rousseau, F. Froebel	extreme progressivists
growing apperceptive mass	addition of new mental states or ideas to a store of old ones in subconscious mind	J. F. Herbart, E. B. Titchener	many teachers and administrators
identical elements	promotion of acquisition of desired S-R connections	E. L. Thorndike	J. M. Stephens, A. I. Gates
conditioned responses or reflexes	promotion of adhesion of desired responses to appropriate stimuli	J. B. Watson	E. R. Guthrie
reinforced or conditioned responses	successive, systematic changes in organisms' environment to increase the probability of desired responses (operants)	C. L. Hull	B. F. Skinner, K. W. Spence
transposition of insights	promotion of insightful learning	M. Wertheimer, K. Koffka	W. Köhler
tested insights	aid students in trial-and-error, goal-directed learning	B. H. Bode, R. H. Wheeler	E. E. Bayles
continuity of life spaces, experience, or insights	help students restructure their life spaces — gain new insights into their contemporaneous situations	Kurt Lewin, E. C. Tolman, J. S. Bruner	R. G. Barker, A. W. Combs, H. F. Wright, M. L. Bigge